AF431663

Sieges and the Defence of Fortified Places by the British and Indian Armies in the XIXth Century

By Colonel Sir Edward T. Thackeray,
V.C., K.C.B. (Late R.E.)

Originally published in the Royal Engineers Journal
Vol. XIX, 1914 through Vol. XXIII, 1916.

Compiled and edited by Gary Menchen

2023
Waterville, Maine
pagesofpages.com

ISBN: 979-8-9855566-8-1 (paper)

Contact: editor@pagesofpages.com

The image on the cover is "British troops storm Ghuznee, after the Kabul Gate is blown up by the Bengal Sappers & Miners." ca. 1840. From the National Archives (UK) via Wikimedia.

Introduction

Sir Edward Talbot Thackeray, V.C., K.C.B., the author of this survey of nineteenth century sieges and defences of fortifications, was born October 19, 1836. His first cousin, the novelist William Makepeace Thackeray, obtained for him a cadetship in the Honourable East India Company's service in 1852[1] He spent several years at Addiscombe, and received a commission in the Bengal Engineers in December 1854. He was posted to the Bengal Sappers and Miners in 1857.

Thackeray was actively involved throughout the duration of the Indian Mutiny, including the advance on and siege of Delhi. He was still 20 years old when he earned his Victoria Cross on the roof of the Delhi magazine. It was under direct fire from mutineers trying to retake or destroy the building. Thackeray climbed onto the magazine's burning roof and, by pouring bags of water down onto the fire inside the magazine as well as onto portions of the roof itself that had caught fire, prevented its destruction. His actions, along with those of another officer, a Lieut. Renny, who threw shells with lighted fuses into the fortification (and also received a Victoria Cross), prevented the explosion of the magazine. His award was granted in 1862.

For cool intrepidity and characteristic daring in extinguishing a fire in the Delhi Magazine enclosure, on the 16th of September, 1857, under a close and heavy musketry fire from the enemy, at the imminent risk of his life from the explosion of combustible stores in the shed in which the fire occurred.

He became commandant of the Bengal Sappers and Miners in 1879, was awarded army rank of colonel in 1884, and retired in 1888. He moved to Italy in 1898, and died there, 1927, age 90.

Thackeray was a participant in several of the actions described in this book: the siege of Delhi, the capture of

---

[1] Thackeray, Edward T., "William Makepeace Thackery. Some Reminiscences, 1850-1862." *Cornhill Magazine.* N.S. XXXVIII (1915): 39-43.

Lucknow under Colin Campbell in March of 1858, and then, in 1879, with the capture of Kabul.

There is an unusually long biographical notice of Thackeray published in the *Royal Engineers Journal* N.S. Vol 42, 1928. By the time of his death he was the senior V.C. by more than twenty years, and one of the few remaining survivors of the East India Company's Service.

The subject matter of this collection - sieges and the defence of fortifications - is particularly the province the military engineers, and these papers were written for an audience of military engineers. As such they have little to say about the portions of battles where engineers were not directly involved. However, with Lucknow and Delhi, where he was himself an active participant, there is considerably more incidental detail than with other operations.

It is not certain that these articles have ever been published in book form. They were certainly intended for regular publication, and the biographical notice in the *Royal Engineers Journal* mentions the series as appearing in book form, but if that happened it is a very rare book. The British Library holds a bound volume of offprints; that is the only holding of the title recorded in the WorldCat catalog.

In this volume the texts from the 23 different issues of the journal are shown as chapters. Some actions a covered in multiple chapters, such as Sebastopol, Delhi and Lucknow. Some individual chapters survey multiple actions, such as the first chapter here. The contents for each chapter are given in the Table of Contents.

Thackeray's other publications include the following:

Views of Kabul and Environs from Pictures Taken by the Photograph School of the Corps of Bengal Sappers and Miners. Printed for private circulation, 1881. xxvii, 75p.

With 30 photographic plates. Thackeray was the compiler of this volume. Very rare - in the preface Thackeray wrote that it was intended for the officers who had served in the campaign of 1879-80. It can be viewed on-line on the Library of Congress website: search for it by title.

From Assam to Kashmir. Notes on Sport and Travel. Privately printed, 1893.

Two Indian Campaigns, in 1857-58. Chatham: Royal Engineers Institute, 1896. iv, 130p.

Biographical Notices of Officers of the Royal (Bengal) Engineers. London: Smith, Elder, 1900. x, 276p.

Reminiscences of the Indian Mutiny (1857-58) and Afghanistan (1879). London: Smith, Elder, 1916. vi, 181p.

There is also a six-part series, "A subaltern in the Indian Mutiny : containing some letters of Lieutenant Edward Talbot Thackeray, Bengal Engineers, afterwards Colonel Sir E.T. Thackeray..." published in the *Royal Engineers Journal* in 1930 and 1931. The letters are very interesting, being quite detailed and written amid the events. This is another case where there is indication that they were intended to be published in book form, but the only citations located appear to be bound offprints.

Table of Contents

Introduction		i
1	Asseerghur 1803; Gawilghur 1803; Asseerghur 1819; Cadiz 1810	1
2	The Lines of Torres Vedras	15
3	First and Second Sieges of Badajoz; Ciudad Rodrigo	21
4	Third siege of Badajoz	41
5	Siege of Burgos, September, 1812	59
6	Siege of San Sebastian, July, 1813	72
7	Second siege of Bhurtopore, 1825; Defence of Khelet-i-Ghilzai 1841-42; Siege of Ghazni, 1839; Siege of Mooltan, 1848	92
8	Great Siege of Sebastopol 1854-5	112
9	The Siege of Sebastopol (continued)	128
10	The Siege of Sebastopol (continued)	138
11	The Siege of Sebastopol (continued)	154
12	The Siege of Sebastopol February to April 1855; Attacks in June 1855	174
13	Siege of Delhi	200
14	Siege of Delhi (continued)	214
15	Defence of Lucknow May-November 1857	229
16	Relief of Lucknow by Outram and Havelock, in 1857	251
17	Relief of Lucknow by Outram and Havelock (continued)	259
18	The Second Relief of Lucknow	268
19	The Capture of Lucknow, April 1858	285
20	The War with China, 1860. Capture of Pekin	296
21	Capture of Magdala, 1868	304
22	Capture of Kabul, 1879	308
23	The Siege of Ladysmith	315

CHAPTER ONE

The following accounts of Sieges of the British and Indian Armies in the 19th century have been arranged and compiled in a comparatively abbreviated form. They commence with the Capture of the Fortress of Asseerghur in November, 1803, and will be continued in consecutive numbers of the *R.E. Journal*. Many histories and books on military subjects have been referred to, and the sources of information from which the accounts of the sieges are derived will, as far as is possible, be mentioned.

It is not proposed, or intended, that the descriptions of the various sieges should be given in very minute detail, and it would be impossible within the scope of a work of this kind to relate more than the salient points of the sieges. But it is hoped that the accounts —even in their abbreviated form—may be of interest to officers of the Corps, to officers of other branches of the Service, and to subscribers to the *R.E. Journal*.

In the present number the following sieges are dealt with :—

(1). The Capture of Asseerghur, November, 1803.
(2). Siege of Gawilghur, December, 1803.
(3). Siege of Asseerghur, March, 1819.
(4). Blockade of Cadiz, February, 1810.

In compiling the accounts of the above sieges the following works have been consulted :—*History of the Madras Engineers*, by Colonel H. M. Vibart, R.E. (by kind permission) ; *Wellington's Despatches ;* Napier's *History of the Peninsular Wars*.

E.T.T.

---

(1).

Capture of Asseerghur (*October*, 1803).

The first siege of Asseerghur took place during the first Mahratta War in 1803.

The British force under Wellesley having totally defeated at the Battle of Assye the enemy under Scindia and the Bhonsla in September, Colonel Stevenson, as reported in the following despatch, advanced upon the Fortress of Asseerghur and captured it after a short siege.

The fort is situated 2 miles from the end of the great western ranges of the Satpoora Hills, and 16 miles north of Boorhanpore. It is placed in one of the principal passes from the Deccan into Hindustan, and the natural defence that it receives from a precipice of rock on almost every side has been increased by a thick and lofty rampart of masonry—which is built on the summit of the rock—and by large cavities with guns, which at the time of the capture of the fortress by Colonel Stevenson in the month of October, 1803, commanded the country in every direction.

The general height of the position above the plain is 750 ft., and the total circumference including the upper and lower forts is 4,600 yards, or considerably over $2\frac{1}{2}$ miles.

The third enclosure, which contains the lower fort, is called Malighur.

The following despatch from Major-General Wellesley to the Governor-General of India gives a detailed account of the capture of this fort :—

CAMP, *6th November*, 1803.

To the GOVERNOR-GENERAL.

" I now proceed to give your Excellency a detailed account of Colonel Stevenson's operations against Asseerghur.

On the 16th October he advanced to Asseerghur, and encamped 3 miles south of the fort. The remains of the enemy's infantry had fled towards the Nerbudda on the previous day, in the state which I reported them to be, in my letter of the 24th October ; and Colonel Stevenson determined to attack Asseerghur.

On the 18th he reconnoitred the fort, attended by a squadron of cavalry and the piquets of the Native infantry ; and having seen a favourable opportunity, attacked the pettah and carried it, and made a lodgment within 150 yards of the lower wall of the fort. In the evening he reinforced the troops by a battalion. On the 19th all the preparations were made for carrying on the siege ; and two batteries were ready to open at 2 o'clock in the afternoon of the 20th ; one to breach the upper wall, and another of four brass 12-pounders, to destroy the defences of the lower wall.

On the 18th Colonel Stevenson had sent a flag of truce to the killadar to summon him to surrender the fort, to which message he did not receive a decided answer. The communication was continued, but Colonel Stevenson did not relax his operations against the fort, as there was reason to believe that the negotiation was carried on only to give time to Dowlat Rao Scindiah to come to his relief. Before opening the batteries, Colonel Stevenson apprised the killadar of the terms on which he should surrender the fort ; which were that the garrison should march out with their private property, and be allowed to go where they might think proper, and that their arrears should be paid to the amount of 20,000 rupees.

After the batteries had opened about an hour, a white flag was shown from the walls of the fort, which was the signal that had been agreed upon in case the terms should be accepted ; hostages were sent down, and an engagement made that the fort should be delivered up on the following morning. It was accordingly evacuated ; the garrison carried off their property in security, and received the sum agreed to be paid to them.

Colonel Stevenson mentions in high terms the conduct of the officers and troops under his command ; and I cannot omit to take the opportunity of expressing to your Excellency my sense of the merits of Colonel Stevenson and of the body of troops under his command. Upon every occasion I received from the Colonel the most cordial and zealous assistance ; and the troops under his command are in the highest state of discipline and order, and fit for any service in which they can be employed.

On the 16th, 9 officers, 4 sergeants, and 1 matross, formerly in the service of Dowlat Rao Scindiah, delivered themselves up to Colonel Stevenson under your Excellency's proclamation of the 29th August.

I have the honour to enclose a return of the killed and wounded of the troops under the command of Colonel Stevenson, during the operations against Asseerghur. Hereafter I shall have the honour of transmitting return of the ordnance, stores, grain, and other property captured in that fort.''

(2).

Siege of Gawilghur (*December*, 1803).

The second siege dealt with is that of Gawilghur which took place during the same campaign. It was undertaken by Major-General Wellesley himself, and a full and detailed account of his operations is given in the following despatch to the Governor-General in India :—

Camp at Deogaum, 15th December, 1803.

To the Governor-General.

" After the Battle of Argaum I determined to lose no time in commencing the Siege of Gawilghur. I accordingly marched on and arrived at Ellichpoor on the 5th instant, and halted there the 6th ; in order to establish a hospital there for the wounded in the Battle of Argaum.

The fort of Gawilghur is situated in a range of mountains between the sources of the rivers Pooma and Taptee. It stands on a lofty mountain in this range, and consists of one complete inner fort which fronts to the south, where the rock is most steep ; and an outer fort, which covers the inner to the north-west and north. This

3

outer fort has a third wall, which covers the approach to it from the north by the village of Labada. All these walls are strongly built, and fortified by ramparts and towers.

The communications with the fort are through three gates ; one to the south with the inner fort ; one to the north-west with the outer fort and one to the north with the third wall. The ascent to the first is very long and steep, and is practicable only for men ; that to the second is by a road used for the common communications of the garrison with the countries to the southward ; but the road passes round the west side of the fort, and is exposed for a great distance to its fire ; it is so narrow as to make it impracticable to approach regularly by it, and the rock is scarped on each side. This road also leads no further than to the gate. The communication from the northern gate is direct from the village of Labada, and here the ground is level with that of the fort ; but the road to Labada leads through the mountains for about 30 miles from Ellichpoor ; and it was obvious that the difficulty and labour of moving ammunition and stores to Labada would be very great.

However, after making inquiry at Ellichpoor it appeared both to Colonel Stevenson and me, that this point of attack was, upon the whole, the most advantageous, and we accordingly adopted it.

Colonel Stevenson had equipped his corps at Asseerghur for the Siege of Gawilghur, for which service it had long been destined ; and I therefore determined that he should make the principal attack by Labada, while I should cover his operations with my own division and all the cavalry ; and if possible assist them by other attacks to the southward and westward. On the 6th inst. the 1st Batt. 2nd Regiment, under Lieut.-Colonel Chalmers, and two companies of the 94th, and the 1st Batt. of the 6th, under Capt. Maitland, were detached ; the former to drive the enemy from the ground which they occupied to the southward of the fort ; and the latter to seize the fortified village of Damergaum, which covers the entrance of the mountains by the road by which Colonel Stevenson was to pass towards Labada, and to protect the parties sent forward to reconnoitre and repair the roads in the mountains. Both these detachments succeeded.

On the 7th both divisions marched from Ellichpoor ; Colonel Stevenson into the mountains by Damergaum, and my division towards the southern face of the fort of Gawilghur. From that day till the 12th, on which Colonel Stevenson broke ground near Labada, the troops in his division went through a series of laborious services, such as I never before witnessed, with the utmost cheerfulness and perseverance. The heavy ordnance and stores were dragged by hand over mountains, and through ravines, for nearly the whole distance, by roads which it had been previously necessary for the troops to make for themselves.

On the 12th at night, Colonel Stevenson erected two batteries in front of the north face of the fort ; one consisting of two iron 18-pounders, and three iron 12-pounders, to break the outer fort and third wall ; and one consisting of two brass 12-pounders, and two 5-in. howitzers, to clear and destroy the defences on the point of attack.

On the same night the troops of my division constructed a battery for two iron and two brass 12-pounders on the mountain under the southern gate, with a view if possible to breach the wall near that gate ; or at all events to draw the enemy's attention to that quarter. Unfortunately the iron guns could not be moved into the battery, notwithstanding the utmost exertions of the troops ; and the fire of the brass guns produced but little effect.

The fire of all these batteries opened on the 13th in the morning ; and on the 14th, at night, the breaches in the outer walls were practicable. All the arrangements were then made for storming on this day. Lieut.-Colonel Kenny, of the 11th Regiment, commanded the party for the storm, consisting of the flank companies of the 94th Regiment, and of the Native Corps in Colonel Stevenson's Division, supported by the 94th Regiment, and Lieut.-Colonel Haliburton's Brigade, with Lieut.-Colonel Maclean's Brigade in reserve. At the same time I made two attacks from the southward to draw the enemy's attention from that quarter ; one, under Lieut.-Colonel Wallace, consisting of the 74th Regiment, 5 companies of the 78th and 1st Batt. 8th Regiment, on the southern gate ; and one under Lieut.-Colonel Chalmers, consisting of 5 companies of the 78th and the 1st Batt. 10th Regiment, on the north-west gate. These last attacks could be of no service, except to draw the enemy's attention from that from the north ; unless they should succeed in blowing open the gates ; and till they should communicate with detachments from Colonel Stevenson's Corps, as they had no other means of entering the fort. All the troops advanced at about ten in the morning. The detachment under Lieut.-Colonel Chalmers arrived at the north-west gate at the moment when the enemy were endeavouring to escape through it, from the detachment of Colonel Stevenson's Corps, which had been sent to communicate with Colonel Chalmers ; and he entered without difficulty.

The wall of the inner fort, in which no breach had been made, was then to be carried. After some attempts upon the gate of communication between the inner and the outer fort, a place was found at which it was possible to escalade the wall. Capt. Campbell, with the light infantry of the 9th Regiment, fixed the ladders against this place, escaladed the wall, opened the gate for the storming party, and the fort was shortly in our possession. The enemy's garrison was numerous. It consisted of Rajpoots, and a great part of Beny Singh's Regular Infantry, which had escaped from the

Battle of Argaum, commanded by Beny Singh, himself. They were all well armed with the Company's new muskets and bayonets. Vast numbers of them were killed, particularly at the different gates. This service has, I hope, been performed, with small loss on our side. No officer has been killed ; and but few wounded, that I have heard of, excepting Lieut.-Colonel Kenny, of the 11th Regiment, and Lieut. Young, of the 2nd of the 11th. In the performance of this service all the good qualities of British troops have been conspicuous to a degree which I have seldom witnessed. In bringing on their ordnance and stores to the point of attack, the troops of Colonel Stevenson's Division performed the most laborious work with a zeal for the service, and patience and perseverance never surpassed ; and when opposed to the enemy, their conduct showed the same gallant spirit that has carried the British troops through so many difficulties in the course of the war.

Although the most laborious and the most brilliant part of the service did not fall to the lot of the troops of my division, I have to apprise your Excellency that they performed the part allotted to them in a manner perfectly satisfactory to me ; and Lieut.-Colonel Wallace, Lieut.-Colonel Chalmers, and Capt. Beauman, commanding the Artillery, have received my thanks for the manner in which the two former led their divisions to the attack, and the latter exerted himself, to forward the service of the department.

I shall hereafter have the honour of transmitting to your Excellency a list of the killed and wounded, and returns of the ordnance and property captured in the fort."

(3).

Siege of Asseerghur (March, 1819).

In 1819 it was again found necessary to capture Asseerghur, and a force for this purpose was assembled under Brigadier-General Doveton and consisted of :—
Three regiments of Native cavalry.
Three and a-half battalions of European infantry.
Seven battalions of Native infantry.
Also a division brought down from Malwa by Malcolm composed of 1 regiment of cavalry, 4 battalions of Native infantry, with horse artillery and trains of both forces. Besides this, a further train was on its way detached from Sangor under Brigadier-General Watson. There were altogether 28 guns, 15 mortars and 19 howitzers.

The pettah is situated to the west of the fort in a hollow intersected by numerous ravines, and is commanded by the lower fort. The pettah was carried by assault at daybreak on March 18th, 1819, by the columns under Brigadiers Sir John Malcolm and Doveton.

Doveton's Column, commanded by Colonel Fraser and led by H.M.'s Royal Scots, entered the pettah by the south-west gate at head of the Buttakerah Nullah ; Malcolm's Column entered by the high road from Boorgaum, through a gap in the hills which covers the pettah on the north-east. The enemy were taken by surprise, made little opposition, and our troops soon established themselves under cover of the houses, with a trifling loss occasioned by fire from the lower fort.

The Engineer Department was established in a large bombproof pagoda in the centre of the pettah, and the troops occupied the street in advance, which runs parallel to the fort. On March 23rd the Engineers reconnoitred the east front of the fort to fire on ground for General Doveton's Encampment.

On March 27th the Ram Bagh under the north-east angle of the upper fort was occupied, and the Engineer Depôt stationed there.

On April 7th, the breaching batteries opened on the retaining walls, and with the assistance of a third breaching battery a practicable breach was nearly effected.

On April 8th the breaching batteries opened at daybreak. About 11 a.m. orders were received to cease fire, the killadar, Jeswant Rao Lar, having agreed to an unconditional surrender.

(4).

BLOCKADE OF CADIZ (February, 1810).

The fourth siege of the present series is that of Cadiz. In this instance the French were the besiegers whilst the British formed part of the defending force.

Before giving the details of this siege, it may be well to recall briefly the events which led up to it. It was in October, 1807, that Napoleon laid his first steps for the future conquest of Spain, by signing a secret convention with the Spanish minister for the partition of Portugal between France and Spain. For this purpose 28,000 French troops were to be sent into Spain for the ultimate occupation of Portugal, whilst an additional 40,000 were to be cantoned at Bayonne as a support to the first Corps. The natural result followed. Portugal was easily overrun by the Allies whilst the French reinforcements entered Spain and secured several of the Northern fortresses. Meanwhile the dissensions of the Spanish Royal Family provided Napoleon with a pretext for dethroning the Spanish Bourbons and for replacing them by his brother Joseph. This act was, however, immediately followed by a general uprising of the Spanish people, during which the people of Cadiz compelled the French warships there to surrender, and the levies of Andalusia forced General Dupont and 23,000 men to lay down their arms at Baylen. Sir Arthur Wellesley, also, landed with a British force and, after the Battle of Vimiera, Junot—who was in command of the French—agreed to evacuate the country. Napoleon now seriously turned his attention to the subjugation of Spain. In January, 1809, the British force under Sir John Moore was compelled to retreat and re-embark at Corunna and, although in the following July, Sir A. Wellesley again defeated the French at Talavera, by the end of the year they were virtually masters of Spain. In January, 1810, they entered Seville, overran Andalusia and pushed on to capture Cadiz. The city was at the time utterly unprepared for attack and there were under 1,000 men in the Isle of Leon. Fortunately General Alburquerque, on his own initiative and contrary to the orders he had received, realized the vital importance of saving the town. Pushing on with the greatest rapidity and by forced marches, he outmanœuvred and outstripped the French, and on the 2nd of February, after a march of over 260 miles he entered the Isle of Leon with 8,000 men.

Defeated in his attempt to surprise Cadiz, Victor spread his troops round the margin of the bay and commenced works of contravallation, 25 miles in length. Although the towns, the islands, the castles, the harbours, and rivers thus enclosed are too numerous, and in their relative bearings too intricate for minute description, the leading features shall in due course be given.

The blockade comprised three grand divisions, separately entrenched, namely, Chiclana, Puerto Real, and Santa Maria. The first resting its left on the seacoast was carried across the Almanza and Chiclana Rivers to the Zuraque, being traced for 8 miles along a range of thickly wooded hills bordering a marsh from 1 to 3 miles broad : both the line and marsh were traversed by those rivers, and by many navigable water courses and creeks, all falling into the Santi Petri, a natural channel connecting the upper harbour of Cadiz with the open sea. This channel, 9 miles long, 200 or 300 yards wide, and of depth to float a seventy-four, was the first Spanish line of defence. In the centre, the bridge of Zanzo, by which the only road to Cadiz passes, was broken and was also defended by batteries on both sides. On the right hand the Caraccas, or Royal Arsenal, situated on an island in the harbour mouth of the channel, and on account of the marsh not open to attack save by water or by bombardment, was covered with strong batteries and served as an advanced post. On the left hand the Castle of Santi Petri, also built upon an island, defended the sea-mouth of the channel.

Beyond the Santi Petri was the Isla de Leon, a vast triangular salt marsh, but having one high strong ridge in the centre, about 4 miles long, on which the town of Isla stands ; this ridge within cannon shot of the Santi Petri offered the second line of defence.

At the apex of the Isla stood the Torre Gardo, from whence a low narrow isthmus 5 miles long connected it with the rocks on which

Cadiz is built.   Across the centre of the isthmus, a cut, called the Cortadura and defended by the large unfinished fort of Fernando, offered a third line of defence.   The fourth and final line was the land front of Cadiz, regularly fortified.

On the Chiclana line, the hostile forces were only separated by the marsh. The Spaniards possessed the Santi Petri, but the French, having their chief depôts in the town of Chiclana, could always command the marsh, and might force the passage of the channel. For the Chiclana, Turaque and Almanza Creeks were navigable beyond the lines of contravallation, the thick woods behind furnished means of constructing an armed flotilla, and the Santi Petri itself, on both sides, could only be approached by water off the high road ; or at best by narrow footpaths leading between the salt pans of the marsh.

The French centre, called the Puerto Real Division, extended from the Turaque on the right for a distance of 7 miles. This line ending at the town of Puerto Real was traced along a ridge skirting the marsh, so as to form with the position of Chiclana a half-circle. Puerto Real was entrenched ; but a tongue of land 4 miles long projected from it perpendicularly towards the isthmus of Cadiz, being cloven in its whole length by the creek or canal of Trocadero.   It separated the inner from the outer harbour, and at its extreme points stood the village of Trocadero, and the fort of Matagorda ; opposed to which there was, on the isthmus of Cadiz, a powerful battery called the Puntales.

From Matagorda to Cadiz was above 4,000 yards ; but from Puntales it was only 1,200, and was therefore the nearest point to Cadiz, and to the isthmus, and the most important post of defence. From thence the French could search the upper harbour with their fire, or throw shells into the Caraccas and the fort of Fernando ; while their flotilla, safely moored in the Trocadero Creek, could quickly reach the isthmus and turn the Isla, with all the works between it and the city ; nevertheless the Spaniards dismantled and abandoned Matagorda.

The Third or Santa Maria Division of blockade followed the sweep of the bay. Reckoning from the San Pedro on the left, to the Castle of Santa Catalina, the extreme point of the outer harbour on the right, was about 5 miles. The town of Santa Maria, built at the mouth of the Guadalete in the centre of this line, was entrenched, and the ground about Santa Catalina was extremely rugged.

Beyond these lines, which were connected by a covered way concealed by thick woods and finally armed with 300 guns, the towns of Rota and San Lucar de Barameda were occupied ; the first, situated on a cape of land opposite to Cadiz, was the northern point of the great bay or roadstead ; the second commanded the mouth of the Guadalquiver. Behind these lines of blockade, Latour

Maubourg occupied Medina Sidonia with a covering division, his left being upon the upper Guadalete, his advanced posts watching the passes of the Sierra di Ronda.

General William Stewart reached Cadiz with 2,000 men the 11th February; 1,000 more joined him from Gibraltar, and all were received with enthusiasm. The Portuguese troops were equally well received, and soon 4,000 Anglo-Portuguese, and 14,000 Spanish regulars were behind the Santi Petri.

The ships recovered at Ferrol had been transferred to Cadiz, and thus were in the bay 23 men-of-war, four of the line and three frigates being British. The *Euthalion* and *Undaunted* also arrived from Mexico, with six millions of dollars, and thus money, troops, and a fleet were suddenly collected at Cadiz. Yet to little purpose. Procrastination, jealousy, ostentation, and a thousand absurdities marred every useful measure, and there was so little enthusiasm among the people that no citizen was enrolled, or armed, or volunteered either to labour or to fight.

Stewart's first measure was to recover Matagorda. In the night of the 22nd a detachment consisting of 50 seamen and Marines, 25 artillerymen and 67 of the 94th Regiment, pushed across the channel during a storm, took possession of the dismantled fort and effected a solid lodgment : the French cannonaded the work with field artillery all the next day, yet the garrison supported by the fire of Puntales, was immovable, and the remainder of February passed without any event of importance. Early in March the city wanted provisions, especially fresh meat, and a tempest beating on the coast from the 7th to the 10th of March, drove three Spanish and one Portuguese sail of the line, a frigate and from 30 to 40 merchantmen on shore between San Lucar and St. Mary's. One ship of the line was taken, the others were burnt and part of the crews brought off by boats from the fleet ; but many men, amongst others a part of the 4th English Regiment, fell into the hands of the enemy, together with an immense booty.

On the 15th the enemy's outposts at Santi Petri were driven in by Major Sullivan, of the 79th, to cover an attack meditated against the Trocadero, but the design was baffled by the surf in one quarter and the difficulty of crossing a shoal in another. In the same month Mr. H. Wellesley, Minister Plenipotentiary, arrived ; and on the 24th General Graham, coming from England, assumed the chief command of the British troops and immediately caused an exact military survey of the Isle to be made. It then appeared that the force hitherto assigned for its defence was quite inadequate. Twenty thousand soldiers, with redoubts and batteries, requiring the labour of 4,000 men for three months, were absolutely necessary ; the Spaniards had only worked beyond the Santi Petri, and there without judgment. Their batteries in the marsh were ill-placed, their entrenchments at the sea-mouth were contemptible ; the caraccas though armed with 150 guns was full of dry timber and could be easily burnt by carcasses. The interior defences of the Isla were quite neglected. Matagorda and the Trocadero had been abandoned, but the batteries beyond the Santi Petri had been pushed to the junction of the Chiclana road with the Royal causeway ; that is to say 1½ miles beyond the bridge of Zanzo, and consequently exposed without support to flank attacks both by water and land.

It was in vain that the English engineers presented plans and offered to construct the works, the Spaniards would never consent to pull down a house or destroy a garden ; their procrastination paralyzed their Allies, and would have lost the place had the French been prepared to press it vigorously.

Additional reinforcements reached Cadiz the 31st, and both sides continued to labour at their lines ; but the Allies worked slowly and without harmony, the people's supplies were interrupted, scarcity prevailed, many persons were forced to quit the city and 2,000 Spanish troops were detached by sea to Ayamonte to collect provisions on the Guadina.

Matagorda was small, of a square form, without a ditch, without sufficient bombproofs, and having one angle projecting towards the land ; it could only bring seven guns to bear, yet though frequently cannonaded it had been held 55 days, and now impeded the completion of the French works. A Spanish seventy-four supported with an armed flotilla moored on the flanks, and co-operated in the defence ; but at daybreak on the 21st heavy batteries, hitherto masked by some houses on the Trocadero, sent a hissing shower of hot shot upon the ships and drove them for shelter to Cadiz. Then the fire of 48 guns and mortars of the largest size were concentrated on the little fort, and the feeble parapet disappeared in a moment before the crushing flight of metal. The naked rampart and the undaunted hearts of the garrison remained ; yet the men fell fast, and the enemy shot so quick and close, that a staff bearing the Spanish flag was broken six times in an hour. The colours were then fastened on the angle of the work itself, to the discontent of both soldiers and sailors who besought their officers to hoist the British ensign, attributing their slaughter to their fighting under a foreign flag. Thirty hours this tempest lasted, and 64 men out of 140 had fallen, when General Graham, finding a diversion he had projected impracticable, sent boats to carry off the survivors. A bastion was then blown up under the superintendence of Major Lefebure, an engineer of great promise, but he also fell, the last man whose blood wetted the ruins thus abandoned.

Matagorda Point was soon covered with batteries by the French, but the war languished in front of Cadiz.

In May some French prisoners cut the cables of two hulks at Cadiz and drifted in a heavy gale to the French side ; they beat off two of the craft sent after them by throwing cold shot from the decks, and about 1,500 saved themselves, despite of the fire from the allied fleet, and from the batteries. Cadiz was now a scene of great disorder. The English General was hampered by the perverse spirit of the authorities, and the Spanish troops were daily getting more inefficient from neglect.

Blake was then called to command in the Isla, and his presence produced some amelioration in the condition and discipline of the troops ; and at his instance the British Engineers commenced a regular system of redoubts for the defence of the Isla. English reinforcements continued to arrive, and 4,000 Spaniards joined the garrison now within the lines ; but such was the state of the Spanish troops, such the difficulty of arranging plans, that hitherto the taking of Matagorda had been the only check given to the enemy's works.

In July the British force in Cadiz was increased to 8,500 men, and Sir Richard Keats took command of the fleet ; the French, intent upon completing their lines and constructing flotillas, made no attacks. The preparations at Matagorda constantly and seriously menaced Cadiz, and a British division was necessarily kept there ; for the English Generals were well assured that some fatal disaster would otherwise befall the Spaniards. Graham's Division might have been set free instead of being cooped up without any counter-balance in the number of French troops employed to blockade. The latter aided indirectly, and at times directly, in securing Andalusia, and if not at Chiclana, must have been covering Seville as long as there was an army in the Isla ; but Graham merely defended Cadiz.

In November, 1810, while the Spaniards were entirely occupied with the debates in congress, the French works were finished : their chain of forts was completed, each fort having a ditch and palisades with a week's provisions. Soult came to San Lucar, and his flotilla there and at Santa Maria, Puerto Real, and Chiclana, being all ready for action he proceeded to concentrate. On the last night of October 30 pinnaces and gunboats, slipping out of the Guadalquiver, eluded the allied fleet, passed along the coast to Rota, and from thence, aided by shore batteries, fought their way to Santa Maria and the San Pedro River. But to avoid the danger of doubling Matagorda the vessels were transported overland on rollers, and 130 armed vessels and transports were thus safely assembled in the Trocadero Canal. At the Trocadero Point there were immense batteries, and some notable pieces of ordnance, invented by Colonel Villantwys, called cannon-mortars. These huge engines, one of which was afterwards placed in St. James's Park, were cast at Seville, and being placed in slings, threw projectiles over Cadiz, a distance of more than 5,000 yards. To obtain this flight the shells were partly filled with lead, and their charge was too small for an effective explosion, yet they alarmed the city and were troublesome to the shipping.

Soult's design was to ruin by superior fire the fort of the Puntales then to pass the straits with his flotilla, and establish his army between the Isla and the city ; nor was this plan chimerical, for on the side of the besieged there was neither conceit nor industry. New drafts made by Wellington had reduced Graham's force to 5,000 men, and in October the fever broke out ; but as Soult's preparations became formidable, reinforcements were diawn from Gibraltar and Sicily, and at the end of the year, 7,000 British, Germans and Portuguese were still behind the Santi Petri. To insure naval superiority, Admiral Keats drew all the armed craft from Gibraltar. To secure the land defence, Graham urged the Regency to adopt certain plans, and he was warmly seconded ty Sir Henry Wellesley ; but neither their entreaties nor the inconvenience of the danger could overcome the apathy of the Spaniards ; their troops were wanting in discipline, clothing and equipment and only 16,000 men of all arms were effective on a muster roll of 23,000. The labour of the British troops far from being assisted was impeded, and December ended before Graham, after many altercations, could even obtain leave to put the interior line of the Cortadura in a state of defence.

When in February, 1811,* Graham knew that Soult had gone to Estremadura he undertook to drive Victor from his lines. Troops sailing from Cadiz were to disembark in rear of the French and be joined by the garrison of Tarifa under Major Brown and by 3,000 Spaniards from San Rouque under General Beguines. Contrary winds delayed the expedition, and the despatch vessels carrying counter-orders to Brown and Beguines being likewise retarded, those officers advanced, the first to Medina, the second to Casa Vieja. Victor got notice of the design and kept close in his works, until he heard of this failure in the combinations, when he sent troops to retake Medina and the Casa. At the same time 12,000 men from the Northern Govern-ments reached him and his whole force being 20,000, he had 15,000 in the lines ; the remainder were at San Lucar, Medina, and other ports. This was known at Cadiz, but 10,000 infantry and 600 cavalry were again embarked, being this time to land at Tarifa, and march straight on Chiclana. General Layas was left in command of the Isla with orders to throw a bridge over the Santi Petri near the sea-mouth.

On the 22nd the British troops passed their port in a gale, and landed at Algescias, marched to Tarifa the next day, and were joined by the 28th Regiment, and the flank companies of the 9th and 82nd Regiments. Thus more than 4,000 effective troops including 2 companies of the 20th Portuguese, and 180 German hussars were assembled under Graham ; all good and hardy troops, and himself a daring old man and of a ready temper for battle. The Captain-General, La Peña, landed on the 27th with 7,000 Spaniards, and Graham to preserve unanimity ceded the command, although it was contrary to his instruction. Next day a march of 12 miles carried

* Official abstract of military reports MSS.

them over the ridges which separate the plains of San Roque from those of Medina and Chiclana, and being then within 4 leagues of the enemy's posts the troops were reorganized. The vanguard was given to Lardizabal, the centre to the Prince of Anglona; the reserve, composed of two Spanish regiments and the British troops, was confided to Graham: the cavalry of both nations, formed in one body, was under Colonel Whittingham, then in the Spanish service.

Before this Beguines and the partidas had driven the French into Casa Vieja and Medina; but General Cassaque being reinforced had retaken both places and entrenched Medina, acting as a covering force to the river. Victor manned his works at Rota, Santa Maria, Puerto Real and the Trocadero, with a mixed force of Juramentados and regular troops; but he assembled 11,000 good soldiers near Chiclana between the roads of Couil and the Medina, to await the unfolding of the Allies' project which was not delayed.

La Peña having 12,000 infantry, 800 horsemen and 24 guns turned towards the coast and drove the French from Vejer de la Frontiera. The following evening he continued his movement and on the morning of the 5th after a skirmish, in which his advanced guard of cavalry was routed by a French squadron, he reached the heights of Barosa being then 4 miles from the sea-mouth of the Santi Petri. Then followed the bloody Battle of Barosa which is fully described in the XIIth book of Napier's *Peninsular War*. The battle lasted only $1\frac{1}{2}$ hours, but 50 officers, 60 sergeants, 1,100 British soldiers, and more than 2,000 French were killed and wounded: 6 guns and an eagle, 2 generals, both mortally wounded, together with 400 other prisoners fell into the hands of the victors.

All the passages in this extraordinary battle were broadly marked, and La Peña's contemptible weakness was surprisingly contrasted with the heroic vigour of Graham whose attack was rather an inspiration than a resolution, so wise, so sudden, was the decision, so conclusive the execution.

After the Battle of Barosa violent disputes arose in Cadiz. La Peña in an address to the Cortes claimed the victory for himself; he said that the arrangements previous to the battle were made with the knowledge and approbation of the English General, and the latter's retreat to the Isla was the real cause of failure.

Graham incensed at this proceeding wrote a letter to the British envoy in which he exposed La Peña's misconduct: he refused with disdain the title of Grandee of the First Class voted to him by the Cortes, and when Lascy used expressions relative to the action personally offensive he enforced an apology with his sword. Having thus shown himself superior to his opponents at all points, the gallant old man relinquished his command to General Cooke, and joined Lord Wellington's Army.

CHAPTER TWO

With Graham's departure from Cadiz, the principal interest in the defence ceases, and although the siege dragged on till 1812, it ultimately proved unsuccessful.

In the present number it is proposed to deal with the Lines of Torres Vedras, which are referred to by Sir J. T. Jones in his *Sieges in Spain* as " a triumph of the British Nation."

The idea of fortifying the hills round Lisbon seems to have first occurred to the Duke of Wellington towards the end of 1809, when he realized how untenable was his position at Badajoz, and how necessary it would be for him to devise some different means of defence to enable him to resist the overwhelming masses which he foresaw would shortly be hurled against him by Napoleon. In his memorandum to Sir R. Fletcher dated October 20th, 1809, he commences with a clear summing up of the situation, and then instructs Colonel Fletcher to examine and report upon the defensive capabilities of the position under 21 separate headings. As Sir R. Fletcher's report confirmed Wellington's opinion, work was at once commenced upon the Lines, and was continued without a break right up to the time when the British Army, closely pursued by the French, entered the outer line of defence on the 8th of October, 1810.

The position thus fortified consisted of three distinct lines of defence.

The first extending from Alhandra on the Tagus to the mouth of the Zizandre on the sea coast, was, following the inflection of the hills 29 miles long.

The second traced at a distance varying from 6 to 10 miles, in rear of the first, stretched from Quintella on the Tagus to the mouth of the St. Lorenza, being 24 miles in length.

The third intended to cover a forced embarkation, extended from Passo d'Arcos on the Tagus to the tower of Junguera on the coast. Here an outward line, constructed in an opening of 3,000 yards, enclosed an entrenched camp, the latter being designed to cover an embarkation with fewer troops if such an operation should be delayed by bad weather. This second camp enclosed Fort St. Julian whose high ramparts and deep ditches defied an escalade, and were armed to enable a rear guard to resist any force. From Passo d'Arcos to the nearest part of the second line was 24 miles ; from the first line it was two marches, but the principal routes lay through Lisbon, where means to retard the enemy were prepared.

Of these stupendous lines the second, whether for strength or importance, was the principal; the other two were subsidiary—the third being a mere place of refuge. The first line was originally designed as an advanced work, to stem the primary violence of the enemy, and to enable the army to take up its ground on the second line without hurry or pressure; but, while Massena remained inactive on the frontier, it acquired strength which was so much augmented by the rain, that Wellington resolved to abide the attack there permanently.

It offered five distinct positions from right to left as follows:—

1st. From Alhandra to the head of the valley of Calandrix. This portion 5 miles long was a continuous and lofty ridge defended by 13 redoubts, and for 2 miles was rendered inaccessible by a scarp 15 to 20 ft. high. It was guarded by Hill's Corps, and flanked from the Tagus by a flotilla of gunboats manned by British seamen.

2nd. From the head of the valley of Calandrix to the Pé de Monte. This portion also of 5 miles, presented two salient mountains forming the valley of Aruda, that town being exactly in the mouth of the pass. Only three feeble redoubts incapable of stopping an enemy were constructed here, and the defence was entrusted to the light division.

3rd. The Monte Agraça. This lofty mountain overtopped the adjacent country, and from its summit the whole of the first line could be seen. The right was separated from the Aruda position by a deep and blind ravine ; the left overlooked the village and valley of Zibriera; the centre overhung the town of Sobral: the summit was crowned by an immense redoubt armed with 25 guns, round which three smaller works armed with 19 guns were clustered. The garrisons amounting to 2,000 men were supplied by Pack's Brigade ; and on the reverse slope about 4 miles in length, Leith was posted in reserve.

4th. From the valley of Zibriera to Torres Vedras. This portion 7 miles long was at first without works, because it was only when the rains had set in that the resolution to defend the first line permanently was adopted. But the ground, rough and well defined, having a deep valley in front watered by the Zizandre now a considerable river, presented a fine field of battle.

Here Spenser and Cole, reinforced with a sixth division formed of troops recently come from England and Cadiz, were stationed under the immediate command of Wellington, whose quarters were fixed at Pero Negro, just under the lofty Secora Rock, on which a telegraph was erected to communicate with every part of the line.

5th. From the heights of Torres Vedras to the mouth of the Zizandre, the right flank of this portion and a pass in front of the town of Torres Vedras were secured by a great redoubt mounting 40 guns, and by smaller forts judiciously planted so as to command all the approaches. From these works to the sea a range of moderate heights was crowned with minor redoubts ; but the chief defence there, after the rains had set in, was to be found in the Zizandre, unfordable and overflowing so as to form an impassable marsh. Such were the defences of the first line, strong, but at several points defective ; and there was a paved road, running parallel to the foot of the hills through Torres Vedras, Sobral and Aruda to Alhandra, which gave the enemy an advantage.

The second and most formidable line also will be described from left to right.

1st. From the mouth of the St. Loureñca to Mafra. In this distance of 7 miles there was a range of hills, naturally steep, artificially scarped, covered by a deep and in many parts impracticable ravine. The salient points were secured by forts which flanked and commanded the few accessible points ; but the line was extensive and a secondary post was fortified a few miles in the rear so as to secure a road leading from Eseceria to Cintra.

2nd. The Tapadas or Royal Park of Mafra. Here there was some open but strong ground, which with the Pass of Mafra was defended by a system of 14 redoubts constructed with great labour and care, well considered with respect to the natural features, and in some degree connected with the above-mentioned secondary post : the Sierra de Chypre, covered with redoubts, was in front and obstructed all approaches to Mafra itself.

3rd. From the Tapadas to the Pass of Bucellas. In this space of 10 or 12 miles forming the middle of the second line, the country is choked by the Monte Chique, the head of which is in the centre of, and overtops all the other mountain masses. A road conducted along a chain of hills, high and salient through less bold than any other part of the line, connected Mafra with the Cabeça, and was secured by a number of forts. The country in front was exceedingly difficult, and behind was a parallel and stronger ridge which could only be approached with artillery by the connecting road in front ; but to reach that, the Sierra de Chypre on the left, or the defile of the Cabeça must have been carried. Now the latter was covered by a cluster of redoubts constructed on some inferior rocky heads in advance ; they commanded all the approaches, and from their artificial and natural strength were nearly impregnable. The Cabeça itself and its immediate flanks were secure in their natural precipitous strength ; so likewise were the ridges connecting the Cabeça with the Pass of Bucellas, wherefore, save the blocking of one mule path they were untouched.

4th. From Bucellas to the low ground about the Tagus. The defile of Bucellas, rugged and narrow, was defended by redoubts on each side, and a ridge, or rather a collection of impassable rocks, called the Sierra de Serves, stretched to the right of it for 2 miles without a break, and then died away by a succession of ridges into the low ground on the bank of the Tagus. These declivities and the flat bank of the river offered an accessible opening, 2½ miles wide. It was laboriously defended indeed by redoubts, water-cuts, retrenchments, and was carefully connected with the heights of Alhandra ; yet it was the weakest part of the line, and dangerous from its proximity to the valleys of Calandrix and Aruda.

Five roads, practicable for guns, pierced the first line of defence ; two at Torres Vedras, two at Sobral, one at Alhandra ; but as two of these united again at the Cabeça, there were only four points of passage through the second line. Hence the aim and scope were to bar these roads, and strengthen the favourable fighting positions between them without impeding the movements of the army ; the loss of the first line therefore would not have been injurious, save in reputation, because the retreat was secure upon the second and stronger line ; moreover the guns of the first line were all of inferior calibre, mounted on common truck carriages, immovable and useless to the enemy. The allies' movements were quite unfettered by the works, but those of the French Army were impeded by the Monte Junta, which rising opposite to the centre of the first line, threw out a spur, called the Sierra de Baraqueda, in a slanting direction towards the Torres Vedras Mountain, and only separated from it by the Pass of Ruña, which was commanded by heavy redoubts. Massena had therefore to dispose his army on one or the other side of the Baraqueda which could not be easily passed ; nor could a movement over it be hidden from the allies on the Monte Agraça, who from thence could pour down simultaneously on the head and tail of the passing columns with the utmost rapidity, because convenient roads had been previously prepared, and telegraphs established for the transmission of orders.

Such were the lines which, in the words of Sir John Jones, " are without doubt the finest specimen of a fortified position ever effected. Every objection heretofore urged against lines fail in application to those. From their peninsular situation there is no possibility of manœuvring on the flanks, cutting off the supplies, or getting in rear of them : in the details of the work there is no pedantry of science ; no long lines of fortification for them without strength ; mountains them-selves are made the prominent points ; the gorges alone derive their total strength from retrenchments. The quantity of labour bestowed on them is incredible, but in no part has the Engineer done more than his duty ; assisted nature, assisted the general, and assisted the troops, and for each arm has procured a favourable field of action. For the militia there are nearly unattackable posts to guard the passes ; for the infantry, admirable fields of battle, suited to ensure and to profit by victory ; for the cavalry, spacious plains to which the enemy must arrive through passes rendered impracticable to their cavalry and artillery. No movement either forward or lateral is cramped ; on the contrary, one chief beauty of these lines is the facility afforded to communication . by a system of judicious and well-planned roads, the distance between each point and each corps of troops has been one-half shortened ; and from the precaution of having these roads commanded by works not to be reduced without artillery, they become useless to an enemy in case of accident or partial success ; and on the great scale, Nature has contributed much to this object by placing Monte Junta immediately in front of the centre of the line, the ramifications of which, extending to the very works, render the enemy's movements in front of the lines tedious and difficult, and give to a body of troops posted within, a superiority of movement rendering them equal to twice the numbers without.''

These celebrated lines were great in conception and execution, more in keeping with ancient than modern military labours ; and it is clear that the defence was not dependent, as some French writers suppose, upon the first line. If that had been stormed the standard of Portuguese independence would still have floated securely amidst the rocks of the second line. But to occupy 50 miles of fortification, to man 150 forts, and work 600 guns, required many men, and numbers were not wanting. A great fleet in the Tagus, a superb body of Marines sent out from England, the civic guards of Lisbon, the Portuguese heavy artillery corps, the Militia and ordnance of Estremadura, furnished a powerful reserve to the Regular Army. The Native gunners and the Militia supplied all the garrisons of the forts on the second, and most of those on the first line ; the British Marines occupied the third line ; the Navy manned the gunboats on the river, and aided in various ways the operations in the field. The recruits from the depôts, and the calling in of all the men on furlough, rendered the Portuguese Army stronger than it had yet been, while the British troops reinforced from Cadiz and England, and remarkably healthy, presented such a front as a general would desire to see in a dangerous crisis.

It was however necessary to have the appearance of even greater strength, and Wellington therefore arranged with Romana, that without much attention to the wishes of his own government, he should join the allies with 6,000 men. Fortune aided the English general's efforts to increase the distance between Massena and Soult, and to diversify their objects at the moment he had concentrated the

greatest force at the most important point ; for before Septembe
more than 120,000 men were rationed within the lines, 70,000 bein
Regular troops.

Massena was surprised at the extent and strength of works whic
he had only heard of five days before, and it is scarcely necessary t
dwell upon the remarkable way in which they achieved their objec
nor to show how they practically proved to be the turning point in th
Peninsular War. The French Army when it arrived before ther
numbered over 50,000 men flushed with victory, and although this forc
was further reinforced by another 10,000, Sir John Jones estimates tha
only some 40,000 men were left when Massena on the 5th of Marcl
determined to retire out of Portugal so as to save his army fron
complete destruction. Even then, although he conducted his retrea
in a masterly manner, his broken, starving troops were in no way ;
match for their victorious adversaries. For one month Lore
Wellington constantly harassed his retreating troops allowing then
no respite, until he finally drove them over the frontiers in a state o
sickness and misery which ultimately destroyed more of them thar
any partial action could have done. No decisive action was fough
during this pursuit, as in Wellington's own words he preferred " tc
harass them and send them out of the country as a rabble when from
want of organization and from sickness, they will not be able to act
for many months, and to keep my own army entire, rather than
to weaken myself by fighting them, and probably be so crippled,
as not to have the ascendant over fresh troops on the frontiers."

Finally, on the 5th of April the French Army recrossed the Spanish
frontier, and Wellington halting his troops at Alfaiates gave up the
pursuit.

CHAPTER THREE

The retreat of the army under Marshal Massena having virtually freed Portugal from the French, Wellington began to contemplate extensive and decisive operations in Spain. Before being able to carry these out, however, it was necessary for him to recapture Almeida and Badajoz, which had been taken by Marshal Soult whilst the Allies were still occupied with the defence of Lisbon. As soon therefore as Massena had crossed the frontier Wellington invested Almeida and after the defeat of the French at Fuentes d'Onor its retention by them was rendered practically hopeless. Unfortunately the carelessness of some of the subordinate generals allowed General Brennier, the Governor, to escape in safety with the garrison after he had successfully ruined the fortifications, but its fall allowed Wellington to turn his whole attention to Badajoz. He soon realized that, although its capture would tend greatly to the security of the Portuguese provinces on the left of the Tagus, it would not enable him by any direct operations to weaken the strong hold the French had obtained on the south of Spain. He rather proposed, if Badajoz should fall, to attack Ciudad Rodrigo, and thus render secure the Beira and the northern districts of Portugal.

Sir John Jones in his *Sieges in Spain* describes the fortress of Badajoz as follows :—" Badajoz is a large fortified town situated on the left bank of the Guadiana ; which river is there from 300 to 500 yards broad and washes about one-fourth of the enceinte of the place, rendering it nearly inattackable ; the defences to the land consist of eight large well-built regular fronts, with a good covered way and glacis, but the ravelins unfinished. The fronts have whole revetments, and the escarp of the bastions exceeds 30 ft. in height, that of the curtains being much lower : in advance of these fronts are two detached works ; one called the Pardaleras, at 200 yards distant, is a crown work ; its escarps are low, its ditches narrow, and its rear badly closed ; the other, called the Picurina, is a strong redoubt at 400 yards in advance of the town. On the N.E. at the angle formed by the junction of the river Rivillas with the Guadiana, rises a hill to the height of 120 ft., the summit of which is crowned by an old castle, and its walls naked, weak, and but partially flanked, here form part of the enceinte of the place.

The space contained within the castle is considerable, and various projects have at different times been under consideration for occupying it by works, but nothing had ever been carried into effect ; indeed the defences of the castle had been unaccountably neglected ; two or three fieldpieces only being mounted on its walls, and those without the shelter of proper parapets.

Immediately opposite the castle, on the other side of the Guadiana, at a distance of 500 yards, are situated the heights of Christoval, rising to nearly the elevation of the castle ; and as the terreplein of the castle is an inclined plane towards the Guadiana, every part of it is seen from the Christoval Heights ; to prevent an enemy readily availing himself of this advantage in any attack of the town, a fort has been constructed on them ; its figure is nearly that of a square of 300 ft. ; the scarp is well built of stone, and is 20 ft. in height. The communication between the town and Fort Christoval is very open to interruption, being either by a bridge 600 yards in length, subject to be enfiladed, or by boats for which there is no security."

From the above it will be seen that the task before Wellington was an exceedingly formidable one, but he determined to lay immediate siege to the fortress if any plan of attack could be evolved which would not require more than 16 days' open trenches. This was all the time that could be considered available, as in that period, including the time required to complete the necessary siege preparations, Marshal Soult would be able to collect a sufficient force to raise the siege. The proper point of attack was one of the south fronts, but to approach either of them would have entailed the reduction of the Pardaleras outwork which would have necessitated the opening of the trenches at a greater distance than usual from the fortress. To carry out this plan of attack would have needed a period of at least 22 days and, in addition, it was realized that the means provided were wholly insufficient to ensure success.

Under these circumstances the Chief Engineer, Colonel Fletcher, proposed to breach the castle, while batteries established on the right bank of the Guadiana took the defences in reverse. False attacks against the Pardaleras and Picurina were to be made by reopening Soult's trenches, and it was necessary to reduce San Christoval before the batteries to take the castle in reverse could be constructed. With this object in view Capt. Squire was directed to break ground there on the night of the 8th of May. The moon shone brightly, he was ill-provided with tools and exposed to a destructive musketry fire from the fort and to shot and shell from the town ; nevertheless he worked with great loss until the 10th of May when the French made a furious sortie and carried the battery. They were immediately driven back by the reserves, but the Allies pursued too far, . and being taken in flank and front with grape lost 400 men. By this time five engineers had fallen and 700 officers and soldiers of the Line had been sacrificed, and only one small battery against an outwork was completed ! On the 11th it opened, and before sunset the fire of the enemy had disabled four of its five guns, and killed many more of the besiegers ; nor could any other result be expected, since the concert essential to success in double operations, whether in sieges or the field, was neglected. Squire's single work was exposed to the undivided fire of the fortress, up to the time of the approaches against the castle being commenced ; and two distant batteries which had been constructed at the false attacks scarcely attracted the notice of the enemy. To check further sallies, a second battery was erected against the bridgehead, but this was also over-matched, and intelligence having been received that the French Army was in movement, the progress of all the works was arrested by Beresford. On the 12th, believing that this information was premature, he directed the trenches to be opened against the castle. But the intelligence proved to be true, and being confirmed at 12 o'clock the same night, the working parties were again drawn off and measures taken to raise the siege.

On the night of the 13th all the batteries were dismantled and on the night of the 14th such materials as could not be moved were burned. Part of the Army had already marched to Valverde to oppose Marshal Soult who had already reached Llerena, and on the 15th the remainder of the besieging force moved to join it. Sir John Jones remarks that this raising of the siege was in truth most fortunate, as at that period the strength of Badajoz was not duly appreciated, nor was it realized that the means prepared for the attack were altogether too inconsiderable. " The besieging corps itself," he adds, " was too small, particularly to attack Christoval ; from which, and the want of entrenching tools, a sufficient extent of ground to oppose a proper front to the enemy could not be opened the first night and gave an opportunity for the sortie." He also points out the inexperience of the Portuguese gunners and the numerical and other inferiority of the besiegers' guns, and he concludes by saying that, had the enemy not caused the siege to be raised " after a great sacrifice of men, in other feeble attempts, it would have brought itself to a conclusion from inability to proceed."

As mentioned above, the last troops drew off from Badajoz on the 15th and on the 16th Marshal Beresford defeated Soult at Albuera. As soon as the retreat of the enemy was known on the morning of the 18th, the cavalry was sent in pursuit of them, and on the same day Major-General Hamilton's Portuguese Division resumed the blockade of Badajoz, on the south of the Guadiana.

There is no operation in war more certain than a modern siege if the rules of art are strictly followed ; and unlike the ancient sieges in that particular it is also different in this, that no operation is less open to irregular daring, because the course of the engineer can neither be hurried nor delayed without danger.

Wellington knew the Siege of Badajoz in form required longer time and better means than were at his disposal ; but he was compelled either to incur danger and loss of reputation, which is loss of strength, or to adopt some compendious mode of taking the place. The time he could command, and time is in all sieges the greatest point, was precisely that which the French required to bring up a force sufficient to disturb the operation. Their doing so depended upon Marmont, whose march from Salamanca to Badajoz through Baños or the Gata could not be stopped by Spencer, seeing that those defiles were commanded by the French positions ; it was possible also at that season to ford the Tagus near Alcantara, and more than 20 days' free action against Badajoz could not be calculated upon. The battering-gun carriages used in Beresford's siege were damaged ; the artillery officers asked 11 days to repair them, and the scanty means of transport for stores were diminished by carrying the wounded from Albuera. Fifteen days of open trenches, and nine days of fire was all that could be expected, and with good guns, plentiful stores, and a corps of regular Sappers and Miners this time would have sufficed ; but none of these things were available.

Of the guns some were of soft brass and false in their bore ; the shot were of different sizes and the largest too small ; the Portuguese gunners were inexperienced, there were but few British artillerymen, fewer engineers, no sappers or miners, and no time to teach the troops how to make fascines and gabions. Regular approaches by the Pardaleras and the Picurina could not be attempted ; Beresford's line of attack on the castle and Fort Christoval were therefore adopted, avoiding the errors of that general ; that is to say the double attacks were to be pushed simultaneously and with more powerful means. San Christoval might then be taken, and batteries from it sweep the interior of the castle, which was meanwhile to be breached ; something also was hoped from the inhabitants, and something from the effect of Soult's retreat from Albuera. In this hope the work was begun. Major Dickson, an artillery officer, conspicuous for talent, prepared with unexpected rapidity a battering train of thirty 24-pounders, four 16-pounders, and twelve 8-in. and 10-in. howitzers used as mortars by placing them on trucks. Six iron Portuguese ship guns were forwarded from Salvatierra making altogether fifty-two pieces ; a convoy of engineer stores arrived from Alcacer do Sal ; and some British artillery came from Lisbon to be mixed with the Portuguese, making a total of 600 gunners. The regular engineer officers present were 21 in number ; 11 volunteers from the Line were joined as assistant engineers ; and a draft of 300 picked infantry, including 25 artificers of the staff corps, strengthened the force immediately under their command.

Hamilton's Portuguese Division was already before the town, and on the 24th May at the close of evening, Houston's division, increased to 5,000 men by the 17th Portuguese Regiment and the Tavira and Lagos Militia, invested San Christoval. The flying bridge was then laid down on the Guadiana, and on the 27th Picton's Division arrived from Campo Mayor, crossed the river by the ford above the town, and joined Hamilton, their united force being about 10,000 men. The covering army which included the Spaniards was under Hill, and spread from Mezida to Albuera ; the cavalry pushed forward in observation of Soult, and when intelligence arrived that Drouet was effecting a junction with that marshal, two regiments of cavalry, and two brigades of infantry quartered at Coria as posts of communication with Spencer, were called up to reinforce the covering army.

Phillipon had used the respite given him to level Beresford's trenches, repair his own damages, and obtain small supplies of wine and vegetables from the people of Estremadura, who were still awed by Soult's vicinity. Within the place all was quiet, for the citizens did not now exceed 5,000 souls, and when the place was invested parties of the townsmen, mixed with soldiers, were observed working to improve the defences. Wherefore, as retrenchments behind the intended points of attack would prolong the siege, a large telescope was placed in the tower of La Lippe at Elvas, with which the interior of the castle was plainly seen and all preparations discovered.

In the night of the 29th ground was broken for a false attack against the Pardaleras ; and the following night 1,600 workmen, with a covering party of 1,200, sunk a parallel against the castle on an extent of 1,100 yards, without being discovered by the enemy, who did not fire until after daylight. The same night 1,200 workmen, covered by 800 men, opened a parallel 450 yards from San Christoval and 700 yards from the bridgehead. On this line one breaching and two counter-batteries were raised against the fort and bridgehead to prevent a sally ; a fourth battery was also commenced to search the defences of the castle, but the workmen were discovered and a heavy fire struck down many of them.

On the 31st the attack against the castle, the soil being very soft, was rapidly pushed forward without much interruption ; but the Christoval attack, carried on in a rocky soil with earth brought from the rear, proceeded slowly and with considerable loss. This day the artillerymen from Lisbon came up on mules, and the engineers hastened the works. The direction of the parallel against the castle made the right gradually approach the point of attack, by which the heaviest fire of the place was avoided ; yet so great was the desire to save time that before the suitable point of distance was attained, a battery of fourteen 24-pounders with six large howitzers was marked out.

On the Christoval side the batteries were not finished before the night of the 1st June, for the rocky soil required that the miners should first level the ground for platforms ; and the garrison having mortars of 16 and 18-in. diameter mounted on the castle sent every shell amongst the workmen. These huge missiles would have ruined the batteries on that side altogether, if the latter had not been on the edge of a ridge from which most of the shells rolled off before bursting ; yet so difficult is it to judge rightly in war that Phillipon stopped this fire thinking it thrown away ! The work was also delayed by the bringing of earth from a distance, and woolpacks purchased at Elvas were used instead. However in the night of the 2nd all the batteries were completed and armed with 43 pieces of different sizes, 20 being pointed against the castle : the next day the fire opened but the windage caused by the smallness of the shot rendered it ineffectual at first and five pieces were soon rendered unserviceable. Towards evening the practice became steadier, the fire of the fort was nearly silenced, and the covering of masonry falling from the castle wall discovered a perpendicular bank of clay. Next night the parallel against the castle was prolonged, and a battery for seven guns traced out 650 yards from the breach. On the 4th the garrison's fire was increased by several additional guns, and six pieces of the besiegers were disabled.

Christoval was now much injured and some damage was done to the castle from one of the batteries on that side ; but the guns were so soft and bad that the rate of firing was greatly reduced in all the batteries. In the night the new battery was armed, the damaged works repaired, and next day the enemy having trained a gun in Christoval to plunge into the trenches on the castle side, the parallel was deepened and traverses constructed to protect the troops. Fifteen pieces still played against the castle, yet the bank of clay although falling away in flakes remained always perpendicular : one damaged gun was repaired on the Christoval side but two more had become unserviceable.

In the night the parallel against the castle was again extended and a fresh battery traced out 520 yards from the breach ; on the Christoval side also some new batteries were opened and some old ones abandoned. During this night the garrison began to entrench themselves behind the castle breach and two additional pieces from Christoval plunged into the trenches with great effect. On the other hand the besiegers' fire had broken the clay bank, which took a slope nearly practicable, and the stray shells set fire to the houses nearest the castle, but three more guns were disabled. On the 6th there were two breaches in Christoval, the principal one seeming practicable, and a company of grenadiers with twelve ladders were directed to assault it, while a second company turned the fort by the east. Three hundred men from the trenches were at the same time pushed forward by the west side to cut the communication between the fort and the bridgehead. while a detachment with a gun moved into the valley of the Gebora to prevent any passage of the Guadiana by boats.

First Assault of Christoval.

Major McIntosh, of the 85th Regiment, led the stormers, being preceded by a Forlorn Hope, under Lieut. Dyas, of the 51st ; and guided by the engineer, Forster, reached the glacis and descended the ditch without being discovered. The French had cleared the rubbish away, the breach had still 7 ft. of perpendicular wall, and above it were pointed beams of wood, and carts chained together, large shells being also arranged along the ramparts to roll down. The Forlorn Hope finding the opening impracticable was retiring with little loss, when the main body which had been exposed to a flank fire from the town as well as a direct fire from the fort, came leaping into the ditch with ladders. Then an effort was made to escalade at different points but the ladders were too short, and the garrison, consisting of only 75 men besides the gunners, made so stout a resistance, and the confusion and mischief caused by the bursting of the shells was so great, that the assailants finally retired with the loss of more than 100 men.

This failure was attributed by some to the breach being impracticable from the first, by others to confusion after the main body had entered. It is however evident that from inexperience, accident or other causes, the combinations for the assault were not well calculated ; the storming party was too weak, the ladders few and short, the breach was not scoured by the fire of the batteries. The attack was also ill-combined, for the leading troops were repulsed before the main body entered the ditch. The intrepidity of the assailants was admitted by all sides, yet it is a great point in such attacks that the supports should form one body with the leaders : the sense of power derived from numbers is a strong incentive to valour, and obstacles insurmountable to a few vanish before a multitude.

During the night the iron guns were placed in battery before the castle, but two more of the brass pieces became unserviceable, and the following day three others were disabled. The bank of clay, however, sloped more, and Capt. Patton, of the engineers, examined it closely ; he was mortally wounded in returning yet lived to report it practicable. The French as usual cleared away the ruins, and with bales of wool and other materials formed interior defences.

They likewise arranged huge shells and barrels of powder with matches fastened to them along the ramparts, placed chosen men, each supplied with four muskets, to defend the breaches, and in that order fearlessly awaited another attack, which was soon made. For intelligence now arrived that Drouet was close to Lierena, and Marmont on the move from Salamanca, so that another attack on Christoval was ordered. This time 400 British, Portuguese, and French men of the Chasseurs Britaniques, carrying 16 long ladders, were employed ; the supports were better closed up ; the appointed hour was 9 instead of 12 ; and more detachments were distributed on the right and left to distract the enemy's attention, cut off his communication with the town, and improve success.

Second Assault of Christoval.

Major McGeechy commanded the stormers, the Forlorn Hope was again led by the gallant Dyas, accompanied by the engineer, Hunt. A little after 9 o'clock the first troops bounded forward, and were closely followed by the support under a shattering musketry which killed McGeechy, Hunt, and many men, but the others with loud shouts jumped into the ditch ; then the French scoffingly calling to come on rolled the barrels of powder and shells down, and the musketry made fearful havoc. The two leading columns united at the main breach, the supports also came up, confusion arose about the ladders, of which only a few could be reared, and the enemy standing on the ramparts bayoneted the foremost, overturned the ladders, and again poured their destructive fire upon the crowd below. When 140 had fallen the order to retire was given. After this failure the breach in the castle remained to be stormed : but the stormers could not there gather in force, between the summit and the interior entrenchment, unless Christoval was taken and its guns used to clear the castle of obstacles ; this would have taken several days, and Soult was now ready to advance and on the 1st a blockade was therefore substituted for the attack.

This siege, in which 400 officers and men fell, violated all rules. The working parties were too weak, the guns and stores too few, the point of attack ill-chosen ; the defences were untouched by counter-fire, and the breaching batteries too distant for the bad guns ; howitzers on trucks were poor substitutes for mortars, and the sap was not practised ; lastly the assaults were made before the glacis had been crowned and a musketry fire established against the breach.

It was not strange that the siege failed. It was strange and culpable that the British Government after such long wars should have sent an engineer corps into the field so ill-organized and equipped that all the officers' bravery and zeal could not render it efficient. The very tools used especially those supplied from the Storekeeper-

General's Department were unfit for work ; the captured French cutting instruments were eagerly sought for in preference ; and when the soldiers' lives and the honour of England were at stake English cutlery could not bear comparison with French !

Want of foresight has also been objected to the general, inasmuch as he might have previously obtained a good battering train from England. But in the Lines, the conduct of the English and Portuguese Governments led him to think rather of embarking than besieging a frontier fortress ; moreover the extreme badness of the Portuguese guns was not known before trial, and the time between Soult's capture of Badajoz and the siege was not sufficient for bringing out an English battering train. It may also be taken as a maxim that in the requirements of war no head was ever strong enough to fore-calculate all.

The second Siege of Badajoz terminated on the 9th of June but the blockade was kept up until the 16th. The junction of the two French armies under Marshals Marmont and Soult then rendered a retreat necessary and the fortress again became open. There was however, no collision between the armies, but on the 22nd of June the French pushed forward a strong reconnaissance which proved unsuccessful. After this both forces remained quiet for above a month, and it was during this period of inactivity that the preparations for the attack on Ciudad Rodrigo were commenced and that the battering train and siege stores were ordered up the Douro from Lisbon.

But it was not until the 8th of August that Wellington reached the Coa, intending first a close blockade of the fortress and finally a siege, but he was too late, the place having been re-victualled for two months on the 6th by Bessière's convoy. The blockade was therefore necessarily relinquished and the troops were quartered near the sources of the Coa and Agueda, close to the line of communication between Marmont and Dorsenne, and in a country where there was still some cover. From thence, if the enemy advanced in superior numbers, there was a retreat to a strong country and to a position of battle near Sabugal, from which the communication with Hill was direct. Nor was the rest of Beira much exposed, as the Allies could send detachments to the valley of the Mondego by Guarda in time to secure the magazines at Celorico ; but the battering train and line of supply from Lamego was unprotected. In these positions the preparation for the siege went on until Wellington learned, contrary to his former belief, that Dorsenne's disposable force was above 20,000 good troops, and Ciudad Rodrigo could not be attacked in face of both that force and of Marmont's Army. Then, changing his plans, he again resolved to blockade the place and to be ready to strike a sudden blow against the fortress, or against the enemy's troops. For it was the foundation of his hopes, that, as the French could not long keep in masses for want of provisions, so he could check those masses on the frontier of Portugal, and always force them to concentrate or suffer the loss of some important post.

Early in September, Marmont pushed a detachment from Plasencia through the passes, surprised a British cavalry piquet, and thus opened his communications with Dorsenne. Wellington had, however, already formed his blockade, and three of his brigades reinforced by a Portuguese regiment were posted on the Ponçul, beyond Castello Branco, to protect the magazines on that line. The battering train then reached Villa Ponte, the troops made gabions and fascines, and 200 men of the Line were instructed as sappers ; the Almeida Bridge on the Coa was permanently repaired, and Almeida was again restored as a place of arms for guns and stores.

During the first arrangements for the blockade in September, 1811, the garrison had made excursions to beat up the quarters of the British cavalry and to obtain provisions from the villages.

Mr. Stuart's exertions had improved the revenue ; the ranks of the infantry were filled up by the return of deserters and by fresh recruits, which, with the reinforcements from England, had raised the Allied Army to upwards of 80,000 men, 56,000 being English. The number under arms, however, did not exceed 24,000 Portuguese and 33,000 British (of which 5,000 were cavalry), with 90 pieces of artillery. This was due to the fact that 22,000 men were in hospital, owing to the increasing sickness acquired in the Alentejo, so that, after deducting Hill's Corps, Wellington could not bring above 44,000 men of all arms to the blockade of Ciudad. But Marmont alone could in a few days bring quite as many to its succour ; and Dorsenne had from 20,000 to 25,000 men available, because the French reinforcements having relieved the old garrisons in the north the latter had joined the army in the field. An aggravating sense of all his difficulties was pressed on the English general when he compared his own situation with that of the enemy. Neither his necessities nor his money could procure due assistance from the Portuguese, while the French generals had only to issue their orders to the Spaniards, through the prefects of the provinces, and all kinds of aid possible to be obtained were surely provided on the day and at the place indicated. In the midst of these cares Wellington was suddenly called into military action. Ciudad Rodrigo again wanted food, and Marmont, who had received 11,000 men from France and had 50,000 under arms, concerted with Dorsenne a combined operation for its succour.

Siege of Ciudad Rodrigo.

After the Allies came to Beira in 1811, Dorsenne and Marmont being reinforced became separately equal to Wellington, and, together, too strong. Soult, master of Andalusia, had a movable reserve of 20,000 men, Suchet gained ground in Valencia, the Asturias were reoccupied by Bonnet, and the army of the centre was reorganized. To besiege Ciudad Rodrigo in form was hopeless, and the rumour of Napoleon's arrival made the English general look once more to the lines of Torres Vedras ; but when the certainty of a Russian war removed this fear, the capture of Ciudad Rodrigo became possible. There was then a good battering train in Almeida ; the line of communication with Oporto was completely organized and shortened by improving the navigation of the Douro ; Rodrigo itself was weakly garrisoned, and the French ignorance as to the state of the Allies' preparations gave hope of a surprise. It was, however, only from surprise that success could be expected, and it was not the least of Wellington's merits that he concealed his preparations for so long a period. No other operation was open, and yet he could not remain inactive because around him the whole fabric of the war was falling to pieces from the folly of the governments he was serving. If he could not effect a blow against the French while Napoleon was engaged in the Russian War, the Peninsula would be lost.

To surprise a third-rate fortress with a weak garrison seems a small matter in such grave circumstances, but in reality it was the first step in a plan which saved the Peninsula when nothing else could have saved it. Wellington knew the Valley of the Tagus could not long support the Army of Portugal and the army of the centre ; he knew by intercepted letters that Marmont and the King were at open war upon the subject, and he judged that if he could surprise Ciudad Rodrigo, the Army of Portugal would, for the sake of provisions and to protect Leon uncovered by the departure of the Imperial Guards, concentrate in that province.   This first step would therefore break the bar Napoleon had raised to offensive operations. For to keep magazines in reserve for sudden expeditions, feeding meanwhile as they could upon the country, was the French manner, and hence want of provisions never obstructed their moving upon important occasions ; yet Wellington thought the tempestuous season would render it difficult for Marmont when thus forced into Leon to move with great masses ; wherefore he proposed if Rodrigo fell to march by Villa Velha to Estremadura and suddenly besiege Badajoz also, the preparations to be secretly made in Elvas under protection of Hill's Corps.   This was the second step and one of promise, because of the jealousies of the marshals, the wet season, and his own combinations which would prevent the concentration of the French armies and prevent them from keeping together if they did unite. If Badajoz fell, he designed to leave a force to cover it against the army of the centre and fight Soult in Andalusia.   For he judged that Marmont could not, in default of provisions, pass beyond the Guadiana, nor follow him before the harvest was ripe ; neither did he fear him in Beira, because the torrents would be full, the country a desert, and the Militia aided by a small regular corps and covered by Almeida and Ciudad Rodrigo, would be sufficient to prevent any serious impression on Portugal during the invasion of Andalusia.

This plan, subtle and vigorous, was the more daring because his own troops were not in good plight. He had indeed received reinforcements, but the infantry had served at Walcheren and exposure to night air or even slight hardships threw them by hundreds into the hospital, while the new regiments of cavalry, inexperienced and not acclimatized, were found, men and horses, so unfit for duty that he sent them to the rear. The pay of the army was three months in arrear, the supplies, brought up with difficulty, were very scanty —half and quarter rations were often served, sometimes the troops were without any bread for three days consecutively, and their clothing was so patched that scarcely a regiment could be known by its uniform. Chopped straw, the only forage, was very scarce, the regimental animals were dying of hunger, corn was rarely distributed save to the generals and staff, and even the horses of the artillery and the old cavalry suffered ;—the very mules of the commissariat were pinched and the muleteers eight months in arrears of pay. The cantonments about the Coa and Agueda were unhealthy from the rains, 20,000 men were in hospital, and after making deductions for other drains, only 54,000 of both nations, including garrisons and posts of communication, were under arms. To finish the picture, a sulky apathy in the Portuguese Regency was becoming more hurtful than the former active opposition. Yet these distresses Wellington with surprising subtlety turned to the advantage of his present designs ; for the enemy were aware of the misery in the army and their imagination magnified it ; and as the allied troops were scattered for relief from the Gata Mountains to the Douro, from the Agueda to the Mondego, immediately after the battering train entered Almeida, both armies concluded that the guns were to arm that fortress as a cover to the extended country quarters which necessity had forced upon the British general. Not even the engineers employed in the preparations knew more than that a siege or the simulation of a siege was in contemplation ; but when it was to be attempted, or that it would be attempted at all, none knew ;— even the Quartermaster-General, Murray, was suffered to go home on leave with the full persuasion that no operation would take place before spring.

In the new cantonments abundance of provisions and dry weather (for in Beira the first rains generally subside during December) stopped the sickness and restored 3,000 men to the ranks ; and the privations had in no manner weakened the moral courage of the troops. The old regiments were incredibly hardy and experienced in all things necessary to sustain their strength and efficiency, the staff was well practised ; and Lord Fitzroy Somerset, Military

Secretary, had established such an intercourse between the head-quarters and the battalion chiefs that the latter had, so to speak, direct communication with the General-in-Chief upon all the business of their regiments, a privilege which stimulated the enthusiasm and zeal of all.

The favourable moment for action so long watched for by Wellington came at last. An Imperial decree had again remodelled the French armies. The army of the south was recomposed in six divisions of infantry and three of cavalry, exclusive of the garrison of Badajoz. Marshal Victor returned to France discontented, for he was one of those whose reputation had been abated by this war, and his divisions were given to eight generals and the younger Soult. The army of the north was exceedingly reduced in numbers, for the Imperial Guards, 17,000 strong, being required for the Russian War, marched in December to France. All the Polish battalions, the skeletons of the cavalry regiments, and several thousand choice men destined to fill the ranks of the Old Guard were drafted ; so that not less than 40,000 of the best soldiers were withdrawn, and the maimed and worn-out men being sent to France at the same time, the force in the Peninsula was diminished by 60,000 men. Marmont having been ordered to abandon the Valley of the Tagus and fix his head-quarters at Valladolid or Salamanca, Ciudad Rodrigo, the sixth and seventh governments, and the Asturias, were also placed under his authority. Montbrun being then near Valencia and Soult's attention distracted between Tarifa and Hill's pursuit of Drouet, the French were employed over an immense tract of country. Marmont also, deceived by the seemingly careless winter attitude of the Allies, left Rodrigo unprotected and Wellington instantly gave orders for the attack of the devoted fortress.

The Siege.

Thirty-five thousand men, cavalry included, were disposable for this enterprise. The materials for the siege were placed at Gallegos, Villa del Cierro, and Espeja, and the ammunition was at Almeida. From those places the hired carts and mules were to bring up the stores to the park ; 70 pieces of ordnance had been collected, but from the scarcity of transports only 38 guns could be brought to the trenches, and these would have wanted their due supply of ammunition, if 8,000 shot had not been found amidst the ruins of Almeida. A bridge was commenced the 1st January at Marialva near the confluence of the Azva with the Agueda, 6 miles below Ciudad, and to secure it piles were driven into the bed of the river above and below, to which the trestles were tied. The fortress was to have been invested on the 6th, but the native carters were two days moving over 10 miles of flat and excellent road with empty carts, and it was dangerous to find fault because they deserted on the slightest offence.

When the place was closely examined, it was found that two convents which flanked and strengthened the bad Spanish entrenchments round the suburbs had been fortified ; and on the greater Teson an enclosed and palisaded redoubt, called Francisco, was constructed and supported by two guns and a howitzer placed on the flat roof of a convent having the same name. All the ground was rocky except on the Tesons, and though the ramparts were there better covered by outworks and could fire more heavily on the trenches, it was, following the English general's views, most assailable, because elsewhere the batteries must have been placed on the edge of the counterscarp before they could see low enough to breach : this would have been a tedious process, whereas the smaller Teson furnished the means of striking over the crest of the glacis at once, and a deep gully offered cover for the mines.   It was therefore resolved to storm Fort Francisco, form a lodgment there, open the first parallel along the greater Teson, place 33 pieces in counter-batteries to ruin the defences and drive the besieged from the convent of Francisco. Afterwards working forward by the sap, it was proposed to construct breaching batteries on the lesser Teson and blow in the counterscarp, while seven guns, battering a weak turret on the left, opened a second breach with a view to turn any retrenchment behind the principal breach.

Carlos d'España and Julian Sanchez were pushed to the Tornes in observation, while four British divisions and Pack's Portuguese laboured at the siege ; but on the right bank of the Agueda there was neither fuel nor cover and the troops therefore kept their quarters on the hither bank, having, although a severe frost and fall of snow had set in, to ford the river each day by divisions in succession, carrying their provisions cooked. To obviate the difficulty of obtaining country transport the English general had previously constructed 800 carts drawn by horses, which were now his surest dependence for bringing up ammunition ; and so many delays were anticipated from the irregularity of the native carters and muleteers and the chances of weather, that he calculated upon an operation of 24 days.   Yet he hoped to steal this time from his adversaries.

On the 8th January the Light Division and Pack's Portuguese forded the Agueda 3 miles above the fortress, and making a circuit took post beyond the great Teson, where they remained quiet during the day, and as there was no regular investment the enemy did not think the siege was commenced. But in the evening the troops stood to their arms, and Colonel Colbourne, now commanding the 52nd, having assembled two companies from each of the British regiments of the Light Division stormed the redoubt of Francisco ; this he did with so much fury that the assailants appeared to be at one and the same time, in the ditch, mounting the parapets, fighting on the top of the rampart, and forcing the gorge of the redoubt, where the explosion of one of the French shells had burst the gate open. Of the defenders a few were killed, not many, and the remainder, 40 in number, were made prisoners. When the post was thus taken with the loss of only 24 men and officers, Elder's Caçadores were sent to labour on the right of it because the fort itself was instantly covered with shot and shells from the town ; this tempest continued during the night, but at daybreak the parallel, 600 yards in length, was sunk 3 ft. deep, the communication over the Teson was completed, and the siege advanced several days by this well-managed assault.

On the 9th the First Division took the trenches in hand, the place was encircled by posts to prevent any external communication, and at night 1,200 workmen commenced three counter-batteries for eleven guns each, under a heavy fire of shells and grape. Before daylight the labourers were under cover, and a ditch was also sunk in the front to provide earth for the batteries, which were made 18 ft. thick at top to resist the very powerful artillery of the place.

On the 10th the Fourth Division relieved the trenches and 1,000 men laboured, but in great peril, for the besieged had an abundance of ammunition and did not spare it. In the night the communication from the parallel to the batteries was opened, and on the 11th the Third Division undertook the siege. That day the magazines in the batteries were excavated and the approaches widened ; but the enemy's fire was destructive, and the shells came so fast into the ditch in front of the batteries that the troops were withdrawn and the earth raised from the inside. Great damage was also sustained from salvos of shells with long fuzes, whose explosion cut away the parapets in a strange manner ; and in the night the French brought a howitzer to the garden of the convent of Francisco with which they killed many men and wounded others.

On the 12th the Light Division resumed work, the riflemen profiting from a thick fog covered themselves in pits which they dug in front of the trenches and from thence picked off the enemy's gunners ; yet the weather was so cold and the besieged shot so briskly that little progress was made.

The 13th the same causes impeded the labourers of the First Division. Scarcity of transport also baulked the operations. One-third only of the native carts had arrived and the drivers were very indolent ; much of the 24-pound ammunition was still at Villa de Ponte, and intelligence arrived that Marmont was collecting his forces to succour the place. In this difficulty it was resolved to hasten the siege by opening a breach with the counter-batteries, which were not quite 600 yards from the curtain, and then to storm the place without blowing in the counterscarp ; in other words to overstep the rules of science and sacrifice life rather than time, for the capricious Agueda might in one night flood and enable a small

French force to relieve the place. The whole army was therefore brought up from the distant quarters and posted in the villages on the Coa ready to cross the Agueda and give battle.

In the night of the 13th the batteries were armed with 28 guns, the second parallel and the approaches were continued by the flying sap, and the Santa Cruz Convent was surprised by the Germans of the First Division, which secured the right flank of the trenches.

The 14th the enemy who had observed that the men in the trenches always went off in a disorderly manner on the approach of the relief, made a sally and overturned the gabions of the sap ; they even penetrated to the parallel, and were on the point of entering the batteries when a few of the workmen getting together checked them until a support arrived and the guns were saved. This affair, coupled with the death of the engineer on duty and the heavy fire from the town, delayed the opening of the breaching batteries ; yet at 4.30 in the evening 25 heavy guns battered the *"fausse braye"* and rampart, and two pieces were directed against the convent of Francisco. Then was beheld a spectacle at once fearful and sublime. The enemy replied to the assailant's fire with more than 50 pieces, the bellowing of 80 large guns shook the ground, far and wide, the smoke rested in heavy volumes upon the battlements of the place, the shells hissing through the air seemed fiery serpents leaping from the darkness, and the distant mountains faintly returned the sound. And when night put an end to this turmoil the quick clattering of musketry was heard like the pattering of hail after a peal of thunder, for the 40th Regiment then carried the convent of Francisco by storm and established itself in the suburb.

Next day the ramparts were again battered and fell so fast that it was judged expedient to commence the small breach at the turret ; wherefore in the night five more guns were mounted. At daylight the besiegers' batteries recommenced, but at 8 o'clock a thick fog compelled them to desist ; nevertheless the small breach had been opened and the place was summoned but without effect. At night the parallel on the lower Teson was extended and a sharp musketry was directed from thence against the great breach ; the breaching battery as originally projected was also commenced, and the riflemen of the Light Division continued from their pits to pick off the enemy's gunners.

On the 17th the fire on both sides was very heavy, and though the wall of the place was much beaten down, several of the besiegers' guns were dismounted, their batteries injured, many men killed, General Borthwick, Commandant of Artillery, wounded, the sap entirely ruined, and the riflemen in the pits overpowered with grape : yet towards evening the latter recovered the upper hand and the French could only fire from the more distant embrasures. In the night the battery intended for the lesser breach was armed and that on the lower Teson raised so as to afford cover in the daytime.

On the 18th the besiegers' fire was resumed with great violence, the turret was shaken at the small breach, the large breach became practicable in the middle, and the enemy commenced retrenching it. The sap made no progress, the superintending engineer was badly wounded, and a 24-pounder, having burst in the batteries killed several men. In the night the battery on the lower Teson was improved, and a fieldpiece and howitzer being placed there kept up a constant fire on the great breach to destroy the French retrenchments. On the 19th both breaches became practicable, Major Sturgeon closely examined the place and a plan of attack was formed on his report ; the assault was then ordered and the battering guns were turned against the artillery of the ramparts.

Assault of Ciudad Rodrigo.

This operation confided to the Third and Light Divisions and Pack's Portuguese, was organized in four parts.

1st. Right Attack.—A company of the 83rd and the Second Caçadores posted in some houses near the bridge were to cross the river and escalade an outwork in front of the castle where there was no ditch, but where two guns commanded the junction of the counterscarp with the body of the place. The 5th and 94th Regiments, posted behind the convent of Santa Cruz and having the 77th in reserve, were to enter the ditch at the extremity of the counterscarp, to escalade the "*fausse braye*" and scour it on their left as far as the great breach.

2nd. Assault of the Great Breach.—One hundred and eighty men, protected by the fire of the 83rd Regiment and carrying hay-bags to throw into the ditch, were to move out of the second parallel and to be followed by the storming party, which was again to be supported by Mackinnon's Brigade of the Third Division.

3rd. Left Attack.—The Light Division posted behind the convent of Francisco, was to send three rifle companies to scour the *fausse braye* to the right and so connect the left and centre attacks. At the same time a storming party. preceded by the Third Caçadores with hay-sacks and followed by Vandeleur's and Barnard's Brigades, was to make for the small breach, and when the *fausse braye* was carried to detach to their right in aid of the main assault, to their left to force a passage at the Salamanca Gate.

4th. False Attack.—This was an escalade to be made by Pack's Portuguese on the St. Jago Gate at the opposite side of the town.

Colonel O'Toole, of the Caçadores, commanded the right attack. Five hundred Volunteers, under Major Manners, of the 74th, the Forlorn Hope, under Lieut. Mackie, of the 88th, composed the storming party of the Third Division. Three hundred Volunteers, led by Major George Napier, of the 52nd, with a Forlorn Hope of 25 men under Lieut. Gurwood, of the same regiment, formed the storming party of the Light Division.

All the troops reached their posts without seeming to attract the attention of the enemy, but before the signal was given, and while Wellington, who in person had been pointing out the lesser breach to Major Napier, was still at the convent of Francisco, the attack on the right commenced and was instantly taken up along the whole line. Then the space between the troops and the ditch was at once covered with soldiers and ravaged by a tempest of grape from the ramparts. The storming parties of the Third Division jumped out of the parallel when the first shout arose, but so rapid had been the movements on their right, that before they could reach the ditch, Ridge, Dunkin, and Campbell, with the 5th, 77th, and 94th Regiments, had already scoured the *fausse braye*, and were pushing up the great breach amidst the bursting of shells, the whistling of grape and musketry and the shrill cries of the French, who were driven fighting behind the retrenchments. There they rallied, and aided by the musketry from the houses made hard battle for their post ; neither side would give way, and yet the British could not get forward, and men and officers falling in heaps choked up the passage, which from minute to minute was raked with grape from two guns flanking the top of the breach at the distance of a few yards : thus striving and trampling alike upon the dead and the wounded these brave men maintained the combat.

On the left the stormers of the Light Division, who had 300 yards to clear would not wait for the hay-bags, but with extraordinary swiftness running to the crest of the glacis jumped down the scarp, a depth of 11 ft., and rushed up the *fausse braye* under a smashing discharge of grape and musketry. The ditch was dark and intricate, the Forlorn Hope inclined towards the left, the stormers went straight to the breach which was so narrow at the top that a gun placed across nearly barred the opening ; there they were rejoined by the Forlorn Hope and the whole body rushed up, but the head of the mass crushed together as the ascent narrowed, staggered under the fire, and with the instinct of self-preservation snapped their own muskets though they had not been allowed to load. Major Napier struck by a grape shot fell at this moment with a shattered arm, but he called on the men to use their bayonets, and all the unwounded officers simultaneously sprung to the front, thus the required impulse was given and with a furious shout the breach was carried. Then the supporting regiments coming up in sections abreast gained the rampart, the 52nd wheeled to the left, the 43rd to the right, and the place was won.

During this contest, which lasted only a few minutes in the breach, the fighting at the great breach had continued with unabated violence ; but when the stormers and the 43rd came pouring along the rampart towards that quarter the French wavered, three of their expense magazines exploded at the same moment, and then the Third Division with a mighty effort broke through the retrenchments. The garrison indeed fought for a moment in the streets, yet finally fled to the castle, where Lieut. Gurwood, who though severely wounded in the head had entered amongst the foremost at the lesser breach, received the Governor's sword.

Now into the streets plunged the assailants from all quarters, for O'Toole's attack was also successful, and at the other side of the town Pack's Portuguese, and the reserves meeting no resistance had entered. Throwing off the restraints of discipline the troops committed frightful excesses ; the town was fired in three or four places, the soldiers menaced their officers and shot each other ; many were killed in the market place, intoxication soon increased the tumult, and at last, the fury rising to absolute madness, a fire was wilfully lighted in the middle of the great magazine, by which the town would have been blown to atoms but for the energetic courage of some officers and a few soldiers who still preserved their senses. Three hundred French had fallen, 1,500 were made prisoners, and the immense stores of ammunition, with 150 pieces of artillery including the battering train of Marmont's Army, were captured. The Allies lost 1,200 men and 90 officers in the siege, of which 650 and 60 officers were slain or wounded at the breaches.

Generals Crauford and Mackinnon, the former an officer of great ability, were killed, and with them died many gallant men ; amongst others, a captain of the 45th, of whom it has been felicitously said that " three generals and seventy other officers had fallen, yet the soldiers fresh from the strife only talked of Hardyman." General Vandeleur, leading the Light Division after Crauford fell, was badly wounded, so was Colonel Colbourne and a crowd of inferior rank ; and unhappily the slaughter did not end with the battle, for the next day as the prisoners and their escort were marching out by the breach an accidental explosion took place and numbers of both were blown into the air.

To recompense an exploit so boldly undertaken and so gloriously finished Lord Wellington was created Duke of Ciudad Rodrigo by the Spaniards, Earl of Wellington by the English, Marquis of Torres Vedras by the Portuguese ; but it is to be remarked that the Prince Regent of Portugal had, previous to that period, displayed great ingratitude in the conferring of honours on the British officers.

Observations.

1st. This siege lasted only twelve days, half the time originally calculated upon by the English general. Owing to the heavy fire from the place the works were more slowly executed than might have been expected ; the cold also had impeded the labourers, but with a less severe frost the trenches would have been under water because in open weather the water rises everywhere to within 6 in of the surface. The worst obstacle was the disgraceful badness of the cutting tools furnished from the Storekeeper-General's Office in England, the profits of the contractor seemed to be the only thing respected ; the engineers eagerly sought for French implements because the English tools were useless.

2nd. Wellington's audacity in storming the redoubt of Francisco, and breaking ground on the first night of the investment ; his greater audacity in storming before the fire of the place had been even abated, or the counterscarp blown in were the true causes of the sudden fall of the place. Success depended more upon the courage of the troops than the skill of the engineer ; and when the general terminated his order for the assault with this sentence, "Ciudad Rodrigo *must* be stormed this evening," he knew well that it would be nobly understood. Yet the French fought bravely on the breach, and by their side many British deserters, desperate men, were bayoneted.

3rd. A perpendicular descent of 16 ft. cut off the great breach from the town, and the bottom was planted with sharp spikes and strewn with live shells. The houses behind were loopholed and manned with musketeers, and on the flanks there were cuts, not very deep or wide, and the French had left the temporary bridges over them ; but they had parapets so powerfully defended that it was said that the Third Division could never have carried them had not the Light Division taken the enemy in flank : an assertion perhaps easier made than proved.

4th. The neglect of the lesser breach was a great error. Narrow and high, a slight addition to its defences would have rendered it impracticable. Moreover the small breach was flanked at a short distance by a demi-bastion with a parapet which, though little injured, was abandoned the moment the head of the storming party forced its way on to the rampart. But the real defence of Ciudad was outside ; when it fell Marmont's errors at Elbodon became manifest. Neither can that marshal be justified for having left so few men in Ciudad Rodrigo as with a garrison of 5,000 the place could never have been taken.

CHAPTER FOUR

Third British Siege of Badajoz, *March*, 1812.

After the capture of Ciudad Rodrigo, Lord Wellington was once more in a position to turn his attention to Badajoz. It was known that Marmont's battering train had been captured in Rodrigo, and for this reason an irruption of the French into Portugal during the absence of the Allies could be attended with no permanent ill-effects, as they had no heavy artillery with which to reduce either Ciudad Rodrigo or Almeida. Towards the end of January therefore Lieut.-General Leith with the 5th Division marched into Rodrigo to form a garrison whilst the defences were repaired and strengthened, and on the 5th of March, the breaches having been rendered perfectly defensible and the place having been in some degree provisioned, it was finally handed over to the Spaniards. Meanwhile preparations for the attack on Badajoz were secretly proceeding : the battering train and Engineers' stores were embarked at Lisbon for a fictitious destination, transferred to smaller vessels at sea, landed at Alcacer do Sal, and thence transported overland to Elvas. Fascines and gabions were also made at Elvas as if intended for the works there, and every preparation was pushed on for the final attack on the fortress. On the 16th of March all was in readiness for the siege ; the 3rd and 4th Divisions crossed the Guadiana by a pontoon bridge which had been thrown across the river some 4 miles below the town, and invested Badajoz without meeting with any opposition from the enemy.

The fortress itself was garrisoned by a mixed force of French, Russian and Spanish troops, 5,000 in all including sick, and a reconnaissance showed that it had been greatly strengthened since the attack of the preceding year. Phillipon making himself felt in every direction, had scoured the vicinity of the place, destroyed many small bands, carried off cattle almost under the guns of Elvas and Campo Mayor, and his spies were abroad from Ciudad Rodrigo to Lisbon and from Lisbon to Ayamonte. He had made an interior retrenchment in the castle and augmented the number of its guns; the rear of Fort Christoval was also better secured, and a covered communication from the fort itself to the work at the bridgehead was nearly completed. Two ravelins were constructed on the south side of the town, a third was commenced, and likewise counter-guards for the bastions; but the eastern front next the castle, which was in other respects the weakest point, was without any outward protection save the stream of the Rivillas. A " cunette " or second ditch had been dug at the bottom of the great ditch, which was also in some parts filled with water; the gorge of the Pardalleras was enclosed, and the work connected with the body of the place from whence powerful batteries looked into it. The three western fronts were mined, and on the east the San Roque Bridge was built up to form an inundation 200 yards wide, which greatly contracted the space by which the place could be approached. All the inhabitants had been ordered to lay up food for three months, and two convoys with provisions and ammunition had entered the place on the 10th and 16th of February; the stores of powder and supply of shells were, however, inadequate.

Wellington finding the old attack against Christoval impracticable, desired to assail one of the western fronts, which would have been scientific; but the Engineers pointed out that he had neither mortars, miners, nor guns, nor the means of bringing up sufficient stores for such an attack. Indeed the want of transport had again forced the Allies to draw stores from Elvas to the manifest hazard of that fortress, and hence here, as at Ciudad Rodrigo, time was necessarily paid for by loss of life, or rather the crimes of the politicians were atoned for by the blood of the soldiers. It was finally resolved to attack the bastion of Trinidad because, the counter-guard there being unfinished, that bastion could be battered from the hill on which the Picurina stood. The first parallel was to embrace the Picurina, the San Roque, and the eastern front in such a manner that counter-batteries might destroy all the armament of the southern fronts which bore against the Picurina Hill. The Picurina itself was to be battered and stormed, and from thence the Trinidad and Santa Maria Bastions were to be breached. All the guns were then to be turned to open a third breach in the connecting curtain which was known to be of weak masonry, and thus a storming party could turn any retrenchment behind the great breaches. In this way the inundation could be avoided, and, although a French deserter declared that the ditch was 18 ft. deep at this point, such was the General's confidence in his troops that he resolved to storm the place without blowing in the counterscarp.

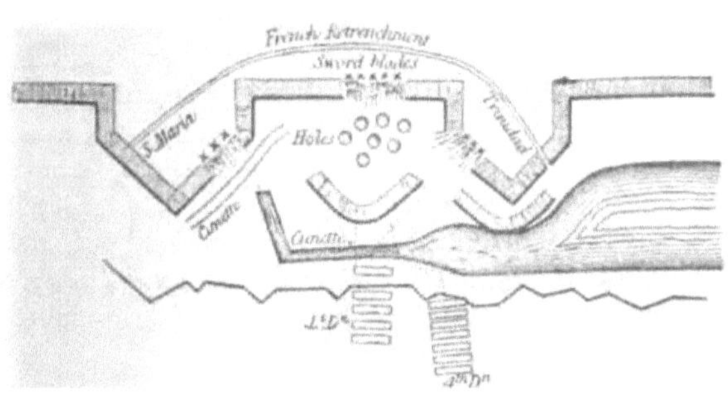

SIEGE OF
BADAJOS
1812 
Mines
San Vincent
Pardaleras
Portugui
Bridgehead
Guadiana R.
Christoval
S.ta Maria
Castle
Picurina
Trinidad
Rivillas
San Roque
Communication
Wilson's attack
Picurina
French Guns
3.d Div.n
San Michel
PLAN OF BREACHES
French Retrenchmens
Sword Holes
S.ta Maria
Trinidad
Holes
Holes
Ravelin
Cunette
L.t D.n
4.th D.n

Dickson's battering train of 52 pieces included sixteen 24-pound howitzers for throwing shrapnel shells, but this missile was little prized by Wellington, and partly to avoid expense, partly from a dislike to injure the inhabitants, neither in this nor in any siege did he use mortars.

Of 900 gunners present 300 were British, the rest Portuguese, and there were 150 sapper volunteers from the 3rd Division, not skilful but of signal bravery. The Engineers' Park was behind the heights of St. Michael. Picton had direction of the siege—·Colville, Kempt, and Bowes alternately commanded in the trenches—the Engineer officers Burgoyne* and Squire conducted the attack, and during the night of the 17th, 1,800 men, protected by a guard of 2,000, broke ground 160 yards from the Picurina. A tempest stifled the sound of the pickaxes, and, though the work was commenced late, a communication 4,000 ft. in length was formed and a parallel 600 yards long, 3 ft. deep, and 3 ft. 6 in. wide was opened. When day broke the Picurina was reinforced, and a sharp musketry interspersed with discharges from some field pieces aided by heavy guns from the body of the place was directed on the trenches.

In the night of the 18th two batteries were traced out, the parallel was prolonged right and left, and the previous works were improved. The garrison raised the parapets of the Picurina, lined the top of the covered way with sandbags and planted musketeers to gall the men in the trenches, who replied in a like manner.

On the 19th, Wellington having secret intelligence that a sally was intended, ordered the guards to be reinforced. Nevertheless at 1 o'clock some cavalry came out by the Talavera Gate, and 1,300 infantry under General Viellande, filed unobserved into the communication between the Picurina and the San Roque—100 men were prepared to sally from the Picurina itself, and all these troops jumping out at once drove the workmen before them and began to demolish the parallel. Previous to this outbreak the French cavalry had divided and commenced a sham fight on the right of the parallel, the smaller party, pretending to fly and answering Portuguese to the challenge of the piquets were allowed to pass, and, elated by the success of this stratagem, galloped to the Engineers' Park, 1,000 yards behind the trenches, where they cut down a few men before help came. Meanwhile the troops at the parallel having rallied upon the relief which had just arrived beat the enemy's infantry back even to the castle. In this hot fight the besieged lost above 300 men and officers, the besiegers only 150, but Colonel Fletcher, Chief Engineer, was badly wounded and several hundred entrenching tools were carried off, for Phillipon had promised a high price for each ; yet this turned out ill as the soldiers neglected the fight to gather tools.

* Afterwards Field Marshal Sir John Burgoyne, G.C.B.

After the action a reserved squadron of dragoons and six field pieces were always stationed behind St. Michael, and a signal post was established to give notice of the enemy's movements.

Wet and boisterous weather harassed the workmen, flooded the trenches, and retarded progress, but on the 19th the parallel was entirely opened, and on the 20th enlarged ; next night it was extended across the Seville road and three counter-batteries were commenced.

On the 20th a slight sally had been repulsed, and during the night another battery against the San Roque was commenced and the battery against the Picurina was finished. Yet heavy rain again retarded the works, and the besiegers, having failed in an attempt to drain the lower parts of the parallel by cuts, made an artificial bottom of sandbags. The besieged, thinking the curtain adjoining the castle was the true object of attack, threw up an earthen entrenchment in front, and commenced clearing away the houses behind it.

Vauban's maxim that a preliminary investment is the first requisite in a siege had been neglected at Badajoz to spare labour, but the great master's art was soon vindicated by his countryman, Phillipon finding the right bank of the Guadiana free, made a battery in the night for three field pieces and at daylight raked the trenches : the shots pitching into the parallel swept it in the most destructive manner for the whole day, and the loss would have been terrible if the soft nature of the ground had not prevented the ricochet of the bullets. Orders were immediately sent to the 5th Division, then at Campo Mayor, to invest the place on that side, but these troops were distant and misfortunes accumulated. In the evening rain filled the trenches, the flood of the Guadiana sank twelve of the pontoons of the fixed bridge and broke the tackle of the flying bridges ; the provisions for the army could not then be brought over, the guns and ammunition were on the right bank and the siege was on the point of being raised. In a few days, however, the river subsided, some Portuguese craft were brought up to form a flying bridge, the pontoons saved were employed as rowboats, and the communication was thus secured for the rest of the siege without accident.

On the 23rd the besieged were working on their entrenchment covering the front next the castle, and the besiegers were fixing platforms, when at 3 o'clock sudden rain filled the trenches, saturated earth fell away, the works crumbled, and the attack was entirely suspended. Next day the place was invested beyond the Guadiana by the 5th Division, and the weather being fine the batteries were armed with ten 24-pounders, eleven 18-pounders, and seven $5\frac{1}{2}$-in. howitzers, all of which opened on the 25th ; they were vigorously answered, and a howitzer was dismounted and several

artillery and Engineer officers were killed. Nevertheless the Sa
Roque was silenced, the Picurina garrison so galled by the mark
men that none dared to look over the parapet, and as the extern
appearance of that fort did not indicate great strength Gener
Kempt was ordered to assault. The outward seeming was, howeve
very fallacious, the fronts were well covered by the glacis, the flan
deep, the rampart at 14 ft. from the bottom of the ditch was pr
tected with thick slanting palings, and above them there was a
earthen slope of 16 ft. A few palings had been knocked off th
covered way and the parapet was slightly damaged, but it was r
paired with sandbags and the ditch was profound, narrow at th
bottom, and flanked by four splinter-proof casemates. Seven gur
were mounted, the entrance by the rear was protected by three row
of thick paling, and the garrison was 200 strong—every man havin
two muskets. The top of the rampart was garnished with loade
shells to push over, a retrenched guard-house formed a secon
internal defence, and small mines and a loopholed gallery under th
counterscarp, intended to take the assailants in rear, were begur
but not finished.

Five hundred men of the 3rd Division assembled for the attack
Kempt ordered 200 under Major Rudd, of the 77th, to turn the for
on the left—an equal force under Major Shaw, of the 74th, to tur
the fort by the right—and 100 men from each of these bodies were t
enter the communication with San Roque, and intercept succou
coming from the town. The flanking columns were to make a join
attack on the fort, and the hundred men remaining formed a reserv
under Capt. Powis, of the 83rd. The Engineers, Holloway, Stanway
and Gipps, having 24 Sappers bearing hatchets and ladders, guide
these columns, and 50 of the Light Division provided with axes wer
to move out of the trenches at the moment of attack.

ASSAULT OF PICURINA.

At 9 o'clock, the night being fine and the arrangements skilfull
made, the two flanking bodies moved forward. The distance wa
short and the troops quick, but the fort black and silent before, nov
seemed a mass of fire. The assailants running to the palisades i
the rear with undaunted courage endeavoured to break through
and, where the destructive musketry and the thick pales rendere
their efforts useless, they strove to get in by the faces of the work
yet the depth of the ditch and the slanting stakes still baffled them
The enemy also shot fast and fatally, and the crisis being imminen
Kempt sent the reserve headlong against the front ; then the figh
and the carnage became terrible, and a battalion coming out fron
the town to the succour of the fort was encountered and beaten b
the party on the communication. The guns of Badajoz and th
castle now opened, the guard of the trenches replied with musketry

rockets were thrown up by the besieged, and the shrill sound of alarm bells mixed with the shouts of the combatants increased the tumult. Still the Picurina sent out streams of fire by the light of which dark figures were seen struggling on the ramparts ; for Powis had escaladed where the artillery had beaten down the pales, and the other assailants throwing ladders in the manner of bridges from the brink of the ditch to the slanting stakes also mounted, and all were fighting hand to hand.

The axe-men of the Light Division, compassing the fort like prowling wolves, soon discovered the gate and hewing it down broke in by the rear, but the struggle still continued. Powis, Holloway, Gipps, and Oates, of the 88th, fell wounded on or beyond the rampart— Nixon of the 52nd was shot 2 yards within the gate—Shaw, Rudd, and nearly all the other officers had fallen outside—and it was not until half the garrison were killed that Gaspar Thiery, the Commandant, surrendered with 86 men ; the others rushing out of the gate endeavoured to cross the inundation and were drowned.

Phillipon thought that the Picurina would have delayed the siege five or six days, and had the assault been a day later this would have happened ; for the loopholed gallery in the counterscarp and the mines would then have been completed, and the body of the work was too well covered by the glacis to be quickly ruined by fire. He was baffled by this heroic assault which lasted an hour, and cost 4 officers and 40 men killed, 15 officers and 250 men wounded, and so vehement was the fighting, that the garrison had not time to roll over the shells and combustibles arranged on the parapet.

When the Picurina was taken three battalions advanced to secure it, and though a great turmoil and firing from the town continued until midnight, a lodgment in the works and communication with the first parallel were established, and the second parallel was commenced ; yet at daylight the redoubt was so overwhelmed with fire from the town that no troops could remain and the lodgment was entirely destroyed. In the evening the Sappers effected another lodgment on the flanks, the second parallel was then opened in its whole length, and the next day the counter-batteries on the right of the Picurina exchanged a vigorous fire with the town, by which one of the besiegers' guns was dismounted.

In the night of the 27th a new communication from the first parallel to the Picurina was made, and three breaching batteries were traced out ; one for twelve 24-pounders, to breach the right face of the Trinidad Bastion, occupied the space between the Picurina and the inundation; a second for eight 18-pounders, to breach the left flank of the Santa Maria Bastion, was on the site of the Picurina; a third on the prolonged line of the front to be attacked contained three shrapnel howitzers to scour the ditch and prevent the garrison working in it. At daybreak these works furnished with gabions and sandbags, were lined with musketeers who galled the workmen employed on the breaching batteries, and the cannonade was brisk on both sides. Two of the besiegers' guns were dismantled, the gabions placed in front of the batteries to protect the workmen were knocked over and the musketry became so destructive that the men were withdrawn from the front and threw up earth from the inside.

On the night of the 27th the second parallel was extended to the right, with the view of raising batteries to ruin San Roque, destroy the dam that held up the inundation, and breach the curtain behind but the Talavera road proved hard, and the moon shone so brightly that the labourers were quite exposed and the work was relinquished On the 28th the screen of gabions before the batteries was restored the workmen renewed their labours outside, the parallel was improved and the besieged withdrew their guns from San Roque. Yet their marksmen still shot from it with great exactness, and the plunging fire from the castle dismounted two howitzers in one of the counter-batteries which was therefore dismantled. The enemy had also during the night observed the tracing string which marked the direction of the sap in front of San Roque, and a daring fellow, creeping out just before the workmen arrived, brought it in the line of the castle fire whereby some loss was sustained ere the false direction was discovered.

In the night the dismantled howitzer battery was re-armed with 24-pounders to play on the San Roque, and a new breaching battery was traced out on the site of the Picurina against the flank of the Santa Maria Bastion. The second parallel was also carried by the sap across the Talavera road, and a trench excavated for riflemen in front of the batteries.

On the 29th, a slight sally made on the right bank of the river was repulsed by the Portuguese, but the sap at San Roque was ruined by the enemy's fire, and the besieged continued to raise the counter-guard and ravelin of the Trinidad and strengthen the front attacked. The besiegers armed two batteries with 18-pounders which the next day opened against Santa Maria with but little effect, and the explosion of an expense magazine killed and hurt many men.

During the siege Soult, having little fear for the town yet expecting a great battle, was carefully organizing a powerful force to unite with Drouet and Danican. These generals had occupied the district of La Serena to keep open the communication with Marmont by Medillo and Truxillo ; but Graham and Hill forced them into the Morena, while Morillo and Penne Villemur, lying close on the Lower Guadiana waited an opportunity to fall on Seville when Soult should advance ; and there were other combinations to embarrass the French Marshal.

Marmont was concentrating his army in the Salamanca country, and it was rumoured he meant to attack Ciudad Rodrigo. Wellington was disturbed by this information. The flooding of the rivers would prevent a blockade and he knew Marmont had not obtained a battering-train ; but the Spanish generals and Engineers had neglected the new works of Ciudad Rodrigo ; Almeida was in a bad state, and the project of invading Andalusia was likely to be stopped by these embarrassments.

On the 30th it became known that Soult was coming from Cordova. Then the 5th Division was brought over the Guadiana, Power's Portuguese Brigade and some cavalry only being left to maintain the investment on the right bank, and the siege was urged vehemently. Forty-eight pieces were in constant play and the sap against San Roque advanced ; yet the enemy was equally diligent, his fire was destructive and his ravelin and counter-guard on the menaced front visibly advanced. By the 1st of April the sap was close to San Roque, the Trinidad crumbled, and the flank of the Santa Maria which was casemated and had hitherto resisted the batteries, also began to yield. By the 2nd, the face of the Trinidad was very much broken, but at the Santa Maria, the casemates being laid open, the bullets were lost in the cavities, and the garrison commenced a retrenchment to cut off the whole of the attacked front from the town.

During the night, a new battery against the San Roque being armed, two officers and some Sappers glided behind that outwork, gagged the sentinel, placed powder barrels and a match against the dam of the inundation, and retired undiscovered ; yet the explosion did not destroy the dam and the inundation remained. Nor did the sap make much progress because of the French musketeers ; for though the marksmen sent against them slew many, they were reinforced by means of a raft with parapets which crossed the inundation, and men also passed by the communication from the Trinidad Gate.

On the 3rd, guns were turned against the curtain behind the San Roque, but the masonry proved hard, ammunition was scarce, and as a breach there would have been useless while the inundation remained, the fire was soon discontinued. The breaches in the bastion were now greatly enlarged, and the besieged assiduously laboured at the retrenchments behind them, and converted the nearest houses and garden walls into a third line of defence. All the houses behind the front next the castle were also thrown down, and a battery of five guns intended to flank the ditch and breach of the Trinidad was commenced on the castle hill outside the wall ; the besiegers therefore traced a counter-battery of 14 shrapnel howitzers to play upon that point during the assault, and the crisis was fast approaching. The breaches were nearly practicable, but Soult having joined Drouet and Danican, was advancing, and as the Allies were not in sufficient force to assault the place and give battle at the same time, it was resolved to leave two divisions in the trenches and fight at Albuera : Graham therefore fell back towards that place, and Hill, destroying the bridge at Merida, marched from the Upper Guadiana to Talavera Real.

To gain time being now, as in war it generally is, the essential ingredient of success, the anxiety on both sides redoubled, yet Soult was still at Llerina on the morning of the 5th when the breaches were declared practicable. The assault was therefore ordered ; but though Leith's Division was brought up to assist, a very careful personal examination caused such doubts in Wellington's mind that he delayed until a third breach should, as he originally designed, be opened between the Trinidad and Maria Bastions. This could not be commenced before morning, and in the night the enemy laboured assiduously behind the openings, regardless of the showers of grape with which the batteries scoured the ditch and breaches. Next morning the guns were turned against the Trinidad curtain, and the bad masonry crumbled so fast that in two hours a yawning break was seen, and Wellington having again examined the points of attack renewed his orders for the assault. Then the soldiers eagerly made ready for a combat, so fiercely fought, so terribly won, so dreadful in all its circumstances that posterity can scarcely be expected to credit the tale.

So sensible was the English General of Phillipon's firmness and the courage of his garrison that he spared them the affront of a summons, yet, seeing the breach strongly entrenched and the enemy's flank fire still powerful, he would not in this dread crisis trust his fortune to a single effort. Eighteen thousand daring soldiers burned for the signal, and he, unwilling to lose the services of one, gave to each division a task such as few generals would have the hardihood even to contemplate. For on the right Picton was to file out of the trenches, cross the Rivillas River and scale the castle walls, 18 to 24 ft. in height, furnished with all means of destruction and so narrow at top that the defenders could easily reach and overturn the ladders. On the left Leith was to make a false attack on the Pardaleras, but a real assault on the distant bastion of San Vincente, where the glacis was mined, the ditch deep, the scarp 30 ft. high, and the parapet held by bold troops provided each with three loaded muskets that the first fire might be quick and deadly.

In the centre, the 4th and Light Divisions, under Colville and Andrew Barnard, were to march against the breaches. They were furnished like the 3rd and 5th Divisions with axes and ladders, and preceded by storming parties of 500 men each with their respective forlorn hopes ; the Light Division was to assault the bastion of Santa Maria, the 4th Division to assault the Trinidad and the curtain, and the columns were divided into storming and firing parties, the former to enter the ditch the latter to keep the crest of the glacis.

At first only one brigade of the 3rd Division was destined to attack the castle, but just before the assault a sergeant of Sappers deserted from the French and reported that there was but one communication from the castle into the town, wherefore the whole division was directed to assail in mass.

To aid these great attacks General Power's Portuguese were to make a feint from the other side of the Guadiana, and Major Wilson, of the 48th, was to storm the San Roque with the guards of the trenches ; this general outline was filled up with many nice arrangements, some of which were followed, others disregarded, for it is seldom all things are attended to in a desperate fight. Nor was the enemy idle. While it was yet twilight some French cavalry issued from the Pardaleras, escorting an officer who endeavoured to look into the trenches with a view to ascertain if an assault was intended; but the piquet on that side jumped up, and firing as it ran drove him and his escort back into the works. Then darkness fell and silently the troops awaited the signal.

ASSAULT OF BADAJOZ.

Dry but cloudy was the night, the air thick with river mist, the ramparts and the trenches unusually still ; yet a low murmur pervaded the latter, and in the former the lights were seen to flit here and there while the deep voices of the sentinels at times proclaimed that all was well in Badajoz. The French, confiding in Phillipon's well-known skill, watched from their lofty station the approach of enemies whom they had twice before baffled, and now hoped to drive a third time blasted and ruined from the walls. The British standing in deep columns were as eager to meet that fiery destruction as the others were to pour it down, and both were alike terrible in their strength, their discipline, and the passions awakened in their resolute hearts. Former failures there were to avenge, and on both sides leaders who furnished no excuse for weakness in the hour of trial. The possession of Badajoz had become a point of personal honour with the soldier of each nation, but the desire for glory with the British was dashed by a hatred of the citizens on an old grudge ; and recent toil and hardship with much spilling of blood had made many incredibly savage. The wondrous power of discipline bound the whole together as with a band of iron, and in the pride of arms none doubted their might to bear down every obstacle that man could oppose to their fury.

At 10 o'clock the castle, the San Roque, the breaches, the Pardaleras, the distant bastion of San Vincente were to have been assailed simultaneously, and it was hoped the strength of the enemy would weaken within that fiery girdle. But many are the disappointments of war. An unforeseen accident delayed the attack of the 5th Division, and a lighted carcass thrown from the castle, falling close to the 3rd Division led to its discovery and compelled the troops to anticipate the signal by half an hour. Then, everything being suddenly disturbed, the double columns of the 4th and Light Divisions also moved silently and swiftly against the breaches, and the guard of the trenches rushing forward with a shout encompassed the San Roque with fire, and broke in so violently that scarcely any resistance was made.

But a sudden blaze of light and the rattling of musketry indicated the commencement of a more vehement combat at the castle. Picton, having been hurt by a fall in the camp and expecting no change in the hour, was not present, and consequently General Kempt led the 3rd Division. Having passed the Rivillas in single files by a narrow bridge under a terrible musketry fire he had re-formed, and running up a rugged hill reached the foot of the castle, where he fell severely wounded, and as he was carried back to the trenches met Picton who was hastening to take the command. Meanwhile the troops spreading along the front had reared their heavy ladders, some against the lofty castle, some against the adjoining front on the left, and with incredible courage ascended amidst showers of heavy stones, logs of wood and bursting shells rolled off the parapet, while from the flanks the enemy plied his musketry with fearful rapidity, and in front with pikes and bayonets stabbed the leading assailants or pushed the ladders from the walls, and all this was attended with deafening shouts and the crash of breaking ladders, and the shrieks of crushed soldiers answering to the sullen stroke of the falling weights.

Still swarming round the remaining ladders those undaunted veterans strove to be the first to climb, until all being overturned the French shouted victory, and the British, baffled but untamed, fell back a few paces and took shelter under the rugged edge of the hill. There, the broken ranks were somewhat re-formed, and the heroic Ridge springing forward seized a ladder and calling with stentorian voice on his men to follow, once more raised it against the castle, yet to the right of the former attack where the wall was lower and an embrasure offered some facility. A second ladder was soon placed alongside of the first by the Grenadier Officer Canch, and the next instant he and Ridge were on the rampart, the shouting troops pressed after them, the garrison amazed and in a manner surprised were driven fighting through the double gate into the town and the castle was won. A reinforcement from the French reserve then came up, a sharp action followed, both sides fired through the gate and the enemy retired.

All this time the tumult at the breaches was such as if the very earth had been rent asunder. The two divisions had reached the glacis just as the firing at the castle commenced, and the flash of a single musket discharged from the covered way as a signal showed them that the French were ready ; yet no stir was heard and darkness filled the breaches. Some hay-packs were thrown, some ladders placed, and the forlorn hopes and storming parties of the Light Division, 500 in all, descended into the ditch without opposition ; but then a bright flame shooting upwards disclosed all the terrors of the scene. The ramparts crowded with dark figures and glittering arms were on one side, on the other the red columns of the British, deep and broad, were coming on like streams of burning lava ; it was the touch of the magician's wand, for a crash of thunder followed and with incredible violence the storming parties were dashed to pieces by the explosion of hundreds of shells and powder barrels.

For an instant the Light Division stood on the brink of the ditch amazed at the terrific sight, but then with a shout that matched even the sound of the explosion the men flew down the ladders, or disdaining their aid leaped reckless of the depth into the gulf below— and at the same moment amidst a blaze of musketry that dazzled the eyes, the 4th Division came running in and descended with a like fury. There were only five ladders for the two columns which were close together, and a deep cut made in the bottom of the ditch was filled with water from the inundation ; into that watery snare the head of the 4th Division fell, and it is said that above a hundred of the Fusiliers—the men of Albuera—were drowned in it. Those who followed checked not, but, as if such a disaster had been expected, turned to the left, and then came upon the face of the unfinished ravelin which being rough and broken was mistaken for the breach and instantly covered with men ; yet a wide and deep chasm was still between them and the ramparts, from whence came a deadly fire wasting their ranks. Thus baffled they also commenced a rapid discharge of musketry and disorder ensued ; for the men of the Light Division, whose conducting Engineer had been disabled early and whose flank was confined by an unfinished ditch, rushed towards the breaches of the curtain and the Trinidad, which were indeed before them but which the 4th Division had been destined to storm. Great was the confusion, for the ravelin was quite crowded with men of both divisions, and while some continued to fire others jumped down and ran towards the breach ; many also passed between the ravelin and the counter-guard of the Trinidad, the two divisions got mixed, the reserves which should have remained at the quarries also came pouring until the ditch was quite filled, the rear still crowding forward and all cheering vehemently. The enemy's shouts were also loud and terrible, and the bursting of shells and grenades, the roaring of guns from the flanks, answered by the iron howitzers from the battery of the parallel, the heavy roll and horrid explosion of the powder barrels, the whirring flight of the blazing splinters, the loud exhortations of the officers, and the continued clatter of the muskets made a maddening din.

Now a multitude surged up the great breach as if driven by a whirlwind, but across the top glittered a range of sword-blades, sharp-pointed, keen-edged on both sides, and firmly fixed in ponderous beams chained together and set deep in the ruins ; and for 10 ft. in front the ascent was covered with loose planks studded with sharp iron points, which moved when any attempt was made to cross them and the soldiers falling forward on the spikes rolled down upon the ranks behind.   Then the Frenchmen, shouting at the success of their stratagem and leaping forward, plied their shot with terrible rapidity, for every man had several muskets, and each musket in addition to its ordinary charge contained a small cylinder of wood stuck full of wooden slugs, which scattered like hail when they were discharged. Once and again the assailants rushed up the breaches, but always the sword-blades, immovable and impassable, stopped their charge, and the hissing shells and thundering powder barrels exploded unceasingly.   Hundreds of men had fallen, hundreds more were dropping; still the heroic officers called for new trials, and sometimes followed by many, sometimes by a few, ascended the sides, and so furious were the men themselves that in one of these charges the rear strove to push the foremost on to the sword-blades willing even to make a bridge of their writhing bodies, but the others frustrated the attempt by dropping down ; and men fell so fast from the shot, that it was hard to know who went down voluntarily and who were stricken, and many stooped unhurt who never rose again.

At the beginning of this dreadful conflict, Andrew Barnard had with prodigious efforts separated his division from the other and preserved some degree of military array ; but now the tumult was such that no command could be heard distinctly except by those close at hand, and the mutilated carcasses heaped up on each other and the wounded struggling to avoid being trampled upon broke the formations, order was impossible.   Officers of all ranks, followed more or less numerously by the men, were seen to start out as if struck by sudden madness and rush into the breach which yawning and glittering with steel seemed like the mouth of a huge dragon belching forth smoke and flame.   Gathering in dark groups and leaning on their muskets the troops looked up in sullen desperation at the Trinidad, while the enemy stepping out on the ramparts, and aiming their shots by the light of the fire-balls which they threw over, asked as their victims fell, why they did not come into Badajoz.

In this dreadful situation, while the dead were lying in heaps and others continually falling, the wounded crawling about to get some shelter from the merciless shower above, and withal a sickening stench from the burnt flesh of the slain, Capt. Nicholas, of the Engineers, was observed by Lieut. Shaw, of the 43rd, making incredible efforts to force his way with a few men into the Santa Maria Bastion. Shaw immediately collected 50 soldiers of all regiments and joined him, and although there was a deep cut along the foot of that breach also, it was instantly passed and these two young officers led their gallant band with a rush up the ruins ; but when they had gained two-thirds of the ascent a concentrated fire of musketry and grape dashed nearly the whole dead to the earth. Nicholas was mortally wounded and the intrepid Shaw stood alone. With wonderful coolness he looked at his watch, and saying it was too late to carry the breaches rejoined the masses at the other attack. After this no further effort was made at any point, and the troops remained passive but unflinching beneath the enemy's shot which streamed without intermission ; for of the riflemen on the glacis, many leaping into the ditch had joined in the assault, and the rest, raked by a cross-fire of grape from the distant bastions, baffled in their aim by the smoke and flames from the explosions, and too few in number, entirely failed to quell the French musketry.

About midnight when 2,000 brave men had fallen, Wellington who was on a height close to the quarries, ordered the remainder to retire and re-form for a second assault ; he had heard the castle was taken, but thinking the enemy would still resist in the town was resolved to assail the breaches again.

This retreat from the ditch was not effected without further carnage and confusion, the French fire never slackened, a cry arose that the enemy was making a sally from the distant flanks, and there was a rush towards the ladders. Then the groans of the wounded, who could not move and expected to be slain, increased, and many officers who had not heard of the order, endeavoured to stop the soldiers from going back ; some would even have removed the ladders but were unable to break the crowd.

All this time Picton was lying close to the castle, and either from fear of the loss of a point which ensured the capture of the place, or that the egress was too difficult, made no attempt to drive the enemy away from the breaches. On the other side however the 5th Division had commenced the false attack on the Pardaleras, and on the right of the Guadiana the Portuguese were sharply engaged at the bridge, thus the town was girdled with fire, for Walters' Brigade having passed on during the feint on the Pardaleras, was escalading the distant bastion of San Vincente. His troops had advanced along the banks of the river and reached the French guard-house at the barrier gate undiscovered, the ripple of the waters smothering the sound of their footsteps ; but just then the explosion in the breaches took place, the moon shone out, the French sentinels discovering the columns, fired, and the British soldiers springing forward under a sharp musketry began to hew down the wooden barrier at the covered way. The Portuguese panic-stricken, threw down the scaling ladders, the others snatched them up again and forcing the barrier jumped into the ditch ; but the guiding Engineer officer was killed, there was a cunette which embarrassed the columns, and the ladders proved too short, for the walls were generally above 30 ft. high. The fire of the enemy was deadly, a small mine was sprung beneath the soldiers' feet, beams of wood and live shells were rolled over on their heads, showers of grape from the flank swept the ditch, and man after man dropped dead from the ladders.

Fortunately some of the defenders had been called away to aid in recovering the castle, the ramparts were not entirely manned, and the assailants discovering a corner of the bastion where the scarp was only 20 ft. high, placed three ladders there under an embrasure which had no gun and was only stopped with a gabion. Some men got up with difficulty, for the ladders were still too short, and the first man who gained the top was pushed up by his comrades and drew others after him until many had won the summit ; and though the French shot heavily against them from both flanks and from a house in front, their numbers augmented rapidly and half the 4th Regiment entered the town itself to dislodge the French from the houses, while the others pushed along the ramparts towards the breach and by dint of hard fighting successively won three bastions.

In the last of these combats Walker leaping forward sword in hand at the moment when one of the enemy's cannoneers was discharging a gun, was covered with so many wounds that it was wonderful that he could survive, and some of the soldiers immediately after perceiving a lighted match on the ground cried out that it was a mine ! At that word, such is the power of imagination, those troops who had not been stopped by the barriers, the ditch, the high walls, and the deadly fire of the enemy, staggered back appalled by a chimera of their own raising ; and in this disorder a French reserve under General Veillande drove on them with a firm and rapid charge, pitching some men over the walls, killing others outright, and cleansing the ramparts even to the San Vincente. There, however, Leith had placed Colonel Nugent with a battalion of the 38th as a reserve, and when the French came up shouting and slaying all before them, this battalion, 200 strong, arose and with one close volley destroyed them ; then the panic ceased, the soldiers rallied, and in compact order once more charged along the walls towards the breaches ; but the French, although turned on both flanks and abandoned by fortune did not yet yield. Meanwhile the portion of the 4th Regiment which had entered the town was strangely situated. For the streets were empty and brilliantly illuminated and no person was seen, yet a low burr and whispers were heard around, lattices were now and then gently opened, and from time to time shots were fired from underneath the doors of the houses by the Spaniards, while the troops with bugles sounding advanced towards the great square of the town. In their progress they captured several mules going with ammunition to the breaches ; yet the square itself was as empty and silent as the streets. The tumult at the breaches was however like the crashing thunder, and showed plainly that the fight was still raging there, and hence, quitting the square the troops attempted to take the garrison in reverse by attacking the ramparts from the town side, but they were received with a rolling musketry, driven back with loss, and resumed their movement through the streets. At last the breaches were abandoned by the French, other parties entered, desultory combats took place, Viellande and Phillipon, the latter of whom was wounded, seeing that all was lost, passed the bridge with a few hundred soldiers and entered San Christoval, which was surrendered next morning upon a summons to Lord Fitzroy Somerset, for that officer had with great readiness pushed through the town to the drawbridge before the French had time to organize further resistance. But even in the moment of ruin the night before, the noble Governor had sent some horsemen out from the fort to carry the news to Soult, and they reached him in time to prevent a greater misfortune.

Of the excesses committed by the troops, and the violence which resounded for two days and nights in the streets of Badajoz it is unnecessary to write in this article. On the third day, when the city was sacked, when the soldiers were exhausted by their own excesses, the tumult rather subsided than was quelled; the wounded men were then looked to and the dead disposed of. Five thousand men and officers fell in this siege, and of these, including 700 Portuguese, 3,500 had been stricken in the assault, 60 officers and more than 700 men being slain on the spot. The five Generals, Kempt, Harvey, Bowes, Colville, and Picton, were wounded, the first four severely ; 600 men and officers fell in the escalade of San Vincente, as many at the castle, and more than 2,000 at the breaches, each division there losing 1,200 !

When it is realized that this frightful carnage took place in a space less than a hundred yards square—that the slain died not all suddenly nor by one manner of death—that some perished by steel, some by shot, some by water, that some were crushed and mangled by heavy weights, some trampled upon, some dashed to atoms by the fiery explosions—that for hours this destruction was endured without shrinking and the town was won at last, the invincible courage of the British can be more clearly appreciated. And it is entirely wrong to suppose that the French were unworthy enemies, as the garrison stood and fought manfully and with good discipline. Yet who shall do justice to the bravery of the British soldiers ! the noble emulation of the officers ! Who shall measure out the glory of Ridge, of Macleod, of Nicholas, of O'Hare of the 95th, who perished on the breach at the head of the stormers, and with him nearly all the volunteers for that desperate service ! Who shall describe the martial fury of that desperate rifleman, who, in his resolution to win,

thrust himself beneath the chained sword-blades and there suffered
the enemy to dash his head to pieces with the ends of their muskets
Who can sufficiently honour the intrepidity of Walker, of Shaw, o
Canch, or the hardiness of Ferguson of the 43rd, who having in forme
assaults received two deep wounds was here, his former wounds stil
open, leading the stormers of his regiment, the third time a volun
teer, the third time wounded ! No age, no nation ever sent fortl
braver troops to battle than those who stormed Badajoz, and Lorc
Wellington's passionate outburst of grief when he heard of the
night's havoc was but a fitting tribute for the loss of his gallant
soldiers.

CHAPTER FIVE

Early in September, 1812, Wellington, desirous of sheltering his troops from the extreme heat, had sent four divisions and the cavalry to the Escurial and to St. Ildefonso, whence they could join Hill by the Valley of the Tagus, or Clinton by Arevolo. When, however, he learnt that King Joseph had decided to retreat upon Valencia, that Soult had abandoned Cordova and that Clinton was falling back before Clausel, he ordered the 1st, 5th, and 7th Divisions, Pack's and Bradford's Portuguese brigades, Ponsonby's light horsemen and the heavy German cavalry, to move rapidly on Arevolo, and on the 1st of September he quitted Madrid himself to take command. Yet his army had been so diminished by sickness that only 21,000 men, including 3,000 cavalry, were assembled in Arevolo. He could scarcely feed the Portuguese soldiers, who were also very ill-equipped, and their Government failed in transmitting either money or stores.

On the 4th, the Allies quitted Arevolo, on the 7th they entered Valladolid, and the Gallicians, who had returned to the Esla when Foy retreated, were ordered to join the Portuguese Army.

But the Gallicians did not obey the order, and the French retreated slowly up the beautiful Pisuerga and Arlanzan Valleys, which, in spite of the stories about French devastation, were carefully cultivated and filled to repletion with corn, wine, and oil. Nor were they deficient in military strength. Off the high road, on both sides, ditches and rivulets impeded the troops, while cross ridges continually furnished strong parallel positions flanked by the lofty hills on either side. In these valleys Clausel baffled his great adversary in the most surprising manner. Each day he offered battle, yet on ground which Wellington was unwilling to assail in front, partly because he momentarily expected the Gallicians to join him, but chiefly because of the steady decrease of his own army from sickness, which, combined with the hope of ulterior operations in the south, made him unwilling to lose men. By flank movements he dislodged the enemy, yet darkness fell each day ere they were completed and the morning sun always saw Clausel again in position. At Cigales and Dueña in the Pisuerga Valley, at Pampliega in the Valley of the Arlanza and at other places the French general offered battle, until he finally covered Burgos on the 16th by taking the strong position of Cellada del Camino.

But 11,000 Spanish infantry, 300 cavalry and 8 guns had now joined the Allies, and Wellington would have attacked on the 17th had not Clausel, able, wary, and skilful, observed the increased numbers and retired in the night to Frandovinez. His rear guard was, however pushed sharply back next day to the heights of Burgos, and during the following night he passed through that town leaving behind him large stores of grain. Caffarelli, who had come down to place the Castle of Burgos in a state of defence, now joined him, and the two generals retreated upon Briviesca, where they were immediately reinforced by that reserve which the Emperor, with such an extraordinary foresight, had directed to be assembled and exercised in the Pyrenees in anticipation of Marmont's disaster. The Allies entered Burgos amidst great confusion, for the garrison of the castle had set fire to some houses impeding the defence of the fortress, the conflagration spread widely, and the partidas—who were already gathered like wolves round a carcass—entered the town for mischief. Mr. Sydenham, an eye-witness and not unused to scenes of war, thus describes their proceedings, " What with the flames and the plundering of the guerillas, who are as bad as the Tartars and Cossacks, I was afraid Burgos would be entirely destroyed, but order was at length restored by the manful exertions of Don Miguel Alava."

SIEGE OF THE CASTLE OF BURGOS.

Caffarelli had placed 1,800 infantry besides artillery men in the castle, and the Governor, Dubreton, was of such courage and skill that he surpassed even the hopes of his sanguine and warlike countrymen. The castle and its works enclosed a rugged hill, and between it and the river the city of Burgos was situated. An old wall with a new parallel and flanks constructed by the French, offered the first line of defence ; the second line was an earthwork of the nature of a field retrenchment and was well palisaded ; the third line was similarly constructed and contained the two highest points of the hill, on one of which was an entrenched building called the White Church, and on the other the ancient keep of the castle ; this last was the highest point, entrenched and mounted with a heavy casemated work called the Napoleon Battery. Thus there were five separate enclosures, and the Napoleon Battery commanded everything around it save to the north where, at a distance of 300 yards, there was a second height scarcely less elevated than that of the fortress. This point, called the Hill of San Michael, was defended by a large horn-work with a sloping scarp 45 ft. high, and a counterscarp not less than 10 ft. high ; it was unfinished and only closed by strong palisades, but it was under the fire of the Napoleon Battery, was well flanked by the castle defences, and covered in front by slight entrenchments for the out piquets. Nine heavy guns, eleven field pieces and six mortars or howitzers were mounted in the fortress, Clausel's reserve artillery and stores were also deposited there, and the armament could therefore be increased.

First Assault.

All the bridges and fords over the Arlanzan were commanded by the batteries, and two days elapsed ere the Allies could cross ; but on the 19th, the passage of the rivers being effected above the town by the 1st Division, Major Somers Cocks, supported by Pack's Portuguese, drove in the French outposts on the Hill of San Michael. During the night the same troops, reinforced by the 42nd Regiment, stormed the horn-work after a murderous conflict. The Highlanders who bore the ladders under the command of the Engineer Pitt placed them very well, splicing them together to meet the great height of the scarp, yet the stormers were beaten back with great loss, and would have failed if the gallant Cocks with the 79th had not forced an entrance by the gorge. The garrison was thus cut off and must have surrendered if Cocks had been well supported, but he was only followed by the 2nd Battalion of the 42nd, and the French being still 500 broke through and escaped. The affair was censured, the troops complained of each other, and the loss was above 400, whilst that of the enemy did not exceed 150.

Wellington was now able to examine the defences of the castle. He found them feeble and incomplete, and yet his means were so scanty that he relied more upon the enemy's weakness than upon his own power ; for it was said that the garrison wanted water, and that their provision magazines could be burned. Upon this information he adopted the following plan of attack :—

Twelve thousand men composing the 1st and 9th Divisions and the two Portuguese brigades were to undertake the works ; the rest of the troops, 20,000 exclusive of the partidas, were to form the covering army. The trenches were to be opened from the suburb of San Pedro, and a parallel formed in the direction of the Hill of San Michael. A battery for five guns was to be established close to the right of the captured horn-work. A sap was to be pushed from the parallel or as near to the first wall as possible without being seen into from the upper works, and from this point the Engineer was to proceed by gallery and mine.

When the first mine was completed, the battery on the left of San Michael was to open against the second line of defence, and the assault was to be delivered against the first line. If a lodgment was formed the approaches were to be continued against the second line and the battery in San Michael was to be turned against the third line in front of the White Church, as the defences there were exceedingly weak. Meanwhile a trench for musketry was to be dug along the brow of San Michael, and a concealed battery was to be prepared within the horn-work itself with a view to the final attack on the Napoleon Battery. Headquarters were fixed on Villa Tore. Colonel Burgoyne conducted the operations of the Engineers, and Major Dickson those of the artillery which consisted of three 18-pounders and the five iron 24-pound howitzers only, and it was on account of these slender means, rather than because of the weak defence of the fortress, that this line of attack was chosen.

When the horn-work fell a lodgment was commenced in the interior, and was continued vigorously, although under a destructive fire of grape and shells on the workmen who were digging the musketry trench in front of the first battery. On the 22nd the fire of the besieged was redoubled, but the besiegers worked with little loss and their musketry galled the enemy. During the night the first battery was armed with two 18-pounders and three howitzers, and the secret battery within the horn-work was commenced. Wellington, deviating from his first plan, then resolved to try an escalade against the first line of defence, and selected a point half-way between the suburb of San Pedro and the horn-work. At midnight 400 men provided with ladders marched from under the hill on which the horn-work stood, to the attack of the wall which was from 23 to 25 ft. high but had no flanks; this was the main column, and a Portuguese battalion was also assembled in the town of Burgos to make a combined flank attack on their side.

Second Assault.

The assault was commenced by the Portuguese but they were driven back by the fire of the common guard alone, and the principal escalading party, composed of detachments from different regiments under Major Lawrie, 79th Regiment, got into disorder in passing a hollow way 50 yards from the wall, and had no success. The ladders were indeed placed and the troops entered the ditch, but in a state of confusion ; Lawrie was killed, the bravest soldiers who first mounted the ladders were bayoneted, and the ladders were reared and overturned several times ; combustibles were also cast down in abundance, and the British, giving way, left half their number behind. The wounded were brought off next day under a truce, and it was said that the French found the plan of the siege upon the body of a dead officer ; certain it is that this disastrous attack stimulated the enemy's courage and produced a bad effect on the Allies, some of whom had been also greatly dispirited by the previous assault on the horn-work.

SIEGES AND THE DEFENCE OF FORTIFIED PLACES.

SKETCH OF THE SIEGE OF BURGOS, 1812.

The hollow way which had led to the disorder amongst the escalader
and which at 50 yards' distance ran along the front of defence, w:
converted into a parallel and connected with the suburb of San Pedr
the trenches were made deep and narrow to secure them from th
plunging fire of the castle, and musketeers were planted to keep dow
the enemy's fire ; but heavy rains caused great inconvenience to th
troops, and, though the allied marksmen got the mastery over thos
of the French immediately in their front, the latter, having a raise
palisaded work on their own right which in some measure flanke
the approaches, killed so many of the besiegers that they wei
finally withdrawn. During the night a flying sap was commence
from the right of the parallel, and was pushed to within 20 yards (
the first line of defence ; but the directing Engineer was killed, an
with him many men, for the French plied their musketry sharpl
and rolled large shells down the steep side of the hill. The head (
the sap was indeed so unprotected as it approached the wall, that
6-ft. trench added to the height of the gabion above scarcely gav
cover to the workmen. The gallery of the mine was therefore opene
and worked as rapidly as the inexperience of the miners, who wei
merely volunteers from the Line, would permit.

A concealed battery within the horn-work of San Michael bein
now completed, two 18-pounders were removed from the first batter
to arm it, and they were replaced by two iron howitzers which opene
upon the advanced palisade below to drive the French marksme:
from that point. When they had fired 140 rounds without success
the project was abandoned, and the ammunition was so scarce tha
the soldiers were paid to collect the enemy's bullets. This day :
zigzag was also commenced in front of the first battery down th
face of San Michael, so as to obtain a footing for a musketry trenc
to overlook the enemy's defences below ; and though the workmei
were exposed to the whole fire of the castle at the distance o
200 yards and suffered severely, the work went steadily on.

On the 26th the gallery of the mine was advanced 18 ft. and the
soil was found favourable, yet the men in passing the sap were hit
fast by the French marksmen, and an assistant engineer was killed
During the night the parallel was prolonged on the right to within
20 yards of the enemy's ramparts with a view to a second gallery
and mine, and musketeers were planted there to pick off the enemy's
marksmen and to protect the sap ; at the same time the zigzag on
the Hill of San Michael was continued, and the trench there was
completed with little loss under cover of gabions, although the
whole fire of the castle was concentrated on the spot.

On the 27th the French were seen strengthening their second line,
and they had already cut a step along the edge of the counterscarp
for a covered way, and had palisaded the communication. The
besiegers likewise finished the musketry trench on the right of their

parallel and opened the gallery for the second time. But the first mine went on slowly and the men in the sap were galled by stones, grenades, and small shells which the French threw into the trenches by hand ; the artillery fire also knocked over the gabions of the musketry trench on San Michael so fast that the troops were withdrawn during the day.

During the night a trench of communication, forming a second parallel behind the first, was begun and nearly completed from the Hill of San Michael towards the suburb of San Pedro, and the musketry trench on the hill was deepened. Next day an attempt was made to perfect this new parallel of communication, but the French fire became heavy, and the shells which passed over came rolling down the hill again into the trench, so that the work was deferred until night and was then perfected. The rolling back of the shells continued to gall the troops, yet the whole of the trench was filled with men whose fire was incessant. The first mine was now loaded with more than a thousand pounds weight of powder, the gallery strongly tamped for 15 ft. with bags of clay and all was ready for the explosion and Wellington ordered the third assault.

Third Assault.

At midnight the hollow road 50 yards from the mine was lined with troops to fire on the defences, and 300 stormers were assembled there attended by others who carried tools and materials to secure the lodgment when the breach should be carried. The mine was then exploded, the wall fell and an officer with 20 men rushed forward to the assault. The explosion was not so efficacious as it ought to have been, yet it brought the wall down, the enemy was stupefied, and the Forlorn Hope consisting of a sergeant and four daring soldiers, gained the summit of the breach and stood there until the French, recovering from their panic, drove them back again pierced with bayonet wounds. Meanwhile the officer and 20 men, who were to have been followed by a party of 50 and these by the remainder of the stormers, missed the breach in the dark and finding the wall unbroken retired and reported that there was no breach ; the main body immediately regained the trenches, and before the sergeant and his men returned with streaming wounds to tell their tale, the enemy was reinforced. Scarcity of ammunition stopped the artillery practice against the breach during the night and the French raised a parapet behind it, placing obstacles sufficient to deter the besiegers from renewing the assault at daylight.

This failure arose from the darkness and the want of a conducting engineer ; out of four regular officers of that branch engaged in the siege, one had been killed, one badly wounded, and one was sick ; the fourth was therefore necessarily reserved for the carrying on the works. The aspect of affairs was gloomy. Twelve days had elapsed since the siege commenced, one assault had succeeded, two had failed; 1,200 men had been killed or wounded, little progress had been made, and the troops generally showed symptoms of despondency—especially the Portuguese who seemed to be losing their ancient spirit. Discipline was relaxed, the soldiers wasted ammunition; the work in the trenches was avoided or neglected both by officers and men; insubordination was gaining ground, and reproachful orders were issued, the guards only being noticed as presenting an honourable exception. In this state it was essential to make some change in the operations, and as the French marksmen in the palisaded work below were now so expert as to hit everything seen, the howitzer battery on San Michael was reinforced by a French 8-pounder, and this mischievous post was at last demolished. The gallery of the second mine was also pushed forward, and a new breaching battery for three guns was constructed behind it, so close to the enemy's defences that the latter screened the work from the artillery fire of their upper fortress. But the parapet of the battery was only made musket-proof, because the besieged had no guns on the lower line of this front. In the night the three 18-pounders were brought from the Hill of San Michael without being discovered, and although a very galling fire of muskets hampered the workmen, they persevered until 9 o'clock, when the battery was finished and armed. But at that moment, the watchful Dubreton brought a howitzer down from the upper works and with a low charge threw shells into the battery; then making a hole through a flank wall he threw out a light gun which sent its bullets whizzing through the thin parapet at every round, and at the same time his marksmen plied their shot so sharply that the Allies were driven from their pieces without firing. More French cannon being now brought from the upper works, the defences of the battery were quite demolished, two of the gun carriages were disabled, a trunnion was knocked off one of the 18-pounders, and the muzzle of another was split. It was in vain that the besiegers' marksmen, aided by some officers who considered themselves good shots, endeavoured to quell the enemy's fire; the French being on a height were too well covered and remained masters of the fight.

During the night a second and more solid battery was formed a little to the left of the ruined one, but the French observed it at daylight, and their fire plunging from above knocked down the parapet so rapidly that it was relinquished. Recourse was then again had to the galleries and mine and to the breaching battery on the Hill of San Michael; the two serviceable guns were therefore removed towards the upper battery to beat down a retrenchment formed by the French behind the old breach. It was intended to place them upon this new position during the night of the 3rd, but the weather was very wet and stormy, and the workmen, those of the guards only excepted, abandoned the trenches; hence at daylight the guns were still short of their destination and nothing more could be done until the following night.

On the 4th, at 9 o'clock in the morning, the two 18-pounders and three iron howitzers again opened from San Michael's, and at 4 o'clock in the evening, the old breach being cleared of all incum· brances and the second mine strongly tamped for explosion, a double assault was ordered. The 2nd Battalion of the 24th British Regiment under Capt. Hedderwick was selected and formed up in the hollow way, having one advanced party under Lieut. Holmes pushed forward as close to the new mine as was safe, and a second party under Lieut. Fraser in like manner pushed towards the old breach.

Fourth Assault.

At 5 o'clock the mine was exploded with a terrific effect, blowing many of the French into the air and breaking down 100 ft. of the wall ; the next instant Holmes and his brave men rushed through the smoke and crumbling ruins, and Fraser quickly fought his way on to the summit of the old breach ; opposed with spears he was seen to tear one from the hands of an enemy and to leap into the midst of the hostile mass followed by his men. The supports followed closely and both breaches were carried with loss to the assailants of 37 killed and 200 wounded, seven of the latter being officers and amongst them the Commanding Engineer. During the night lodgments were formed in advance of the old, and on the ruins of the new breach, yet very imperfectly and under a destructive fire from the upper defences. This happy attack revived the spirits of the army, vessels with powder were coming coastwise from Corunna, a convoy was expected by land from Ciudad Rodrigo, a supply of ammunition sent by land by Sir Horne Popham reached the camp, the howitzers continued to knock away the palisades in the ditch, and the battery on San Michael's was directed to open a third breach, at a point where the first line of defence was joined by the second.

This promising state of affairs was of short duration.

On the 5th, at 5 o'clock in the evening, while the working parties were extending the lodgments, 300 French came swiftly down the hill and sweeping away the labourers and guards from the trenches, killed or wounded 150 men, got possession of the old breach, destroyed the works and carried off all the tools. During the night the Allies repaired the damage and pushed saps from each flank, to meet in the centre near the French line and serve as a parallel to check future sallies ; the howitzers also continued their fire from San Michael against the palisades, and the breaching in the horn-work opened, but the guns being unable to see the walls sufficiently low down soon ceased to speak, and the embrasures were masked. On the other hand the besieged were unable, from the steepness of the castle hill, to depress their guns sufficiently to bear on the lodgment of the breaches in the first line, but their musketry was destructive, and they rolled down large shells to retard the approaches towards the second line.

On the 7th the besiegers got so close to the wall below that the howitzers above could no longer play without danger to the workmen, wherefore two French pieces taken in the horn-work were substituted and did good service. The breaching battery on San Michael's being altered also renewed its fire, and at 5 o'clock had broken 50 ft. off the parapet of the second line, yet the enemy's return was heavy and another 18-pounder lost a trunnion. During the night block carriages with supports for the broken trunnions were provided, and the disabled guns were enabled to recommence their fire with low charges. A constant rain now filled the trenches, the communications were injured, the workmen negligent, the approaches to the second line went on slowly, and again Dubreton came thundering down from the upper ground driving the guards and workmen from the new parallel at the lodgments, levelling all the works, carrying off all the tools, and killing or wounding 200 men. Colonel Cocks, promoted for his gallant conduct at the storming of San Michael, restored the fight and repulsed the French, but fell dead on the ground he had recovered.

After this severe check the approaches to the second line were abandoned and the trenches were extended so as to embrace the whole of the fronts attacked. The battery on San Michael had meantime formed a practicable breach 25 ft. wide, and the parallel at the old breach of the first line was prolonged by zigzags on the left towards this new breach, while a trench was opened to enable marksmen to fire upon the latter at 30 yards distant. Nevertheless another assault could not be risked, because the great expenditure of powder had again exhausted the magazines, and without a new supply the troops might have found themselves without ammunition in front of the French Army which was now gathering head near Briviesca. Heated shot were, however, thrown at the White Church with a view to burn the magazines ; and the miners were directed to drive a gallery on the other side of the castle against the church of San Roman, which was pushed out a little beyond the French external line of defence on the side of the city.

On the 10th when the besiegers' ammunition was nearly all gone, a fresh supply arrived from Santander, but no effect had been produced upon the White Church and Dubreton had strengthened his works to meet the assault ; he had also isolated the new breach on one flank by a strong stockade extending at right angles from the second to the third line of defence.

The fire from the Napoleon Battery had compelled the besiegers again to withdraw their battering guns within the horn-work, but the attempt to burn the White Church was relinquished, although the gallery against San Roman was continued. In this state things remained for several days with little change, save that the French, in spite of the musketry from the nearest zigzag trench, had scarped 8 ft. at the top of the new breach and formed a small trench at the back of it.

On the 15th the battery in the horn-work was again armed, and the guns pointed to reach the wall of the Napoleon Battery ; they were, however, overmatched and silenced in three-quarters of an hour and the embrasures were once more altered so that the guns might bear on the breach in the second line. Some slight works and counter-works were also made on different points, the besiegers being principally occupied repairing the mischief done by the rain, and pushing the gallery under San Roman, where the French were now distinctly heard talking in the church ; the mine was therefore formed and loaded with 900 lbs. of powder.

On the 17th the battery of the horn-work was renewed, the fire of the 18-pounders cleared away the enemy's temporary defences at the breach, the howitzers damaged the rampart on each side, and a small mine was sprung on the extreme right of the lower parallel, with a view to take possession of a cavalier or mound which the French had raised there, and from which they had killed many men in the trenches ; it was successful and a lodgment was effected, yet the enemy returned in force and compelled the besiegers to abandon it again. On the 18th the new breach was rendered practicable and Wellington ordered it to be stormed. The explosion of the mine under San Roman was to be the signal, the church was also to be assaulted, and at the same time a third detachment was to escalade the works in front of the ancient breach and thus connect the attacks.

Fifth Assault.

At 4.30 the springing of the mine at San Roman broke down a terrace in front of that building, yet with little injury to the church itself ; the latter, however, was resolutely attacked by Colonel Browne at the head of some Spanish and Portuguese troops, and though the enemy sprung a countermine which brought the building down, the assailants lodged themselves in the ruins. Meanwhile 200 of the foot guards with strong supports poured through the old breach in the first line and escaladed the second line, beyond which in the open ground between the second and third lines, they were encountered by the French, and a sharp musketry fight commenced. At the same time a like number of the German legion under Major Wurmb, similarly supported, stormed the new breach on the left of the guards so vigorously that it was carried in a moment, and some men mounted the hill above and actually gained the third line. Unhappily at neither of these assaults did the supports follow closely, the Germans, cramped on their left by the enemy's stockade, extended their right

towards the guards, and at that moment Dubreton came dashing
like a torrent from the upper ground and quickly cleared the
breaches. Wurmb and many other brave men fell, and the French
gathering round the guards who were still unsupported, forced them
beyond the outer line ; more than 1,000 men and officers were killed
or wounded in this combat, and the next night the enemy recovered
San Roman by a sally.

The siege was thus virtually abandoned. The French were indeed
beaten out of San Roman again, and a gallery was opened from that
church against the second line ; but these were mere demonstra
tions, and the contemporary events which compelled a victorious
army to abandon the siege of a small fortress, strong in nothing but
the skill and bravery of the Governor and his gallant soldiers, need
not be related in this work which is occupied only with the siege of
the place.

———————

So vast and intricate an art is war, that the apothegm of Turenne
will always be found applicable : " he who has made no mistakes
in war, has seldom made war." Some military writers, amongst
them the celebrated Jomini, blame the English general because, with a
conquering army and an insurgent nation at his back, he, during the
three months after his victory at Salamanca, attempted nothing
more than the unsuccessful Siege of Burgos. This censure is not
entirely unfounded and the King certainly escaped very easily from
Madrid ; yet there are many points to be argued ere the question
can be decided. The want of money, progressively increasing, had
become almost intolerable. The army was partly fed from Rodrigo,
partly from the Valley of the Pisuerga ; Hill's troops were fed from
Lisbon ; the Portuguese from their own country ; the Spaniards always
lived like the French by requisition ; the British professed to avoid
that mode, and their movements were therefore subservient to this
principle and must be judged accordingly ; want of money was
want of motion.

The objection may be more that, as Burgos did not yield, it would
not have yielded under any circumstances without a vigorous defence.
This is not so certain ; the prolonged defence of the castle was due to
some errors of detail in the attack as well as to want of sufficient artillery
means. In respect of the great features of the campaign, it may be
assumed that Wellington's judgment on the spot and with a full
knowledge both of his own and his adversary's situation, is of more
weight than Jomini's, however able and acute, for he knew nothing
of the difficulties.

It is said Sir Howard Douglas, on being consulted, objected
to the proceeding by gallery and mine against an outward, a middle,
and an inward line of defence, as likely to involve a succession of

tedious and difficult enterprises, which even if successful would still leave the White Church and the castle to be carried ; that this castle, besides other artillery armament, was surmounted by a powerful battery of heavy guns, bearing directly upon the face of the horn-work of San Michael, the only point from which it could be breached, and until it was breached the Governor, a gallant man would certainly not surrender. It could not, however, be breached without a larger battering train than the Allies possessed, and would not as he supposed be effected by mines ; wherefore, proposing to take the guns from two frigates then lying at Santander, he proffered to bring them up in time. In this reasoning Wellington partly acquiesced, but he expected success from the scarcity of water in the castle and the facility of burning the provision magazines ; he also trusted to good fortune. Towards the end of the siege, however, and too late, he got the guns from Santander.

CHAPTER SIX

SIEGE OF SAN SEBASTIAN, *July*, 1813.

In June, 1813, the Anglo-Portuguese troops were detailed by
Lord Wellington to cover the Siege of San Sebastian, and the blockade
of Pampeluna, while the Spanish divisions attacked Santona on the
coast, and the Castles of Daroca, Morella, and Zaragoza in the interior.
Pasages was the only port near the scene of operations suited for
the supply of the army, but as it was between the covering and
besieging armies, the stores and guns once landed were in danger
from every movement of the enemy ; the Deba River between San
Sebastian and Bilbao was unsuitable for large vessels, and no permanent
depôt could be established nearer than Bilbao. At that port therefore, and at St. Auder and Corunna, the great depôts of the army
were fixed, the stores being transported to them from the establishments in Portugal. But the French held Santona, their privateers
interrupted the communication along the coast of Spain, and Ameri-
can privateers did the same between Lisbon and Corunna. The intercourse between San Sebastian and the ports of France was scarcely
molested, while the most urgent remonstrances failed to procure a
sufficient naval force on the coast of Biscay. It was in these circumstances that Wellington commenced the Siege of San Sebastian.

This fortress, built on a low sandy isthmus, had the harbour on
one side, the river Urumea on the other. Behind it rose the Monte
Orgullo, a rugged cone 400 ft. high washed by the ocean, its
southern face, covered with batteries and overlooking the town,
being cut off from the latter by defensive walls. It was crowned by
the small castle of La Mota which was itself commanded at a distance
of 1,300 yards by the Monte Olea rising beyond the Urumea.
The land front was 350 yards wide, stretching quite across the isthmus,
and it consisted of a high curtain or rampart very solidly constructed,
strengthened by a lofty casemated flat bastion or cavalier placed
in the centre, and by half-bastions at either end. A regular hornwork was pushed out from this front ; and 600 yards beyond the
hornwork the isthmus was closed by the ridge of San Bartolomeo, at
the foot of which stood the suburb of San Martin.

On the opposite side of the Urumea were certain sandy hills called

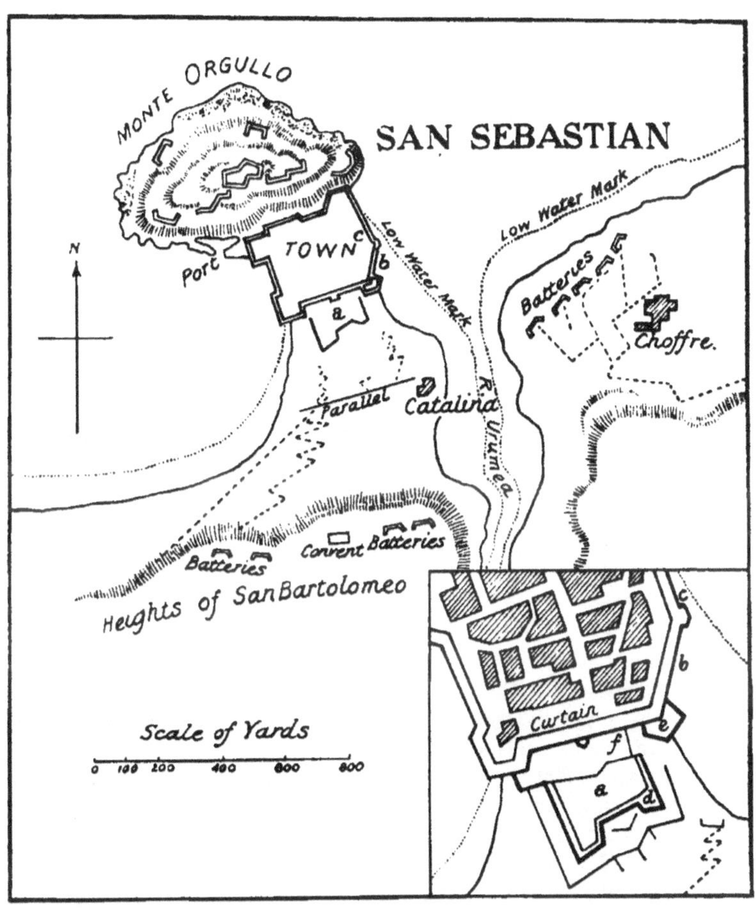

the Choffres, through which the road from Pasages passed to the wooden bridge over the river, and thence by the suburb of Santa Catalina, along the top of a sea wall which formed a *fausse braye* for the hornwork. The flanks of the town were protected by simple ramparts ; one washed by the water of the harbour, the other by the Urumea, which at high tide covered four of the 27 ft. of this height of the wall. This was the weak side of the fortress, for though covered by the river there was only a single wall badly flanked by two old towers and the half-bastion of San Elmo, which was situated at the extremity of the rampart close under the Monte Orgullo. There was no ditch, no counterscarp, no glacis ; the wall could be seen to its base from the Choffre Hills, at distances varying from 500 to 1,000 yards ; and when the tide was out the Urumea left a dry strand under the rampart as far as St. Elmo. However the guns from the batteries of Monte Orgullo could cover this strand. The other flank was secured by the harbour, in the mouth of which was a rocky island called Santa Clara, where the French had established a post of a few men.

Before the Battle of Vittoria, San Sebastian was nearly dismantled; many of the guns had been removed to form battering trains or to arm similar ports on the coast, there were no bomb-proofs, palisades, or outworks; the wells were foul, and the place supplied by a single aqueduct. Joseph's defeat restored its importance as a fortress. Emanuel Rey entered it the 22nd June, with the escort of the convoy which quitted Vittoria the day before the battle. The town was then filled with emigrant Spanish families, ministers, and other persons attached to the court; the population ordinarily 8,000, was increased to 16,000 and confusion prevailed. Rey pushed by necessity, immediately forced all persons not residents to march at once to France, granting them a guard of 100 men; the people of quality went by sea, the others by land, and fortunately all arrived for the partidas would have given them no quarter.

Rey then burned the wooden bridge and both the suburbs, and commenced fortifying the heights of San Bartolomeo, which the Spaniards attacked on the 29th and were repulsed.

On the 1st July the Governor of Gueteria abandoned the place and secretly left a lighted train which exploded the magazine and destroyed many of the inhabitants. His troops, 300, entered San Sebastian, and at the same time a vessel from St. Jean de Luz arrived with 56 cannoneers and some workmen, the garrison was thus increased to 3,000 men, and all persons not able to provide sustenance for themselves were ordered to quit the place. On the 3rd the frigate *Surveillante*, with a sloop, and some small craft blockaded the harbour; yet the French vessels from St. Jean de Luz continued to enter by night. The same day the Governor made a sally with 1,100 men to obtain news, and after some hours' skirmishing returned with a few prisoners. On the 9th Graham arrived with a corps of British and Portuguese troops. Before his arrival the French had constructed a redoubt on the heights of San Bartolomeo, and connected it with the convent of that name which they also fortified. These outworks were supported by posts in the ruined houses of San Martin behind, and by a low circular redoubt formed of casks on the main road half-way between the convent and the hornwork. Hence to reduce the place, working along the isthmus it was necessary to carry in succession three lines of defence covering the town, and a fourth at the foot of Monte Orgullo, before the Castle of La Mota could be assailed. These works had 76 pieces mounted, and others were afterwards obtained by sea from France.

The besieging army consisted of the 5th Division under Oswald, the independent Portuguese brigades of J. Wilson and Bradford, reinforced by detachments from the 1st Division, artillerymen, some seamen commanded by Lieut. O'Reilly of the *Surveillante*, and 100 regular Sappers & Miners (now for the first time used in the sieges of the Peninsular), making in all nearly 10,000 men. There was a new battering train, originally prepared to besiege Burgos, consisting of fourteen iron 24-pounders, six 8-in. brass howitzers, four 68-pound iron carronades, and four iron 10-in. mortars; six 24-pounders lent by the ships of war, and six 18-pounders which had moved from the army from Portugal, making altogether 40 pieces, commanded by Colonel Dickson. The distance from the siege depôt at Pasages to the Choffres was 1½ miles of good road, and a pontoon bridge was thrown over the Urumea River above these hills ; but from thence to the height of Bartolomeo there was more than 5 miles of very bad road.

Early in July the fortress had been twice closely inspected by Major Smith, the Engineer who had so ably defended Tarifa. He proposed a plan of siege, founded upon the facility furnished by the Choffres, to destroy the flanks, rake the principal front, and form a breach with the same batteries ; the works being at the same time secured, except at low water, by the Urumea. Counter-batteries on the left of that river, were to rake the line of defence in which the breach was to be formed ; and against the castle and its outworks he relied principally upon vertical fire. This plan would probably have reduced San Sebastian in a reasonable time without any remarkable loss of men ; Wellington approved of it, though he doubted the efficacy of the vertical fire and he ordered the siege to be commenced. Although anxious to save time, he did not urge the Engineer beyond the rules. *Take the place in the quickest manner, yet do not from over-speed fail to take it.*

During the night of the 10th two batteries were commenced against the convent, and the redoubt of San Bartolomeo; and next night four batteries, to contain twenty of the heaviest guns and four 8-in. howitzers, were marked out on the Choffre sandhills, at distances varying from 600 to 1,300 yards from the eastern ramparts of the town. Two attacks were established, one on the right bank of the Urumea for the Portuguese brigades ; one on the left bank for the 5th Division.

On the 14th a French sloop entered the harbour with supplies, and the batteries of the left attack opened against San Bartolomeo throwing hot shot into that building. The besieged responded with musketry from the redoubt, with heavy guns from the town, and with a field piece which they had mounted on the belfry of the convent itself. On the 15th Sir Richard Fletcher took command of the Engineers. This day the batteries set the convent on fire, silenced the musketry of the besieged, and so damaged the defences that the Portuguese of the 5th Division were ordered to feel the enemy ; they were however repulsed with great loss, the French sallied, and the firing did not cease until nightfall.

On the 17th the convent being nearly in ruins, the assault was ordered. The storming party was formed in two columns. Detachments from Wilson's Portuguese, supported by the Light Company of the 9th British Regiment, and three companies of the Royals, under General Hay, were destined to assail the redoubt ; General Bradford leading the other column, composed of Portuguese, supported by three companies of the 9th under Colonel Cameron were to assail the convent.

ASSAULT OF SAN BARTOLOMEO.

At 10 o'clock in the morning two heavy 6-pounders opened against the redoubt, and a sharp musketry fire from the French, announced their resolution to fight. The allied troops were assembled behind the crest of the hill overlooking the convent, and the first signal was given ; but the Portuguese advanced so slowly at both attacks that the supporting columns of the 9th Regiment, passing through them, fell upon the enemy with the usual impetuosity of British soldiers. Cameron leading his grenadiers downhill was exposed to a heavy cannonade from the hornwork, but he gained the cover of a wall 50 yards from the convent and there awaited the second signal. His rapid advance, which threatened to cut off the garrison from the suburb, caused the French to abandon the redoubt ; Cameron's force then cleared the wall and assaulted both the convent and the houses of the suburb. At the latter a fierce struggle ensued and Capt. Woodham of the 9th was killed in the upper room of a house, but the grenadiers carried the convent with such rapidity that the French unable to explode some small mines, hastily joined the troops in the suburb. There the fighting continued, and the affair was becoming doubtful, when the remaining companies of the 9th Regiment arrived, and the suburb with much fighting was won. At the right attack the company of the 9th though retarded by a ravine, a thick hedge, the slowness of the Portuguese, and a heavy fire, entered the abandoned redoubt with little loss ; but all the troops were then, contrary to Oswald's orders, rashly led against the cask redoubt, and were beaten back by the enemy. The French lost 240 men. On the British side the companies of the 9th under Cameron alone lost 7 officers and 60 men killed or wounded, and the whole operation though successful was an error. The battery on the Urumea was not opened, so that either the assault was precipitated or the battery was not necessary, but the loss justified the conception of the battery.

When the action ceased, the Engineers made a lodgment in the redoubt ; and commenced two batteries for eight pieces to rake the hornwork and the eastern rampart of the place. Two other batteries, to contain four 68-pounder carronades and four 10-in. mortars, were also commenced on the right bank of the Urumea. The besieged then threw up traverses on the land front to meet the raking fire of the besiegers, and the latter dragged four pieces up the Monte Olea to fire into the Mirador and other batteries on the Monte Orgullo. During the night a lodgment was made on the ruins of San Martin ; the batteries at the right attack were armed, and two additional mortars dragged up the Monte Olea ; on the 19th all the batteries of both attacks were armed, and that night two approaches were commenced from the suburb towards the cask redoubt, from whence the French were driven.

On the 20th the whole of the batteries opened fire, the greatest part being directed to form the breach.

Smith's plan was similar to that followed by Marshal Beresford a century before. He proposed a lodgment on the hornwork before the breach should be assailed, but he unknowingly fixed the breaching point precisely where the wall had been most strongly rebuilt after Berwick's attack. This was the first fault, yet a slight one, because the wall did not resist the batteries very long ; it was a more serious matter that Graham, at the suggestion of the commander of the artillery, began his operations by breaching. Smith was opposed to it, but Fletcher acquiesced reluctantly, on the understanding that the destruction of the defences was only postponed, an understanding afterwards forgotten.

The result of the first day's firing was not satisfactory. The weather was bad, the guns mounted on ship carriages failed, one 24-pounder was rendered unserviceable by the enemy, another useless by an accident, a captain of Engineers was killed, and the besiegers' shot had little effect upon the solid wall. During the night however the ship guns were mounted on better carriages, and a parallel across the isthmus was projected. but the greater part of the workmen sought shelter in the suburb of San Martin, and when day broke only one-third of the work was performed.

On the 21st the place was summoned, but the Governor refused to receive the letter, and the firing was resumed. The main wall still resisted, yet the parapets and embrasures crumbled away, and the batteries on Monte Olea plunged their fire into the hornwork, with such effect, although at 1,600 yards distance, that the besieged having no bombproofs were forced to dig trenches to protect themselves. The counter-fire directed solely against the breaching batteries was feeble, but at midnight a shell thrown from the castle into the bay gave the signal for a sally, and during the fire which ensued several French vessels with supplies entered the harbour. This night the besieged also isolated the breach by cuts in the rampart and other defences. On the other hand the besiegers' parallel across the isthmus was completed, and in its progress laid bare the mouth of a drain, 4 ft. high and 3 ft. wide, containing the pipe of the aqueduct cut off by the Spaniards. Through this narrow opening Lieut. Reid of the Engineers, a young and zealous officer, crept as far as the counterscarp of the hornwork, but there finding the passage closed by a door returned without an accident. Thirty barrels of powder were then placed in the drain, 8 ft. being stopped with sandbags to form a globe of compression, which was designed to blow sufficient rubbish over the counterscarp to fill the narrow ditch of the hornwork.

On the 22nd the fire from the batteries, unexampled by its rapidity and accuracy, opened what appeared to the besiegers a very practicable breach in the eastern flank wall. The counter-fire of the besiegers then slackened, yet the descent into the town from the breach was more than 12 ft. perpendicular, and the garrison was seen from Monte Olea diligently working at the interior defences to receive the assault. The besiegers now placed four 68-pound carronades in battery to play on the defences of the breach, but the general fire slackened because the guns were greatly enlarged at the vents with constant firing.

On the 23rd, the sea blockade being null, the French vessels returned to France with the badly wounded men ; and that day the besiegers judging the breach between the towers quite practicable, turned the guns to break the wall on the right of the main breach. Smith opposed this, urging that no advantage would be gained by opening a second opening to get to which the troops must first pass the great breach, that time would be lost to the besiegers, and there was a manifest objection on account of the tide and the depth of water at the new point attacked. His counsel was overruled and in the course of the day, the wall being thin and the fire heavy and quick, a second breach 30 ft. wide was rendered practicable. Then the fire of the besieged being much diminished, the 10-in. mortars and 68-pound carronades were turned upon the defences of the great breach. The nearest houses were soon in flames which spreading rapidly destroyed some of the defences, and menaced the whole town with destruction, and the assault was ordered for the next morning ; but when the troops assembled the burning houses appeared so formidable that the attack was deferred. The batteries then fired again, partly on the second breach, partly on the defences, partly to break the wall in a third place between the half-bastion of St. John on the land front and the main breach.

During the night the vigilant Governor mounted two fieldpieces on the cavalier in the centre of the land front, and he still had on the hornwork a light piece, and two casemated guns on the flank of the cavalier. Two other field pieces were mounted on an entrench-ment, and a 24-pounder looked from the Tower of Las Mesquitas ; two 4-pounders were in the Tower of Hornos, two heavy guns were on the flank of St. Elmo, and two others placed on the right of the Mirador.

Thus 14 pieces were still available for defence, the retaining sea wall, or *fausse braye*, which strengthened the Urumea flank of the hornwork and between which and the river the storming parties must necessarily advance, was covered with live shells to roll over on the columns, and behind the flaming houses near the breach other edifices were loopholed and filled with musketeers. However the fire extended rapidly and fiercely, greatly injuring the defences ; the French withdrew their guns until the moment of attack, while the British artillery officers declared they could silence the enemy's fire in daylight, and keep the parapet clear of men Graham thereupon renewed the order for

The Assault.

During the night of the 24th 2,000 men of the 5th Division filed into the trenches on the isthmus. This force was composed of the 3rd Battalion of the Royals under Major Fraser, detailed to storm the great breach ; the 38th Regiment under Colonel Greville for assail-ing the lesser and most distant breach ; and the 9th Regiment under Colonel Cameron, to support the Royals. A detachment selected from the Light Companies of all these battalions was placed in the centre of the Royals under the command of Lieut. Campbell of the 9th Regiment ; he was accompanied by Lieut. L. Machell of the Engineers and a ladder party and was to sweep the high curtain after the breach should be won.

From the trenches to the point of attack was more than 300 yards along a contracted space, the ground was strewed with rocks covered by slippery seaweed, the tide had left large and deep pools of water—the parapet of the hornwork was entire as well as the retaining wall—the parapets of the other works and the two towers which closely flanked the breach, although injured were far from being ruined, and the walls and defences were fully manned. The difficulties indeed were obvious.

While it was still dark the storming columns moved out of the trenches, and the mine in the drain was exploded against the counter-scarp and glacis of the hornwork with great effect. The garrison astonished by this unlooked for event abandoned the flanking parapet, and the Allies rushed onwards, the storming party for the main breach leading and suffering more from the fire of the batteries on the right of the Urumea, than from the enemy. Major Fraser and Lieut. Harry Jones of the Engineers first reached the breach, and as the enemy had fallen back in confusion behind the ruins of the burning houses, those brave officers rushed up expecting that their troops would follow, but not many did for it was extremely dark, and the natural difficulties of the way had contracted the front and disordered the column in its whole length, the soldiers, straggling and out of wind, arrived in small disconnected parties at the foot of the breach. The foremost gathered near their gallant leaders, but the depth of the descent into the town, and the volumes of flame and smoke which still issued from the burning houses behind awed the stoutest, and more than two-thirds of the column harassed by the flank fire, had broken off at the demi-bastion to commence a musketry combat with the enemy on the ramparts.

Meanwhile the shells from the Monte Orgullo fell rapidly, the French rallied and with a smashing musketry from the ruins and loopholed houses assailed the head of the stormers, while the men in the towers took them on the flank ; and from every quarter came showers of grape and hand grenades, shattering them in a terrible manner.

Fraser was killed on the flaming ruins, the intrepid Jones stood there a while longer amid a few heroic soldiers, hoping for aid, but none came, and he and those with him were struck down ; Lieut. Machell was killed early, and the ladder bearers fell or were dispersed. Thus the rear of the column was in confusion before the head was beaten, and it was in vain that Greville of the 38th, Cameron of the 9th, and many other regimental officers attempted to rally their discomfited troops and refill the breach ; it was in vain that Lieut. Campbell breaking through the tumultuous crowd with the survivors of his chosen detachment, mounted the ruins—twice he ascended, twice he was wounded, and all around him died. The Royals endeavouring to retire, got intermixed with the 38th and with some of the 9th, who had unsuccessfully tried to pass them and get to the lesser breach. Then swayed by different impulses, pent up in the narrow way between the hornwork and the river, the mass reeling to and fro could neither advance or retire until the shells and musketry, constantly plied both in front and flank, had thinned the concourse when the trenches were regained in confusion. At daybreak a truce was agreed to for an hour, during which the French, who had already recovered the gallant Jones and some of the wounded men from the breach, carried off the more distant sufferers lest they should be drowned by the rising of the tide; but during the contest some grenadiers rushed out of the breach and stabbed several wounded soldiers lying there.

Five officers of the Engineers including Sir Richard Fletcher, and 44 officers of the Line with 520 men, had been killed, wounded, or taken prisoners in this assault, the failure of which was signal. The causes were obvious and may be classed thus :—

1st. Deviation from the original project of siege and from Wellington's instructions.

2nd. Bad arrangements of detail.

3rd. Want of vigour in the execution.

Wellington having visited the Choffre trenches on the 22nd had confirmed his first approval of Smith's plan, and gave that officer final directions for the attack finishing thus " *Fair daylight must be taken for the assault.*" These instructions were repeated by Smith in the proper quarter, and were not followed ; no lodgment was made on the hornwork, the defences were nearly entire both in front and flank, and the assault was given in darkness. Smith had ascertained by calculation and consultations with the fishermen, that the ebb of tide would serve exactly at daybreak on the 24th ; yet the assault was only made the 25th and before daylight, when the high water, contracting the ground, increased the obstacles and forced the assaulting column to march in a narrow front and a long line, thus making a difficult progress. The rules of art being thus neglected the operation failed.

During the night the troops filed out of the long narrow trenches, a tedious operation, and were at once exposed to a fire of grape from their own batteries on the Choffres. This fire should have ceased when the mine was sprung, but owing to the darkness and noise the latter was neither seen nor heard, and though the Portuguese advanced to the ditch, where a vigorous escalade would probably have succeeded, they had no ladders. The stormers of the great breach marched first filling up the way, and rendering the second breach, as Smith had foretold, useless, and the ladder bearers never got to their destination.

There was also a neglect of moral influence. Deferring the assault from the 24th to the 25th, expressly because the breach was too difficult, rendered the troops uneasy ; they suspected hidden danger. In this mood emerging from the trenches they were struck by the fire of their own batteries; and then wading through deep pools of water, or staggering over slippery rocks, and being close under the enemy's flanking works where every shot told with fatal effect, how could they succeed ? A second and more vigorous assault on the great breach might have been effected by a recognized leader ; but no general or staff officer went out of the trenches, and the isolated exertions of the regimental officers failed.

Wellington repaired immediately to San Sebastian. The causes of failure were apparent, and he would have renewed the attack, but was compelled from want of ammunition to defer it, until powder and additional ordnance, should arrive. Next day other events caused him to resort to a blockade, and the battering train was transported to Pasages, two guns and two howitzers only being retained on the Choffre and Monte Olea. This operation was completed during the night of the 26th, but at daybreak the garrison made a sally from the hornwork, surprised the trenches and swept off 200 Portuguese and 30 British soldiers. To avoid a repetition of this disaster the guards of the trenches were concentrated in the left parallel, and patrols only were sent out, but one of these also was cut off on the 1st August. Thus terminated the first part of the Siege of San Sebastian in which the Allies lost 1,300 soldiers and seamen, exclusive of Spaniards during Mendizabel's blockade.

Renewed Siege of San Sebastian.

Villette's demonstration against Louga on the 28th July had caused the ships laden with the battery train to put to sea, but on the 5th August the guns were re-landed and the works against the fortress resumed.

The old trenches were repaired, the heights of San Bartolomeo were strengthened, and the Convent of Antigua, built on a rock to the left of those heights, was fortified and armed with two guns to scour the open beach and sweep the bay. The siege however languished for want of ammunition ; and during this forced inactivity the garrison received supplies and reinforcements by sea, repaired their damaged works, made new defences, filled their magazines, and put 67 pieces of artillery in a condition to fire. Eight hundred and fifty men had been killed or wounded since the commencement of the attack in July ; but fresh men came by sea, and more than 2,600 good soldiers were still present under arms.

However the general firing was severe upon the castle and the town works and the defences were damaged ; the French guns were nearly silenced, additional mortars were mounted at the Choffre, making in all 63 pieces of which 29 threw shells, and the superiority of the besiegers was established. Now however the Urumea was discovered to be fordable by Capt. Alexander Macdonald of the Artillery, who had waded across in the night, and passed close under the works to the breach. A few minutes would suffice to bring the enemy into the Choffre batteries, and therefore to save the guns from being spiked their vents were covered at night with iron plates fastened by chains.

This day the materials and ordnance for six pieces, to take the defences of the Monte Orgullo in reverse, were sent to the island of Santa Clara ; and from the Choffre some guns played on the retaining wall of the hornwork ; but with low charges to shake down any mines constructed there without destroying the wall itself, which offered cover for troops in an assault. The trenches at the isthmus were now wide and good, the sap was pushed close to the hornwork ; and the sea wall, supporting the high road into the town, which had in the first assault lengthened the run and cramped the columns, was broken through to give access to the strand and shorten the approach to the breaches. The crisis was now at hand, and during the night of the 29th a false attack was ordered, to make the enemy spring his mines. This desperate service was executed by Lieut. Macadam of the 9th Regiment ; the order was sudden and no volunteers were demanded, no rewards offered, no means of excitement resorted to ; yet such is the inherent bravery of British soldiers, that 17 men of the Royals, the nearest at hand, immediately leaped forth ready and willing to encounter what seemed certain death. With a rapid pace, all the breaching batteries firing hotly at the time, they reached the foot of the breach unperceived, and then mounted in extended order shouting and firing ; the French were too steady to be imposed upon, their musketry laid the party low, and their commander returned nearly alone to the trenches.

On the 30th the sea flank being open from the half-bastion of St. John to the most distant of the old breaches, 500 ft., the Choffre batteries were turned against the castle and the other defences of the Monte Orgullo. The battery on the isthmus in conjunction with the fire from the Choffre, also demolished the face of the St. John's Bastion and the end of the high curtain above it ; thus the whole of that quarter was in ruins. The San Bartolomeo batteries then broke the demi-bastion of the hornwork, and Wellington after examining the defences decided to make a lodgment and ordered the assault for the following day at 11 o'clock, when the ebb of the tide would leave space between the hornwork and the water. The galleries in front of the advanced batteries on the isthmus were now pushed to the sea wall ; and three mines were formed with the double view of opening a way for the troops to reach the strand, thus rendering useless any subterranean works the enemy might have made in that part. At 2 o'clock on the morning of the 31st they were sprung, and opened three wide passages ; these were immediately connected, and a traverse of gabions, 6 ft. high, was run across the mouth of the main trench on the left, to screen the opening from the grape shot of the castle. Everything was now ready for the assault, but before describing that terrible event it will be fitting to show the exact state of the besieged in defence.

Graham had been before the place for 52 days, during 30 of which the attack was suspended. All this time the garrison had laboured incessantly ; and though the besiegers' fire appeared to have ruined the defences of the enormous breach in the sea flank such was not the case. A perpendicular fall behind of more than 20 ft. barred progress ; and beyond, amongst the ruins of the burnt houses, was a strong counter-wall 15 ft. high, loopholed for musketry and parallel with the breaches, which were also cut off from the sound part of the rampart

by traverses at the extremities. To evince their confidence, the besieged celebrated the Emperor's birthday by crowning the castle with
a splendid illumination, encircling it with a fiery legend to his honour
in characters so large as to be distinctly read by the besiegers.

On the 19th after a delay of 16 days the battering train arrived
from England, and 15 heavy pieces were placed in battery, 8 at the
right attack, 7 at the left during the night of the 22nd. A second
battering train came on the 23rd augmenting the number of pieces
of various kinds to 117, but with characteristic negligence this
enormous armament had been sent out from England with no more
shot and shell than would suffice for one day's consumption.

In the night of the 23rd the batteries on the Choffre were reinforced with four long pieces and four 68-pound carronades; the
left attack had six additional guns. Ninety sappers & miners had
come with the train from England, the seamen under Lieut. O'Reilly
were again attached to the batteries, and part of the field artillerymen
were brought to the siege. The Choffre batteries were also enlarged
to contain 48 pieces, and two batteries for 13 pieces were begun on
the heights of Bartolomeo. These last were to breach at 700 yards
distance the faces of the left demi-bastion of the hornwork, that of
St. John on the main front, and the end of the high curtain; for
these works rising in gradation one above the other, were in the same
line of fire. The approaches by the isthmus were pushed forward
by sap, but the old trenches were still imperfect; and before
daylight on the 25th, the French coming from the hornwork, swept
the left of the parallel, injured the sap, and made some prisoners.

On the night of the the 25th, the batteries were all armed on both
sides of the Urumea, and on the 26th 57 pieces opening with a general
salvo, continued to play with astounding noise and rapidity until
evening. The fire from the Choffre Hills destroyed the revetment
of the demi-bastion of St. John, and nearly ruined the towers at the
old breach together with the wall connecting them; but at the
isthmus the batteries, although they injured the hornwork, made little
impression on the main front, from which they were too far distant.

Wellington, present at this attack and discontented with the
operation, then ordered a battery for six guns to be constructed
amongst some ruined houses on the right of the parallel, 300 yards
from the main front. Two shafts were also sunk with a view to
drive galleries for its protection against the enemy's mines; but
the sandy soil made this work slow.

Early on the 27th the boats of the squadron under Lieut. Arbuthnot
of the *Surveillante*, carrying 100 men of the 9th Regiment under
Capt. Cameron, attacked the island of Santa Clara. The troops
landed with some difficulty under a heavy fire, but a lodgment
was made with the loss of only 28 officers and men, of whom 18 were
seamen.

In the night the French sallied against the new battery on the isthmus ; but were met with the bayonet by men of the 9th Regiment under Colonel Cameron on the very edge of the trenches. The attempt failed but it delayed the arming of the battery. At daybreak the renewed fire of the besiegers was extremely heavy, and the shrapnel shell were supposed to be very destructive ; but the practice with that missile was uncertain, the bullets frequently flew amongst the guards in the parallel and one struck the field officer. In the course of the day another sally was commenced, but the enemy being fired upon did not persist. The trenches were now furnished with banquettes and parapets as fast as the quantity of gabions and fascines would permit ; but the work was slow because the Spanish authorities neglected to provide carts to convey the materials from the woods, and this hard labour was performed by Portuguese soldiers.

Wellington visited the works again, and the advanced battery was armed with four guns and opened next morning ; but an accident prevented the arrival of one gun, the enemy dismounted another, and only two instead of six guns as Wellington had designed. smote the demi-bastion of St John, and the end of the high curtain.

The only really practicable way into the town was by the narrow end of the high curtain above the half-bastion of St. John. About the middle of the great breach stood the Tower of Los Hornos, still capable of some defence, and beneath it a mine charged with 12 cwt. of powder. The streets were all trenched and furnished with traverses to dispute the passage and cover the retreat to the Monte Orgullo ; to reach the main breach it was also necessary to form a lodgment in the hornwork, or pass as in the former assault, under a flanking fire of musketry for 200 yards ; and the first step was close under the sea wall at the salient angle of the covered way, where two mines charged with 800 lbs. of powder were prepared.

Besides these retrenchments and mines, the French had still some artillery in reserve. One 16-pounder mounted at St. Elmo flanked the left of the breaches on the river face ; a 12 and an 8-pounder, preserved in the casemates of the cavalier, were ready to flank the land face of the half-bastion of St. John ; many guns from the Monte Orgullo could play upon the columns, and there was a 4-pounder hidden on the hornwork to be brought into action when the assault commenced. Neither the resolution of the Governor or the courage of the garrison was abated ; but the overwhelming fire of the past few days had reduced the number of fighting men ; and Rey who had only 250 men in reserve, demanded of Soult whether his brave garrison should be exposed to another assault. " The army would endeavour to succour him " was the reply, and he abided his fate.

STORMING OF SAN SEBASTIAN.

To assault the breaches without having destroyed the enemy's defences, or established a lodgment on the hornwork, notwithstanding the increased fire and greater facilities of the besiegers, was obviously a repetition of error. And the same generals who had before publicly disapproved of such operations, now more freely dealt out censures, not ill-founded, but very indiscreet since there is much danger when doubts expressed by their commanders reach the men. Wellington thought the 5th Division had been thus discouraged. He was incensed and demanded 50 volunteers from each of the 15 regiments composing the 1st, 4th, and Light Divisions, *"men who could show other troops how to mount a breach."* Such was the phrase employed, and 750 gallant soldiers instantly marched to San Sebastian in answer to the appeal. Colonel Cooke and Major Robertson led the Guards and Germans of the 1st Division ; Major Rose commanded the men of the 4th Division ; Colonel Hunt, who had already earned his promotion at former assaults, was at the head of the fierce rugged veterans of the Light Division ; yet there were good officers and brave soldiers in the 5th Division.

It being at first supposed that Wellington designed only a simple lodgment on the great breach, the volunteers and one brigade of the 5th Division only were ordered to be ready ; but at a council held at night, Major Smith maintained that the orders had been misunderstood, as no lodgment could be formed until the high curtain was gained. General Oswald, being called to the council, was of the same opinion ; whereupon the remainder of the 5th Division was brought to the trenches ; and General Bradford having offered the services of his Portuguese brigade, was told he might ford the Urumea and assail the farthest breach if he thought it advisable.

Leith had now resumed command of the 5th Division, and directed the attack from the isthmus ; but he was extremely offended with the volunteers, and would not allow them to lead the assault ; some he spread along the trenches to keep down the fire of the hornwork, the remainder was held in reserve with Hay's British and Sprye's Portuguese brigades of the 5th Division. To Robertson's brigade the assault was confided; it was formed in two columns, one to attack the old breach between the towers, the other to storm the bastion of St. John and the end of the high curtain. The small breach on the extreme right was left for Bradford's Portuguese, who were on the Choffre Hills ; some large boats filled with troops were directed to make a demonstration against the sea line of the Monte Orgullo, and Graham overlooked the whole operations from the right bank of the river.

Heavily the morning of the 31st broke, a thick fog hid every object and the besiegers' batteries could not open until 8 o'clock ;

from that hour however a constant shower of missiles was poured upon the besiegers until 11, when Robertson's brigade quitted the trenches, and passing through the openings in the sea wall was launched against the breaches. While the head of this column was still gathering on the strand, 30 yards from the salient angle of the hornworks, 12 men under a sergeant, whose heroic death has not sufficed to preserve his name, rushing forward leaped upon the covered way with intent to destroy the enemy's mines. The French startled by this sudden assault fired the train prematurely ; but though the sergeant and his followers were all destroyed and the high sea wall thrown with a dreadful crash upon the head of the advancing column, not more than 40 men were crushed by the ruins, and the rush of the troops was scarcely checked.   The Forlorn Hope had before passed beyond the play of the mine, and now hurried along the strand amidst a shower of grape and shells, the leader, Lieut. Macquire, of the 4th Regiment, conspicuous by his long white plume, his fine figure and his dash, bounding far ahead of his men in all the pride of youthful strength and courage ; but at the foot of the great breach he fell dead, and the stormers swept over his body, many died however with him, and the passage of wounded men to the rear was incessant.

This time there was a broad strand left by the retreating tide, and the sun had dried the rocks, but the latter still disturbed the order and closeness of the formation, and the main breach was 200 yards distant. The French seeing the first mass pass the hornwork, regardless of its broken bastion, crowded to the river face and poured their musketry into the second column as it rushed along a few yards below them ; but the English returned this fire without slackening their speed. Then the batteries of Monte Orgullo and the St. Elmo sent down showers of shot and shell, the two pieces on the cavalier swept the face of the breach in St. John, the 4-pounder mounted in the hornwork was suddenly mounted on the broken bastion and poured grape shot into the rear. Thus scourged with fire from all sides, their array broken alike by the shot and by the rocks they passed over, the troops reached their destination. The first column soon reached the top of the great breach, but the unexpected gulf below could only be passed at a few places, and the deadly French muskets clattering from the loophole and wall beyond, strewed the crest of the ruins with dead. In vain the following multitude, covering the ascent, sought entrance at every part ; to advance was impossible and slowly sinking downwards the mass remained stubborn and immovable on the lower part of the breach. There they were safe from the musketry in front ; but from isolated points, especially from Los Hornos under which the great mine was placed, the French still assailed them with small arms, and from Monte Orgullo came shells and grape without intermission.

At the half-bastion of St. John the access to the top of the high curtain being quite practicable, the efforts to force a way were more persevering and constant, and the slaughter was in proportion, for the traverse on the flank was defended by French grenadiers who would not yield. The two pieces on the cavalier itself swept the front of the opening, and the 4-pounder and musketry from the hornwork swept the river face.

Some Sappers and a working party attached to the assaulting columns endeavoured to form a lodgment ; but no artificial materials had been provided, and most of the labourers were killed before they could form the loose rocky fragments into a cover. During this time the counter-fire of the British artillery killed many ; and the reserve brigades of the 5th Division were pushed on by degrees to feed the attack, until the left wing of the 9th Regiment only remained in the trenches. The volunteers, who had been with difficulty restrained in the trenches, called out to know why they had been brought there if they were not to lead the assault. These men who had given such offence to Leith that he would have kept them altogether from the assault, being now let loose went like a whirlwind to the breaches and the crowded masses swarmed up the face of the ruins ; but on reaching the crest line they came down again like a falling wall, crowd after crowd were seen to mount, to totter, to sink, the French fire was unabated, the smoke floated away, and the crest of the breach bore no living man !

Graham standing on the nearest of the Choffre batteries, beheld this frightful destruction with a stern resolution to win at any cost ; and he was a man to have put himself at the head of the last company and die sword in hand upon the breach, rather than sustain a second defeat ; and neither his confidence nor his resources were exhausted. He directed an attempt to be made on the hornwork, and turned all the Choffre batteries and one on the isthmus, that is to say the concentrated fire of 50 heavy pieces, upon the high curtain. The shot ranged over the heads of the troops now gathered at the foot of the breach ; and the stream of missiles thus poured along the upper surface broke down the traverses and in its fearful course, shattering all things, strewed the ramparts with the bodies of the defenders. When this flight of shot first swept over the heads of the soldiers a cry arose from some inexperienced people " to retire because the batteries were firing upon the stormers"; but the veterans of the Light Division under Hunt were not men to be so disturbed ; and in the very heat and fury of the cannonade they effected a solid lodgment in some ruins of houses actually within the rampart on the right of the great breach.

For half an hour this horrid tempest smote against the works and the houses behind ; and when it ceased the clatter of the French muskets showed that the fight was renewed. At this time also the 13th Portuguese Regiment, led by Major Snodgrass, and followed by a detachment of the 24th under Colonel Macbean, entered the river from the Choffre. The ford was deep, the water rose above the waist, and when the soldiers reached the middle of the stream which was 200 yards wide, a heavy gun struck the head of the column with a shower of grape, the havoc was fearful but the survivors closed up and moved on. A second discharge from the same piece tore the ranks from front to rear, still the regiment moved on, and amidst a confused fire of musketry from the ramparts and of artillery from St. Elmo, from the castle and from the Mirador, landed on the left bank and rushed against the third breach. Macbean's men following with equal bravery reinforced the great breach 80 yards to the left of the other, although the line of ruins seemed to extend the whole way.

Then the fighting became fierce and obstinate again at all the breaches ; but the French musketry still rolled with deadly effect, the heaps of slain increased, and once more the great mass of the stormers sunk to the foot of the ruins unable to win ; the living sheltered themselves as they could, and the dead and wounded lay so thickly that it could hardly be judged whether the injured or uninjured were the most numerous.

It was now evident that the assault must fail unless some accident happened ; for the tide was rising, the reserves all engaged, and no greater effect could be expected from men whose courage had been already pushed to the verge of madness. · In this crisis fortune intervened. A number of powder barrels, live shells, and combustible materials which the French had accumulated behind the traverses for their defence, caught fire. Soon a bright consuming flame wrapped the whole of the high curtain, a succession of loud explosions were heard, hundreds of the French grenadiers were destroyed, the rest were thrown into confusion ; and while the ramparts were still enveloped with suffocating eddies of smoke, the British soldiers broke in at the first traverse. The defenders bewildered by this terrible disaster, yielded for a moment, but some rallied and a close desperate struggle took place along the summit of the high curtain ; the fury of the stormers, whose numbers increased every moment, could however not be stemmed. The French colours on the cavalier were torn away by Lieut. Gethin, of the 11th Regiment ; the hornwork, the land front below the curtain, the loopholed wall behind the great breach were all abandoned ; the soldiers of the Light Division who had already established themselves in the ruins on the French left, penetrated to the streets, and the Portuguese at the small breach mixed with British who had wandered to that point seeking for an entrance, burst in on their side.

Five hours the dreadful battle had lasted at the walls, and now the stream of war went pouring into the town. The undaunted Governor still disputed the victory for a short time with the aid of his barricades ; but several hundreds of his men were cut off and taken in the hornwork, and even to effect a retreat behind the line of defences which separated the town from the Monte Orgullo was difficult ; however a crowd of his troops flying from the hornwork along the harbour flank of the town, broke through a body of the British which had reached the vicinity of the fortified convent of Santa Téresa. This post was the only one retained by the French in the town, and it was thought that Monte Orgullo might have been carried, if a general to direct the troops had been at hand ; but whether from wounds or accident no officer of that rank entered the place until long after the breach had been won ; the battalion chiefs were thus embarrassed for want of orders, and a thunderstorm coming down from the mountains with unbounded fury immediately after the place was carried, added to the confusion of the fight.

The capture of the town was marked with much violence and brutality and although many officers exerted themselves to preserve order, and many men were well conducted, the rapine and violence commenced by villains spread ; the camp followers soon crowded into the place, and the disorder continued until the flames following the steps of the plunderer, put an end to his ferocity by destroying the whole town. Three generals, Leith, Oswald, and Robinson, had been wounded in the trenches; Sir Richard Fletcher, Chief Engineer, a brave man who had long served his country honourably, was killed ; Colonel* Burgoyne, Second Engineer, was wounded, and the carnage at the breaches was appalling. The volunteers though brought late into action had nearly half their number struck down ; most of the regiments of the 5th Division suffered in the same proportion, and the whole loss since the renewal of the siege exceeded 2,500 officers and men.

When the town was taken the steep and rugged Monte Orgullo with its citadel remained to be assailed. It presented four batteries connected with masonry in first line ; and from the extremities ramps protected by redans led to the Santa Téresa Convent, which offered a salient point of defence. On the side facing Santa Clara, and behind the Orgullo were some sea batteries, and if all these works had been of good construction and guarded by fresh troops, the second siege would have been difficult. But the force of the garrison was shattered by the recent assault, most of the Engineers had been killed, the Governor and many others wounded, 500 men were sick or hurt, the soldiers fit for duty did not exceed 1,300, and they had 400 prisoners to guard.

The castle was small, the bombproofs scarcely sufficed to protect the ammunition and provisions, and only ten guns remained in a condition for service, three of which were on the sea line. There was very little water, and the troops had to lie out on the naked rock, exposed to fire, or only covered by inequalities of ground ; Rey and his brave garrison were however resolute to fight, and they received

* Afterwards Field Marshal Sir John Burgoyne, G.C.B.

nightly by sea small supplies of ammunition. Wellington arrived the day after the assault. Regular approaches could not be carried up the steep naked rock, he doubted the power of vertical fire, and ordered batteries to be formed on the captured works of the town, intending to breach the enemy's remaining lines of defence, and then storm the Orgullo. Meanwhile seeing the Santa Téresa would enable the French to sally by the rampart on the left of the Allies, he composed his first line with a few troops strongly barricaded, and placed a supporting body in the market place with strong reserves on the high curtain and flank ramparts. But from the convent, which was actually in the town, the enemy killed many of the besiegers ; and when after several days it was assaulted, they set the lower parts on fire and retired by a communication made from the roof to a ramp on the hill behind. All this time the flames were licking up the houses, and the Orgullo was overwhelmed with a vertical fire of shells.

On the 3rd September the Governor was summoned but his resolution was not to be shaken, and the vertical fire was therefore continued day and night. The British prisoners suffered as well as the enemy ; for the officer commanding in the castle irritated by the misery of the garrison, cruelly refused to let the unfortunate captives make trenches to cover themselves. The French complained that their wounded and sick men lying in an empty magazine with a black flag flying, and having the English prisoners with their red uniforms placed around to strengthen the claim of humanity, were fired upon.

Guns for the new batteries were now brought, by night, from the Choffre across the Urumea ; but the difficulty of struggling with the water in the darkness was great and transport by day was carried out although within reach of the French batteries which fortunately did not fire. The flaming houses impeded the works, but the river furnished cover for marksmen to gall the French, and the guns on Santa Clara were augmented and worked by seamen. With the besieged, ammunition was scarce, the vertical fire subdued their energy, and the besiegers laboured freely until the 8th. then 59 heavy pieces opened at once from the island, the isthmus, and the hornwork, and the Choffre, and in two hours the Mirador and the Queen's battery were broken, the French fire extinguished, the hill torn and furrowed in a frightful manner ; the bread ovens were destroyed, a magazine exploded, and the castle crowded with men was overlaid with the falling shells. Then the Governor proudly bending to fate surrendered. On the 9th this brave man and the garrison reduced in number, and leaving 500 wounded in the hospital, marched out with the honours of war. The Spanish flag was hoisted under a salute of 21 guns, and the siege terminated after 63 days of open trenches, just when the tempestuous season commencing would have rendered a continuance of the sea blockade impossible.

CHAPTER SEVEN

THE SECOND SIEGE OF BHURTPORE, 1825.

Towards the close of the year 1824, trouble again arose in the
Native state of Bhurtpore, not far from Agra, through the usurpation
of the " gaddi " by one Doorjan Lal, who imprisoned the rightful
heir, recognized by the British on the death of the Rajah, Runjert
Singh of Bhurtpore.

Sir David Ochterlony, well knowing the temper and intrigue of
which this city was the centre, collected a force at once, and moved
against Doorjan Lal.   Lord Amherst, however, ignored the danger,
and refused to ratify Sir David's action, and ordered him to withdraw
and break up the army.   This gave Doorjan his opportunity, which
he made the most of, in collecting arms, powder, artillery, and sending
round messages to the Central Indian States to support him.   He
soon made his position exceedingly strong ; and relying on the
prestige of the invulnerability of his fortress (gained 20 years before
when it withstood four assaults by Lord Lake's Army which lost
3,000 men in futile efforts), he now defied the British openly.   This
constrained the Government to take vigorous action, before he was
actually joined by the other states, who were ready to move, but
who were then merely looking on.   In December, 1825, therefore, a
force of some 27,000 men, with a large siege train, moved against
Bhurtpore, under Lord Combermere, then Commander-in-Chief ;
and by the 11th of that month the city was invested by a cordon
15½ miles long.   On the 18th of December, three companies of
Goorkhas (Sirmoor Rifles) reached Muttra, which was held by some
of our cavalry, and next day joined the camp of the main army
before Bhurtpore.   The same high mud walls which had baffled Lord
Lake still surrounded the city, and the Motee Jheel still supplied
water to the moat.   Guns innumerable crowned the walls, and
25,000 Jats, Pathans and Rajputs defended the city, with its immense
store of treasure.

The first act in this siege was a fortunate one, for a rapid move of
a portion of Lord Combermere's left wing surprised the enemy in
the act of cutting the dam which admitted the waters of the Motee

Jheel into the moat, and thus prevented it from becoming a terrible obstacle.

Nine days were spent in survey and reconnaissance which resulted in the Commander-in-Chief's decision to attack from the east, while making a feint of coming from the south-west as Lord Lake had done.

Under cover of this feint the cordon was drawn still closer, two important positions were taken up, and parallels were opened some 600 yards from the walls.

The duty of reconnoitring and seizing the " Kaddam Kandi," a temple situated in a wood within 400 yards of the so-called " Long-Necked Bastion," was carried out by a column consisting of the Grenadiers of the 59th Foot, five companies of the 21st Native Infantry, 100 of the Sirmoor Battalion, two troops of cavalry, and two howitzers. On reaching the wood, the Goorkhas were sent forward to clear it and hold the further edge, while a passage was dug through some banks for the guns.

The enemy retreated at once, and a heavy but ineffective fire was opened from the walls. The Goorkhas were then sent forward to reconnoitre the ditch, while the 59th replied to the fire from the temple walls and banks. The reconnaissance completed, the Goorkhas were withdrawn to hold the " Kaddam Kandi " Temple with the 59th. At the same time 100 men of the Sirmoor Battalion, under Lieut. Kirke, attached as skirmishers to General Reynell's Column of the 14th Native Infantry and 23rd Native Infantry, operating to the right of the first-named column, were successful in obtaining possession of a walled garden and in repulsing a vigorous sortie from the Soorajpur Gate with slight loss. These two positions now formed our advanced posts, and were held by the Goorkhas almost throughout the operations.

The first parallel was commenced on the 23rd December, and the following day all women and children, other than those of the Royal Family, were allowed to pass out ; at the same time a force of cavalry from the city succeeded in cutting their way out through our lines.

The regular siege now opened, the Goorkhas acting as covering parties and holding the advanced posts.

On the 26th it appeared as if the enemy's guns were more or less silenced, and the second parallel was opened within 250 yards of the ditch, while on the 28th December the approaches were almost within 20 yards of the moat. But the enormously strong earth walls defied our hammering. On the left of General Nicholls' column 14 heavy guns had battered one of the curtains for nearly a week without making any impression, and the same thing had happened at the other points we hoped to breach, in spite of the large number of heavy guns brought to bear on the place —every siege gun in Upper India having been collected for the purpose.

So on the 6th January, 1826, resort was found necessary to mining. The bombardment, however, continued till the 17th January to distract attention from this new work. Parties of the Sirmoor Battalion were continually used to guard those in the mines, and more than once our miners met those of the enemy countermining, where severe hand-to-hand fighting occurred ; on one occasion a party of sixty of the enemy were surprised under the counterscarp by sixteen of the Goorkhas who killed a number of Jats. The naick of this party was promoted on the spot by Lord Combermere.

On the night of the 15th a mine was sprung to the left of the Long-Necked Bastion opposite which General Nicholls' column lay in their trenches. This was rumoured to have made a practicable breach, and Capt. Carmichael, the General's A.D.C., taking with him an Engineer officer, six of the 59th Grenadiers, and five of the Sirmoor Battalion, actually did manage to scramble to the top to reconnoitre and report on what they could see inside in the way of obstacles. This was done at noon when the enemy apparently were not very vigilant ; the party gained the top, threw in some 50 hand grenades, fired three rounds, took a deliberate look well into the interior, before the astonished enemy recovered their surprise, and returned with the loss of only one grenadier. Later a similar piece of work was done at another reported breach by Havildar Mawanchand and 12 Goorkhas of the battalion, the former being promoted at once for the success of the undertaking.

The long-looked-for time for the assault was now close at hand. Another mine had successfully been sprung under a curtain in the Long-Necked Bastion, bringing down a mass of wall with some guns on top, and a huge mine of 10,000 lbs. of powder under the North-East, or Pathan Bastion, opposite General Reynell's point of attack, was completed on the 17th January. It was arranged that the firing of this mine was to be the signal for the final assault, which was to be in three main columns—General Nicholls against the breach in the Long-Necked Bastion, with two small columns, detached, one to attack the extreme left breach, the other, under Colonel Wilson, was to escalade at a point midway between the two great bastions ; another, under General Reynell, was to assault the North-East Bastion ; while on the extreme right a column under Colonel Delamain, with which was a detachment of the Nassera battalion, was to assault the Jugeenah Gate, which was partially breached. Lieut. Spottiswoode with 100 Goorkhas was to cover the advance of the Reserve Column under General Adams, who was to enter by the Muttra Gate immediately after the storm. Lieut. Kirke with the remainder of the Goorkhas was to cover General Reynell's stormers.

Before dawn on the 18th January, 1826, all the stormers were in their places in the advanced trenches, awaiting the springing of the mines, while the defenders, with an intimation of what was going forward, opened a heavy fire at daybreak. Word went down our line that all was ready. A mine at the Jugeenah Gate was sprung first, and then that in the counterscarp of the North-East Bastion, and all were awaiting the firing of the train for the demolition of that work. These explosions brought the garrison crowding to the walls, some 800 Pathans rushing to the parapets of the huge North-East Bastion, which it was their particular duty to defend. Immediately the mine under this with its 10,000 lbs. of explosives was fired ; the ground heaved and rocked, and with a dull heavy roar half the bastion lurched and rose slowly in the air, followed by clouds of thick pungent smoke, carrying up guns, gabions, Pathans, banners, swords and matchlocks, to be strewn in their descent a mass of mangled flesh and broken metal. Three hundred of the defenders had been blown to pieces, and those in our advanced trenches also suffered somewhat, a number being hopelessly buried by the descending débris.

As soon as the smoke cleared away, with loud cheers Reynell's and Nicholls' stormers rose and dashed at their respective breaches, at the top of which the defenders fought desperately. They were, however, beaten back, and the entire line of hitherto impregnable walls was in our hands. Brigadier Edwardes, who led the assault at the Long-Necked Bastion had been killed, and the brigade suffered such losses that they could not penetrate beyond the bastion which they had won, till Fagan's Brigade arrived to reinforce them ; then the whole swept forward into the city, and the place was soon in British hands.

Doorjan Lal managed to cut his way out through a cordon of the 14th Foot but was overtaken and captured by our British cavalry. The casualty list on the part of the enemy was reported as upwards of 13,000 of whom 4,000 perished in the assault alone ; while the total British loss was 1,000.

In the Divisional Orders by General Nicholls, of the 19th January, 1826, he says : " The handsome and gallant advance of the 59th Foot was followed—indeed emulated—by the 31st Native Infantry, the Light Infantry of the 37th Native Infantry, the Grenadiers of the 30th Native Infantry, and the detachment Sirmoor Battalion. The service which fell to the troops was essential, and it was gallantly and effectively performed. Capt. Orchard, 37th, and Herring and Mercer, 35th, and Fisher's Sirmoor Battalion are requested to receive the Major-General's very best thanks for the exertions so cheerfully made by their respective battalions."

The army dispersed towards the end of January and a General Order later directed that the word " Bhurtpore " should be borne on the standards and colours of all the corps which were employed at the capture of that fortress.

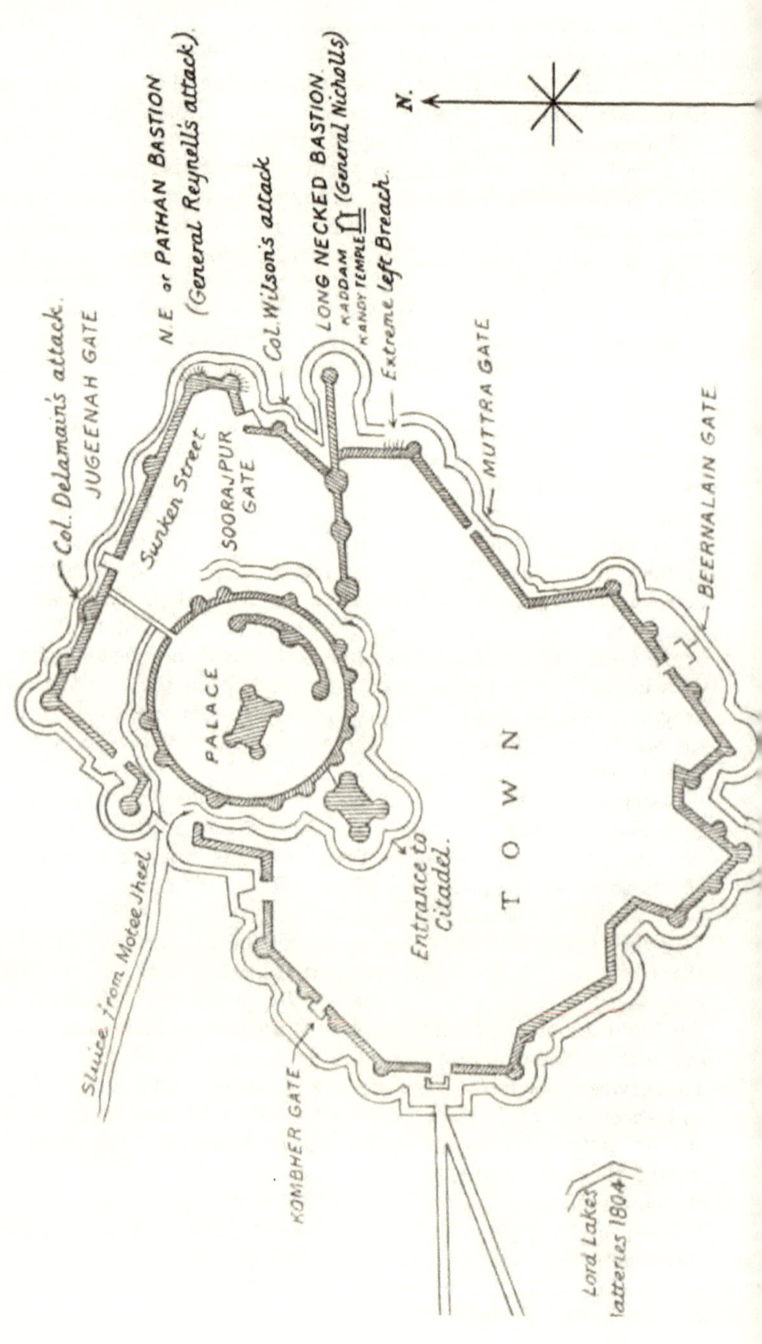
Col. Delamain's attack.
JUGEENAH GATE
N.E. or PATHAN BASTION
(General Reynell's attack).
Col. Wilson's attack
LONG NECKED BASTION.
KADDAM
KANDY TEMPLE (General Nicholls)
Extreme left Breach.
N.
Sunken Street
SOORAJPUR GATE
PALACE
MUTTRA GATE
BEERNALAIN GATE
Entrance to Citadel.
T O W N
Sluice from Motee Jheel
KOMBHER GATE
Lord Lakes batteries 1804

Defence of Khelat-i-Ghilzai, 1841-42.

Khelat-i-Ghilzai is a small fort built on a high flat-topped hill, rising abruptly from the plain, about 150 ft. above its level—situated 87 miles from Kandahar, 134 from Ghazni, and 229 from Kabul. From the centre of this table-land rises, to about a height of 100 ft., a small conical hill which formed the citadel.

The garrison consisted of 600 of the 3rd Regiment of Infantry, in the service of Shah Shujah; three companies of the 43rd Bengal N.I., under Capt. Webster and Lieut. Trotter; 40 European artillery, 23 Native Sappers & Miners; Major Leech, Bombay Engineers, Political Agent; Dr. Campbell Mackinnon; Lieut. H. Milne attached to Shah Shujah's force as Commissariat Officer and Lieut. T. Studdert, Bengal Engineers, Executive Engineers; Lieut. David Gaussen and Lieut. Robert McKean, about 950 in all—under Capt. John Halkett Craigie.

This noble little garrison maintained their position during the whole winter, from November, 1841, until relieved by Colonel Geo. Peter Wymer on the 26th May, 1842, although exposed to cold and privation unequalled by any of the victorious troops in Afghanistan.

On the 21st May, 1842, they repulsed in a most gallant and determined manner a fierce assault that was made on their position by a large body of Ghilzais, variously estimated by themselves from 5,500 to 7,000 men. Capt. Craigie in his despatch dated 21st May, 1842, says " that Khelat-i-Ghilzai was attacked at a quarter before four o'clock this morning in two places, viz. at the long neck to the north-east, and at an outwork constructed last winter by the Sepoys, to give a raking fire in rear of the barracks. The enemy advanced to the assault in the most determined manner, each column consisting of upwards of 2,000 men, provided with 30 scaling ladders, but after an hour's fighting were repulsed and driven down the hill, losing five standards (one of which was planted three times in one of the embrasures) and the whole of which are now in our possession.

*   *   *   *   *

" The greatest gallantry and coolness were displayed by every commissioned, non-commissioned officer, and private (both European and Native) engaged in meeting the attack of the enemy, several of whom were bayoneted on the top of the sandbags forming our parapets. On our side I am happy to say only six Sepoys were wounded, viz. two of the detachment 43rd N.I. and four of the 3rd Infantry.

" A body of about three hundred of the enemy were driven back, took shelter under the rocks below the outwork, but were immediately dislodged by a company of the 3rd Infantry, which I detached for that purpose."

They left 104 dead bodies at the foot of the defences, and within a few days after the assault the Political Agent ascertained that the number of killed, and of wounded men who died immediately after the action, considerably exceeded four hundred.

Siege and Capture of Ghazni, 1839.

Ghazni is a walled town with a deep ditch, situated in a plain surrounded by high mountains, by a spur of one of which it is commanded. In the centre of the town is a hill about 300 ft. high, on which is the citadel. A small stream runs near and round the town, and there are numerous walled gardens occupied by the Afghans.

At the time of the first Afghan war in 1839, the fort was garrisoned by from 3,000 to 4,000 men under Hyder Khan, the son of Dost Mahomed, and the Ameer of Afghanistan had therefore calculated rightly upon the British force being delayed for some time before it. He and his emissaries had had no difficulty in deceiving MacNaghten as to its strength and the nature of the resistance likely to be offered, and so completely was the latter deceived by the information supplied, that the day before Ghazni was reached he declared the place to be empty. Acting on this information the Commander-in-Chief and his staff rode on ahead to enter the deserted fort and they were only undeceived when fired on and compelled to return. Two forces under the Ghazni chiefs, Abdul Ruhman and Gul Mahomed Khan, had meanwhile marched parallel to the British all the way from Khelat-i-Ghilzai, one on each flank, at a distance of from 12 to 15 miles, with the object, not of immediate attack, but of taking advantage of the anticipated check to our troops at Ghazni, and of any confusion that might result therefrom. It cannot be denied therefore that when our troops reached Ghazni and found it strongly guarded, their position was critical in the extreme. Not only was the food supply short, but the breaching guns also had been left behind and there was only one battery of 24-pounder howitzers with the force, and these were useless for battering purposes. In their dilemma, the Envoy and the Commander-in-Chief (Sir John Keane) called upon the Chief Engineer (Capt. G. Thomson, of the Bengal Engineers) to reconnoitre and report.

He did so, and placed two alternatives before Sir John Keane, viz. either to blow open a gate and immediately assault, an operation the success of which may be doubtful and generally attended with heavy loss, or to mask the fort by a small corps, and with the rest of the army advance and attack Dost Mahomed. The latter alternative was abandoned, as the army was without the necessary supplies, and the proposal to assault was approved. A party of engineers was told off to the desperate duty of blowing in the gate in connection with which the following extracts from the diary of Lieut. James Broadfoot are of interest :—" A bag of 300 lbs. of powder was to be laid at the Kabul Gate, protected by the fire of the batteries and by the Goorkhas. The gate was to be blown open, and a storming party, composed of four European regiments was to advance immediately. I volunteered to carry the bag, as did Pigou ; but the latter was refused. Later in the day William* came, very excited, and told me he was not to go, the corps having been stopped on the pretence that the Shah was not sufficiently protected. He nearly threw up his commission in the Shah's service, but at last went away to try to join his old corps as a volunteer. Batteries and embrasures were made and the guns put in position, and then daylight was awaited. At last Peat and the powder party appeared, when the eastern horizon was just strong enough to show the hills in strong relief. The garrison opened fire on them ; the covering party extended on the edge of the ditch replied ; a few minutes afterwards a large volume of smoke above the walls and a rushing sound showed that the explosion had taken place. The head of the storming party now appeared with Brigadier Sale, doubtful whether to proceed or not. In this emergency I offered to go on to see if the explosion had been effectual. Being allowed I ran on towards the gate ; my anxiety to get on, and the constant whirring of balls past my head, made every step appear a mile. A little farther on I got into the range of the camel battery, and had to creep along to avoid our own balls. At last I met Durand† and shouted " Has it failed ? " He called out, " No, no." I then ran back so fast that my breath was entirely taken away. Peat and Macleod were stretched under a little tomb half-way, the former groaning heavily. He had been rolled over and over by the explosion, and was much shattered.

My report having been made the advance was ordered. I then ran on to the head of the column and entered with it, exposing myself to a severe reprimand. From the advance of the powder party not a quarter of an hour had elapsed, yet it seemed an age. On our way to the gate a shower of matchlock balls was kept up from the fort, with an occasional round shot, while our own artillery was thundering in our rear. Once within the darkness of the archway the fire stopped, the men gathered close, and sent up a magnificent cheer, in which we all joined and thus was our first step gained. A rush was made at the gate—the vicinity of which was nearly deserted— and it was carried with small opposition.

The colours were then planted on the four corners of the palace. The firing in the town was as constant as ever, few people asking quarter, and

---

* Lieut. William Broadfoot, of the 1st European L.I., now the Roya. Munster Fusiliers. he was then attached to Shah Shujah's force.

† Afterwards Major-General Sir Henry Durand, K.C.S.I., C.B., Lieutenant-Governor of the Punjab.

no one giving it."   Lieut. Broadfoot describes how he saw men jumping from walls 30 ft. high, or sliding down ropes, or hunted through the streets by soldiers with their bayonets close to their backs. Outside, the cavalry killed about 100 or 200 men, and 1,700 prisoners were made.

The result of the capture was decisive ; it was worth many lakhs of rupees paid by political officers to secure immunity from attack, or to induce treason in the enemy's camp.   The Afghans learnt for the first time that the English could strike a heavy blow, and respected them accordingly.   Dost Mahomed behaved under the circumstances with his accustomed bravery.   He had brought his troops from Kabul to oppose the advancing force, and finding that his men were shaken by the news from Ghazni, he rode amongst them, Koran in hand, begging them to support him so that at least he might die with honour, after which they might if they pleased join Shah Shujah.   It was in vain ; his men deserted him, and with his family and a small remnant of his force he fled to Bamian.

Our army found the Amir's guns at Arghandeh, and, advancing by regular stages, occupied Kabul on August 7th, 1839, and seated Shah Shujah on his throne, without opposition on the one hand, but on the other, without the slightest popular enthusiasm.

It should be mentioned in connection with the capture of Ghazni that whilst serving as an Engineer officer through the first Afghan war it fell to the lot of Lieut. Durand to undertake the duty of blowing in the gate of the fortress, an operation rendered necessary by the absence of any siege train.   In reference to this brilliant episode it may be remarked that in the obituary article which appeared in *The Times* newspaper on the occasion of Sir Henry Durand's tragic death, more importance was laid on his share in the work than it appears he really deserved. This called forth a remonstrance from Lord Keane, who wrote : " The credit of blowing in the gate was entirely due to Capt. Thomson,* the Chief Engineer.   Lieut. Durand performed his part of firing the train with great coolness and self-possession, being fully exposed to the enemy's fire from the ramparts while he applied the match to the fuze, which he had some difficulty in lighting."

Lieut. James Broadfoot, in his notes on the siege, writes thus : " Whilst to Capt. Thomson is due the credit for planning the demolition of the gate of Ghazni and the immediate assault of the fortress, to Lieut. H. M. Durand must be assigned that of successfully carrying out the instructions.   He exhibited there the greatest coolness and gallantry in the most dangerous situation.   After the powder was laid and all ready, the port fire did not light as it should have done,

* The late Lieut.-Colonel George Thomson, Bengal Engineers.

100

and he had to blow the slow match and port fire until at last it ignited. He then watched it burning for some time before returning to cover." The other engineer officers engaged in this arduous duty were, Capt. Peat, Bombay Engineers, and Lieut. (afterwards Lieut.-General) Macleod, Bengal Engineers. At Ghazni, indeed, it may be said that the army was indebted for its safety to its engineer officer, Capt. G. Thomson.

Sir John Keane—afterwards Lord Keane of Ghazni—did not fail to do justice to Thomson. He wrote : " To Capt. Thomson, of the Bengal Engineers, much of the success of this brilliant *coup de main* is due. A place of the same strength, and by such simple means as this highly talented and scientific officer recommended to be tried, has, perhaps never before been taken, and I feel I cannot do justice to Capt. Thomson's merits throughout."

Again in his General Orders, Sir John said : " The scientific and successful manner in which the Kabul Gate—of great strength—was blown up by Capt. Thomson, in which he reports having been most ably assisted by Capt. Peat, Bombay Engineers, and Lieuts. Durand and Macleod, of the Bengal Engineers, in the daring and dangerous enterprise of laying down powder in the face of the enemy, and the strong fire kept up on them, reflects the highest credit on their skill and cool courage, and His Excellency begs Capt. Thomson and officers named will accept his cordial thanks."

SIEGE OF MOOLTAN, 1848.

In April, 1848, two well-known, able, and popular officers— Mr. Vans Agnew, of the Civil Service and Lieut. Anderson of the 1st Bombay Fusiliers, had been sent with a large escort by the Lahore Government, to support an incoming Sikh Governor, Sirdar Khan Singh, and this at the request of the retiring Governor, Mulraj.

On the morning of the 18th April, the two officers were riding unarmed out of the fort when they were attacked by the soldiers of Mulraj, and both were severely wounded. They were carried to a strong Mahomedan building called the Eedgurh—a short distance from the city walls—in which they were lodged. Mulraj, who was present, rode away without offering any assistance. Next day the escort proved faithless and Mr. Vans Agnew and Lieut. Anderson were attacked by a furious and excited mob and brutally murdered.

Sir Henry Lawrence, who was the British Resident at the head of the " Lahore Durbar," was in England on sick leave at the time, and the absence of his determined leadership made itself felt disastrously.

The movable column at Lahore was not launched against Mooltan immediately, and instead of this, four columns of disaffected Sikhs, led not by men like Sir Henry Lawrence, but by Sirdars of doubtful loyalty—amongst whom Sher Singh was pre-eminent—were sent against a Sikh chief with whose cause the rank and file of the force were in ardent sympathy.

These Sikh columns, moreover, did not reach Mooltan till some eleven weeks after the murder of the two Englishmen, at which date the rebellion at Mooltan was beginning to take on the character of a religious and national war.

At this time Lieut. Herbert Edwardes was the Political Agent in charge of the Derajat. No sooner did this young officer—a disciple and friend of Sir Henry Lawrence—receive Vans Agnew's letter asking for help, than, without asking for orders from Lahore, he swept across the Indus at the head of wild Pathan levies, and with the aid of Colonel Van Cortlandt and the Nawab of Bahawalpur succeeded in driving Mulraj into Mooltan, which he thought he might succeed in capturing if speedily reinforced by " Napier* and some guns " ; for both of which he begged in vain.

Forced into action by the energy of their subordinate, and by the danger of their position, the British authorities at last despatched a column under General Whish to co-operate with him and the Sirdars in attacking Mooltan. The force arrived at Mooltan after the middle of August.

The strong fortress of Mooltan could only be taken by breaching its walls and to do this large guns and heavy ammunition were needed. Carriage, however, was exceedingly difficult to obtain, while the boats and boatmen of the Ravi and the Sutlej were quite unfit to be entrusted with so precious a convoy. Major Robert Napier*—the Chief Engineer of the Force—remembered the pontoon boats at Ferozepore, and thought that they might be used for this purpose if put into suitable hands, although unwieldy and not designed to carry freight through difficult waters.

He sent for Lieut. Alexander Taylor,† and asked him if he would undertake to carry the heavy artillery and engineering stores more than 200 miles down the Sutlej in his bridge boats. The young engineer replied in a delighted affirmative.

On the 30th July the heavily-laden flotilla started for its long row from Ferozepore to Adamwahan, 40 miles from Mooltan. The Chief Engineer and Alex Taylor travelled with it. Neither Taylor nor the boatmen knew the river ; the boats were cumbersome, and there were many difficulties and obstacles during the journey, owing to rapids, shallows, rocks, sand banks, storms, and floods.

The flotilla, however, safely reached its destination—Adamwahan, opposite Bahavalpore—in little more than a fortnight, arriving on the 15th August ; its contents were disembarked by the Sappers &

* Afterwards Field Marshal Lord Napier of Magdala, G.C.B., G.C.S.I., R.E. (late Bengal).
† Afterwards General Sir Alexander Taylor, G.C.B., R.E. (late Bengal).

Miners, who had marched thither from Loodianah at 48 hours' notice. Steep and firm banks were found, beside which the water was sufficiently deep to allow the boats to come alongside ; and the precious cargo, of which nothing had been lost *en route*, was gradually unladen and heaped in gigantic piles on what seemed to be *terra firma*.

Without siege materials it would have been impossible to inaugurate a siege, and it was only owing to Taylor's energy in moving the stores further inland, that these were saved, as the whole area on which the ammunition had been heaped, owing to the water undermining its base, shortly after collapsed into the rushing stream.

Day by day more siege material arrived but so great was the amount required that it was not till the 4th September that the engineer and artillery parks received their full equipment.

Immediately after the arrival of the complete siege train, General Whish issued a proclamation inviting the inhabitants and garrison to surrender unconditionally, within 24 hours of the firing at sunrise on the 5th of a Royal salute in honour of Her Most Gracious Majesty the Queen of Great Britain, and her ally, His Highness the Maharajah Dhuleep Singh.

" On the morning of the 5th, accordingly," writes Taylor, " the force turned out, and the artillery fired a Royal salute from 24-pounders. Before the sixth round, we received Mulraj's reply—a 14-pound ball, said to contain Whish's proclamation ! The direction was good, but it fell short and hurt no one. Mulraj had spoken ; and preparations for the siege were at once commenced."

On the 6th September a Council of War was held, during which the general plan of the siege operations was fixed. The plan adopted after much discussion—two other projects having been negatived— was that a trench should be run from the north-easterly angle of Herbert Edwardes' camp to a point called Ram Terut, a mile further to the north-east, and that this trench should be used as a base from which to advance on the city.

The town of Mooltan lies in the midst of a desert. Its climate in summer is exceedingly hot. Though rain rarely falls, the city and its environments, which are exceedingly wealthy, are richly provided with artificial canals of running water.

Between the walled gardens, enclosing country houses, lie dirty villages, temples, tombs, mosques, brick kilns, ravines, and fragments of mere jungle ; ground, easy to defend and most difficult to clear.

The suggested trench was a " first parallel " ; it was destined to afford cover from which the troops might advance over the difficult ground lying between it and some position from which the town wall could be distinctly seen and breached.

The first step in the realization of this plan was made next day (7th September). At dawn, working parties, numbering in all 2,800 men, left their camps and set themselves to trench work. The composition of General Whish's Army now gave rise to complications. It contained 20,000 men of all arms ; 13,000 of these were Irregulars, largely Herbert Edwardes' Pathans, men who would dig trenches for themselves, fight anywhere and against any odds, but would not put a spade into the ground for the defence of others ; against this their pride rebelled, it was contrary to " custom." The burden of the digging was therefore thrown on the Native Regulars and the British regiments. It was found, however, that the latter could not face the sun, it simply struck them down. These difficulties were met by two expedients ; the British troops were permitted to work at night, and the Pathans were allowed to carry out a separate set of parallels of their own ; " this separate attack was conducted by Lieut. Lake, assisted by Lieuts. Charles Pollard* and Frederick Maunsell†, two young Engineers, " whose cool bravery and indefatigable zeal won the admiration of us all." writes Herbert Edwardes ; who adds : " The same remark would, however, apply to the whole Engineer staff at Mooltan—a finer body of men was never collected in any Indian Army."‡

The rebels set themselves to work at the same time to entrench themselves in the vicinity of the city. " So," writes Herbert Edwardes, " there were two armies throwing up works within a few hundred yards ; the rebels with little science, but unbounded zeal, rearing stockades, piling up felled trees and the woodwork of wells and houses, for the defensive warfare in which the soldiers of the Punjab excel ; the British approaching with laborious discipline to the attack which, at the proper moment, would burst from the trenches like a flood, and sweep all obstacles away."

Presently the process of dislodging the enemy from the aforesaid defences, houses, gardens, etc., began. The house-to-house and hand-to-hand fighting that ensued was of a most desperate and determined character.

We read of the cool courage with which the officers of the engineers placed scaling ladders and laid explosive bags close under the fire of the enemy's muskets ; of the rush of the soldiers surging over garden walls, or leaping from these walls on to trees, from the boughs of which they dropped into the midst of the enemy ; of confused attacks on unknown ground ; of hundreds of Mulraj's soldiers being heaped beneath the mango trees in walled enclosures ; and of our own many heroic dead. Ever to the fore in the midst of these brave assailants was Robert Napier, chivalrous, cool, and fertile in resource.

Sometimes driven back, often brought to a temporary standstill.

* The late General Charles Pollard, R.E. (late Bengal).
† General Sir Frederick Maunsell, R.E., K.C.B. (late Bengal).
‡ *A Year on the Punjab Frontier*, by Major Herbert B. Edwardes, C.B. 2 vols. Richard Bentley, London, 1851. 2nd edition, ii., p. 513.

the invading tide of British soldiers nevertheless pressed steadily on, taking point after point of vantage, until on the 13th of September, the engineers stood on the destined breaching ground—the summit of a cone in one of the suburbs, which rose within 600 yards of the Bloody Bastion, and from which the masonry of that tower could be seen for at least two-thirds of its height. Without loss of time, and protected by seven batteries already erected in its rear, the Sappers & Miners set to work on the great Breaching Battery.

All was going well. The day of the assault seemed to be within measurable distance, when on the morning of the 14th September came the news that Sher Singh—the chief of our allies, the Lahore Sirdars —had gone over to the enemy during the previous night taking the column of 4,300 Sikhs with him.

The transference of so great a weight from one arm of the scales to the other so altered the relative strength of the two armies that General Whish was obliged to suspend operations. The projected attack was abandoned for the time being ; our hardly-won positions within breaching distance of the walls ; the streets, houses, and fortified posts, just taken ; our own batteries and trenches—all were deserted ; and the British Army fell back in the direction of Bahawalpore, whence it drew its supplies, there to await reinforcements which were immediately ordered from Bombay.

There is no doubt that this step was necessary. Major Napier, who was among the wounded, gave it as his professional opinion that the force at General Whish's disposal after the desertion of Sher Singh was insufficient for the successful execution of his plans, and in this opinion he was supported by the most experienced officers in the camp.

The first act in this retrograde movement was the withdrawal of the guns, ammunition, etc., from the Great Breaching Battery and its neighbourhood. This was done at nightfall on the 14th, under cover of the falling darkness, and without molestation from the enemy. By some oversight no orders had been issued to the engineers for the removal of their large depôt of tools and engineering materials.

The loss of these stores would seriously affect the park equipment, and Taylor resolved to recover them if possible. Taking a sufficient number of camels and workmen, and a few of the Park Guard, he sallied out into the darkness, and made his way towards the city. On arriving at a reasonable distance from the Breaching Battery, he halted his escort and rode on alone. On reaching its neighbourhood he was pleased to find that it was still the target for the enemy's fire, for this showed that the British withdrawal had been unobserved, and that it was still believed to be in our possession. He went up to it, and found it unoccupied. He signalled to his men to advance to the Engineer depôt, and the tools were soon in the hands of their lawful guardians. The camels were quickly laden and their heads turned homewards, and the party eventually reached the engineers' camp safely, not without adventures, but without serious molestation. The rescue was accomplished only just in time ; next morning the whole of the area abandoned was in the hands of the Sikhs.

To prevent Mulraj's rebellion from growing into a Sikh war, by entrusting the Sikh Durbar with the task of quelling it, had been the political object of the Siege of Mooltan. This object was defeated by the defection of the Sikh Sirdar, Sher Singh, after whose desertion it was clear that a second Sikh struggle for national independence was inevitable. It was further clear, that the struggle would not take place at Mooltan, but in the home proper of the Sikhs, the country north of the Munjha, lying between the Chenab and the Jhelum, where fighting on an imposing scale might be expected.

These circumstances made the Siege of Mooltan, *per se*, a matter of secondary importance ; it was all-important, however, that the heavy artillery collected there should be set free soon, for it would be urgently needed in the north. It was because all the available troops in Northern India would be wanted by the Commander-in-Chief to meet the new emergency, that the reinforcements necessary to the renewal of the siege were ordered from the south, *i.e.*, from Bombay.

In the meantime General Whish's Army temporarily abandoned its position. On the 15th September the forces of the Nawab of Bahawalpur, those of Van Cortlandt, and the Irregulars commanded by Herbert Edwardes, fell back to their new camp in and near the village of Suraj Kund, some 5 miles south of Mooltan. A few days later the British troops took up a position on their left. " Our camp," says Alex Taylor, writing from it on the 14th November, " was pitched in the midst of high jungle or underwood, some 8 ft. in height, but by dint of hard labour the ground to our front had been cleared to a distance of about 600 yards, and we are now in a tolerably good fighting position."

The removal from one camp to another of the great quantity of siege material collected was a large undertaking. Innumerable country-carts, gathered together for the purpose, plied backwards and forwards between the two camps, under the protection of 2,000 Irregular Horse and six guns, commanded by Lieut. Richard Pollock,* who defended the convoy from the flanking attacks of Sher Singh's Sikh horsemen. In spite of all efforts, however, sufficient carriage to move so much heavy ammunition was not forthcoming. Edwardes' Irregulars saved the situation. Each of his 1,500 horsemen took a cannon-ball—a 16-pounder—into his keeping,

---

* The late Major-General Sir Richard Pollock, K.C.S.I.

and either holding it in his hand, or slinging it across his saddle, carried it to the new depôt.

The siege was raised on the 14th September, and not renewed till the 21st December. This long period of inaction—more than three months—was one of great anxiety. Opposite General Whish's small heterogeneous army rose the battlements of the city of Mooltan, which was overlooked by one of the strongest citadels in Northern India, manned by 15,000 men who fought with halters round their necks ; while for some time Sher Singh, who never came to terms with Mulraj, or was allowed by him to enter the city, lay with his fanatical soldiery to the north-east. It was with feelings of intense relief that the British Army saw this storm cloud move northward, for, had those traitors, Mulraj and Sher Singh, been loyal to each other, and had they attacked the British camp simultaneously, things must have gone hardly with it. It was known at the time that Mulraj was intriguing with Dost Mohamed and others of our Trans-Indus foes, to whom he promised Peshawur and the lands west of the Indus, if they would invade the Derajat, and thus force the British Army to move away from Mooltan.

During this interval the engineers under Major Napier prepared busily for the future resumption of siege operations. A store of gabions and fascines on an immense scale was made ; in December the Engineer Park of which Taylor had charge possessed the enormous number of 15,000 gabions and 12,000 fascines, as well as a number of ingenious mechanical contrivances for facilitating the siege operations, and invented by the Director.

On the 30th November Colonel Cheape,* the Chief Engineer of the Punjab Army, arrived, and took over the general direction of the siege operations. Detachments of the troops from Bombay were now beginning to arrive at Mooltan, and by the 21st December, the numbers of the besieging army were complete.

On the 27th, the British Army, moving *en masse*, retook the suburbs they had abandoned at the end of the first siege, and entrenched their position north-eastward as far as Mulraj's garden palace, Am Khas, 500 yards from the north-eastern angle of the fort. The rebels were driven in at the Delhi Gate, and positions seized on heights suitable for battering the south-eastern walls and the Bloody Bastion ; the breaching battery destined to deal with the latter being only 120 yards from it. As these batteries were completed they began to pour their shot and shell against the walls which they were designed to breach.

On the 30th the Grand Mosque within the citadel—the rebels' chief powder magazine, and hitherto believed to be *bombproof*—was

* Afterwards General Sir John Cheape, G.C.B., Colonel Commandant, R.E. (Bengal).

pierced by a shell and blown up. The explosion was terrific ; an immense volume of smoke and débris rose in the air, and overspread the sky. " At a vast height," writes Herbert Edwardes,* " the heavy cloud stood still, like some great tree, and its shadow fell at night over the camp below. All action was suspended, every eye was turned up in awe, and watched the strange vision sink and disappear."

Finally, on 2nd January, 1849, the breaches having been declared practicable, a successful assault was delivered, and the city fell into British hands. Not the citadel, however, into which Mulraj withdrew with 4,000 picked men, leaving the rest of his army outside to die or escape as fate might decree.

Two breaches had been made in the south-easterly portion of the battered city wall :—one in the Bloody Bastion, and the other near the Delhi Gateway. The column destined to assault the latter was led by Robert Napier ; while the perilous honour of guiding the Bombay Column up to the breach in the Bloody Bastion and through it fell, at the Chief's request, to Alexander Taylor.

The latter breach was carried by the 1st Bombay Fusiliers, Lieut. Anderson's regiment, to whom the place of honour in the avenging column was given as a right. Sergt. John Bennet, of the same regiment, planted the regimental colour on the crest of the breach, and stood beside it until it was torn and tattered by bullets. The place was found to contain another trench inside, but this was also taken after a bloody struggle.

" Then, from every crowded height and battery whence the excited struggle had been watched, rose the shouts of applauding comrades, and through the deafening roar of the musketry which pealed along the ramparts and marked the hard-earned progress of the victorious columns through the streets, both friend and foe might distinctly hear that sound, never to be forgotten—the ' Hurrah ' of a British army after battle " ; so writes one who was present. By nightfall the army was in entire possession of the city.

The following additional account of the Siege of Mooltan, with some details of the construction of the trenches and batteries, is taken from the Biographical Notice of General Sir John Cheape, G.C.B., who was the Chief Engineer of the Army :—

" The city of Mooltan is situated 4 miles from the present left bank of the Chenab, enclosed on three sides by a wall from 10 to 20 ft. in height, but open towards the south, where the dry bed of the old Ravee intervenes between the town and the citadel.

The original town consisted of two islands which are now crowned by the citadel and city, at an elevation of about 50 ft. above the surrounding country. The fortifications were dismantled in 1854,

* Major-General Sir Herbert Edwardes, K.C.S.I.

but the fort still remains a place of considerable strength, occupied by a European garrison. Within the city proper, narrow and tortuous streets, often ending in *culs de sac*, fill almost the whole space ; but one broad bazár—constructed by the British immediately after the annexation—runs from end to end. Mooltan is a place of great antiquity. The principal buildings include the shrines of the Mohammedan saints Baha-oo-din, Ruku-ul-alam, lineal descendants of the Prophet, which stand in the citadel. Close by are the remains of an ancient Hindu temple called Paládpuri, blown down by the explosion of the powder magazine during the siege of 1849.

On Christmas Day General Whish had occupied his old position, and the Bombay force under the command of Brigadier the Hon. H. Dundas next day formed on his left.

On the 27th the enemy in the suburbs were attacked by four columns. Brigadier Dundas commanding the left, moved round the left of the first original parallel, and drove the enemy successfully from the Maya Temple, and the mound called the Sidi Lal ke Bed, and the Baghi Bagh. Brigadier Casson advanced against Ram Tirat and compelled the enemy to evacuate the Mandi Awa and drove them out of the suburbs into the city.

The right column occupied without any loss the suburbs and buildings east and north-east of the citadel, and the brick kilns with their entrenchments.

General Whish had decided on attacking the north-east angle of the citadel in regular form, but Brigadier Cheape advocated an attack upon the suburbs and town. This was considered too great a risk, but a diversion on the south-east side was resolved upon. There was therefore a right and a left attack ; the first fell to the Bengal gunners, the latter was shared with the Bombay artillerymen. The numbering of the batteries was that of the engineers, which included both Bengal and Bombay batteries.

December 28th. Right Attack.—A ravine to the right of Shams-i-Tabiz occupied the day before was converted into a battery, No. XI., for six 8-in. mortars, which moved out of park that evening and opened this morning at 700 yards from the outer wall of the fort. The infantry posts were loopholed. At dusk No. X. for two 24-pounders to destroy the upper defences of the north-east face of the citadel, and No. XII. for two 8 and three 10-in. howitzers to enfilade the face commanding the town, were marked out.

Left Attack.—No. I., three 10 and four 5½-in. mortars (Bengal) were established during the night on the Mandi Awa. No. II. for six 18-pounders to breach the curtain near the Khuni Burj at about 120 yards, was traced out, but not completed, material having to be conveyed from a distance. In the morning a heavy matchlock fire prevented more than the revetting of the finished portion. No. I. opened in the evening and continued during the night.

December 29th. Right Attack.—Nos. X. and XII. commenced and completed during the night as also connecting trenches with Shams-i-Tabiz. They were armed and opened during the day and trenches widened.

Left Attack.—On the previous day Edwardes and Lake had relieved the Bombay troops of the posts about Sidi Lal ke Bed, and the latter closing to the right had their left posts in the suburbs about the Khuni Bhurj. No. II. was completed by midnight, but the first gun was not brought in until daybreak, and a company of the 9th Bombay Native Infantry was unable, after several attempts, to bring in a second. Several gunners were wounded.

December 30th. Right Attack.—Magazine for No. XII. was commenced and completed.

Left Attack.—No. II., completed during the night and opened at daybreak. No. V., for two 6-pounders, was commenced and armed by daybreak among the houses near the Delhi Gate, to destroy the town wall defences at about 200 yards. Two Bombay 18-pounders and two 8-in. howitzers were placed behind a mud wall opposite the Delhi Gate, and opened with effect upon the gateway. The mud wall coming down, a sandbag battery was put up.

At 10 a.m., this day a shell from a mortar laid by Lieut. Newall in No. XI. Battery fell upon the principal magazine near the southern face of the fort, a mosque which had been appropriated for that purpose, and which blew up, opening an extensive crater in the ground through the inner wall. General Whish in his report compares it to the explosion at the Siege of Hattras, March 1st, 1817. When the smoke and dust had cleared away the enemy resolutely resumed their fire.

January 1st, 1849.—On this day the Commanding Engineer at noon reported the Khuni Bhurj as looking well, though not likely to be a good breach, and recommended the assault, if it were to be made here, to be done at once.

Right Attack.—No. IX. completed. Repairs to batteries during the day.

Left Attack.—The fire of the four right* guns of No. II. was turned from the curtain on to the Bhurj itself. No. VIII. Battery armed and opened fire. Capt. Siddons examined the breach in the early morning, and reported it practicable though steep. That at the Delhi Gate was said to be sufficiently practicable for an attempt.

The troops told off for the assault left camp after noon in two columns ; the right under Brigadier Markham, to attack the Delhi Gate ; the left under Brigadier Stalker, to attack the Khuni Bhurj.

The Bombay column was completely successful, the leading party

* This was done by Lieut. (afterwards Lieut.-General) Pollard, Bengal Engineers, without interfering with the direct fire of the left pieces.

crowning the breach found the communication with the Bhurj interrupted, but with the aid of two ladders procured by Lieut. Oliphant* and his sappers, they got over a low house into it, driving out the enemy.

The other parties forced their way through the town, taking possession of the Pak, Haram, and Bohar Gates, which were held during the night. Major Scott was wounded. That under Markham, on getting to the Delhi Gate, found the lower part of the wall, previously concealed from view too high for escalade. Capt. Smyth, with great decision withdrew the leading companies under cover. This column had to find its way in through the other breach, whence it followed the eastern face of the town to the Delhi Gate. The Daulat Gate was taken next morning. Major Napier (afterwards Lord Napier of Magdala) commanded the engineers here. Capt. Garforth was dangerously, Lieuts. A. Taylor and J. A. Fuller severely, wounded ; the latter by an explosion of a magazine near the Bohar Gate."

Thus fell the town and citadel of Mooltan, after a resolute defence and severe fighting. The Mulraj was put on his trial for the murder of an official, and being found guilty was sentenced to death ; but this penalty was afterwards commuted for that of transportation. The district at once passed under British rule.

* Afterwards Major-General Oliphant, R.E. ; died in 1898.

CHAPTER EIGHT

THE GREAT SIEGE OF SEBASTOPOL, 1854–55.

When the Allies in Bulgaria finally determined upon the western and not the southern coast of the Crimea as the place of their landing, it was taken for granted, though not perhaps committed to writing, that this resolve carried with it the ulterior design of moving southward along the coast, and operating against the northern defences of Sebastopol. The assumption was a natural one ; since Sebastopol Bay made it impossible for an invader established on the western side to attempt an attack, except from the north.

Long before, and prior indeed to the actual commencement of the war, Capt. Drummond, of the *Retribution*, had ventured to give firm counsel upon this subject ; and the knowledge which he had acquired while lying at anchor in the roadstead of Sebastopol enabled him to speak with great weight. Both Capt. Drummond and Capt. Willes (who was acting with him at the time of the survey) conceived themselves able to report decisively in favour of an attack upon the Star Fort as a means of achieving the great object of the Allies. If, even before the invasion they were warranted in fixing upon the Severnaya or " North Side " as the true point of attack, much more was it now, September, 1854, to be concluded in favour of such a choice, since the Allies by their successful landing, followed up by the result of the battle of the Alma, had fastened already on that very part of the coast from which they could conveniently assail the Star Fort ; and moreover it was fairly to be reckoned, that if the Allies should go straight to their end, without turning aside or interposing fresh marches between themselves and the enemy, the momentum they had gathered from their victory might carry them through the defences without necessitating a siege.

Bivouacking now on the Belbec, the Allies were at last within gunshot of the fortress they had come over sea to confront ; and the period during which it had been possible to keep the question open being close to its end, they were called upon to determine whether they would at once prepare to deliver the attack, or give up their old plan of campaign.

On the northern side of Sebastopol Bay, and facing the sea forts which covered the town and harbour, there were not only other sea forts of great size and power but also some barracks, some magazines, and a factory worked by the Government. This aggregate of buildings, or the quarter on which they stood, was known amongst Russians by the name of the Severnaya and by the English as the " North Side."

The sea forts were not so constructed as to be the means of defence against an invader coming down upon them by land from the north ; but on the high ground above, though still at a distance of only a few hundred yards from the bay, there was a dilapidated work, called by the English the Star Fort, which had been constructed in 1818. It was of octagonal shape with sides from 190 to 230 yards long ; and of its eight angles, every other one was supplied with a little bastion or caponière having an earthen parapet, whilst three out of the four remaining angles of the octagon were furnished with small bonnettes or barbettes, each taking three guns. The profiles of the bastion were 14 ft. high and 10 ft. thick. The bastion which looked towards the roadstead was retrenched at its gorge by a cavalier. The fort was surrounded by a ditch 12 ft. deep and 18 ft. broad with revetment in masonry and a glacis.

Of the 47 guns with which the work was armed only 12 could be of service in the expected attack from the north. The fort was commanded and even looked into from the heights towards the north. In and near this work, from the day of the landing on the 14th of September, down to the evening of the 24th, the Russians had toiled night and day, at one time with a force of 1,500 workmen. Their object was not only to repair and strengthen the Star Fort itself, but also to provide generally for the defence of the plateau against an enemy advancing from the Belbec. By those who knew that these hurried works went on under the direction of Colonel Todleben it will be easily inferred that they were planned with a consummate skill ; but what even he found means to achieve in ten days could not but fall very short of what was needed. One of Todleben's objects was to throw up works which might prevent the enemy from turning the Star Fort on the eastern flank, but for the execution of this part of his plan there was no time.

By the morning of the 25th there were altogether twenty-nine guns in battery and available for the defence against the expected attack from the north. The two north-western batteries were however liable to be destroyed by the guns of the Anglo-French fleet ; * and the trench connecting one of them with the fort could be enfiladed and taken in rear by the fire from the same quarter.† Indeed the position of the ground and of the Russian works was such that in every stage of an attack undertaken against the Star Fort, the seamen and the ships of the Allies would be able to take a great part.‡

In order to cover the retreat of the Russians, some of their ships were placed in such positions as to be able to sweep with their broadsides the slopes on the north of the roadstead. The form of the ravines descending from the Star Fort was such that upon two if not upon three, of the approaches from the side of the Belbec, the assailants might come up to the ditch without first incurring a cannonade of any great force or duration.

With regard to the forces available for the defence, it may be said that if the Allies had advanced against the Star Fort on the morning of the 25th they would have encountered there and on the ground adjoining a battalion of militiamen, a company of sappers and so large a body of sailors—withdrawn for that purpose from the ships and from the defence of the South Side—as would bring up the whole number to 11,000.§ The sailors were for the most part, badly armed, some of them having old flint and steel muskets, and others, it seems, only pikes and cutlasses. This was the force which extended along a front of a mile, was to defend the fort and the plateau against a victorious army of from 50,000 to 60,000 men, supported and actively aided by their fleets. The defenders were, however, commanded by one whose name will be long illustrious in the annals of Russia. For the present it suffices to say of Admiral Korniloff that he was a chivalrous, resolute and devoted seaman who, with hardly any hope of any better success than that of an honourable death, had determined to defend the plateau and the fort to the last extremity.

The officer who planned and directed the works of defence was Colonel Todleben and he was of opinion that the plateau and the fort could not have been successfully defended against the attack which the Allies had the means of making. The situation of the defenders, he says, notwithstanding all they had done, and notwithstanding their heroic resolves was nothing less than desperate ; ‖ and he declared that the complete success of the expected attack by the Allies would have been inevitable. Lord Raglan and Sir Edmund Lyons came in fact to the same conclusion as Colonel Todleben, and it is not possible in this short account of the

* Todleben, *Defense de Sebastopol*, Vol. I., p. 233.
† Ibid.
‡ Ibid.
§ Todleben 11,350.—*Defense de Sebastopol*, Vol. I., p. 227.
‖ *Defense de Sebastopol*, Vol. I., p. 230–33.

memorable siege to discuss the reasons for the Allies relinquishing the proposed attack on the North Side.

The Allies were not ignorant that the possession of the North Side would at once enable them to cannonade the enemy's shipping. Nor again did they fall into the error of supposing the Star Fort of itself to be a formidable work. By far the gravest of the obstacles to the plan of assailing the North Side was the want of a safe harbour on that part of the neighbouring coast which was north of the Sebastopol Bay. It was said that the attack might take time, and that pending the operations, the fleets might be so driven from the coast by stress of weather as to put the Allies in peril for their supplies.

So inextricably were the Allies engaged in the expedition, and so deeply were they committed in the face of Europe to the duty of achieving their end, that whatever might have been their wisdom originally in resolving to touch the Crimea, ordinary prudence now seemed to command that they should follow up the victory with swiftness, and always in that venturesome temper which was the only one fitted for their enterprise. For refuge as well as for glory they needed the port of Sebastopol. But if the relinquishment of the North Side was not to be justified on military grounds, there was still this to be said for the measure ; it was a way out of the trouble.

On the day after the battle of the Alma Lord Raglan proposed to Marshal St. Arnaud, the Commander-in-Chief of the French Army, " at once to advance to the Belbec, cross that river, and then assault the forts." The Marshal answered that " his troops were tired and that it could not be done."* It must also be added that the further efforts of Sir Edmund Lyons to induce the Marshal to agree to an attack on the position of the Star Fort met with no success.

Notwithstanding the failure of these efforts, Lord Raglan was thoroughly qualified to deal with the emergency in which the Allies would find themselves placed if the French should persist, as they did, in their unwillingness to assail the Star Fort.

At the time of the earliest deliberations on the subject, Lord Raglan had been disposed to think that Sebastopol ought to be attacked on the south ; and although he had ceased to dwell upon the idea from the time when the west coast was chosen for the place of landing, it recurred to him on the morrow of the Battle of the Alma when he found himself encountered at the French headquarters by a refusal to attack the Star Fort. He then conceived that if the French should persist to the last in their refusal, he at least might avert that utter cessation and collapse of the whole enterprise which their determination threatened to produce by

* Statement of Sir E. Lyons.

persuading them (as a substitute for the old plan which they were then abandoning) to join with him in marching across the country to the south coast, and there establishing a new base of operations, from which to attack Sebastopol on its south side.

The unwillingness of the French to attack the north side of Sebastopol had brought the Allies into straits so hard, that with all its rashness the plan of defiling round the east of Sebastopol might be regarded as the least of the evils from which a choice could be made. Rightly looked at " the flank march," for so the movement is called, was a perilous, a desperate expedient, by which Lord Raglan sought to find an alternative for the enterprise declined by the French and avert a collapse of the whole undertaking.

From causes which will be spoken of later, the French Army, without any fault of its own was, for the moment, paralyzed ; and the English Army, on the other hand, being ready for action and under a General resolved to force on the enterprise, there was a great temptation to clutch at a plan which would relieve the French Army from all immediate demands on its energies, and cast the load on the English. The plan of the flank march fulfilled these conditions ; for it spared the French from the task which seemed to await them on their right front, and invested the English General with the leadership, and the virtual control of the proposed operation.

But although it was as an escape from a dilemma that the flank march is best to be justified, it is not believed that Lord Raglan himself thought ill of the measure. Without ever wavering in his opinion that the victory on the Alma should be followed up by pursuing the old plan, and attacking the Severnaya or north fort, he yet thought that he saw such good features in the alternative plan as to be able to fall back upon it with contentment. Apparently he was not much impressed with the hazardous character of the flank march ; and on the other hand he certainly thought that, if once the Allies should be established on the south coast, they would then be on the best ground for attacking Sebastopol.

For the purpose of informing himself upon any question of military engineering, Lord Raglan had at his side an accomplished and gifted adviser. Sir John Burgoyne was a general of Engineers now serving on the Staff of the Army which Lord Raglan commanded. His experience of war was very great. It began with the first year of the century at Malta. In 1806 he was serving in Sicily. He was Commanding Engineer with General Fraser's expedition to Egypt, and was at the assault on the lines of Alexandria, and the Siege of Rosetta. He was with Sir John Moore at Messina and in Sweden in 1808, and was with him the same year in the Peninsular. He was at Corunna. He blew up the bridge of Benevente in the presence of the enemy.   He was with Sir Arthur Wellesley in 1809, and at the passage of the Douro.   He served in the lines of Torres Vedras. He blew up Fort Conception in presence of the enemy.   He was at Busaco, at the first siege of Badajoz, at Elboden, and at the siege and capture of Ciudad Rodrigo.   He was at the second siege and capture of Badajoz, and was present at the assault and escalade of the castle.   He was Commanding Engineer at the siege and capture of the Forts of Salamanca and at the battle.   He was Commanding Engineer at the capture of Madrid, and the Retiro, and also at the siege of Burgos where he was wounded.   At Vittoria he had a horse shot under him.   He was wounded at the assault of San Sebastian where he conducted the siege as Commanding Engineer.   He was also at New Orleans.   He had therefore a vast experience, connecting his name with a glorious period of English history ; and the value of this advantage was not, as often happens in the least counteracted by failure of energy.   As might be expected he was a master of military engineering science ; but his mind ranging freely beyond his own branch of the service, had become stored with the many kinds of knowledge which concern the whole business of war. Of course it might have been thought that the judgment of a man deeply versed in the business of sieges should be more or less warped by his science ; but Sir John Burgoyne had so much breadth of view, and so general a knowledge of war that he was little likely to err in that direction.

Sir John Burgoyne held strongly that the project of an attack upon the south side of Sebastopol had many and great advantages, and also that the Star Fort was far too strong to be carried by a *coup de main.*

Before the battle of the Alma, Lord Raglan requested Sir John to put his opinion in writing ; and, in the course of the same day, the English Commander was furnished with this memorandum :—

"CAMP ON THE ALMA, 21ST *September,* 1854.

" I would submit that unless some impending circumstances occur which cannot now be foreseen, the combined armies should at once move round to the south side of Sebastopol, instead of attacking Fort Constantine ; by which the following advantages may be anticipated :—

" 1. That instead of attacking a position naturally strong and of limited extent to which a powerful support will be given by Fort Constantine, which is a permanent fortification, though by no means formidable if, insulated, the enemy would have to defend a very extensive line, divided by valleys, and, from every information, very imperfectly, if at all entrenched, and which would probably be forced rapidly.

" 2. As the advance is from the north, our attack will rather be expected on that side, and not on the south.

" 3. Even supposing Fort Constantine* to be taken, although it will open the shipping, dockyard, etc., to cannonading, it will not ensure entire possession of the important establishments until after a second operation, which may still require to move round to the south, while the enemy will retain free and open communication to the place.

" 4. There is every reason to believe from the appearance of the maps, and what may be expected to be the formation of the ground that there is a very strong position between the sea at Balaclava, and along the valley of the Tchernaya, that would most efficiently cover the Allied Armies during the operation, but which is too extensive to be taken up by the garrison.

" 5. That the communication with the fleet, which is, in fact, our base of operations, would be much more secure and commodious by the small harbour of Balaclava, and the bays near Chersonese, than on the open coast to the north, and with the advantage of a good road to the attacks and a very flat country to pass to them from the bays near Chersonese.

" 6. Under ordinary circumstances such a movement would have the effect of exposing the communication of the army to be cut off ; but in this case the idea is to abandon the communication from the north altogether, and establish a new one to the shipping in the south which would be moved round for that purpose.

"J. F. BURGOYNE, Lieut.-General."

Sir John Burgoyne, by Lord Raglan's direction, then propounded the flank march to Marshal St. Arnaud, and Lord Raglan himself held a conference with the Marshal on the evening of the 24th Marshal St. Arnaud it seems, though not without some hesitation had already made up his mind to accept it. On this subject therefore, neither one nor the other of the two commanders had need to use words of persuasion. They agreed to attempt the flank march.

At the time of this conference, Marshal St. Arnaud was in a dying state although he forced himself to sit rigidly up in an armchair and on the night between the 26th and 27th September he ceased to hold his command and made over his trying and important duties to General Canrobert, a general with a brilliant reputation established in African warfare.

On this night the Marshal had thrown off the cholera, but other ailments still caused from time to time cruel suffering alternating with periods of prostration. From the moment he resigned the command he longed with great intensity to leave the Crimea, but before he embarked Lord Raglan went to his bedside to bid him adieu.

Almost the last of the Marshal's acts whilst on shore gave proof

* By Fort Constantine Sir John Burgoyne probably meant the Star Fort. Fort Constantine was one of the sea forts, but at this period of the invasion the name was often applied by mistake to the Star Fort.

of that freedom from vindictiveness which was one of the features of his character. Before he embarked he offered a present—his Russian carriage and horses—to General Bosquet, an officer of great repute in the French Army who even at that parting moment was regarded by the Marshal as his enemy. Covered by a tricolour flag, he was carried on board ship by the seamen of the *Berthollet* on the 29th September, and placed in the cabin prepared for him. This was in the morning, and although he no longer suffered pain, between noon and sunset he died.

During the seven days after the Battle of the Alma which were passed by the Allies in caring for their wounded and in marching to the southern coast of the peninsular, men faithful to their Czar and their country, and so endued with courage as to be able to exert their whole power of mind and body under a weight of disasters which seemed hardly short of mere ruin, were entering upon a task of great moment, and destined to be famous in history. Expecting the attack of a victorious host, and abandoned by their own defeated army, an admiral* with some thousands of sailors and workmen, all guided by the skilled engineer† whose achievement has made him illustrious, were preparing the defence of Sebastopol.

Towards the south-western extremity of the Crimea there is an arm of the sea, with a breadth of from 1,000 to 1,500 yards which stretches in from the west to a distance of $3\frac{1}{2}$ miles. This deep narrow bay is the roadstead of Sebastopol. On the north the roadstead is bounded by the slopes and ledges on which stand the forts and buildings constituting the Severnaya or " North Side of Sebastopol." There was reason for believing that even so late as the 25th September, though much had been done since the day of the landing, the Star Fort, the key of the North Side, could not have been successfully defended against a resolute attack by the Allies.

The plateau on the south and south-west of the bay is heart-shaped and is called the Chersonese. Its eastern end is much higher than the western and on this—the landward—side, it is abruptly divided from the plain by an acclivity rising from a height of from 500 ft. to about 700 ft., and extending for a distance of about 8 miles from north to south (in a straight line) so as to form a continuous buttress to the plain. This acclivity as well as the easternmost crest of the table-land or plateau at its top, is called Mount Sapouné.

The only great break in the steepness thus dividing the table-land of the Chersonese from the plain is at the point some 3 miles from the southern coast called the " Col de Balaklava." Along a distance of about 4 miles in a straight line, beginning from its north-easterly angle near the Inkerman bridge and going thence westerly, the

* Admiral Korniloff.
† General de Todleben.

plateau is washed for the first half-mile by the Tchernaya, and lower down by the waters of the Sebastopol bay ; but the rest of the water boundary is the open sea. The side of the Chersonese which lies towards the north is deeply jagged by creeks or bays throughout its whole length, from the Inkerman bridge on the east to Cape Chersonese on the west ; but on the south and south-western side of the plateau its shore line has a different character and it is only after passing the plateau that an inlet can be found. This inlet is called the Port of Balaklava. The length of the plateau from its easternmost side to Cape Chersonese is about 10 miles.

Throughout its extent the plateau is scarred by ravines. Some of these are deep and precipitous. They run, for the most part in a direction from the south-east to the north-west, and several of them are prolongations of the openings which form the many creeks and bays indenting the north and north-west of the plateau.

Of these creeks there is one which stretching deep in from the roadstead from north to south had become the port of Sebastopol or as the English used to call it the " Man-of-War Harbour." In this port mighty fleets could be sheltered.

Including the eastern suburb which is called the Karabel Faubourg, Sebastopol may be regarded as standing upon a semi-circular tract of ground, subtended by the great bay or roadstead, and split into two segments by the " Man-of-War Harbour " in such a manner that the western segment included Sebastopol proper, with the Admiralty, the public buildings, the arsenal, and town ; whilst the eastern segment—that is the Karabel Faubourg—contained among other buildings, the docks, great Government storehouses, some barracks on a large scale, and a church.

The separation of the town from its faubourg was rendered more complete by the steepness and depth of the ravine which descended into the Man-of-War Harbour. The configuration of land and water which thus split off the faubourg from the main town was a great source of embarrassment to the defenders, and was not the only obstacle in the way of their lateral communications, for there was another ravine which subdivided the town, and another again which cut the suburb in two. These ravines as well as the ridges and knolls on which the place stood, sloped down with more or less abruptness to the water's edge. The long hill on which the main part of the town stood, is 200 ft. above the level of the sea.

Of the streets in the town two were spacious, and in these stood the principal buildings. The rest of the streets were narrow. On the highest spot in the town stood the Naval Library, and on the top of the building was an observatory.

In the times immediately preceding the invasion the numbers

collected within the town and its suburbs had been in general about 42,000, but 35,000 of these belonged to the fleet or the army.

At the time of the invasion, the entrances both north and south of the great bay or roadstead, and both its shores within, to a distance of more than 2 miles, were studded with fortified works. Of these, some indeed, were only great earthworks, but others, and those the chief ones, were huge casemated forts, having stone-work revetments. These sea forts and batteries were—On the north side, Fort Constantine and Fort Michael, both stoneworks, the work called " Number Four," the " Twelve Apostles " and " Paris "; and on the south side the Quarantine Sea Fort, Fort Alexander, the Artillery Fort, Fort Nicholas, and Fort Paul, and lastly the Sviatoslaw Battery. It was to cover Fort Constantine on its landward side, and to prevent the enemy's ships from approaching the shore, that after the breaking out of the war, the Volokhoff Tower (surnamed by our people the " Wasp ") and the Telegraph Battery were erected on the high ground between the Star Fort and the open sea. In all these forts and batteries, without including the Star Fort, there were mounted at the time of the landing 611 guns for the most part of heavy calibre.

The Black Sea Fleet, which lay in the harbour or in the roadstead, consisted of 14 line-of-battle ships, 7 frigates, 1 corvette, 2 brigs, and 11 war steamers besides some other vessels. It carried 1,908 guns, and was manned by 18,500 seamen. There was a boom across the roadstead, at some distance from its entrance. Before the day of the Alma, it was believed by the Russians that these defences alone were quite sufficient to secure the roadstead against an attack from the sea ; and after the sinking of the ships at the mouth of the bay, the Allies acquiesced in this judgment, abstaining throughout the war from any attempt to break in with their fleets. On the eastern side also the Karabel suburb was so bounded by the Careening Bay, and the deep ravine at its head, that in that quarter also, the dominion of the water by the Russians was an obstacle to any attack. Thus relieved from apprehension of attack from the side of the water, the garrison would be able to bring almost their whole strength to bear upon the land defences. On the western side of Sebastopol there was a wide and deep ravine, running parallel with the boundary of the place which could not but be a grave obstacle to besiegers ; and upon the whole the configuration of the ground was such that works on a moderate scale might suffice to prevent an enemy from choosing his point of attack in that direction.

It was towards the south and south-east that the defenders were least helped by nature. Even in these quarters, however, the configuration of the ground was in some respects favourable to the defence ; for the ravines descended into the place in a way which laid them open to the fire of the garrison, especially to fire from the ships ; and everyone of the intervening ridges along which the assailants could best push their attacks was so formed by nature as to offer the defenders an advantageous position for the erection of a fortified work.

Other sources of embarrassment existed which, however—though not in an equal degree—were common to the attack and the defence. Besiegers and besieged alike were sure to be put to great stress by the depth of the ravines, which would more or less split their strength by hampering all lateral movements ; and in event of the conflict taking a form which should make it depend much upon earthworks, both the garrison and their assailants would have to encounter the difficulty of trying to gain cover from ground which was simply hard rock, coated over, where coated at all, with a very thin layer of clay.

The length of the semi-circular line which had to be defended throughout was 4 miles ; and of the defensive posts which might be most advantageously established along this extended line, there were three at the least, so circumstanced that the loss of any one of them would be likely to carry with it the fall of the place.*

Although in the beginning of February, 1854, the works planned for the defence of the west side of the town had been begun, the whole of the Karabel suburb, and even the approach from the south leading into the heart of the place, remained untouched by the spade. After that period, however some works sprang up ; and on the day when the Allies effected their landing, the state of the land defences was as follows :—At intervals along a curved line beginning from the Artillery Fort, and ending at the ground over-hanging the Man-of-War Harbour, there now stood this chain of works : the Artillery Fort, the Land Quarantine Bastion, the Central Bastion, the Schwartz Redoubt, and the Flagstaff Bastion.

With the exception of the Central Bastion, which was still in course of construction, these works had been completed, and were connected with one another by a loopholed wall, which passed, with but little interruption, along the whole of the curved line from the Artillery Fort to the head of the Man-of-War Harbour. Besides these works, the isolated sea fort near Quarantine Bay, and also the Artillery Fort, had been so closed by earthworks at their gorges as to be turned into redoubts, now defended on the land side as well as on the side of the water.

In the Karabel suburb less had been done ; but there also, along a curved line extending from the head of the Man-of-War Harbour

* The position subsequently occupied by the Malakoff, the Redan, and the Flagstaff Bastion. Todleben even says that the loss of the " Central," or of the " Land Quarantine " Bastion would also have been fatal.

to the mouth of the Careening Bay, were already the Redan, the Malakoff Tower, the Little Redan, and finally a single-faced battery for four guns in connection with the stone building in the form of a cross, which stood near the Careening Bay. The works thus defending the Karabel Faubourg were not as yet connected by any intermediate entrenchment ; and the Malakoff, afterwards so formidable, was at this time only a naked horseshoe-shaped tower having five guns at the top, but without the glacis, which were soon afterwards added. At this time the number of guns for the defence of the south side of Sebastopol on its land side amounted to 151. Of these 128 pieces were applied to the defence of Sebastopol proper, and only 23 to that of the Karabel suburb.

The strength of the Czar's forces in the Crimea, according to General de Todleben on the day when the great armada of the Allies was seen to be approaching the coast, may be taken to stand as follows :— The land forces then occupying the peninsular were 54,000 strong.* Of this force, some small portions consisting of about 1,000 men, were local troops ; and another portion to the number of 2,700, was a body of artillerymen permanently stationed at the batteries of the coast defences ; but the rest, amounting in numbers to more than 50,500, were troops belonging to what the Russians called their " active army " and were available for operations in the field wherever their services might be needed. Of these Prince Mentschikoff had under his immediate personal command a force of 38,500 men. These lay posted partly in Sebastopol and partly at other places, but all were so nearly in hand as to be capable of being assembled in time for the battle. The rest of the regular land forces in the Crimea amounted in number to about 12,000 and were stationed under the command of General Khoumatoff in the south-eastern part of the peninsular ; but even these most distant troops were not so far beyond reach as to make it impossible to call them in to headquarters before the critical moment.†

Besides these bodies of men, which were all land forces proper, there were some bodies of marines which had been permanently stationed partly at the several sections into which the land defences had been divided, and partly in furnishing guards for the Admiralty and the hospital. They amounted in number to 2,600. There were besides four " landing battalions " amounting in number to 1,800 men who were posted along the lines of defence.

* 54,208 thus made up :—

Strength of the army (Todleben)	.. ..	51,500
Artillery appropriated to the coast defences	..	2,708
		54,208

† This was proved by the forced march of the Moscow Regiment which having been ordered up soon after the appearance of the Allies on the coast was on the field of the Alma on the morning of the battle.

The seamen of the Black Sea Fleet lying in the harbour numbered 18,500 men. Prince Mentschikoff, as High Admiral was in command of the fleet as well as the army, and in the absence of the Prince, Vice-Admiral Korniloff commanded the naval forces and the roadstead, and the harbour of Sebastopol. The number of workmen whose services could be obtained for the defence of the place amounted to 5,000. Including these the force which Prince Mentschikoff had in the Crimea at the time of the landing therefore was 76,000 men.*

There were thousands of guns of heavy calibre in the arsenal but it was stated that owing to age and other causes, a large proportion of these were useless. Cranes, guns, and engines of all kinds were at the disposal of the defenders, and a body of men, 26,000 in number, who had long been accustomed to work them. There was an abundance of ammunition for all the early necessities of the defence and fresh supplies could always be poured in owing to it not being possible for the Allies to invest the place. At the early period of the siege the Russians squandered their ammunition.

At this time the five thousand workmen at the command of Prince Mentschikoff were busily employed, and the works on the north side especially were pushed on with ceaseless energy ; but it was not until a week after the landing that these approached completion. On the south side the defenders were busied with a fieldwork connecting the Flag Staff and the Central Bastions. Means were also taken for perfecting the telegraphic communication between Sebastopol and the covering army.

When Prince Mentschikoff had advanced to the heights on the Alma with the whole of the forces which afterwards opposed our landing the number of men still forming the garrison of Sebastopol or aiding in its labours amounted to some 32,000. Of these, however, only the gunners at the coast defences, and the militia could be said to form part of the army.

Such was the condition of things at Sebastopol when on the 20th September, the telegraph announced to the garrison that the Allies were advancing to assail Prince Mentschikoff in his position on the Alma Heights.

The result of this great battle and the victory of the Allies is well known, and as we are only dealing with condensed accounts of sieges proper no attempt has been made to describe the great battles of

* 76,375 thus made up :—

The Army	51,500
Local companies	1,000
Stationed Marines	2,666
Seamen of the Black Sea Fleet	18,501
Artillerymen appropriated to the coast defences	2,708
	76,375

Alma, Balaklava, and Inkerman.   For full and detailed descriptions of these battles the reader is referred to the grand classical work, *The Invasion of the Crimea*, Vols. II., III., IV., and V., by the great military historian, A. W. Kinglake, from which work a large portion of this chapter has, by the kind permission of Messrs. Blackwood & Son, been taken.

Admiral Korniloff who was riding with Colonel Todleben towards the sound of the guns, was forced to apprehend, and then to see only too plainly the result of the encounter.   " As I approached," he says, " the firing grew slacker, and I soon perceived that our army was retreating, but retreating in order.   A sad picture it certainly was but the will of the Lord is inscrutable to us."

The next morning, Korniloff assembled a council of admirals and captains to determine what should be done in the straits to which things were brought by the loss of the battle.   Prince Mentschikoff was not present at this council.   Korniloff addressed the assembled admirals and captains.   " Our army," he said, " is falling back on Sebastopol, and therefore the enemy will easily occupy the heights on the south of the Belbec.   He will extend his forces as far as Inkerman* and Holland†, and commanding from those heights the ships of Nachimoff's squadron, he will force the fleet to leave its present position.   By thus altering our order of battle for the fleet, he will make it feasible to force the entrance to the roadstead ; and if at the same time his land forces should take the Star Fort, no resistance on our part, however heroic, will save the Black Sea Fleet from ruin and disgraceful capture.   I therefore propose to put to sea and attack the enemy, crowded as he is off Cape Loukoul. I think that, fortune favouring us, we might disperse the enemy's armada, and thus deprive the Allied Armies of supplies and reinforcements.   In the event of failure, we shall be able to avoid a disgraceful capture ; for supposing we do not succeed in boarding the enemy's ships, we can at all events blow them up when close alongside, together with our own.   Without the co-operation of the fleet, the Allied Armies could not capture the town, if fortified and defended by our troops, until the arrival of a fresh army from Russia, and then with united exertions we might crush the enemy."

The assembled admirals and captains received the proposal of Korniloff in blank silence, and although there were some who assented, the rest disapproved of it.   All probably knew beforehand that the other measure was to be proposed, and that it had the sanction of Prince Mentschikoff, the Commander-in-Chief.

The rejection of Korniloff's measure was followed by the open

* This does not mean the ground where the Battle of Inkerman was fought but the eastern heights overhanging the head of the roadstead.
† The ground thus designated was between the Star Fort and the head of the roadstead.

proposal of that other and very different line of action which was already engaging the thoughts of the council.

That which Capt. Zorin proposed was this: to sink some of the oldest ships across the mouth of the roadstead, and employ the crews of the sunken ships, as well as those of the rest of the fleet in reinforcing the garrison.

Korniloff expressed his dissent from the counter-proposal, but perceiving that the majority of the officers present approved it, and still holding to his own opinion, he dismissed the council, and with these words " Prepare for putting to sea. A signal will be given pointing out what everyone has to do."

But he spoke, the narrator said, with a heavy heart, for he had little hope that the Commander-in-Chief would change the resolve he had imparted to him the evening before. Korniloff however went to Prince Mentschikoff, and declared his intention of putting to sea. To this the Prince peremptorily objected, and he reiterated the order he had given to Korniloff the evening before—the order to close the roadstead by sinking some of the ships. Korniloff when told that he might return to his post at Nicolayaff, however said " It is suicide what you are compelling me to ; but now—to leave Sebastopol surrounded by the enemy is impossible. I am ready to obey you."

Prince Mentschikoff was at this time very secret in regard to his ulterior plan for the disposition of the army ; but for the present he allowed his troops to continue the movement which divided them from the field of the Alma, and retreat fairly into Sebastopol.

In a weakened and tired condition of body, but not, it is said, in a state of dejection, the troops in the course of the 21st September were all brought over the water, and into the town. Thence they were moved to a piece of ground outside which was called the Kooli-koff Field. There they bivouacked. At 4 o'clock in the afternoon, the ships of the fleet including those that were doomed, began to move into their places, and at half-past ten at night all were in their ordered places. In the night the orders for the scuttling of the ships were obeyed, and at the dawn of the morning of the 23rd there were only to be seen some bare masts in the places where the *Siropol*, the *Varna*, and the *Silistria* had been lying the day before. Soon afterwards the *Oorgil* and the *Selaftroil* went down, and at 8 o'clock the *Flora* also disappeared, but the *Three Holy Fathers*, a 130-gun ship, was still erect. The commander of the steam frigate the *Thunder-Bearer* was commanded to fire into her sides, in order to " shorten her agony." At a quarter before one the sacred man-of-war reeled. For a moment—so pious men thought—the waves fell away recoiling, then closed, and bore the ship down.

But it must be acknowledged that the sinking of the ships was a wise measure. It fulfilled two great purposes. It not only closed the entrance of the roadstead against the Allies, but also, by putting a sure and visible end to the career of the fleet at sea, it brought to bear upon the land defences, that strength of 18,000 fit men, and those almost boundless resources in the way of materials which the Navy was able to furnish; Prince Mentschikoff's idea of at once shutting out the invading fleets, and turning his own navy into a town garrison by the short expedient of sinking some ships, was a conception boldly and ruthlessly formed, and one well adapted for its twofold end.

Of the celebrated flank march made by the Allied Armies in September it is not necessary to refer, as only the siege operations are being dealt with. It is sufficient to say that the march was successfully carried out without hindrance by the Russians, and that the town and port of Balaklava was seized and held.

In the course of the 25th Prince Mentschikoff with the whole of his force took up a position in the neighbourhood of Otarkoi; and the next day after leaving a detachment* in the country of the Upper Belbec, he yet further withdrew the main army, and completed his retreat to the Katcha.

There, day after day, he remained with his army, concerting no measures with the people he had left in Sebastopol for the defence or relief of the place, and suffering the garrison to live on for a time in ignorance of the region where he and his troops were reposing. So far from threatening or even observing the invaders, not only did he not know on which coast of the Crimea (the west or the south) they were operating, but when at last he once more put himself in communication with the garrison, it was to them that he looked for his tidings.

---

* A force of cavalry and infantry under Jabrokritzky amounting altogether to 13,000 men.

CHAPTER NINE

THE SIEGE OF SEBASTOPOL (*continued*).

Vice-Admiral Korniloff was an able administrator and thoroughly understood the duties of a naval commander ; but was not gifted with the faculty of designing apt plans for the conduct of the war.

But if the army was wanting in this the time of trial, there had come to Sebastopol, as a guest, a man so gifted by nature as to be able to fill the void ; and able moreover to make people bend to his judgment, confessing that his was the guidance which would best meet the emergency ; yet, curiously enough, until some four or five weeks before the time of the landing of the Allies, the name of Lieut.-Colonel de Todleben had scarcely been heard of in Sebastopol.

Colonel de Todleben was born in one of the Baltic provinces lying within the dominions of Russia, and to Russia accordingly he had ever devoted himself, but by race, and name, and feature, and warlike quality he was the fellow-countryman of Count Bismarck.

The honour of placing this gifted man on the scene in which he was destined to achieve his renown, must be given to Prince Michael Gortschakoff. Having discovered the capacity of Colonel de Todleben, and knowing how likely it was that the issue of the conflict, which he perceived to be impending, might be governed by a skilful application of the engineer's resources, Prince Gortschakoff determined that he would not only entrust to the colonel the duty of conveying his warnings to the headquarters in the Crimea, but would introduce him to Prince Mentschikoff as an officer capable of being of great use to him in the business of fortification.

Colonel de Todleben was master of the art of military engineering. His devotion to the study of his profession had been unstinted ; and there was a period when his practice of the business of mining had kept him underground during a third part of each year. He had great experience in the trenches before Silistria, and the rough tasks of war in the Caucasus. He was about thirty-seven years old.

During the three weeks which elapsed between Colonel de Todleben's arrival and the appearance of the armada on the coast, he was not only making himself acquainted with the field of the approaching conflict, but also beginning to earn that rare confidence, which afterwards enabled him to guide into a right direction the valour and strength of the garrison.

It may truly be said of this colonel of Sappers, all that was fanciful or for any reason unpractical—all that lay, though only by a little, beyond the immediate future with which he was dealing—he utterly drove out of his mind, and his energies, concentrated for the time upon some object to which they could be applied with effect, were brought to bear upon it with all their full volume and power. Under guidance so firm and sure there could be no waste of energy and no waste of bodily labour.

When the Russian field army undertook its flank march, Colonel de Todleben remained at Sebastopol. Admiral Korniloff and he had come to be as one man. They lived in the same room. What de Todleben judged to be right, the Admiral impelled men to do. If Korniloff was the soul of the cause, the great engineer was its mind.

On the 24th September, the day the Allies were marching on the Belbec with the then apparent intention of attacking the Star Fort, Korniloff assumed the command of the North Side and Colonel de Todleben, whilst still continuing to direct the works going on there, was now also charged to post the troops in the way he deemed the best for resisting the expected assault.

Korniloff did not seriously imagine that with the comparatively small force of 11,000 men under his command, he would be able to offer a successful resistance to a resolute attack directed against the Star Fort by a victorious army with a strength of between 50,000 and 60,000 men. Colonel de Todleben did not deceive him and he did not deceive himself. " From the North Side there is no retreat," Korniloff said to Capt. Gendre. All of us who are there will also find our graves. Death does not terrify me. Only one thing makes me uneasy. If wounded, one cannot defend one's self, and to be taken prisoner ! "

The morning of the 25th brought with it no signs of the expected advance of the Allies against the Star Fort ; but as though to add to the helplessness of the people abandoned in Sebastopol, Prince Mentschikoff had left them without the cavalry required for reconnoitring the enemy ; and it seems that the garrison remained unacquainted with the momentous operation in which the Allies were that day engaging, until it was almost noon. Then, strange to say, they learnt the truth without seeking it. From the Naval Library which stood upon a high knoll in the town of Sebastopol and commanded a far-reaching view, some officers extended their gaze towards a quarter not hitherto thought of as the probable scene of any English or French operations. They looked towards the heights overhanging the head of the roadstead. There, scarlet and glittering under a bright noonday sun, they saw regiments and regiments of the English soldiery moving up along the skirts of the forest to the Mackenzie Heights, and afterwards descending southward into the valley of the Tchernaya. All day, the march was seen going on; and before evening, the heights where the English had first been descried were observed to be alive with dark-coated troops moving on in the same line of march which the scarlet battalions had taken. The import of this movement could hardly be doubtful.

It meant that the Allies were abandoning the valley of the Belbec with design to attack Sebastopol on its south side.

It followed that the Severnaya, which before had been regarded as doomed, was now safe, and that the danger had all at once, shifted from the north to the south of the place.

On the south, the now threatened side, the seamen were commanded by Admiral Nachimoff. Of these for the moment there were few ; for out of the battalions already withdrawn from the ships, no less than eleven were on the North Side, and of land forces there were none except the Militia battalions. Nachimoff was a brave, devoted man ; but the courage he now evinced was of that forlorn sort which consists of blank despair. By cutting apertures in the ship's sides—to be filled up until the last moment by stoppers—he strove to ensure to himself the power of sending his whole squadron to the bottom with little delay.

Vice-Admiral Korniloff continued to be the " Chief of the Staff " of the Black Sea fleet, and remained in command of his naval squadron ; but independently of these functions, the Prince entrusted to Korniloff the command of all the forces, both naval and military, which were to operate on the North Side.

Entrusted with the command of the North Side at the moment when that was the ground believed to be in peril, Korniloff after Lord Raglan's flank march, saw that owing to the Allies so plainly committing themselves to the enterprise of attacking the South Side, the North for the time was comparatively safe.

Korniloff had so much greatness of mind, and was of so generous a nature, that despite the straitening effect of the formalism then predominant in Russia, he was able to understand the occasion. The army, and the commander of all the forces both naval and military, had abandoned the place to its fate. The navy was imprisoned. The peril which beset Sebastopol was great and imminent. On the other hand, Korniloff's orders, if only they were to be obeyed, would prevent him from acting upon the scene of the approaching conflict, and rivet him fast to that North Side which was no longer threatened. Far from accepting the repose thus enjoined by his instructions, Korniloff at once turned away from the quarter whence the danger had passed, and went straight to where the danger was coming. Giving up the command of the North Side to Capt. Bartenoff, and leaving orders for the transport of his eleven sailor battalions from the North to the South, he went on board the *Twelve Apostles*, in order to consult with Admiral Nachimoff for the defence of the main town and arsenal, now so suddenly threatened ; and for the same purpose Korniloff assembled at his lodgings Admiral Nachimoff, General Möller and Colonel de Todleben.

There, arrangements were made for distributing what forces they had along the lines of defence on the South Side. But this was not all that the assembled chiefs did. They came to a great resolve.

Forgetting their mere rank in the army and the navy and remembering only the welfare of their country General Möller and Admiral Nachimoff requested Admiral Korniloff " to undertake the general arrangements for the defence of the town." And Korniloff did not shrink from accepting the command thus proffered him. He observed, it is true, that the land forces would not be under an obligation to obey his orders, but General Möller met this objection by appointing Korniloff the Chief of the Staff of the Sebastopol garrison, and by publishing an instruction which enjoined obedience to all the orders which Korniloff might give the land forces.

The Russians take a just pride in tracing the glory of their defence of Sebastopol to the political courage and the generous self-denial which thus secured unity of command in the gravest hour of danger. Having forbidden the scuttling of the ships as proposed by Admiral Nachimoff, Korniloff with Todleben at his side, devoted his whole energy to the all but desperate purpose of defending the South Side.

The march of the Allies to the south coast was a surprise to the garrison, which had assumed, since the day of the Alma, that the attack would be delivered against the Severnaya, and their energies having been directed in the main to that quarter, they had not found time to do much on the South Side. There, the principal change which had been effected since the landing was the completion of the Central Bastion ; and although the lines along the Karabel Suburb were fully equal in their military value to those which took in the main town, they had received but little accession of strength since the day of the landing.

The Battery of the Point had indeed been begun, and preparations had been made for strengthening the position of the Malakoff Tower ; but little had hitherto been done to this quarter, and the Malakoff on the 25th September, was a mere naked tower, without a glacis, exposed from head to foot, unsupported by the powerful batteries which were intended to flank it, and uncovered as yet by the works which afterwards closed up round its base.

There were no intermediate entrenchments along the line of the
Karabel Suburb to connect with one another the four works either
begun or established. These four works afforded but a weak defence
to the great intervals of ground by which they were divided. Upon
the whole, it may be said that along the arc of 4 miles which encompassed the place on the land side, the part which reached from
the Artillery Bay to the Central Bastion was the only one that could
be considered tolerably secure.

All the rest of the line of defence, and all the works of the Karabel
Faubourg were weak, and could be easily forced. They afforded
hardly any cover for infantry, not even for the reserves ; and the
gunners at the batteries, having for the most part mere barricades
to shelter them or having to serve guns which fired over the parapets,
would have been ruinously exposed.

To defend this weak line Korniloff had indeed as many artillerymen as he needed ; but it seems that the whole number of other
combatants that he could employ in the defence of Sebastopol was
only 16,000. In this force there was an imperfect battalion of
sappers, and a body of 5,000 Militiamen. The rest consisted of
seamen withdrawn from the ships, and had been formed into 16
battalions, of which only four were well trained and well armed.
The remaining battalions were but slightly instructed in the duties
of the land service, and portions of the force were ill armed, some
carrying old flint muskets, and some having no better weapons than
pikes or cutlasses.

With 16,000 combatants of this description, it was hopeless to
try to defend a line of 4 miles against such an attack as might be
made by the victorious army of the Allies ; and this the more so,
since the garrison, split into two by the Man-of-War Harbour and
the deep ravine at its head, would be unable to concentrate upon
any one endangered quarter this little strength that it had. In the
opinion of de Todleben, it was impossible that the attack of the
Allies could be repelled by even the most valiant defence.

The 26th, it is true, passed away without showing that the Allies
(who had this day seized Balaklava) were preparing an attack for
the morrow ; but on the other hand it brought no tidings of the
invading army. " Of the Prince," writes Korniloff on this day,
" nothing is to be heard."

On the morning of the 27th, the garrison was still without tidings
of Prince Mentschikoff and his army. " Thus," so Todleben writes,
" the defenders of Sebastopol had no help that they could reckon
on. It has been seen that it was absolutely impossible for them
to repel the enemy with only the force the garrison consisted of.
So there remained to them no alternative but that of seeking to die
gloriously at the post committed to their bravery."

A solemn ceremony of the Russian Church was ordered to be held along the lines of defence. At an early hour the troops stood ranged in order of battle. Then the priests with images, gonfalons, and crosses, walked in procession along the lines, and performed divine service at each of the bastions, and the troops were sprinkled with holy water. " Let the troops first be reminded of the Word of God," said Korniloff, " and then I will impart to them the word of the Czar."

When the religious ceremony was ended Korniloff made a spirited address to the troops. He said, " The Czar hopes that we shall not give up Sebastopol. Besides we have nowhere to retreat to. We have the sea behind, the enemy in front. Prince Mentschikoff has deceived our enemies and got round them, and when they attack us our army will fall upon their rear. Remember then—believe in no retreat. Let the bands forget to play the retreat ! Let him be a traitor who sounds the retreat ! And if I myself give the order for retreating, kill me with the bayonet ! "

In his addresses to the men of the land service, he added words to this effect : " Your business will be at first to receive the enemy with a well-directed fire of musketry ; and if they should try to mount the batteries, receive them in the Russian style. You well know the work—at the point of the bayonet ! "

Korniloff's address was received with the sound of bursting " Hurrahs ! " which followed him through the lines.

In a work of this kind, it was necessary to give a somewhat lengthy description, although in a condensed form, of the defenders of Sebastopol up to the 28th September, 1854, and to show that the whole bearing of the conduct of the future defence of the place depended upon the resolution and energy of men such as Admiral Korniloff and Colonel de Todleben.

The Siege proper may now be considered to have been entered upon and the details of the operations will be related as far as is possible in the condensed form required by a work of this kind.

Governed as de Todleben was by his conception of two conditions, stress of time on the one hand, and on the other, the command that he had of all the ships' guns and munitions—he went on to frame his plan for strengthening the lines of defence, and with that view resolved " to choose a position as little extended and as near to the town as the nature of the ground would allow, and to arm its principal points with a formidable artillery ; to connect these points one with the other by trenches to be defended by musketry ; to establish there separate batteries, each armed with some pieces of cannon, and in this way to concentrate upon all the approaches of the town a powerful front and flank fire of artillery and musketry, endeavouring to sweep with as much fire as possible all the bendings of the broken ground by which the enemy might approach."[*]

* *Todleben*, Vol. I., p. 259.

The object of the works to be undertaken on this general plan was to provide against the event of an assault at whatever part of the line it might be attempted ; but the way in which they were to produce their result was to be by enabling the garrison to meet every column of assault with a slaughtering fire.

de Todleben was always steadfast in declaring that against an assault of the Allies the garrison had but one defence.   This lay in the volume of shot which the garrison might be able to pour into bodies of troops coming on within grapeshot range ; and one single word, he used to say at the time, was enough to describe his main purpose—" Mitrail ! "

The round shot, the shell, the bayonet, and the rifleman's far-ranging bullet had each, he acknowledged, its use ; and now too if ever in war, the spade and the pickaxe were needed; but still in his mind, these things were chiefly of worth, because they either tended to avert the assault, or else, were more or less auxiliary and conducing to his one cherished purpose of meeting the assaulting column whatever the time, whatever the point of attack, with a pelting blast of mitrail.

There was also open to the defenders of Sebastopol, another and a more hopeful view of the future.   The very sight of preparations for resistance might not only bring the enemy to adopt counter-measures for neutralizing these same preparations, but might even perhaps incline him to delay his attack.   It was in fact hoped that the enemy might be induced to refrain from attacking Sebastopol, with a view to besiege it instead.   The problem as stated by one who toiled at Korniloff's side* was to maintain a line of 4 miles against powerful armies with only a small body of sailors and militia-men ; whilst the way to attempt its solution was by making the defences so formidable as to induce the enemy to forsake the idea of an immediate assault, and proceed to a regular siege.

Besides the task of connecting the still isolated works by intermediate entrenchments, it was necessary to deepen the ditches, to thicken and raise the parapets, to erect traverses, and to strengthen the ground by a great number of new batteries.   Also, if only the enemy would give time enough, the armament along the whole line of defence was to be changed, and the lighter artillery replaced by heavy guns brought from the ships.   Colonel de Todleben determined that the works should go on simultaneously along all the weak parts of the line ; and each day's toil was to be so adjusted that it would not only effect a due approach towards the perfecting, after a time, of the work which had to be executed, but would also bring the impending improvements to such a state every night, that in event of an attack next morning they would still subserve

* Gendre, *Matérieux pour servir*, Chapter III.

the defence ; so that if the enemy should grant a long respite, or if on the other hand he should assail in three days, or in two, or on the very morrow, the works—whether grown to full strength, or assailed whilst yet frail and weak—might in each case do all the good which the limit of time might allow.

And now by the ardour of Korniloff and de Todleben, all things and all people within the place were turned to the business of the defences. There was no ceasing. The people worked by relays. From dawn to sunset, between 5,000 and 6,000 men were busy along the lines of defence. By help of torches, other men, in less numbers, carried on the work through the night.

Colonel de Todleben, it would seem, was instinctively conscious that the power he was wielding depended very much upon his actual presence. He never wrote. He did not even read the communications which poured in upon him; for believing that he saw his way clear without the help of others, and being accustomed as an engineer to let his thoughts take the form of estimates and reckonings, he made as it were a computation, by which he assured himself that the probability of there being important matters in the papers before him, was not great enough to compensate the distraction and expenditure of most precious time which must be occasioned by reading them. It was with his own eyes, with his own voice, that he defended Sebastopol. At a later period when the besiegers could rest their field glasses on the gabions which covered their batteries they grew to be familiar with the aspect of an officer on a black charger, who was constantly seen in the Russian lines of defence ; and they more than once pointed their guns with design to extinguish that untiring activity of one man, which (even from across the space which divided the besiegers and besieged) they could perceive to be of value to the garrison. In that ceaselessly diligent horseman, they saw the great volunteer whose brain was defending Sebastopol.

When the morning of the 28th had dawned, it still appeared that the Allies were undertaking no instant attack, but they were afterwards seen reconnoitring the defences of Sebastopol.

On the same day the deserted garrison of Sebastopol got tidings at last from Prince Mentschikoff's Army, and the officers who brought the message also brought news that the Prince had been reinforced by the arrival of 10,000 men under Khoumatoff, and was hourly expecting from the north fresh accessions of strength.

The next day, the 29th, the Allies were seen to be again reconnoitring, but again refraining from an attack, and the people of Sebastopol as well as the garrison were beginning to draw encouragement from the immense improvement that had been effected in the defences by several thousands of men always working by day and by night.

It was at the Malakoff, and the ground which flanked it on either side that the greatest wonders had been wrought. Admiral Istomin, who commanded there, knew that the post was vital; but also he had been frankly told by Korniloff that it was weak. He had toiled with a ceaseless care, looking closely into all details, and guiding the labours of the multitude which had swarmed night and day round the work.

That simple white tower, the Malakoff, now famous in history, had been so changed in shape by the industry of the last three days, that it now closed high up round the centre of the building, and had not only begun to take the form of a glacis annexed to the original work, but was also the site of a new semi-circular battery which covered the front of the tower. This last battery was connected by entrenchments with the other new works thrown up on both flanks of the Malakoff. Ships of war were so placed in the creeks that their fire could search the ravines which descended into Sebastopol. To ease the passage between the town and the Karabel Suburb, a floating bridge was constructed, nothing was forgotten, nothing neglected, and on the night of the 29th September, the great engineer who had yearned to be in readiness with his pitiless storm of mitrail, might almost lie down to his rest with the contentment of one who had made his purpose sure.

When morning broke on the 30th September, it showed that the Allies were still abstaining from any attack. This was the sixth of the days which had passed since Prince Mentschikoff's Army had been withdrawn from Sebastopol.

In the course of the day the advanced guard of the Russian Army, commanded by General Jabrokritzky, appeared on the North Side; and the sight of his troopers was most welcome to the garrison and inhabitants of Sebastopol, as they imagined that the field army was returning at last to share in the perils and glory of striving to defend the place. But this joy at the time was ill-founded; for although some of Mentschikoff's troops had thus come once more within sight of Sebastopol, and could freely communicate with the town by crossing the ferry, their presence on the north of the roadstead was still far from really meaning that Prince Mentschikoff had resumed active warfare. Unless these newly-seen troops should be suffered to cross the water—and the prospect of such a movement seemed to be shut out by the order for transferring the army's heavy baggage from the South to the North Side—there would still be long difficult marches to divide them from the enemy.

In the course of the day, Prince Mentschikoff came down in person from the Upper Belbec to the Severnaya, but did not pass over the water. He rested in the Severnaya and there received the devoted Admiral who, since the two men last saw each other, had been forced by his love of country to usurp the command of Sebastopol.

Prince Mentschikoff gave assent to the kind of dictatorship which had been created in his absence ; for he treated it as quite natural that Korniloff had been raised to the supreme authority.

After complaining of the weakness of his army, and declaring his belief that the enemy was in great strength, he intimated that he was about to make another movement, and gave Korniloff to understand that he, the Prince, meant to leave Sebastopol to its own resources.

Korniloff remonstrated, and said : " If that takes place then farewell to Sebastopol ! If the Allies decide on some daring action, they will crush us." Prince Mentschikoff then said that he would summon a council of war.

From the first the Russian Army in the Crimea had been scantily provided with skilled officers in the higher grades ; and on the day of the Alma out of the number who were competent a large proportion was killed or disabled, and of the officers of rank who escaped some, at least, were in a great measure shorn of their due authority by the comments and the blame and recriminations which too often follow defeat. As a result for the time at least the army was much out of gear, and it seems probable that the weakness of his army in point of officers was so fully realized by the Prince afterwards that he thought it necessary to withhold his army for a time from the sight of the enemy's outposts.

CHAPTER TEN

THE SIEGE OF SEBASTOPOL (*continued*).

It is time to be passing to the camp of the French and the English. It has been shown what the condition of Sebastopol was during those last days of September, and it may be asked why it was that the invaders, now able to gaze at their ease on the domes of the coveted town, did not move forward to seize it.

On the 27th September, the day the French completed their flank march and the second of the days during which the deserted garrison had been left without tidings of Prince Mentschikoff's Army, both the French and the English pushed forward some troops towards Sebastopol, and from the southern side of the town effected their first reconnaissance of its defences.

Seeing the entrance of the roadstead blocked up, the Allies were not without means of inferring that the resources of the Black Sea Fleet, both in men and material, must become available for the land defences ; and they were witnesses of the energy and haste which the garrison thought it needful to exert in trying to strengthen their lines, for upon the points upon which their field-glasses were directed there were thousands of men and women at work.

The cardinal question which had to be solved was whether the Allies should now follow up their hitherto victorious march, and endeavour to carry Sebastopol by a prompt and determined attack, or whether they should consent to give the enemy breathing time and begin upon a slow plan of warfare resembling a siege.

Before the 27th September closed bold counsel had been offered by Admiral Sir E. Lyons, and the fact is recorded that having made himself in a general way acquainted with the state of the defences which covered the land front of Sebastopol, and believing them to be imperfect and weak, he urged at the English headquarters the expediency of an immediate assault. Lord Raglan was of the same opinion, but the notion of an assault without first reducing the fire of the place by means of heavy artillery was not favoured by Sir John

Burgoyne, and the proposal having been submitted for consideration to the French, General Canrobert refused to adopt the measure.

So now the Allies took a step, not in itself decisive, but tending to govern their fate, by ignoring the all-vital question of time, and adopting a plan, smooth and easy enough at first sight, but which might yet lead to trouble. They requested the naval commanders to land the siege trains. Their purpose was to open the way for assault by first getting down the enemy's fire.*

On the 28th the seamen were busily engaged in landing the siege trains, and at this time Sir George Cathcart began to urge that the attack upon Sebastopol should be of a summary kind. There was however no change of opinion in the French camp. Apparently they were all of one mind, the reason given, among several others, being " that they would have to move under the fire of the enemy's batteries for a space of some 2,000 yards. They would have to traverse ground quite unknown to them. Any attack upon the enemy's defences must be made from an extended diverging circumference ; and the assailing forces would be so split by these deep intersecting ravines, as to become divided into isolated bodies of men incapable of giving one another any mutual help."

The combined arguments of Lord Raglan, Sir Edward Lyons and Sir George Cathcart in favour of an immediate assault were of a most cogent nature. They may be thus summed up : " Here, on this barren shore we stand fastened—inexorably fastened—to the duty of taking Sebastopol ; and for an army in such a predicament as this, the adoption of even a very hardy measure may not only be free from the charge of rashness, but may be commanded by the strictest prudence."

Without the concurrence of Marshal Canrobert there could of course be no assault, and as he did not concur, and any endeavour to shake his decision was clearly hopeless, the question was ended. What the Allies now undertook when they resolved not to assault the place immediately was to open some trench work in which to plant their great guns, and with these to cannonade the fortress. In other words they had determined to enter upon the Siege of Sebastopol. It was with the hope of inducing the Allies to come to this very resolve that the defenders of Sebastopol had been toiling.

The great Engineer who directed the labours of the garrison has declared that the place, at that time, could not have been held against such an attack as the Allies had the power to make ; and this is the judgment of one who, compared with all other men, had the fullest understanding and knowledge of the question on which he was writing.

* Sir John Burgoyne's *Military Opinions*, p. 181.

The condition of things in the Crimea, after the battle of the Alma, was such as might well have contented the Allies had they looked upon the expedition as one to be carried through swiftly, in the first week after the victory. Yet it would be likely to be hard against them, from the moment, when setting themselves against the judgment of Lord Raglan, and Lyons, and Cathcart, they reasoned away their first boldness, and wilfully suffered the enterprise to degenerate into a siege.

In adapting the disposition of their troops to the undertaking now about to begin the Allies had two objects before them ; they had to provide for the duties of the intended siege, and also to secure their forces as well as they could from interruption on the part of the enemy.

With this twofold purpose in view General Canrobert divided his army into two bodies, each consisting of two French divisions. Of these two corps, one only, consisting of the 3rd and 4th Divisions, and placed under the orders of General Forey, was charged with siege duties. It encamped with its front towards the town of Sebastopol, its left resting on the sea, and its right extending to the Harbour Ravine. The French forces drew their supplies from the Bays of Karniesch and Koratch.

On the other hand Lord Raglan devoted everyone of his infantry divisions to the business of the siege,* but his troops were so posted, that while they had thus cast upon them the duty of pursuing the siege, they were also liable to be summoned to the task of defending the Chersonese at its north-eastern angle.

The English Army had its left at the crest of the ravine which divided our lines from the French, and thence it extended eastward to ground not very far distant from the crest of the Saponné Ridge. The English Army drew its supplies from Balaklava, and at first by two routes ; for until the 25th October the Woronzoff Road, as well as by the way of the Col was open to the besiegers.

The task of covering the siege, by defending the Col, and the greater part of the Saponné Ridge, was assigned to the 1st and 2nd Divisions of the French Army under the command of General Bosquet. The Turkish battalions under the orders of the French commander took part in the same duty. General Bosquet, however, did not occupy the more northerly part of the Saponné Heights ; for there the right wing of the English, though also engaged in the siege stood charged to defend the position.

The Allied Armies were to be covered by the sea on the north-west as well as the south ; and on the more southerly portion of the

---

* The infantry forces detached were only one battalion, the 93rd, and some weakly men not in a condition for hard duty, together with one field battery.

Saponné Heights they were to be defended by Bosquet's Corps ; while against any sortie from Sebastopol directed upon the French or English trenches, the besieging forces would of course be their own defenders.

So long as the English drew their supplies from Balaklava it was necessary, of course, that that harbour should be secured ; and this place was on the outside of the natural rampart that guarded the table-land. It therefore required a separate system of defence. For this so far as concerned its eastern approaches, the steep lofty hills, which soon came to be known as the " Marine Heights," were so well fitted as to be capable of being rendered formidable by even the slight works which could quickly be constructed for the purpose ; and a redoubt with a line of breastwork extending athwart the entrance to the gorge by the village of Kadikoi, was to complete the " inner line " of the Balaklava defences. It was afterwards determined that an " outer line " of defence should be constructed by throwing up a chain of small redoubts upon the low range of heights which stretches across the plain at a distance of about a mile and a-half from the gorge leading into Balaklava.

Lord Lucan with his cavalry and horse artillery was stationed in the plain to the north of Balaklava, with orders to patrol to the Tchernaya, and also in the direction of the gorges leading into the valley of Baidan. With the exception of this division of cavalry, the whole of the scant forces entrusted with the defences of Balaklava were placed under the orders of Sir Colin Campbell.

Both the English and the French headquarters were established on the Chersonese—the English in a farmhouse a little to the north of the pass which led up from Balaklava, and the French at a spot further west.

Wharves had at once to be made for the purpose, and the Allies went on in all haste with the toil of landing their siege trains. There was yet the still harder task of bringing up heavy guns from the shore to the front, great stores of ammunition and the loads of material required for the business of the siege work besides all the usual supplies which were needed for the support of their armies.

The French had spacious landing ground in the Bay of Karniesch but it was otherwise with the English, for there soon came the first stress of that want which was destined to be the cause of cruel suffering to their army. The forces, encamped on the Chersonese, were near, it is true, to their port of supply, but not in contact with it. There was a distance of 6 or 7 miles which had to be conquered. And how ? It would seem that the only means of transport available to our engineers were some light bullock carts of the country, amounting at first to forty-six, but reduced by the 20th October to twenty-one ; and the only way this scant command of draught power could be augmented, was by pressing into the service every spare ammunition and baggage horse.

Large bodies of men were landed from the Allied fleets, and they were ordered to take part in the active operations against Sebastopol. The brigade of English seamen then placed under the orders of Capt. Lushington, and Capt. Peel* undertook a battery with his men from the *Diamond*. Large quantities of the armament and other material resources of the fleets were also freely devoted to the same purpose. Numbers of ship's guns of heavy metal were taken from the decks of the men-of-war, and dragged up to the camp by the sailors.

The process of landing battering trains and bringing them up to the front was too difficult to be got through in the short space of time that was thought sufficient when the Allies resolved to enter upon the siege ; and before they were ready to open the first trench, the enemy's field army began to show signs of changing the attitude to which its chief had condemned it since the day of the Alma. Prince Mentschikoff must have been told by his own officers, as early as the 28th or 29th September, that the Mackenzie Height was clear of the invaders, but for several days he made no movement. By the 7th October, however, the Russians had begun to appreciate the fact that, after all, they were once more the undisturbed masters of the Mackenzie Range, including every road and pathway which connected it with the valley of the Tchernaya. So now at last the Russian commander accepted this priceless dominion of territory which secured his communications with Sebastopol and the interior of Russia, but pushed his reconnoitring forces down into the plain, and even to the banks of the stream where the British Cavalry patrolled. At this time, moreover, it began to appear that the forces which constituted the garrison of Sebastopol were daily becoming more bold, for (supporting them in some instances with field guns) the enemy now kept his outposts so firmly on ground far in front of his works, as to hinder the Allies in any attempt to establish batteries at a moderate distance from the place.

The part of the enemy's defences which offered to his assailants the obvious " front for attack " was that slightly curved belt which included the Flagstaff Bastion, the Redan, and the Malakoff Tower. This last work, or rather the ground on which it stood, had been pronounced by Sir John Burgoyne upon his surveying the ground to be the key of Sebastopol. But the Malakoff was not " the key " in such sense as to imply that it was the only key of Sebastopol ; and it was the opinion of General Todleben that the capture of any

* Afterwards Sir William Peel who was in command of the Naval Brigade at the capture of Lucknow in 1858, and who died from small-pox shortly after the siege.

one of the three works—the Malakoff, the Redan, or the Flagstaff Bastion—must have carried with it the fall of the place.

Straitened in their choice of the " front for attack " the Allies determined that they would devote their first efforts to carrying the Flagstaff Bastion and the Redan, and. they hoped that the mastery which might thus be attained would insure, with but little delay, the fall of the Malakoff itself, and all the other defences. It was by the eventual assault of the Flagstaff Bastion and the Redan, that the French and the English expected to be able to carry them. To prepare the way for this enterprise, they not only endeavoured to keep down the fire of these works, but of all the intermediate batteries as well on shore or ship's decks, which helped the defence of the place on its land front. It was also their object to do all they could towards silencing, on the one side, the Central Bastion, and on the other, the Malakoff Tower. The first step towards the execution of this plan was, to draw the investment closer, and to push forward some of the infantry battalions to ground nearer the place ; and this with the view to obtain for the engineers better means of reconnoitring, and also to support the working parties in their endeavour to open trenches at a moderate distance from the enemy's works.

On the 7th October, Lord Raglan assembled the Generals of the Infantry Divisions* and announced to them what he wished to have done ; but the practical conclusion attained by the council was the rejection of Burgoyne's proposal for a closer investment of the place. Lord Raglan seemed to ascribe to the decision of his Divisional Generals, the necessity of confining the operations of the English Army, and apprehended that for the time and until the moment for assault should be ripe, that army must confine itself to such an operation as would enable the engineers to place in battery some guns of long range.

In pursuance of their plan of attempting something against the shipping and the other defences by their long-range guns, the English on the nights of the 7th and the 8th October, began the formation of two half-sunken batteries upon spots very distant from the enemy's line of works.†

After sunset on the same day as that on which the English generals had delivered their opinions, nine French battalions commanded by General Lourmel were pushed forward, and established in a sheltered position, beneath the commanding crest of Mount Rodolph, where the French meant to plant their batteries.

It was on the night of the 9th October that the French were to

* Sir George Brown, the Duke of Cambridge, Sir de Lacy Evans, Sir Richard England and Sir George Cathcart.
† About 2,800 yards from the nearest of the enemy's works.

break ground. Advancing from the ground where Lourmel had established himself, their engineers, with a large body of men told off for the work, were to fasten at once upon the crest of Mount Rodolph ; and this they proposed to do by throwing up a gabionade a few yards in advance of the ground they had selected as the site of their intended batteries. This gabionade was intended as a screen for the subsequent operation of sinking the trenches in which their batteries were to be placed. The night was clear, and a fresh wind blew from the north-east, which prevented the garrison from hearing the sound of the pickaxe. Relays of working parties numbering 1,600, worked all night without being molested, so that when morning dawned, they had thrown up a work 1,100 yards in length at a distance of about 1,000 yards from the Central Bastion.

The enemy often busied himself with sallies at night, and the cannonades with which he assailed the besiegers and their works rarely ceased for any length of time, and were sometimes of much power. In the space of a single hour on the 14th October, 800 cannon shot were fired against the works of the French, resulting in a good deal of damage to the parapets, but killing only two men, and wounding three. Whilst the French, in most places, had beneath them a fair depth of earth, the ground in front of the English was almost bare rock covered with soil a few inches deep.

On the nights of the 10th and 11th October, the English succeeded in opening the trenches on Green Hill, as well as on the Woronzoff Heights ; and it soon appeared that the fire they were preparing was likely to prove much more effective than they had ventured to hope for. By the evening of the 16th October the English had established their batteries and were ready, with the French, to open fire on the following morning.

The English were to be ready to storm the Redan as soon as the French operations should be ripe for a like effort against the Flagstaff Bastion.

The English were put to great straits for want of timber, owing to the platforms sent out with their siege trains being of a new and ingenious kind, which, though promising to serve its end admirably when tried upon a perfect level at Woolwich, turned out to be altogether unfitted for the rocky and uneven ground where our batteries had to be placed. So the platform of the old-fashioned pattern had to be resorted to, and, to meet the emergency most of the few buildings which stood on the Chersonese were quickly stripped of their roofs.

At this time there was a strong desire that the fleets should take part in the attack upon Sebastopol, but there was a difficulty indicating a way in which it would be prudent for their co-operation. On the 15th October a naval conference was held on board the *Mogador* and after much discussion a plan of the naval attack was determined upon on the 16th October. As late as the 5th October, the Russian forces defending the quarter of the Malakoff Tower were judged to be deficient in military strength, and Prince Mentschikoff yielding to the advice of Admiral Korniloff, without calling a council of war, suddenly to the joy of Sebastopol made it known that some twelve battalions should at once be detached from his field army, and be allowed to take part with the garrison in the defence of the place. Two other battalions were also brought over from the north of the roadstead ; and from time to time afterwards, further bodies of infantry detached from Prince Mentschikoff's Army were sent to strengthen the garrison. This resolution of Prince Mentschikoff to send reinforcements from the field army was apparently decided upon in consequence of a step taken by Admiral Korniloff which seemed to provide that in case of Sebastopol falling for want of aid from his army, the truth should be visibly extant. The latter framed and signed a remonstrance against the plan of continuing to withhold the entire field army from the defence of Sebastopol, and Korniloff apparently intended that whether he were destined to survive or to perish along with the fortress, his words should go to the Czar.

By the 6th October more than 25,000 men of the army had joined the sailors to help in the defence, the total amounting to nearly 38,000 doing duty on shore, and in the course of the ten days which followed the 6th October the garrison was yet further reinforced.

During this time Todleben with restless energy had been pressing on the defences ; and it seems to have turned out that the respite of 20 days with which the Allies had been indulging Sebastopol, was just of the length that the garrison needed for bringing the works commenced since the 26th September to a state of all but completion.*

On the evening of the 16th October, the garrison knew that the time of preparation was almost at an end, and that a great cannonade of their works was likely to begin on the morrow. At half-past six a.m. on the 17th October, three shells were to be discharged from one of the French batteries, and then forthwith the Allies were to open fire along the whole line of their works. The following are the details of the Russian guns :—

Guns opposed to the batteries of the Allies .. 118
Guns sweeping the approaches 160
Guns for taking the besiegers when at close quarters
   in front or flank 63

Total .. 341

* Todleben, p. 301.

The signal had not yet been given when at daybreak the Russians were able to see that the Allies during the night had cut their embrasures and that their guns were visible. A body of French tirailleurs with a support pushed forward towards the enemy's lines. Sebastopol beat to arms. The three appointed signal shells were fired. In a minute some English guns opened ; and presently along their whole line of batteries, and along all the enemy's works from the Central to the Flagstaff Bastion, and thence across to the Redan, and thence on again to the Malakoff, a heavy cannonade commenced.

So long as the conflict was one between covered batteries on one side and covered batteries on the other, there could not well be any approach to equality in point of losses between the besiegers and the besieged ; for the Russians were not only forced to keep manned the 223 guns which they had prepared against the expected assaults, but also to have close at hand near the gorges of their bastions the bodies of infantry which they designed to meet the same contingencies. Both the gunners and the infantry were imperfectly sheltered from the fire from the batteries of the Allies and the result was that the troops thus kept in expectation suffered many casualties in killed or wounded, whilst the besiegers on the other hand, were able to keep out of fire the troops with which they meant to assault till the moment for their onset had come.

The instant he heard the opening of the cannonade Korniloff galloped off to the Flagstaff Bastion. Korniloff conversed with the gunners, and to some of them he gave directions as to the pointing of the guns. " Calm and stern," says one of the staff who rode with Korniloff, " was the expression of his face, yet a slight smile played upon his lips. His eyes shone brighter than was their wont. His cheeks were flushed. He carried his head loftily. His thin and slightly bent form had become erect. He seemed to grow in size."

Gaining at length the Central Bastion, Korniloff there found Admiral Nachinoff toiling hard at his duty and seeming to be as much at home in the batteries as though he were on board his own ship. He afterwards visited the work at the Land Quarantine and seeing that the men were suffering from thirst, he gave orders for handing up casks of water to the batteries.

After changing the position of the Moscow battalion by moving it to ground where it would be sheltered from the enemy's fire Korniloff passed the dock-bridge and began to ascend the western slope of the Malakoff. When he came near the seamen on duty in that part of the field they greeted him with loud cheers ; but Korniloff forbade them. He pointed to the crest of Mount Rodolph where all was now hushed, owing to the French batteries having been silenced by the Russian fire, and said to his people, " When the English batteries are as silent as the French yonder, then, and not till then you may cheer."

When Korniloff reached the Malakoff Tower he found that its guns had been silenced and deserted ; but Admiral Istornin still answered the English by a well-sustained fire from the earthworks which covered and flanked the stone building. It occurred to Korniloff that the ground floor of the tower would be suitable for an ambulance or field hospital and he gave directions accordingly. After this Korniloff remained for some time at the foot of the tower. His aide-de-camp begged him to return home ; and in answer he pointed to the ground where the Bontir and Borodino Regiments were stationed, saying, " We will just go to those battalions, and after that we will go home by the hospital road." He still loitered for a few minutes longer, but at length—it was then half-past eleven o'clock—he said " Now let us go." He moved towards the spot under shelter of the breastwork where the horses were awaiting him ; but he had scarcely yet taken four steps when the uppermost part of his left thigh was shattered by a round shot. Gendre raised the head of the wounded chief, and the other officers near coming up and lifting him in their arms, they together laid their Admiral under shelter of the breastwork, between two of the guns. For a moment Korniloff was able to speak, and he said feebly " Defend Sebastopol." He then became senseless. He was carried to the hospital, suffering greatly; but at a moment when he was free from sharp pain, he laid both hands on the head of the Chief of the Staff and said, " Tell everybody how pleasant it is to die when the conscience is quiet." He sent tender words to his wife and children ; and from time to time he prayed thus, " O God ! bless Russia and the Emperor. Save Sebastopol and the fleet ! " Shortly afterwards he became insensible. After a few minutes he ceased to breathe. An effort was made to conceal the death of the Admiral, but upon coming to know the truth, the sailors, and the soldiers too, grieved bitterly for the loss of their trusted chief and dictator. From time to time there had been posted up numbers of general orders, in which Korniloff gave directions tending to relieve the sufferings of the men, and in many ways add to their comfort. These announcements remained on the walls long after the death of the chief whose name was at the foot of them ; and the grateful men as they passed, used to look up and point to the words, and bless the memory of their hero, saying often in that gentle and poetic spirit which is characteristic of the Muscovite people, " Our Admiral still watches over us ! "

It had been originally determined apparently that the attack of the forts should be executed by ships which, keeping always in movement, would deliver their fire in succession and that the attack should commence at half-past six on the morning of October 17th, but at the last moment Admiral Dundas in command of the British

Fleet received a communication from the French Admiral Hamelin that he did not intend to commence his fire before 10 or 11 o'clock, as his shot would not last long, and if expended early, the enemy might think that he was beaten off. Dundas acceded to the reason which Hamelin adduced, and consented to the proposed change of time.

At 7 o'clock on the morning of the 17th Admiral Hamelin to the astonishment of Dundas came on board the *Britannia* and announced a new plan of attack. By this new plan it was laid down that instead of an operation effected by ships kept in motion, the two fleets while engaging the forts, should be anchored in line ; that the array of the French fleet should begin at Chersonese Bay, proceeding thence in a north-north-easterly direction to a point opposite to the centre of the harbour ; and that from thence, but in a line taking a north-easterly direction, the English fleet should be ranged. The French fleet would thus be at a distance of from 1,000 to 2,000 yards from the Quarantine Sea Fort—the nearest of the forts which it proposed to assail—and that the English fleet would have to engage Fort Constantine at ranges equally long.

This was the plan which the French had decided to carry out. Admiral Dundas was so reluctant to adopt a measure which he considered would be mortifying to the self-respect of our Navy that until Admiral Hamelin had declared that the French were determined to adopt this course he withheld his assent.

It was apparently in a spirit of devotion to a forlorn duty that Dundas chose the place in which to put his own flagship ; for when in the course of a conference of admirals and captains that had been previously held, an officer whose opinion was weighty, pointed out that the ship which should be on the extreme right of the English line must of necessity be sunk in one hour, Dundas quietly answered that that post was the one he had reserved for the *Britannia*.

So large a proportion of the defensive works had been designed for the purpose of preventing an enemy's ships from entering the roadstead, that not counting the two small works, the Wasp Tower and the Telegraph Battery, three only of all the water-side forts were so placed as to be able to take part in an engagement with ships keeping clear of the entrance. These three forts were Fort Constantine, Fort Alexander, and the Quarantine Sea Fort.

This being a condensed history of the sieges in which the British and Indian Armies have been engaged, and being limited in size, it has been found necessary to exclude the account of the naval engagements of the 17th and 18th October, the details of which are fully and admirably related in Chapters XVII. and XVIII. of Kinglake's *Invasion of the Crimea*. It will be sufficient to recall that the results of the naval actions were on the whole more favourable to the Russians than to the Allies.

In a categorical form the five results evolved by the conflict may be thus summed up.

1. At ranges of from 1,600 to 1,800 yards, a whole French fleet failed to make any useful impression upon a fort at the water's edge, though its guns were all ranged in open-air batteries, and firing from over the parapet.

2. An earthen battery mounting only five guns, but placed on a cliff at an elevation of 100 ft., inflicted grievous losses and injury on four powerful English ships of war, and actually disabled two of them, without itself having a gun dismantled, and without losing a single man.

3. At ranges of from 800 to 1,200 yards, and with the aid of steam frigates throwing shells at a range of 1,600 yards three English ships in 10 minutes brought to ruin and cleared of their gunners the whole of the open-air batteries (containing 27 guns) which were on the top of a great stone fort at the water's edge.

4. The whole Allied fleet operating in one part of it at a range of from 1,600 to 1,800 yards, and in another part of it at ranges of from 800 to 1,200 yards, failed to make any useful impression upon casemated batteries protected by a good stone wall from 5 to 6 ft. thick.

5. Under the guns of a great fort by the water's edge, which although it had lost the use of its topmost pieces of artillery, still had all its casemates entire, and the batteries within them uninjured, a great English ship lay at anchor at a distance of only 800 yards, and fought for hours without sustaining any ruinous harm.

October 17th.—Whilst the fleets plied their thunder in vain and the guns on Mount Rodolph were still silent, there was one part of the field where the cause of the Allies seemed to prosper. This was in the English batteries. There from break of day our gunners, sailors and landsmen, had been well fulfilling their part. Not only had they sustained with advantage their now single-handed conflict with the Flagstaff Bastion and the " Garden Batteries," but they were fast achieving almost all that could have been hoped from their efforts against that part of the enemy's lines in the Karabel Faubourg which they more especially undertook to assail. The batteries in both Gordon's and Chapman's attacks were so placed and were armed with guns of a calibre which compensated so aptly for the length of the range that after some nine hours of firing, they had established a clear ascendancy over the enemy's ordnance.

Though with somewhat less advantage in that respect, than the French, the English were still upon heights which commanded the

Russian defences, and looked over into their rear. From this cause as well as from the effect of shot bounding in by *ricochet*, our guns from the first, had begun to work a great havoc in those parts of the Russian batteries which lay towards the gorges of their bastions, as well as among the bodies of troops which were posted hard by to await the expected assault.

But this was not all ; for little by little the whole front of the assailed defences in the Karabel Faubourg began to give way under the power of the English artillery. Even from the Allied lines it was easy to see that independently of the effect produced by explosions, the shell or round shot alighting upon a parapet which was no more than a heap of loose particles, wrought changes in its bulk and its form and whirling into the air at every blow a dark column of dust and small earth. Before the day was half spent, the frail ramparts most battered by our artillery had degenerated into shapeless mounds ; and after the first nine hours of the cannonade there was more than one spot where they seemed to be nearly effaced. In the midst of the earth-works thus almost dissolved into dust the stone-built tower of the Malakoff still remained upstanding ; but the work had undergone a fire so powerful that it no longer carried an effective armament. Of its few guns, all ranged in open-air battery at the top of the work, some had been not merely dismounted, but even hurled over the parapet. The stone parapet of the tower also was so shattered, and its splinters flew so destructively, that without incurring an unwarrantable sacrifice, the men at the top of the work could no longer be kept to their guns, and were withdrawn. A well-sustained fire from the guns still poured on the glacis of the work, but the tower itself was silent.

At an early hour in the forenoon when de Todleben surveyed the Redan its defences had fallen into a critical state. Even then several pieces had been dismounted, and numbers of the embrasures were blocked up with ruins. By about 3 o'clock p.m., one-third of the pieces which armed the work had been dismounted. The loss in men had been heavy. The gunners of several pieces had had to be replaced by fresh hands twice. Of 75 men sent to the Redan from one of the ships, 50 were killed or wounded. Yet in spite of the decisive and increasing ascendant thus established against them by the English, the gunners in the Redan stood firm. However appalling the slaughter, the men yet remaining alive and unstricken worked on with a courage which did not droop. The officers did not hesitate to give examples of devotion. They mounted the parapets, and toiled at the repairs to the embrasures.

Soon after 3 o'clock, however, there occurred a disaster which completed the ruin of the work. A shell blew up the powder magazine established in the salient. When the smoke lifted a dire spectacle of ruin was disclosed. At the fore part of the work the parapet had been thrown over into the ditch, and so filled it. The ground was laden with fragments of platforms, with guns dismounted, with gun-carriages overthrown, and shattered. On all sides there were the blackened bodies of men and it was afterwards known that more than 100 had been killed.

The troops which had been kept near the gorge of the Redan in order to meet an assault, all at once fell back for shelter towards the Marine Hospital. " Thenceforth," says de Todleben, " there disappeared all possibility of replying to the English artillery. The defence in that part was completely paralyzed ; and in the Karabelnaya men expected to see the enemy avail himself of the advantage he had gained, and at once advance to the assault.*

But it has to be remembered that whenever the English should be assaulting the Redan, the French were to be assaulting the Flagstaff Bastion. According to the understanding between the French and the English headquarters, the one assault was not to be going on without the other ; and it seems to have been not so much stated in terms, but rather taken for granted, that the silencing for the day of the batteries on Mount Rodolph carried with it a corresponding postponement of any attempt by the French to assault the Flagstaff Bastion. Thus the tender exigencies of the bond which united two mighty states forbade them the full use of their strength. A tacit compact required that their armies should act together in any great operation ; and it chancing at this time, from the mere fortune of war, that the English were in a condition to assault and the French not, it resulted as a natural consequence, that the temporary impotence of the one Power carried with it the abstention of both. What benumbed the Alliance was the Alliance.

After the failure of the 17th October the Allies had determined to undertake a new plan of attack. The French were now to proceed against the Flagstaff Bastion by regular approaches. The English, it was known, with difficult ground in their front, and having but scant means of carrying on extensive siege works, would be able to do but little towards attaining the Redan by regular approaches ; but it was agreed that whenever the French should be ready for the assault of the Flagstaff Bastion, the English at one point or other, should also storm the defences. On the night of the 17th October the French so prolonged their first parallel as to disclose their new plan of proceeding against the Flagstaff Bastion.

It was determined, however, that pending the time which would be occupied in proceeding by regular approaches, the cannonade

* de Todleben, p. 329.

should go on, and on the 18th October the English still maintained the fire of their batteries as the French had not only been repairing the havoc made in their works, but establishing new and powerful batteries ; and as it was known that on the morning of the 19th, they would be in a condition to open their fire with largely increased means, the hour of trial was looked forward to with great interest by the Allies.

But the preparations of the French were under the eyes of Colonel de Todleben ; and he evidently assured himself that, so long as they might continue to assail him from a narrow point of fire, he would be able to keep his ascendant, by meeting their increase of armament with an increase yet greater than theirs. And de Todleben got the ascendancy. Two of the French batteries were visited by the calamity of explosions ; a third was silenced by fire, and at 3 in the afternoon there was no longer any French battery which continued the strife. The English fire was continued with great energy the whole of the day, and directed for the most part against the Redan. At evening the cannonade ceased. No material injury had been done to the works of defence ; but in killed and wounded this day the Russians lost 516 men. Every day from this time until the evening of the 25th October the fire of the Allies was continued, but every day it was met by de Todleben with a ceaseless energy.

The French at this time, with their magazines often exploding, and their batteries often enfiladed by new works thrown up for the purpose were undergoing a trial of such a kind as might tend to make them distrustful of their own engineers. They hardly understood at the time the true root of the evils which beset them, but that which really stood in their path was warlike genius.

Under the direction of de Todleben, the Russians, by fighting their batteries with unsparing valour, and achieving at night immense labours, were able to present to the besiegers every morning a line of defence which was not only strong and unbroken, but even augmented in strength ; and they also found means to provide themselves, as the struggle continued, with a more and more efficient protection against the missiles.

On the 18th (when only the English were firing) the Russians in killed and wounded lost no less than 543 men ; but although during the six days which followed the 19th October, a cannonade equally vigorous was maintained by both the French and the English, yet during that period the average daily loss of the Russians in killed and wounded was reduced to 254. The whole loss in killed and wounded which the Russians sustained from the siege down to the 25th October was officially stated to be 3,834. From the moment when on the morning of the 18th October, de Todleben saw how the French on Mount Rodolph had newly opened the ground along a distance of 400 or 500 yards, he had assured himself that they had determined to assail the Flagstaff Bastion by regular approaches.   As an engineer he entirely approved their decision.   By means of a change in the organization of the night outposts, he was able to inflict much heavier losses than before upon the French working parties ; but he also constructed fresh batteries, so ordering his measures that the nearer they might draw their approaches the more he would be able to ply them with fire, and adhering to his favourite principle, he never ceased to take care that, whenever the moment might come for assaulting the work, any troops employed in the enterprise should be under a storm of mitrail.

CHAPTER ELEVEN

THE SIEGE OF SEBASTOPOL (*continued*).

The Way in which France and England administered to Their Armies.

In this work—only relating to siege work, and not being intended to include any description of the battles fought between the Russians and the Allies—no attempt has been made to describe the Battle of Balaklava fought on the 25th October, with its famous Charge of the Light Brigade, or of the heroic Battle of Inkerman fought on the 5th November.

We may now proceed to a short description of the way in which France and England ministered to their armies in the East.

To say nothing of our English stepping-stone, Malta, the Allied Armies were at first established on the territories of an ally, the shores of the Dardanelles and the Bosphorus, without confronting an enemy. Next, having been moved to Bulgaria they prepared to undertake regular operations in the field by striving to collect with all speed the requisite means of land transport.*

Next, transported by sea to the Crimea, and there landing without opposition, they seemed to have dominion of a country abounding in food for man and beast, and means of land carriage. Then, by their victory on the Alma, they converted their dominion of the country into unresisted possession, and for a moment it seemed that the task of supplying the armies had been happily lightened. But this only lasted for five days ; for by their flank march, commenced on the 25th, the Allies abandoned their conquest of almost all the Crimea, and by descending the Mackenzie Heights, made the step they were taking irrevocable.

Next, intent on the siege, they suffered themselves to be compassed about, and imprisoned upon a small area of barren ground ; and then it became evident that, at least for some time, the life of the troops must depend altogether upon what might be brought to them by sea.

* When the orders came out which suddenly shifted the theatre of war from Bulgaria to the Crimea, Mr. Filder had already collected 5,000 beasts of burden.

But another and even more trying change yet awaited them ; for in November, when already bleak winds and chill rains were sweeping over the Chersonese, it was determined that where the armies were, there they must be prepared to lie for months, and that the French Intendance and the English Commissariat must meet, as best they could, the huge accession of wants that would be created by striving to keep troops alive on the top of the Chersonese Heights throughout a Crim-Tartary winter.

Trusting mainly to their own stores at home not only for articles of equipment and all implements and munitions of war, but also for flour, corn, biscuit, coffee, wine, spirits, and salt meat, they sent out all these things to the shores of the Bosphorus ; there established magazines and hospitals, and thus constituted for their armies a secondary base of operations less remote from the theatre of war than the south coasts of France and England.

For the means of land transport, fresh meat, vegetables, forage, and timber, if needed, they trusted mainly at first, of course, to the resources of the countries occupied by their armies ; but when the Allied Armies suffered themselves to be penned up upon a small barren corner of ground, there was the anxious task of providing them by sea with everything that they needed, however bulky and cumbersome, so that, when disembarked with great labours from the ships, the freights would not only include huge parks of artillery, and munitions of war, but moreover crowd acres and acres with draught and pack horses and mules, with camels, wagons and carts, and herds and flocks awaiting slaughter, with pyramids of grain and flour sacks, mounds of vegetables, ricks of hay and straw, hillocks of charcoal for fuel, and numberless stacks of timber.

Distressing experience proved that a Government buying things for an army from traders at home may not only have to wait, but in spite of all the money it offers, to go on waiting and waiting during a lengthened period. It took five months to supply our troops on the Chersonese with new tents, and even seven months elapsed before they received the whole number of 3,000 tents demanded in the month of November.

It soon became plain that the whole mercantile shipping of England and France, and of all the neutral countries besides, was insufficient to meet at short notice the growing exigencies of the campaign ; so that for long periods together, there were troops, munitions, and stores of all kinds collected for shipment to the East, yet detained at the opposite extremity of Europe for want of vessels to carry them.

For want of means to land or trans-ship goods which had reached their destined ports, they too often remained on board during lengthened periods, and apparently it now and then happened that a vessel left the port she had reached without having completely discharged her cargo, yet continued to go on plying, so that stores and munitions long moved to and fro on the waters. The insufficiency of the steam vessels at the command of the British also proved baneful to the health of the troops by curtailing their supplies of fresh meat and vegetables. Then remained the task of landing the stores, disposing them in magazines, drawing them up to the camp, the task of distributing them, and bringing them into due use. For this the French were more happily circumstanced than the British. Their harbours, Kaniesch and Kazateh, no less than the adjacent landing grounds, were so ample and convenient that with the great number of workmen they had at their command, there was nothing to hinder their disembarkation. The regiments had their own bakers with them, and until wounded or stricken by sickness, the French soldier used his own skill and resource in making the very best of his too meagre ration, and his wretched means of shelter. To the English, on the other hand, the advantages enjoyed by the French were all unhappily wanting. They had not sufficient harbours, and Balaklava constituted a very indifferent port of supply for the vast and ever pressing needs of an army.

To facilitate the landing of cargoes, the British engineers in spite of great difficulties managed to construct some wharves. But from the insufficiency of the harbours, and from the want of hands an accumulation of supplies lay for weeks and months on board the ships, some of which had to be kept in the roadstead outside for want of berth-room within.

Soon too a new exigency began to press hard on the Allies, for the enemy had been receiving great accessions of strength, and on the morning of the 25th October he took the offensive at Balaklava. From that day until the 5th November, Inkerman Day, the Allies were under a peremptory challenge, delivered by an army largely outnumbering them and during this critical period of twelve days, there was not, and could not have been, any thought of having roads made by the small number of British troops, which were performing the enormous tasks of besieging Sebastopol, defending Balaklava, and defending the Heights of Inkerman against the enemy's assembled hosts.

Although resulting in victory, the morning of Inkerman Day brought with it so great a disclosure of the enemy's strength that far from lifting off a weight from the minds of the Allied generals, it quickened their sense of the need that there was for preparing resistance to largely superior numbers. And so Lord Raglan began his measures for converting the road by the Col into a " metalled " highway. Four hundred Turks were employed on this task, and the work made fair progress during the few fine days which succeeded the storm of the 14th ; but the torrents of rain which afterwards fell, and the sickness and deaths which ensued, proved destructive to the hope of completing the work without many more hands.   Of the 400 Turks who had at first been employed, only 150 could now be collected, and even these were in too feeble a state to be capable of performing anything like a full day's work.   No hired labour worth having could be obtained at this season.   The Commissary-General, it is true, was able to hire workmen on the shores of the Euxine and the Bosphorus, and he accordingly imported them by hundreds ; but they died by fifties, and the duty of burying them deep enough to prevent their bodies from tainting the air became an additional task.   Of course under such conditions the work made small progress ; and yet the time had now come when the need of a completed road was most urgent, for torrents of rain were converting the old carriage tracks into a quagmire of tenacious clay.   Again and again the irrepressible truth stood forth that the business of the road was one of life or death to many of our soldiers, if not indeed to the army.

The road, growing worse daily under the action of rain, was before long in such a condition as to be impassable for wagons, unless hauled through the clay by powerful teams.   The change of draught power to the backs of horses or mules would have reduced the transport power, and yet the number and strength of our baggage horses and mules in the Crimea was being reduced daily and in mid-winter was so low as to be almost on the verge of extinction. Cold, wet, and hard work with prolonged want of food were not only killing the transport beasts, but fast weakening the artillery teams, and Mr. Filder was prevented from importing fresh horses and mules, of which he had numbers in readiness, because he knew that if they were landed, the means of feeding them were not available.   Writing on the 29th January, Lord Raglan stated that Mr. Filder complained sadly of the non-arrival of the supplies of hay which he was led to expect he would receive from England periodically.   The Commissary-General, on the 13th September, in his official despatch to the Treasury, wrote :—

" BEFORE SEBASTOPOL, 13*th* *September*, 1854.

" SIR,

Referring to my letter of the (blank) I have the honour to report, for the information of the Lords Commissioners of Her Majesty's Treasury, that the contractors having failed to provide the quantity of hay therein adverted to of proper quality, and under the uncertainty of being able to procure in this country a sufficient supply of forage for the great number of animals belonging to the two Allied Armies, I have the honour to suggest that 2,000 tons of hay be forwarded to Constantinople during the course of the autumn.

" I have the honour, etc.,

" WILLIAM FILDER."

The Treasury officials, however, did not comply with the Commissary-General's urgent request, but on the 10th October they wrote to Mr. Filder apprising him that it "would depend upon his further reports, whether steps should be taken to send out the hay mentioned in the letter of 13th September"; but at the same time they gave instructions for the despatch of a shipload with as little delay as possible. Until the 7th November no further step was taken; and owing partly to this delay and to the lengthened periods of time spent in finding and loading the vessels, the whole month of October passed away before the first cargo went off. Even to the end of November, the quantity of hay despatched from Eng'and's shores "during the course of the autumn" had reached 270, instead of 2,000 tons.

The army of General Canrobert was often, though not always, able to provide itself with good leaven bread, and to this there were added small allowances of rice, coffee, sugar, and salt; but as regards meat the soldiers were poorly fed, so that upon the whole their rations were hardly sufficient to fit them for bearing the hardships of a winter campaign.

The food of the English Army was a subject of anxious and ceaseless care to its chief. In addition to the regulation ration, consisting of either $1\frac{1}{2}$ lbs. of bread, or 1 lb. of biscuit, and 1 lb. of fresh or salt meat, Lord Raglan directed the Commissariat to supply daily to each soldier, as part of his ordinary ration, 1 oz. of coffee and $1\frac{3}{4}$ ozs. of sugar. Some weeks later, when the health of the army became seriously affected, Lord Raglan, upon the advice of the Medical Department, directed that there should be temporarily added to the daily food of the soldier, 2 ozs. of rice or Scotch barley, an extra $\frac{1}{2}$ lb. of meat, and which was cordially appreciated above all a free ration of spirits. In the winter, for want of land transport the issue of rice was for some weeks suspended, and with the approach of winter, and the exhaustion of the supplies of cattle at Eupatoria, the issues of fresh meat became necessarily less and less frequent, the means of sea transport being wanting. As early as the 24th October, Lord Raglan commenced to obtain fresh vegetables for the British troops in sufficient abundance, but owing to delays in sea passages the quantity brought up to camp in good condition proved constantly less than was wanted for the welfare and health of the troops.

In the autumn, Dr. Andrew Smith recommended that large quantities of lime juice should be sent out, and a portion of this supply, 20,000 lbs. in weight, reached Balaklava on the 19th December, but the medical authorities did not apparently know that they had this resource close at hand, for until Lord Raglan interposed, and by that time scurvy had already proved baneful to health and life, no steps were taken for issuing the juice to our soldiers as part of their daily rations.

The French Army was ill supplied with means of shelter, for it mainly used the *tente d'abri*, a low canvas hutch, which is a miserable substitute for the ordinary tent.

Except when unhoused by the whirlwind of the 14th November the English Army was always sheltered by the ordinary bell tents. Still Lord Raglan felt keenly that against the rigours of a winter on the Chersonese, mere canvas would prove a miserably insufficient shelter, and he sent officers to Constantinople, and several ports on the Black Sea, to purchase large quantities of timber, nails, tools, and all the requisites for the construction of huts. But the task of hauling all the timber to the heights of the Chersonese, and converting it into huts was destined to be long retarded by the two great wants oppressing the British Army, want of transport and want of workmen.

An immense supply of all the thick woollen coverings lying on board vessels anchored off Balaklava that seemed best adapted for the soldiers was destroyed by the fury of a tempest. Lord Raglan succeeded in partly counteracting the effects of the tempest by obtaining warm clothes from Constantinople, but the scarcity of land transport between Balaklava and the camp prevented a general distribution.

The administrative arrangements provided for the care of our stricken soldiery were slight, crude, and indeed almost primitive. The London departments provided no efficient ambulance corps, appropriated no well-fitted vessels to the care and transport of our soldiers, sent out no artificers of the kind demanded, refused Admiral Boxer's wise request for a receiving ship at Constantinople. For attendance upon our sick and wounded in hospital, no provision at all was at first made; and in the absence of properly trained hospital orderlies, our people had to rely upon the clumsy old plan of drawing sergeants and soldiers from the ranks for duty as nurses.

Our establishment of hospitals in the Levant extended at one time to the Dardanelles, spreading yet even further to Rhodes as well as Smyrna. For the most part, however, our hospitals in the Levant were established on the shores of the Bosphorus. Of these one for our land-service troops at Koullali received a large number of patients, but by far the greatest part of our Levantine hospital system became concentrated at Scutari.

The supply of things greatly needed for the use of our hospitals was hampered, and for a long time prevented, by the want of decisive authority by those responsible for making the requisite purchases. With the absence of an anterior organization for hospital construction and management, and the want of authority and active brain power to make good past neglect, it can scarcely be wondered at that the endeavours to deal with any very large numbers of sick and wounded men was for a long time baffled.

One of the causes which grievously augmented the sufferings and consequent sickness endured by our troops was the excessive work which the siege cast upon them. When great reinforcements had brought up Canrobert's Army to a strength far exceeding Lord Raglan's, it was suggested that there should be a readjustment of the toil endured by the soldiery. Lord Raglan's appeals to the French commander for a re-distribution of the siege labours between the troops of the two Allied Armies did not certainly encounter a complete and final rejection, but they were invariably met by General Canrobert with reasons for postponing the desired relief, and afterwards by delays still more lengthened than the reasons first suggested appeared to warrant. No dilemma more embarrassing to a General could be imagined. On the one side, a certainty that the sufferings of our troops would continue undiminished, and that many lives would be sacrificed ; on the other, a grave risk of disaster to the whole Allied Army, resulting from want of concord.*

Under these conditions the Allied Armies, still engaged day and night in a siege which they could not forsake, held fast the bleak heights of the Chersonese, and there, uncomplaining, and loyal, awaited the close grasp of winter.

The Storm of the 14th November.

On the evening of the 13th November, after wild storms of wind and rain, a calm set in which continued until an hour before sunrise on the following day ; but then over the open downs on the Chersonese, and the neighbouring coasts, harbours, and road-steads, there swept a violent hurricane accompanied by thunder and lightning, by heavy rain, hail, and sleet, and followed before the day ended by driving snow.

Of the French shipping, one man-of-war, the *Henri IV.*, one despatch boat, and several supply vessels and transports were lost ; but it was upon the British supply ships and the British camp that the disasters fell most heavily. Of the vessels freighted with munitions and stores for our army no fewer than twenty-one were dashed to pieces and totally wrecked, with grievous loss of life, whilst eight besides were dismasted. The *Retribution* (having the Duke of Cambridge on board) had her rudder unshipped, lost two of her anchors, and was long in extreme peril. Even in the little landlocked pool of Balaklava, the shipping there was rudely battered together by the whirling tornado ; whilst, moreover, the captains of vessels

---

* This condensed statement is based upon numerous passages contained in Lord Raglan's Despatches, as well as his private letter.

which had been lying outside, seized the one hope of saving their craft which seemed to be left them, and lawlessly drove their way in, carrying yet more confusion and havoc into a crashing thicket of bulwarks, and masts, and spars.

On shore no less than at sea the hurricane raged. It tore up trees by the roots, and not only were houses unroofed, but even the vast sheets of metal which covered the naval magazines of Sebastopol were partly carried away. Into the camp of the Allies the tempest at once brought " unspeakable misery." *

The tents not only fell, but many of them were torn to pieces and utterly swept away, with all the things they contained. Affrighted horses broke loose, and fled in all directions until struck down by the whirlwind. Wagons were overturned, and great quantities of food and forage which had been brought up to camp were destroyed or spoilt. The hospital marquees presented so great a breadth of canvas to the fury of the blast that in spite of every effort to uphold them, they were amongst the first tents to fall; and then not only men fit for duty, but the wounded, the sick, the dying, became exposed all at once to the biting cold of the blast, and deluged with rain and sleet.† The trenches were quickly flooded. The soldiers were unable to cook their food, for no camp fires could be lit. To this miserable condition of things no remedy could be applied; for the storm made it hard in the extreme to move from one spot to another, and not only men on foot, but the horses of riders attempting to make head against the blast were again and again overthrown. Under the fall of snow which began when the storm was abating, many laid themselves down without having tasted food, and some, benumbed by cold, were found dead next morning in their tents.

Amongst the twenty-one ships wrecked was the *Prince*, a ship containing everything that was most wanted: warlike stores of every description, surgical instruments, guernsey frocks, flannel drawers, woollen stockings and socks, boots, shoes, greatcoats, and all that the Government could devise for the equipment and comfort of the troops.

The *Resolute*, too, suffered total wreck, and she was the principal ammunition ship of our army. Of the Minié ammunition alone, there went down in her no less than 10,000,000 rounds.‡ The loss of provisions and stores on board other wrecked ships was appallingly great, the hay alone destroyed being in quantities that would have sufficed for all the horses and mules of our army for a period of 20 days.§ That loss of hay was one destined to prove calamitous

* *Journal of the Royal Engineers*, p. 53.
† *Ibid.*
‡ *Ibid.*, p. 55.
§ " Mr. Filder's great fear," writes Lord Raglan, " is want of forage for the horses. He lost 20 days' hay by the tempest."

beyond measure. Lord Raglan, however, without losing an hour applied himself to the task of providing for the speedy replacement of his lost stores.

The disastrous 14th November was followed by a brief interval of fine weather; and as early as the 18th Lord Raglan intimated that the camps were "wearing a less desolate appearance." But already the sufferings and privations which the storm had inflicted on our troops, were resulting in an increase of sickness; and the horses, too, in great numbers died from the effects of exposure. Lord Raglan's plans for replacing the stores destroyed by the storm were so prompt and well conceived, that they speedily produced their intended effect, but there were some of the losses, and especially the loss of the hay, which no energy exerted from the Crimea could quickly repair. And it is certain that a large proportion of the hardships endured by our army in the following December and January were due to the hurricane of November.

Sufferings of the Armies.

Of the Russians engaged during winter at the war, a great proportion always lived with a roof overhead, some being in barracks in Sebastopol, some housed in neighbouring villages, some in huts, whilst even the troops out on duty, though suffering cruel hardships, had advantages over their enemy in the opposite camp, not only being accustomed to withstand northern winter, but also having behind them a garrison town and an arsenal. The roads broken up by floods of rain however increased their troubles to such an extent that administrative confusion was rife.

The Russians lying stricken with sickness or wounds were at one time 25,000; and the hospital succour in readiness fell so hideously short of the need, that the number of prostrated sufferers exceeded by more than 9,000 the number of hospital berths.*

The French, as compared with our people, enjoyed great advantages owing to their highly-organized system of war administration, their mastery of the art of campaigning maintained by long practice in Africa, the spaciousness of their harbours and landing places, and above all their ample numerical strength.

They used for shelter the *tente d'abri* consisting of separate slips of canvas which by aid of a short, small stick might be raised some 3 ft. off the ground. This in Africa had proved more or less successful but was too frail a thing as a means of protecting troops against the rigours of a Crimean winter and was denounced with indignation and disgust, for the shelter to be found in their dog-tents was only to be gained by crawling on all fours through the frozen or wet mud and snow without, to the mud and wet snow within.

* *Todleben*, Vol. I., p. 705 *et seq*

Before October had ended, the French War Department brought up or caused to be made a large quantity of warm clothing for Canrobert's troops and as early as the 28th November, a large portion of these supplies was already in camp. But the distribution long remained incomplete. Men in thousands were frostbitten, and many died ; whilst of those who survived, the majority were grievously mutilated ; and indeed it is declared that but few escaped the sad fate of being maimed for life.*

Without shelter in this severe weather, and also too often unfed, the French horses perished by hundreds ; the cavalry were almost dismounted, the artillery and the land-transport trains lost half their teams, and this at a time when double teams were needed for moving even slight loads.

The accustomed rations of the French soldier were scarcely sufficient for any campaign of a kind entailing hard, lasting toil, still less for sustaining him under the hardships of the Chersonese winter. He was from time to time unsupplied with bread. The supplies of fresh meat were not only rare and scant, but of poor quality, while there was no supply at all of fresh vegetables, so that the men had to live upon biscuit and salt meat.

We learn that the admission of patients into the ambulances of General Canrobert's Army were as follows :—In October, 1854, 4,747 ; in November, 8,990 ; in December, 6,432 ; in January, 1855, 9,259 ; in February, 8,298 ; in March, 7,737 ; and in April, 6,323, making altogether 51,786.

It is stated that in the seven months which extended from the 1st October to the end of April, 4,901 men died in the ambulances alone, whilst the deaths in hospital during the four last of these months were 6,557, thus bringing such of the deaths as have not been kept out of sight by the want of monthly returns to the number of 11,458. Within the 20 months November, 1854, to June, 1856, the ambulances of the French, and four only, out of their 23 hospitals, received 23,250† patients afflicted with scurvy.

Lord Raglan's Army at that time was suffering under a great complication of ills. Their outpost duties were always anxious and harassing, their toils with spade and pickaxe fatiguing ; but the men who suffered most were the guards in the trenches, often wet through from the first, who had to be sitting all night in postures which cramped their limbs. To such tasks in the middle of winter our men were too often kept no less than five nights out of six. Very often the weary soldier omitted the task of cooking altogether,

* " War appeared in all its horror ; men exhausted by illness, scarce protected by a few rags of covering, arrived on the beach to be embarked."—*Rapport Officiale*, p. 76.

† " Dans le mois de Février, le scorbut, prend un developpement considerable, et menace d'envahir toute l'armée."—*Rapport*, p. 81.

throwing away his salt beef, or bartering it with the French, and eating his salt pork raw, and thus depriving himself of nourishment or taking food in an uncooked or ill-cooked state, becoming an easy prey to disease. Whether by some misunderstanding, or by the paralyzing effect of cold and privation, many regiments were very slow to appropriate the warm clothing provided for them.

The evils affecting our camp kept on acting and re-acting upon each other with a baneful effect ; suffering from wet and cold, and deprived of due rest by an excessive burden of duties, the soldier more than ever required wholesome and generous food, but benumbed and tired out with the stress of those very hardships which had made him need such a diet he too often shunned the toil necessary for grubbing up fuel and preparing his ration. Worn down by hard toil and wet, suffering from wants so pernicious as to be too surely followed by scurvy, assailed by cholera, dysentery, fevers, and numberless other complaints, the British army underwent appalling losses day by day.

The whole number of officers disabled by battle or sickness soon became very great, and in some regiments but few remained. The Royal Fusiliers at one time had only three officers left, but it was amongst the rank and file that sickness most destructively raged. On the last day of February the army, out of a mean strength of 30,919 for the month, had no less than 13,608 men lying in hospital. Between the beginning of November and the 28th February we lost in hospital 8,898 soldiers.

From time to time, at this period, reinforcements were landing at Balaklava, yet unhappily did not effect a proportionate and sustained augmentation of the number of men under arms ; for the newcomers, all at once subjected to the hardships of the winter campaign, fell sick with great rapidity, so that within a few days, the fresh body of troops became rather a superadded assemblage of hospital sufferers than an actual accession of strength.

Even of the 11,000 men on the Chersonese still able to handle a firelock and keep their names out of the sick list, it must not be imagined that all, or perhaps even a great part, were free from grave bodily ailment ; for there reigned in this suffering army so noble a spirit that many, though ill, refused to increase the labours of their comrades by going into hospital. All their hardships officers and men endured with a heroism unsurpassed in the annals of war, and there is good ground for saying, though of course only in general terms, that the men did not choose to complain of the hardships and privations under which they were suffering.

If the soldier had to endure grievous hardship and bodily suffering, his General's portion was almost unceasing care, for to Lord Raglan every day of his life and " with dreadful exactness ' the morning state ' told all."* His visits to the divisional camps and hospitals impressed him more and more painfully with the extent of the sufferings endured. It was in general by continuous work at his desk that he obtained such distraction from grief as made endurance possible. In the whole multitude of his despatches and letters, general orders, specific directions, memoranda, remonstrances, and minutes that he penned at this time, as stated by the Historian Kinglake, there is not to be found one ill-aimed appeal, one random or misapplied word, one statement disclosing confusion or obscurity in the mind of the writer.

When the sick were carried down for embarkation to the port of Balaklava they often endured long delays and consequent sufferings, which however perhaps in most instances could be traced to want of hands and of space. No adequate arrangements had been made by the Home Government for removing them in vessels which were either sufficiently spacious, or properly equipped for the purpose ; and although they had only to traverse a distance of some 300 miles, the privations and hardships they endured while making the passage, proved often such a cruel addition to their original sufferings that, during the months of December and January respectively, they died in the proportions of 85 and then 90 per thousand.

During a period of only seven months from the 1st October, 1854, to the end of April, 1855, out of an average strength of 28,939, there died in our hospitals, or on board our invalid transports 11,652 men, 10,053 from sickness alone. Of these misfortunes the causes were :—With the French, a scanty allowance of meat and a miserable kind of tent. With the English, excessive toil, an interruption of the land-transport power, resulting in many privations ; and a grievous inadequacy of the means required for watching over the health of an army and tending the sick and wounded. The evil lay—not alone, and not even capitally—in the want of better means for facing a rigorous winter, but rather in the ugly predicament of having to winter at all without long antecedent preparation on bleak, open downs in Crim-Tartary.

In war, as we all know, dire predicaments result often from defeat; but here, strange to say, it was by the joyous path of victory that the Allies placed themselves to meet the winter on a high, barren promontory, without even a hope of keeping themselves alive unless by means brought them in ships from many and distant shores.

* The Quartermaster-General before the Chelsea Board, p. 171.

Improvement in the Health of the English Army.

However, towards the end of February, matters began to improve. Owing to the assistance of a fund called the " Crimean Army Fund," administered by two honorary agents, Messrs. Tower and Egerton, an immense quantity of stores of every description were sent out from England, and a thousand tons of goods were sent out to Kadikoi, the chosen site of their magazines, somewhat more than a mile from the beach.   Owing mainly to the skill and energy with which Tower and Egerton worked, and to their tact and good feeling, our army responded to their exertions in a spirit described as one of " universal goodwill."   The thousand tons of gifts altogether are believed to have represented a value of about £60,000.   The moral effect of these offerings upon the mind of the soldier was good beyond measure, showing the sympathy that united our people at home to their suffering army abroad.   The advance towards good health went on steadily down to the close of the war.   Computed in proportion to force, the decrease since January, 1855, in the number of admissions to hospital became so great during the last month of the occupation of the Crimea in 1856 that it might be indicated without very large error by a ratio of ten to one.   So its numbers slowly augmenting, its toils at last happily lightened, its wants almost all supplied, the army regained health and strength.

THE SIEGE OF SEBASTOPOL FROM NOVEMBER 6TH, 1854, TO FEBRUARY, 1855.

The Allies, as it has been shown, having given their adversaries the priceless respite they needed for the Flagstaff Bastion, and not judging the Sebastopol front to be anywhere else in a state that would warrant assault, now found themselves committed to what seemed destined to prove a long siege.

Instead of approaching their object with that huge preponderance of numbers, before Vauban's time ten to one, which science had declared to be needed for the reduction of a fortress, they were, on the contrary, outnumbered by tens of thousands ; the Allies had confessed themselves unable to invest the fortress on the north, whilst even on the south they were leaving the enemy free to come in or go out as he chose.

By a part of the Russian Army on their flank, and the garrison of Sebastopol entrenched along their whole front, the Allies had allowed themselves to be completely hemmed in on the land side. So long as they had been able to hope that within a few days they would break their way into Sebastopol, the delay suffered would be regarded as only a brief restraint to be followed by a dazzling conquest, and an end to all their troubles ; but the moment they had resolved that the crisis of their enterprise should be indefinitely put off, the Chersonese on which they had alighted, as though it were simply their stepping-stone, seemed thenceforth to be their prison.   With their parallels, " first," " second," and " third," and all their siege apparatus, they still had the air of assailants, yet were not in reality minded to risk striking any prompt blow; and on the other hand, they were subjected to whatever might be adventured against them by an army which they could not shake off, and also by the garrison of a fortress which they had not even tried to invest.   Whatever might be the difficulty of forcibly reducing Sebastopol, an undertaking to withdraw the Allies, and to cover their embarkation, would have been still more formidable, and must have proved an utterly desperate task.

Imagining that the enemy might some day renew his great enterprise of the 5th November, the Ailes constructed, armed, and maintained defensive works on Mount Inkerman; threw up works of countervallation on their left; perfected the eastern and north-eastern defences of Balaklava, and even strengthened yet further the hardly assailable lines which crested the Saponnè Heights on General Bosquet's front.   Thus self-defence entered into the motives which impelled the now harassed Allies to toil day and night at their works.

It was still by the Flagstaff Bastion that the French were at this time hoping they might some day break into Sebastopol.   They did not indeed try to lessen the distance of some 180 yards which parted their most advanced trench from the counterscarp of the opposite bastion, but they did their utmost to perfect the third parallel opened on the 3rd November, and prepare to break down by over-dominant metal the fire that threatened to rage against any column advancing to storm and capture the work.

As is usual with besiegers when prevented in their task of pushing forwards " approaches " by trench work, the French with great diligence resorted to the expedient of mining. They also by degrees saw that their own special task must include a great extension of siege-work towards their left.   They therefore not only made ready to deal with the Flagstaff Bastion, but became step by step the besiegers of all the Sebastopol Front from the line of the Wironzoff Road to the edge of the Quarantine Bay.   To maintain, to improve, and a little advance their approaches, to confront with new batteries an enemy ever restless and aggressive in his use of the pickaxe and spade, and finally to prepare for the object of supporting the French on their right, was all that in the way of siege work the British were able to do. They did no less than their utmost ; yet in face of the mighty defences piled up before them, could not at all make sure that they would be able to win for the French such immunity in the direction of their right front as was given them on the 17th October, when under the fire of our guns the Malakoff Tower was silenced, and the Great Redan lay in ruins.

The strain upon the fortitude of our army by the exigencies of siege work and continuous strife with the enemy, superadded to the task of living or painfully trying to live, was excessive. In the midst of its most grievous straits for want of other means of land transport, one might too often see hundreds of our weary soldiers, every man of them heavily laden, painfully employed in carrying up the supplies over miles and miles of deep quagmire, whilst also at the very same time might be seen on the track by Karani a team reckoning no less than from thirty to forty of our few surviving horses, engaged in dragging up to the front by ploughing through depths of clay some mighty gun intended for the all-demanding siege.

Whilst the suffering and hampered Allies could employ workmen only by hundreds, the Russians kept engaged on their works an organized body of labourers with a varying strength of from six to ten thousand; and if it be remembered that the enormously constructive sources thus possessed by the garrison was wielded by Colonel de Todleben, some conception will be formed of the inferiority in working power which kept down the Allies.

It was with these vast advantages, wielded by consummate genius, that the formidable colonel of Sappers proved able to work his wonders. Not even neglecting that quiet and unmolested " North Side " which a less wary man might have judged to be exempt from all risk, he converted Sebastopol into a mighty fortress prepared for the fight at all points, and defended on the land side alone by great guns already numbering 700, beside all the lesser artillery, held ready at every apt spot to confront storming parties with round shot, and volleys of mitrail. He closed the gorge of the Little Redan, and of the Malakoff, and afterwards that of the Flagstaff Bastion. To make sure that the French would meet with destruction in event of their carrying the Flagstaff Bastion, by means of underground wires he connected the powder magazine of the work with a peaceful spot. As regards the French mining operations, Colonel de Todleben met them by countermines.

By all the works thus accomplished did the great engineer make his fortress secure against any attack the Allies might attempt. But he did not so believe; he believed that with all his resources he could not defend the threatened bastion against a determined attack; whilst moreover he judged that the loss of the work would so split the Sebastopol defences as to ensure the fall of the place. But short of undertaking great sorties, Colonel de Todleben did all that he could to conduct his defence of Sebastopol in an eagerly aggressive spirit, and one might say that he manœuvred with earthworks as others manœuvred with troops.

Another way in which de Todleben maintained his aggressive defence was by sinking and maintaining " rifle-pits." So vexatious a kind of encroachment was not always to be maintained without provoking resistance, and the struggles for rifle-pits occurring in the course of the siege began with the exploit of young Lieut. Tryon, who wrested one of these from the enemy, and thereby won warm praise from both the Allied commanders. de Todleben also caused a sufficing breadth of ground to be scientifically chosen and duly taped out by skilled engineers, then delivered under cover of night, to strong working parties, who would instantly and swiftly entrench it. All this he saw could be done ; and thenceforth the besiegers had cares which resembled in some sort those of people besieged ; for too often the morning disclosed a small bit of what might be called a counter-parallel; and these lodgments soon became oppressive beyond measure. It was on the French, for the English approaches had been less closely pressed, that the lodgments especially frowned.* The explosion de Todleben effected on the 9th February did the French no physical harm, but he was convinced that by the vigour of his countermining operations, he caused the French to mistrust every foot of ground upon which they must tread when marching against the Flagstaff Bastion, and in that way did much to deter them from ever assaulting the work.

There was no resort during the winter to powerful sorties, which, as some able critics thought, the Russians ought to have hazarded, but of small sallies, ventured at night, the garrison made frequent use, so that owing to the hostile pressure which Todleben was always applying the guards of the trenches were constantly kept on the alert.

Another expedient used by the Russians seemed one less meant for the exigencies of actual fighting, than as one for dealing with soldiers surprised, confused, and distracted by a sudden incursion at night-time. At one time they certainly used the lasso, and also the gaff, or some tool resembling a boathook, as their means of first upsetting or otherwise arresting an adversary, and then so pulling him in as to be able to make him a prisoner. This abhorred innovation was so highly resented by the French that General Canrobert, under a flag of truce, made it a subject of complaint addressed to the Russian authorities ; and in a magnanimous spirit of concession, General Osten-Sacken, commanding the garrison, put an end to the practice.

Burgoyne all this while had not ceased to insist that the Malakoff Front was the one more than all others meet for attack and had put forward counsels to that effect. In the face of our dread "Morning States," and the absence of any English succour approaching, he long clung fast to a hope that the honours of attacking the work which he held to be the all-mastering key of the position might accrue to his fellow-countrymen, and even when forced to see that no heavier share of siege work could be laid upon our people, still

* Out of 34 lodgments, which at one time were counted, two only menaced the English.

tried to find a way, by proposing that Canrobert's troops should relieve the British infantry from the task of supporting the Left Attack, and that with the force then set free Lord Raglan should undertake the Malakoff.*

It was on the 20th November that the French had begun to push forward their great mining enterprise, and they had thenceforth conducted it with unwearying energy, their first design being to surprise the enemy by effecting an explosion under the Flagstaff Bastion. Unenlightened, it seems, by either spies or deserters, they worked their way forwards, moving their earth-trucks to and fro. Such work has always to be carried out with every precaution for minimizing noise which can be detected at a considerable distance, and at times located with some accuracy. The foe whom they had challenged by entering on this underground warfare was perhaps one more thoroughly practised, more, highly skilled in its mysteries, more eager to use his resources, than any other man living ; † and before they had burrowed their way to the ground required for their purpose, an enemy like themselves, subterranean, but silent, unheard, unsuspected, was awaiting them in his listening galleries.

The great engineer scarcely awaited the reports of deserters ; for when he saw that the French did not push their approaches beyond the third parallel, he inferred that they would try to work their way underground, and he resolved to meet any such enterprise by a vast system of countermines. At length, on the 30th January, the expected reward of long toil was attained, for then Colonel de Todleben learnt that at the extremity of one of his listening galleries the French could be heard, and he was even able to assure himself that they were piercing ground on a level with that to which he pressed his keen ears when listening for signs of their presence.

In the strife between miner and counterminer, he who first hears his antagonist obtained the ascendant. Todleben with a great self-restraint determined that before he assailed them he would let the French burrow still closer, and thus so reduce the thickness of the interposed clay as to give him the means of overwhelming them by an explosion of only moderate strength.

At length on the 3rd February, the fourth day after the one when the miner's approach was first heard, Colonel de Todleben fired a camouflet, which left undisturbed the whole surface of the ground overhead, but tore its way into the gallery where the French had been heard, killing two of their men as it passed and visibly finding its issue in the open air through ground behind their third parallel, thus showing him where lay the entrance to their system of mines.

* *Journal of the Royal Engineers*, pp. 63, 139.

† At one period of his life General de Todleben had devoted himself with the greatest zeal to the science of mining and at that period a very large proportion of his time was spent underground.

The French chief engineer, however, hoped that they might still draw advantage from their system of underground approaches on which much labour had been expended, because it would enable their miners to open up a line of craters which might afford cover, and perhaps made the beginning of a fourth parallel. He therefore by an explosion threw up one crater of moderate size, but it was seized and crowned and definitively held by the Russians, and the second design of the French being thus defeated, it resulted that so far Colonel de Todleben obtained and kept his ascendant at the seat of the underground war.

The works of defence on Mount Inkerman were by this time complete; and of those which from the first had remained in charge of the British they continued to hold; but the bulk of our troops on the Chersonese lay henceforth compactly disposed between the 2nd French Corps on their right and the 1st French Corps on their left.

Acting in concert, in so far as was possible, and each making good the other's deficiencies, the French and the British Armies began to fulfil the conditions laid down on the 1st January, and constructed two batteries which by means of flanking fires were destined to aid our Allies in their meditated attack on the Malakoff.

After his defeat at Inkerman, General Dannenberg was removed from the command of the 4th Army Corps, and replaced by General Osten-Sacken, and amongst those " reorganizing " directions, which General Niel had brought out, there was one which removed General Forey from the command of the 1st Corps d'Armée, and entrusted it to General Pellissier—an officer destined to reach, though not until some months afterwards, a yet more exalted position.

Under the directions of Lieut. Stopford, of the Royal Engineers, our people in the beginning of December constructed an electric field telegraph ; and towards the close of the same month, Mr. Campbell, a civil engineer, began his operations for making the railway between Balaclava and the camp. In December the command of our fleet passed from Admiral Dundas to Admiral Sir Edmund Lyons.

Although in a measure disorganized by the bloody defeat sustained by the Russians at Inkerman, and by the immense loss of officers, yet so high was the spirit of their people, and so great the firmness, the skill, and the resource of the engineer then directing their energies, that far from yielding to depression, they carried on the defence which almost undid the curse of defeat, and so bore themselves that, after a while, they stood, as some thought, in less jeopardy than the baffled victors of Inkerman. It might indeed have been said of the besieged and the besiegers that during several months each lay at the mercy of the other.

Eupatoria.

Although up to the middle of the month of February, 1855, the Russians may perhaps be said to have obtained some ascendancy in the siege operations before Sebastopol after their defeat at the Battle of Inkerman, they suffered another reverse at Eupatoria, where they were repulsed by the Turks in an attack made on the city of Eupatoria on the 17th February, 1855.

The seaport town, Eupatoria, had surrendered to Admiral Lyons in the earliest hours of the invasion, and the Allies thus established close and friendly relations with not only the people of the town, but also their country neighbours. These countrymen, however, soon found that they were dangerously circumstanced, and when the Russian cavalry came near their homesteads, they hastened to fly from the imagined wrath of their Czar, took shelter within the town, and pastured their flocks in its neighbourhood.

Russian cavalry after a while drew a cordon about Eupatoria on its land side, and took care to maintain it so closely that the flocks in their neighbouring pastures were no longer safe against capture. Some ten thousand head of cattle, which would otherwise have furnished good meat to our suffering troops on the Chersonese, were seized instead by the enemy, and driven off into his camp.

Upon learning that General Khrouleff had carefully explored the ground, and considered it possible to take Eupatoria without grave losses, Prince Mentschikoff not only made up his mind to have the enterprise tried, but to have it conducted by one who, directly in the face of judgment pronounced by his immediate chief (Baron von Wrangel), had formed a counter-opinion, and imparted it to the Commander-in-Chief.

Thus it happened that on the morning of the 17th February, the Russians made a vigorous attack, opening their fire against the defences of Eupatoria with 76 pieces of cannon. It completely disabled one Turkish battery. It killed Selim Pasha, struck down another general and 19 men, brought about several explosions, and the town at last slackening fire seemed to own itself ripe for the assault. In columns of companies two of the chosen Azoff battalions moved forward. They approached to within some 25 yards of the ditch, but were then beaten back by the fire of the place. Soon, however, they rallied, and were advancing once more when stricken again by the fire from the parapet they again began to fall back.

And now a Turkish battalion pressed forwards with bayonets fixed, sprang on the beaten columns retreating across its front, and pushed them northward, and preventing them reaching shelter. With some 200 horsemen, who constituted what was almost the whole of Omar Pasha's landed cavalry, Iskender Bey trotted up on the flank of the beaten battalions, cut them off from the shelter of the Russian burial-ground, and pressed their retreat in the open till one of them, formed up at last in a hollow square, was able to stop the pursuit. The Russian loss was put at 760, and that of the garrison at 387.

This repulse might seem only a trifling discomfiture, yet (as oftentimes happens in war) was destined to gather some weight from the fact of. its proving conclusive. From the moment of Khrouleff's retreat to the end of the war, Russia always acquiesced in' the briefly-delivered arbitrament of the 17th February, and thenceforth left to her foes the absolute, unchallenged ownership of Eupatoria, which by many was believed to be the true key for laying open Sebastopol.

Although the little discomfiture thus sustained by the Russians was only of the kind that soldiers call " a repulse," the Czar Nicholas felt it acutely. By relieving Prince Mentschikoff of the command, he perhaps found some vent to his feelings, yet could not allay his anguish, and continuing to grieve, he fell ill.

The bare sequence of facts ran thus :—The Czar's troops were repulsed by the Turks on the 17th February ; the telegraph soon told him the truth ; and he died on the 2nd March.

CHAPTER TWELVE

The Siege from the Middle of February, 1855, to the Second Week of April.

Colonel von Todleben saw that to defend the Mamelon the new French " approaches " on his left front must be arrested, and that then he might prevent them from acquiring ground whence their batteries would be able to drive off all Russian ships from the eastern part of the Roadstead.

Having taped down beforehand the lines of a newly-planned Redoubt, he moved out on the night of the 21st February with seven battalions commanded by General Khroustchoff, crossed the channel of the Careenage Ravine, ascended to the heights of Mount Inkerman, and under shelter of darkness laid hands on the chosen site.

The men were kept in a state of readiness to lay down their tools, and to take instant part as combatants whenever the need might occur ; but they toiled undisturbed the first night, and when morning broke, it was seen that the cover already obtained by dint of pickaxe and spade, and gabions rapidly filled, was even then solid enough to be good against musketry fire. This work was called the Selinghinsk Redoubt after the name of the regiment that constructed it.

The French did not molest the new work until the early morning of the 24th. They then undertook to assault it with a force of three battalions, supported by two in reserve, and entrusted the command of the troops to General Mayran. The attacking part of the force consisting of one battalion column of Zouaves at each flank, and one of Marines in the centre was under the immediate orders of General Mouet.

When the moon had gone, General Mouet's three battalions

moved forward, and made good their advance with great spirit, driving in both the line of skirmishers, and the line of company columns which formed the front of the Volhynia Regiment, and apparently forcing back also two out of its three massed battalions. The ships in the Roadstead, and even the Karabel batteries soon began to intervene, but the advance of the French was not checked. The battalion of Zouaves on the right of the assailing force was commanded by Colonel Cler, a daring and brilliant officer much liked by our people. At the head of his Zouaves he turned the flank of the Russians, and pushing forwards so vigorously that before long carried the fighting to ground on the left of the growing redoubt.

To meet the stress of battle brought thither, the unengaged column of the Volhynia Regiment was moved laterally by Khroustchoff from his right to the ground on his left where the Russians were most hotly pressed. Before long the four Volhynia battalions, with some men of the Selinghinsk Regiment intermixed, gathered irregularly in advance of the new redoubt, presenting to their assailants a broad, concave front. General Mouet now received several wounds, and finding himself compelled to give up the command he handed it over to Cler, who was called away from the right in order to receive his new charge.

Cler, however, soon returned to his Zouave battalion, taking with him all the troops that he found on his road, and going in person up to the work knocked over the gabions revetting a part of its counterscarp, crossed its ditch, overthrowing the Russians there gathered, and mounted the parapet. But then he learnt that notwithstanding the darkness, the redoubt and its precincts were swarming with troops, and those of the French who had till then remained alive on the parapet were forced back into the ditch, and were there surrounded by Russians coming from all directions. To the fire of musketry there was added the fire from ships in the Roadstead, and even from the Faubourg Defences. But Colonel Cler stood his ground in the fosse hoping that reinforcements might come. But now General Mayran, becoming convinced that his foremost troops were in danger, caused the retreat to be sounded.

Thereupon, Colonel Cler passed back over the counterscarp, led the men acting with him against the host of Russians who were barring his path, clove a way through their ranks with the bayonet or the musket-stock used as a club, and rejoined the rest of the force which General Mouet had led. The French force thus reunited made good its retreat without being pursued.

General Mayran did not bring into action the troops which formed his reserve. The fight lasted an hour.

In killed, wounded, and missing the French lost some 270, and the Russians rather more than 400.*

The French did not renew their attack. Convincing themselves that, if captured, the Selinghinsk Redoubt might be swept by so potent a fire of artillery as would make it untenable, they resolved, however unwillingly, that they must needs stand by whilst the enemy, losing no time, completed and armed his new work. And this bold encroachment effected under their eyes was only the beginning of the counter-approaches, with which the Czar's great engineer was minded to try their patience.

Seizing ground that lay towards the left front of the newly-formed work, on the night of the 28th February he began to construct yet another one of a similar kind which was called the Volhynia Redoubt ; and he lost no time in rendering it stronger every day.

Although the Allies by this time saw the object at which he was aiming, viz., to attempt the fortification of the Mamelon, they still resolved to abstain from storming the newly-reared works which now formidably obstructed their siege, contenting themselves with promising that so soon as the enemy should try to plant any field-work on the coveted Mamelon, they would carry it at once by assault.

Meanwhile their counsels induced them to await the actual happening of the apprehended contingency, and not undertake to avert it. The question whether the Allies should submit to these aggressions was one of course meriting their joint consideration, and accordingly, a council assembled. It included General Canrobert, Lord Raglan, General Bosquet, General Niel, General Birot, Sir John Burgoyne, Sir George Brown, and General Harry Jones. It lasted several hours without coming to any definite resolve. On the following day the council again met and discussed the general progress of the siege. The difficulties of the attack were a good deal dwelt upon, and were acknowledged to be increasing rather than diminishing.

The importance of endeavouring to take what with normal besiegers has commonly been called the first step, that is to invest the place, or in other words to cut off communication between Sebastopol and the Russian field army was much dwelt upon, whilst General Canrobert declared his opinion to be that, if from any cause Omar Pasha should be unable to act upon the rear or flank of the enemy from Eupatoria, he should be requested to come to the Chersonese with two-thirds of his army. Lord Raglan stated his reasons for not sharing the opinion thus formed by General

* *Todleben*, Vol. II., p. 30.

Canrobert.   The French and English engineers did not come to any agreement, and the adjourned conference sat again on the 6th March.

Then the French making no proposal, Burgoyne submitted a memorandum recommending an attack on the Selinghinsk and Volhynia Redoubts with a view to driving the enemy effectively from that part of the ground.

General Canrobert and the French officers attending him did not consider the reasoning by which Sir John Burgoyne supported his opinion to be well founded ; and they at once declared their determination not again to attempt to drive the enemy from his new works.   Whilst the Allies were thus vainly deliberating, their adversary was acting with ceaseless vigour.

The Volhynia work was completed in the course of ten days ; and the armament which the two new redoubts had received on the 10th of March comprised 22 pieces of cannon.*

To have a strong hold on the Mamelon was the object of besieged and besiegers alike, but it had not up to this time been the chosen scene of their efforts.   Lightly held by an outpost of Russian infantry, it had neither been touched by the pickaxe nor assaulted by troops, nor even approached by " approaches " ; but by the morning of the 10th March that state of affairs was fast drawing to an end.

Looking towards the north-west on the morning of the 11th March the Allies saw that during the night, their great adversary had been fastening on the Mamelon, and that there, with the rudiments of a work plainly meant to defend it, he had already saddled the Ridge.   On the following night, the 11th March, the French opened their first parallel, against the new work, not yet one day old; thus almost repeating the all-involving mistake of the previous autumn, that of " besieging " an embryo.

To enter on a course of " approaches " was to give the enemy time.   The Allies before long brought a powerful artillery fire on the growing lunette, but as the French were as yet not minded to undertake an assault they had to bear the torment of seeing or otherwise knowing that every day and night their unwearied adversary was completing his work.   He finished it on the 21st March, and by that time had not only armed it with ten 24-pounder guns, but covered it by the fire of twelve other pieces, planted for that purpose in battery on chosen sites less in advance.

The reason which had prevented Canrobert on the 10th March from consenting to seize the then unfortified Mamelon proved

* *Todleben*, Vol. I., pp. 34, 35.

sufficiently strong to deter him from assaulting the embryo work which had newly grown over its surface.

To our people the notion of suffering the enemy to construct a defensive work on the one path which could lead our Allies to the Malakoff, seemed almost the same as abandoning the main design of the siege ; and to deprecate such acquiescence, our chief engineer drew up a memorandum " on the expediency of occupying the Mamelon " which Lord Raglan imparted to Canrobert*; but all this insistence proved vain ; and the Mamelon, growing daily in strength, continued to remain unassaulted.

Meanwhile Lord Raglan succeeded to a certain extent in allaying the apprehensions of the French commander who thought it possible that when the Allies should open their fire upon Sebastopol, the enemy would attempt a general attack, making a sortie with 20,000 men on the extreme left of the French, and at the same time the right of our position with 40,000 men, and the ground in front of Balaclava with an equal force by a simultaneous movement.

" In those times of trial," said one who best knew Lord Raglan, " he would calmly withhold his assent to all gloomy apprehensions, and throw upon those who conversed with him the spell of his own undaunted nature. Men went to him anxious and perturbed. They came away firm." †

" I think," said Lord Raglan, " our friends are a little uneasy, and are anxious for the arrival of some of the Turkish Army from Eupatoria ; but they continue to have full confidence in their English Allies."

On the night of the 22nd March the enemy undertook an adventure with a much greater number of troops than are commonly charged with the task of making a sortie in darkness. He effected four sorties against his English besieger, thus extending the front of his great night attack, but still threw the main weight of his onslaught on that chosen part of the ground where our French Allies were engaged in sapping their way towards the Mamelon. The night was dark, and a strong wind intercepted the sound of troops marching, when at about 10 o'clock nine battalions of infantry, commanded by General Khrouleff, moved out from the flanks of the Kamtchatka Lunette along the Victoria Ridge ; and another battalion assisting, it was with a strength of no less than 5,500 men that the Russians soon came into action.‡

The French " guards of the trenches," that night were under General d'Autremarre and comprised four battalions.

* Despatch " Secret " to Secretary of State, March 17th, 1855.
† Speech of General Airey to the Board of General Officers.
‡ Khrouleff was the General repulsed by the Turks when assailing Eupatoria.

Though not without some hard fighting, General Khrouleff's battalions recovered the lodgments which their adversary had been suffered to occupy, advanced to the head of the sap, and invaded the foremost " approaches," whence, after encountering a brave and stubborn resistance, they at last drove in the French working parties.   After leaving in the " approaches " thus seized, a large number of sailors who wrought all the havoc they could, Khrouleff's force moved on in pursuit.

Here, however, by this time were gathered the three French battalions which d'Autremarre had within reach ; and his force now opposed to the Russians a resistance so strong that those of them who made bold to adventure beyond the parallel met their deaths, whilst those who remained on its verge soon found themselves engaged in a hot and obstinate fight.

To the enormous preponderance of numbers already enjoyed by the Russians there now came a new and unexpected advantage, for a little body of troops had by this time moved up along the edge of the Woronzoff Ridge ; and then it came to pass that the French whilst engaged against the host in their front suddenly found themselves stricken by a fire from across the ravine, and from ground so far south that it took their troops in reverse. Under this serious trial the French showed great firmness ; and on the other hand the enemy failed to obtain any encouragement from the sight or sound of the fire newly befriending him.

His masses still remained hanging back on the verge of the parallel and apparently with the loss of their headway they lost all their clearness of purpose. There were glimmers of light in the sky which enabled the French to see that their assailants were gathered into bewildered groups, and in need of sure guidance.

The onset had spent its force, and the counter-sway followed. Whether simply, as von Todleben says, obeying their General's repeated signals, or yielding as Niel asserts to the prowess of d'Autremarre's force, the assailants at all points fell back. They were pressed for a while in retreat, but soon found shelter beneath the guns of the fortress.

The field officer that night on duty in the English trenches of " Gordon's Attack " was Colonel Kelly ; and of the 1,200 men under him, one-half at first guarded the third or foremost parallel, which may be said to have crossed the whole breadth of the Woronzoff Ridge, from the Dockyard Ravine on his right to the Woronzoff road on his left.

With 300 of his men Colonel Kelly had furnished the working parties employed that night under the guidance of Colonel Tylden, R.E., and the remaining 300 he kept higher up in reserve. Colonel Kelly had the advantage of having at his side Major Gordon (the directing engineer of the Gordon's or "Right Attack" siege works) who thoroughly well knew the ground.

Directed by Ensign Zavalchine, the attack planned against our right flank was opening with some shots from his skirmishers, when under the orders of Boudischeff, and designed to take effect on our front, a much heavier onslaught began.

Greatly favoured by the darkness, and also by the roar of the wind overpowering the sound of their march, a body of Russian troops, supposed to be about 800 strong, moved out from the lines of Sebastopol, and ascended the Woronzoff Ridge. It was opposed by a small detachment of the 97th Regiment comprising about 80 or 90 men commanded by Capt. Hedley Vicars. During the fighting Gordon who was with Colonel Kelly received a wound from a musket shot which struck his right arm and disabled him ; but Colonel Kelly running forward overtook Capt. Vicars, and was presently moving down alongside him against the enemy's column. It is supposed that baffled by the darkness, the Russians failed to divine the scantiness of the small force that assailed them with a strength of only about one to ten, for when the advance of our soldiery was becoming or had already become a charge the Russians fired a last volley ; and then, still hanging together after the manner of Russians in flight, began to retreat at the double, its rear files turning however and firing back shots as they ran. By one of these shots Capt. Hedley Vicars, who was moving eagerly forward at the side of Colonel Kelly, was killed. Colonel Kelly at last stopped the pursuit, and brought back the 97th detachment to its former post at the trench. From this time, about midnight, until one other hour had passed all was quiet on the Woronzoff Ridge. But again at 1 o'clock in the morning the tumult of more fighting began to make itself heard ; and the seat of conflict this time was a part of the Ridge further west.

During the *mêlée* that ensued, Colonel Kelly saw a group of seven or eight soldiers whom he took in the darkness to be men of his own regiment—the 34th. So going close up to them he directed these men to fall in with the other men. He was met by an uproar of outlandish cries, and found that he had been accosting the enemy. Whilst attempting to defend himself with his revolver, the trigger of which was held fast by the safety-catch, he was felled by blows laid upon him with the butt ends of muskets, and was bayoneted in the right shoulder, in the left hand, and in the right leg and was only saved from being killed by a brave young Russian officer who interposed, and in shielding him became the recipient of some of the fiercely-aimed blows, and caused the wounded Colonel, as a prisoner of war, to be brought safely into the fortress.

The conflict drew to a head on the site of a new mortar battery occupying the trench during its centre. The enemy advanced on this battery from the west, the English from the east, and within it the two forces met, each moving with bayonets fixed alongside the parapet, and of course therefore facing the traverse. At the first traverse the Russians made a protracted stand. Colonel Tylden came up in person, and his own idea apparently was to execute a charge straight forward from east to west along the foot of the parapet ; but our people instead, with a rush, drove their way round the end of the traverse, overthrew at the point of the bayonet all they then found before them, and pursuing, approached the next traverse where the enemy made his last stand. Colonel Tylden by one charge more overcame the resistance they offered, drove all the Russians out of the battery, and pursued them some way along the course of the trench, but the fugitives before very long were all over the parapet and making off towards the Redan.

The two English detachments engaged in this part of the field lost three officers and several men.*

Whilst this combat was raging, yet one other sortie began, and was directed against our Left Attack. A column commanded by Béruleff, about 500 in number, moved out against the foremost trench at the base of Green Hill which was afterwards called the 4th Parallel.

Favoured greatly as had been other columns by the darkness and the roaring of the wind, this column surprised and drove in the detachments of the 20th Regiment which had lined the parapets of the advanced trench. A great number of the assailants entered the two new and incomplete batteries No. VII. and the advanced No. VIII. which had been established in the 3rd Parallel, there surprising the working parties, which under Capt. Montagu, R.E., were engaged in thickening the parapets. Lieut. Carlton, of the 21st Fusiliers, collected his own little force, about 50 in number, adding to it some men of the 57th whom. he found within reach, and then at once opened fire on the hesitating conquerors of the advanced trench who were then brought to bay.

Lord Raglan highly commended the gallantry with which officers and men, called from their toil with pickaxe and spade, had met the successive emergencies, and not confused by the darkness or putting all their trust in cartridges, proved able to drive off the masses one after another by simply the use of the bayonet.

* Capt. the Hon. Cavendish Browne, of the 7th Fusiliers, and Lieut. Jordan, of the 34th, were killed, and Lieut. McHenry, of the 34th, wounded.

Our Allies, all this time, both above and below the earth's surface had been pressing their siege operations against the town of Sebastopol, whilst the British with scantier numbers, and besides on more difficult ground, had been slowly pushing forward their batteries against the Redan and its neighbours. Lord Raglan did not wish to oppose the conjoined wishes of the French and Turkish commanders; and at this time Omar Pasha was brought to the Chersonese with from 15,000 to 18,000 men supported by 30 guns. Towards the end of February the Russians sank six more of their ships in order to more effectually close the Roadstead.

In the command of the Russian forces, Prince Mentschikoff was succeeded by Prince Michael Gortchakoff; and General Osten-Sacken was placed at the head of the Sebastopol garrison.

On the 17th March, the Russians lost their valiant Admiral Istomine, a cannon ball killing him whilst standing by the Kamtchatka Lunette.

Pursuant to the early decision of Lord Palmerston's new administration General Harry Jones on reaching the Crimea was at once put in orders as the commander of our engineers, and Sir John Burgoyne being apprised of the instructions recalling him ceased of course to hold power officially at the seat of war. But Lord Raglan believing at that particular time that the continued aid of Burgoyne would be of great value to the public service, requested the General to remain for a while at headquarters. This Burgoyne did, and it was only in the third week of March that he left the Crimea. Lord Raglan addressed to Burgoyne a letter expressive of the grateful appreciation with which he regarded his services.

The April Bombardment.

The Allies had now in the month of April decided upon a bombardment of Sebastopol on an immense scale, and had expended great efforts, undertaking to deliver their fire with 501 guns which (with the exception of 31) were of great calibre; and for the service of all this artillery they had collected a vast amount of ammunition. Of the 501 pieces only 123 were English, the rest being French; but in aggregate weight of metal, the difference was less; computed in that way the proportion of the French siege power to that of the English was only as sixteen to thirteen.*

Of the 998 guns which by this time they had established in battery, the Russians could bring into action against the now threatened attack, as many as 466, with an aggregate weight of metal which

* " The weight of projectiles thrown by the French pieces of ordnance in one salvo was 15,957 lbs.; by the English, 13,333 lbs.; combined salvo, 29,290 lbs."—*Todleben.* Vol. II., p. 164.

compared with their adversaries, was as twenty-three to twenty-nine. On the whole, it seemed plain beforehand that in this artillery conflict the balance of advantage was strongly against the besieged.

On Monday, the 9th of April, the morning opened with heavy mist, storm, and rain, so that each object was thickly obscured, but nevertheless, soon after daylight, the cannonade was commenced.

In almost every bastion some 20 or 25 minutes were suffered to pass before the Russian batteries opened. At the end of that time the garrison began to answer, but were firing with a rigid economy of ammunition ; and this very unequal interchange of artillery missiles had not gone on for many hours, when the richly-supplied besiegers were seen to be having the mastery. All day, the besiegers went on with their great cannonade, which, even when darkness fell, did not relapse, the defences being plied at night with a powerful vertical fire.

From the 10th, to the close of the 18th April, the Allies continued to work their guns with destructive effect. But the enemy laboured indomitably, always at night-time, though still more or less under fire, and never failed before morning dawned, to repair the broken defences and restore the artillery power.

With some little help from our people, the French siege guns broke down the most precious defences of what was called the " Town Front," and again in the opposite quarter, silenced the two " White Redoubts " on Mount Inkerman, whilst our British artillery mastered the interposed batteries of the Kamtchatka Lunette which had blocked all approach to the Malakoff.

The official narrative tells us that on the eve of this April bombardment General Dacres preferred a request, one not however conceded, that in order to complete his arrangements, the opening of the fire might be postponed for 48 hours.* What caused General Dacres to ask for delay was the backwardness of certain preparations in the Left Attack.

Before evening on the 11th April, the ground had become much more firm than it was on the days preceding ; and when our left siege-train commander directed Capt. Oldershaw, of the Royal Artillery, to take down the guns meant for the arming of the advanced No. VII. he was answered by a cheerful " All right, sir," that had the ring of decisiveness.

With the aid of 300 infantrymen, Capt. Oldershaw opened a road through the parapet of the 2nd Parallel, brought his guns through

* *Journal of the Royal Engineers*, Vol. II., p. 145.

the passway, and before morning, lodged them all safely in the advanced No. VII.

The advanced No. VII. of our Left Attack was the battery destined to be fought on the 13th April by Capt. Oldershaw, and on the 14th by Capt. Henry. It was one of two batteries in the 2nd Parallel of our Left Attack, and was not only in close proximity to the enemy's frowning defences, but was so low down as to be commanded from most of the ramparts. The little advanced No. VII. was placed so forlornly as to be openly inviting a fire of almost indefinite power. The distance of No. VII. from the Crow's Nest (the nearest of the enemy's guns) was only about 700 yards.

On the evening of the 12th, Capt. Oldfield (the officer commanding the artillery of the Left Attack) ordered Capt. Oldershaw to work the No. VII. Advanced Battery on the next day.

Long before sunrise so as to be under cover of darkness Capt. Oldershaw moved down into the work, having with him one subaltern, one surgeon, and 65 gunners. There four guns stood planted in battery, and a fifth one was near them, but lying in its travelling carriage. It was with the four guns already established in battery that Oldershaw undertook to fight.

Capt. Oldershaw now found himself engaged against five batteries, and undergoing the concentrated fire of their twenty heavy guns. For a while the chief's losses in men went on faster than the disabling of his guns ; and there soon came a time when, with three pieces still undisabled, he could barely find sufficient unstricken men to work them. Still, all who could, toiled heart and soul, and one of these was Oldershaw's subaltern, Lieut. W. R. Simpson, a zealous and valiant officer. At this period of the fight, Capt. Oldershaw sent off a messenger to the 1st Parallel to ask for reinforcements.

With all the power left them our gunners still answered the storm of the enemy's fire, but their guns of course after a while had been wrought by incessant discharges to a state of intense, scorching heat, and could only be fired at intervals.

A hollow shot entered the embrasure through which Oldershaw was laying his gun, and achieved what is perhaps unique in the annals of gunnery conflicts ; for killing two, wounding the rest, and yet sparing the Captain himself, it laid the whole of the gun detachment at its feet. The gun was disabled. It had twice before been struck by a shot without becoming unserviceable. So of the four guns with which Oldershaw had begun the conflict, only one now remained intact. With that one gun, however, the Captain still continued to fight.

Capt. Oldershaw had maintained the unequal combat for five hours, when at length a superior officer came down into the battery and directed him to retire.   The detachment at first comprised 65 gunners.   Of these 18 men at the close of the fight had been sent away by Oldershaw with orders to bear off wounded men.   Of the remaining 47, the enormous proportion of 44 were either killed or wounded, so that the remnant of the original body with which Oldershaw at last marched out of the battery mustered only three.

On the day of the fight the Brigadier-General Commanding (afterwards Sir Richard Dacres) rode accompanied by his staff to the tent of Capt. Oldershaw, and there thanked him personally for his exploit of that morning saying, " You fought your battery nobly, and are an honour to your regiment."

The advanced No. VII. was restored and prepared for new fights with so great despatch as to be again in working order on the next day, the 14th April, and its sister work, No. VIII., having at last been armed, the fight of the previous day was renewed.

On that day the advanced No. VII. was commanded by Capt. Henry, of the Royal Artillery, having under him Lieut. Conolly and 35 men.   Capt. Henry engaged the barrack batteries, and they answered him with a power that soon proved him to be hugely overmatched ;   whilst he was also assailed front and flank by the Garden Batteries, besides being placed under the strong enfilading fire of the left face of the Flagstaff Bastion.   Out of his small force Capt. Henry lost two men killed and five wounded.   From each of his 32-pounders he fired about 100 rounds, but one of his guns was after a while disabled.   Kept under a powerful fire for nearly eight hours, the battery and its embrasures suffered havoc.

With their siege guns in this bombardment of ten days the Allies are believed to have fired some 130,000 shots, and to have been answered by the Russians with about 88,000.

Though inflicting on the Russians huge losses, the artillery conflict cost the French and the English together no more than a few hundred men.   Of this loss in killed and wounded a large proportion, as usual, was borne by our sailors.   They were masters of the art of bantering the enemy by making humorous signs to him, sometimes a seaman standing up on the top of the parapet teasing by gestures the Russian officer when seen to be bending his field-glasses on one of the batteries, or by the favourite prank of extinguishing his own mirthful head beneath an inverted bucket.   To say whether this great bombardment did or did not open paths for assault, it is right to hear the voice of authority.   Commanding on this subject more weight than any other man, General von Todleben answers the question.   He wrote that the " French might have advanced to the assault of the Flagstaff Bastion with an absolute certainty of success, and this so much the more since they found themselves at a distance from it of only some hundred paces." After stating that the Allies had planned assaults and failed to execute them he goes on to say :—" It is thus that the Allies failed to profit by the important advantage they had gained ; yet they had it completely in their power to take the Flagstaff Bastion, and that would have carried with it the fall of Sebastopol."

The Siege from the 9th April to the Middle of May.

On the 11th of April the French, and indeed the Allies, sustained a painful loss. Whilst making his way along one of our unfinished trenches, General Bizot was struck by a shot, and the wound some days later proved mortal. Commanding the French engineers he had pursued his huge task with a zeal that never relaxed. General Bizot died on the 15th April, and Lord Raglan together with those of his Staff who could be spared from their imperative duties, showed the feeling with which they regarded the brave engineer by following his remains to the grave.

General Bizot had scarce breathed his last, when the French carried into effect a design he had long entertained, and had long been seeking to execute. At the close of that series of mining operations which he had devised for the purpose, they at length on the evening of the 15th brought about some convulsing explosions, which opened up from below a line of volcano-like craters, at a distance of less than 100 yards from the counterscarp of the Flagstaff Bastion, and thus formed in front of the work a long deep cavity, interrupted, it is true in one place, but forming elsewhere what might almost be called a ravine.

This artificial opening of the ground close to and in front of the Flagstaff Bastion became for the French a beginning of their 4th Parallel, and, though not until after hard struggles, they were ultimately able to establish themselves in the hollow, taking care of course to connect it with their 3rd Parallel, full 100 yards less in advance, by covered lines of way.

Passing yet further west to the front of the Central Bastion, Colonel von Todleben at this time began to construct new works on the zone then dividing his lines from the French, by establishing lengthened chains of rifle-pits which he had taught the Allies to distinguish as "lodgments"; and, as previously on Mount Inkerman, and the Victoria Ridge, General Canrobert appeared to be reluctant to make any resolute stand against the encroachments.

General Pelissier at this time only commanded a corps ; but these as it chanced were the troops challenged and defied by this last growth of new Russian works thrown out in advance of Sebastopol ; and although he was only a subordinate owing obedience to the

Commander-in-Chief, was by nature so constituted as to be in hot rage at the notion of quietly enduring the enemy's audacious encroachments. He seems to have got his way over Canrobert, and was either empowered or suffered to make war against the " lodgments."

Pelissier determined to attack them on the night of the 10th April, but the Russians, on the same evening withdrew their troops from the lodgments, and prepared to ply the new occupants who might soon be there with a powerful fire of artillery from the Central Bastion.

Between 9 and 10 o'clock in the evening the French advanced in some strength, and planted themselves in the then empty lodgments, but were presently assailed by a powerful artillery fire. Under this ordeal the French held their ground firmly during several hours, but not without suffering losses. Then at 2 o'clock in the morning the enemy made a powerful sortie, retook at once two of the lodgments, and did not give himself rest until he had recovered them all. In like manner, on the nights of the 11th and the 12th there was a taking and retaking of these pits ; but on the night of the 13th Pelissier caused them to be attacked in some force and destroyed.

In order to cover a somewhat weak part of his defences by a species of " counter-guard," Colonel von Todleben had established in front of his Schwartz Redoubt another strong chain of lodgments which were to make a beginning of the work designed.

These lodgments Pelissier seized on the night of the 12th April ; but after dark on the 23rd, the strife was renewed. From that last night until the close of the month, the Russians not only remained masters of the lodgments, but deliberately converted them into a new work of counter-approach in the form of a redoubt, and so thrown forward as to be 141 yards in advance of the Russian line of defence and within 116 yards of the French siege works.*

This new work the Sousdal Counterguard was furnished already with nine 6-pounder mortars which, with the fire of the riflemen, were used to annoy the French workmen who toiled in their most advanced trenches.

General Canrobert grudged the loss that would have to be suffered in wresting this Sousdal Counterguard from the enemy, but Pelissier brought his Chief to consent that the attack should be made, and orders were given accordingly.

* Todleben does not deny that the extreme proximity to the enemy's siege works was a defect, but says its position was dictated by the lay of the ground. The new work was executed by troops of the Sousdal Regiment, and thence acquired its name.

On the night of the 1st May, a strong body of French infantry, commanded by General Metterouge, advanced against the work in three columns.

Either in or about the work, the enemy at this time was present with no less than four battalions; but the Russians devoting their care to the task of repairing the havoc done in the daytime by French artillery, were said to have been off their guard, and to have been taken in part by surprise.

Without firing a shot, the assailants made good their advance to the edge of the work, and the centre column at once broke over the parapet intent on the use of the bayonet. Some fighting ensued but did not last long. The centre column prevailing soon drove out the Russians, pursued them some way in their flight, and was master of the counter-approach including its nine little mortars.

With admirable valour and skill the French engineers, under Colonel Guerin, hastened to clench the victory. Reversing the parapets of the captured work, they connected to the use of the French what so lately had sheltered the Russians, and achieved under fire the perilous and difficult task of forming by flying sap the gabionaded approach, full 350 yards long, that would link to their system of trenches the newly effected conquest. The conduct of the French troops, that night, was as Lord Raglan said " very brilliant."

It was not without making sacrifices that the French achieved this conquest of the lodgments. In killed and wounded they lost about 600 officers and men ; the Russians 425.*

On the following day the French strengthened themselves yet further in the conquered work, and afterwards at about 3 o'clock they promptly repulsed a sortie which the Russians attempted against it.

On the night of the 13th, they repulsed a new sortie attempted against the work, as also one made further west.

On the night of the 20th April the enemy had determined to make a sortie to prevent the British from seizing the lodgments confronting the left advanced sap of Gordon's Attack ; but our people anticipated him by 24 hours ; and it was at 9 o'clock on the evening of the 19th April that, commanding in person a detachment of his splendid 77th Regiment, Colonel Egerton assaulted the lodgments These he promptly carried, but suffered some loss, and Capt. Lemprière of his regiment was killed.

In one of the captured lodgments, our engineers resolved to

---

* " The French losses at the Battle of the Alma were not, it seems, quite so great as those they sustained in this combat."—*Niel*, p. 241.

establish a lodgment of their own, and to connect it with the head of their sap. This, though only of course incompletely, they found means to do in three or four hours. They determined that they would not retain the other lodgment ; but some men, eight or ten, were left there on watch for the time.

At about 1 o'clock the Russians advanced with a whole battalion of their famous Vladimir Regiment reinforced by some hundreds of men volunteering from its other battalions. The assailants drove in our covering sentries, and the eight or ten soldiers left watching in the otherwise unoccupied lodgment. Then advancing against the lodgment which our people had resolved to hold fast, the Russian force moved in its strength ; but the British coming up in good time soon drove back the Vladimir troops, thus defeating the enemy's efforts to reconquer what he had lost. Thenceforth accordingly the lodgment thus taken and held remained connected definitely with the siege works of " Gordon's Attack."

But this brilliant achievement cost our people some lives. Whilst forming his troops for the second of the two encounters Colonel Egerton was unfortunately killed. Lord Raglan reported the conduct of the troops to have been admirable. In killed and wounded, all reckoned, the losses were sixty-eight.

The real advantages achieved by these petty enterprises was of a general, not special, kind. They kept the besiegers on the alert, and made it their duty to go on unceasingly with the always harassing task committed to the " guards of the trenches."

Towards the end of the month of April the task of laying down a submarine telegraph cable connecting the Chersonese was brought to completion, and on the 2nd May the arrangements for communication were completed. Thenceforth a few hours sufficed for the passage of messages from either Paris or London to the camps before Sebastopol. There was also laid down a cable which connected the Chersonese with Eupatoria.

Lord Raglan towards the close of this period was happily strengthened in numbers by reinforcements of troops which were placed under his orders.

On the 8th May General de la Marmora, with a part of the 15,000 Sardinian troops despatched to the seat of war, and followed by the rest of the force, was already landing at Balaclava, and placing himself, as agreed, at the British Commander's disposal.

Dr. Russell in his history of the siege says :—" It was impossible to deny to the Russian engineers great credit for the coolness with which they set about repairing damages under fire, but words could not do more than justice to the exertions of our own men, and to the Engineer officers and sappers engaged in this most perilous duty. When an embrasure was struck and injured it was the duty of the sappers to get up into the vacant place and repair the damage, removing the gabions, etc., under fire, and without the least cover from shot, shell, or riflemen. Our Engineer officers had frequently to set the example to their men in exposing themselves when not called upon to do so."

· On May 28th a meeting was held in Pelissier's hut, at which the Generals of the French were present, three of whom were Engineers. On the part of the British, General Jones, R.E., and Colonel Adye, R.A., took part in the proceedings. At the meeting General Pelissier announced his intention of promptly assaulting the Mamelon and the redoubts in front of the Inkerman attack, known as the " Ouvrages Blancs," and requesting that the British should at the same time establish themselves in the Quarries in front of the right attack.

General Jones promised to lodge a force in the Quarries and clear the ground in front at the same time that the French crowned the Mamelon. A good deal of discussion took place for the next few days, at the end of which it was decided that fire should be opened from all the batteries for two days, and that on the evening of the second day the forward movement should take place on all three points simultaneously by signal.

By this time the following additions had been made in the British attacks :—On the left No. 10 Battery for seven guns in the centre of the 2nd Parallel ; No. 11 for eight guns on the extreme left of the same parallel, beyond No. 9 with a communication from it under shelter of the crest of the ravine ; No. 12 for four mortars to the right of No. 9, and No. 13 for four mortars in the 3rd Parallel between Nos. 7 and 8. In the right attack three new batteries had been thrown up, No. 13, or the Sandbag Battery, for four guns in the 2nd Parallel, to the immediate right of No. 12 ; No. 14 for five guns, in the same parallel, to the left of No. 9, and No. 15 for three mortars in a small quarry to the left of No. 12.

During the interval since the April bombardment the 9th Company, Royal Sappers & Miners, had also been added to the strength of the British Forces. On the other hand the following losses had been sustained :—Capts. King, Crofton, Lieuts. Baynes and Carter, killed ; Capt. Owen, wounded, and Capt. Porter and Lieut. Pratt, invalided.

It may here be mentioned that during the month of May a very successful expedition was made to Kertch and Yenikale where the Russians had accumulated vast masses of stores of every description. These were all destroyed, and after a few days spent in carrying devastation in every direction, the force returned to the duties of the siege.

On June 6th all the batteries opened at 3 p.m., and before sunset had done good service, the enemy's works being greatly knocked about. During the night the mortars were kept firing upon all the quarters where the enemy were likely to be engaged in restorations, and on the 7th the artillery fire recommenced at daybreak. At 6 p.m. that evening the signal was given and three simultaneous attacks delivered. One French column was directed against the "Ouvrages Blancs," a second against the Mamelon, and a British column against the Quarries. All three were perfectly successful. The Russians were driven out, and the first steps taken to connect these works with the besiegers' advanced trenches.

As regards the British attack, the troops were commanded by Capt. Shirley, of the 88th, acting as a General Officer. He was assisted by Lieut.-Colonel Tylden, R.E., who guided him as to the points of attack, and the distribution of the troops in the assault. The Royal Engineer officers employed in this brilliant operation, under Lieut.-Colonel Tylden, were Capt. Browne,* and Lieut. Elphinstone † in charge of the working parties, and Lieut. Lowry as guide to the attacking column. Capt. Wolseley ‡ and Lieut. Anderson also served with the working parties.

Lieut.-Colonel Tylden made the following report on the operations :—" The enemy's ' ambuscade ' known as the Quarries, and the adjoining trenches in front of the left of the right attack, were stormed and carried yesterday evening about 7 p.m. by a party of 400 men from the Light and Second Divisions. A good lodgment has been formed on our right of the Quarries, and the communication from the left advanced sap made good. Our troops are at present in occupation of the Quarry lodgment, covering their left, extending from thence to the right along the reverse of the enemy's trench to his salient rifle pit at the centre. The whole of these works have been appropriated for our own use. The enemy's resistance was energetic and determined, evinced, not only in the defence of his Quarries, but in the repeated efforts he made during the night, to retake his trenches by turning their right, as well as by direct attacks. A reserve of 600 men formed the immediate support of the assaulting party, and a working party of 800 men was detailed for the forming of the lodgment.

"Communications, etc., were divided into four different parties, each for a special part of the work. Three of these parties I brought forward in readiness to commence work directly the enemy's trenches were taken, but such was the resistance of the enemy and his numbers, that the assaulting party and their reserve were

---

* Afterwards General Sir J. F. M. Browne, K.C.B., Colonel Commandant, R.E.

† Afterwards Lieut.-General Sir Howard Elphinstone, V.C., K.C.B.

‡ Afterwards Field Marshal Viscount Wolseley, G.C.B., G.C.M.G.

insufficient to hold the captured trenches, and I quite concurred in the necessity of those portions of the working party who were armed being appropriated for this purpose. The last 250 men I kept in reserve in the right ravine communication, and as soon as the advance had been reinforced and regularly posted, I brought this party forward, and with them made the lodgment and communication. The former was effected under the immediate direction of Lieut. Elphinstone, R.E., and when the darkness of the night and critical circumstances under which the lodgment had to be made are considered, I think that this officer deserves the highest praise for the creditable manner in which he executed this service. Capt. Browne, R.E., who was the officer of Engineers in charge of the general superintendence of the work, and of the arrangement of the working parties executed these services to my perfect satisfaction. Capt. Browne speaks in high terms of the conduct of Capt. Wolseley, 90th Regiment, Assistant Engineer, who was employed in forming the communication to the lodgment."

" We have unhappily to regret the loss of Lieut. Lowry, R.E., an officer whose gallantry and untiring zeal, added to the experience he possessed from many months' service in the siege, adds another instance to recent losses in the Corps which we cannot replace, nor sustain without the deepest concern. Lieut. Lowry was the officer who conducted the storming party, which service he performed in the most gallant and conspicuous manner."

To these reports must be added General Jones's remarks on Lieut.-Colonel Tylden, which are as follows :—

" Lieut.-Colonel Tylden, of the Royal Engineers, distinguished himself particularly on this occasion, as well as on every other from the commencement of the siege, always at hand to aid in the repulse of the enemy whenever our works have been attacked."

After repeating Lieut.-Colonel Tylden's encomium on Capt. Browne and Lieut. Elphinstone, etc., he continues :—

" The Sappers & Miners were conspicuous, and by their gallantry and zeal obtained for themselves strong marks of approbation from His Lordship, the Field Marshal Commanding."

The next few days were spent in rendering secure the new acquisitions, and in constructing within them advanced batteries to play upon the line in their rear. Meanwhile fire was kept up more or less vigorously from most of the existing batteries. After a conference between the Artillery and Engineer chiefs of the two armies, which was held in General Jones's hut on June 10th, at which six French and two English Generals were present, plans were submitted for an assault on all points. The Generals-in-Chief, however, decided upon limiting the attack to the Mamelon and the Redan without advancing on the line in front of the French left.

The Attacks on the Mamelon and the Redan.

On June 16th General Jones issued his orders as to the duties of the Royal Engineers on the occasion. The Redan was to be assaulted at three points—the right, centre, and left. The columns were numbered one, two, and three. Each was to be headed by an Engineer officer, with 10 Sappers provided with tools for removing obstacles, behind them a covering party of 100 men, then some men with bags of wool, and after them the ladder party. The main column was to consist of 400 men; to be followed by a reserve of 800 men, and lastly a working party of 400 men. The three columns were to be identical in strength and organization, and captains of Engineers were to accompany the officers commanding.

The following Engineers took part in the operation :—

Lieut.-Colonel J. W. Gordon, attached to Lieut.-General Sir G. Brown, who commanded the entire force.

No. 1 Column.—Major Bent, Lieuts. Murray, Graham, and C. G. Gordon.*

No. 2 Column.—Lieut.-Colonel Tylden, Capt. de Moleyns, Lieuts. James and Donnelly, and Major Campbell, Assistant Engineer.

No. 3 Column.—Capt. Jesse, Lieuts. Fisher, Graves, and Somerville.

There was also a fourth column which was to move towards the Woronzoff Ravine, and enter the works of the place beyond No. 3 Column.

The assaults failed in every direction, no column, either French or English, succeeding in establishing themselves within the enemy's works. There were two causes for these failures. First the attack was made before the fire of the garrison had been sufficiently crushed. Secondly, the French columns on the extreme right, which was intended to penetrate the line to their right of the Malakoff, started before the signal was given. The Russians were therefore fully prepared for the other columns when they left their trenches. The result was, as has been said, complete failure, coupled with severe losses, especially in officers.

Two Engineer descriptions of the British attacks were given, one by Lieut. Graham, who was with No. 1 Column, the other by Lieut. Fisher, who was with No. 3 Column. Graham's report was as follows :—

" In obedience to brigade orders of this day's date " (the 19th June) " I have the honour to inform you that at half-past three o'clock yesterday morning, I was in charge of the ladder party

---

* Afterwards Major-General Charles Gordon, c.b., the hero of Khartoum.

accompanying the storming party, ordered to attack the right flank of the Redan, Brig.-General Sir J. Campbell commanding. On the signal for the attack being given Lieut. Murray, R.E., advanced in rear of the skirmishers towards the left, followed by the ladder party. The skirmishers did not advance beyond the rear spur of the hill, the fire from the Redan, Flanks, and Creek Batteries being too heavy. Lieut. Murray was here severely wounded, and obliged to retire. Lieut.-Colonel Tylden here came forward, and I had just obtained his sanction to advance on the salient instead of on the flank when he too was struck down by grape shot. The skirmishers now advanced towards the salient, followed by the sappers, and the party carrying the woolsacks and ladders, whom I halted in front of the advanced trench, in order that the skirmishers might cover us before we advanced. Finding, however, that the skirmishers could not advance under the formidable fire of grape and musketry from the Redan, I ordered the escalading party to retire into the advanced trench, which they did. After about 10 minutes the officer in command of the storming party, Lord West, told me that he was again about to lead out the skirmishers, and requested that I would take out the ladders. This I accordingly did, and the ladders were again brought to the front. Here, I beg to be allowed to remark on the remarkable steadiness and gallantry of the officers and men of the Naval Brigade, who formed part of the ladder party, and who suffered most severely on this occasion. As it was again found impracticable for the skirmishers to advance, the ladder party again retired, bringing in most of their ladders, though not without severe loss. After this no further attempt was made until the order was received for the supports to retire. I beg to call your attention to the steady conduct of the party of sappers, under Sergt. Coppin, 4th Company, Royal Sappers & Miners, especially to Private F. Perrie."

Lieut. Fisher reported as follows :—

" On a signal being given from the 8-gun battery, No. 9, I observed the skirmishers moved to the front in open order, and almost simultaneously the assaulting column advanced from the right of our position. I immediately led the Sappers to the front, followed by the remainder of the column in due order under Lieut. Graves, R.E. I proceeded at a steady pace to allow time for the ladder party to cross the two old Russian trenches which were in our line of advance. We were exposed to a heavy fire of grape and musketry as we advanced.

" On arriving at the abattis I looked back to see how the ladder party were coming on. I could not see a single ladder, the men having abandoned them or (as I believe was very general) been shot down in advancing. I observed the whole party to be very much reduced. I endeavoured to rally the men, but being unable to get together a sufficient force to attempt an assault in the face of such fire as we were exposed to, I ordered the men to get under cover as fast as possible among the irregularities of ground and shell holes which existed close to the abattis, in the expectation of the supports which I hoped would advance to our relief. Here they were shot down by the Russian soldiers, who stood on the parapet of the Redan to fire, as well as by the grape which continued to sweep through our force. After waiting some time for the supports to come, in vain, I felt with such a handful of men any attempt to assault would be madness. Accordingly I endeavoured to find an officer senior to myself to recommend him to retire. Failing in this I took upon myself to order a retreat into our trenches, which was effected, but I fear our loss was very great. The abattis, though not very thick was almost entirely uninjured by our fire. It stood from 5 to 6 ft. high above the ground. There were small gaps and weak places where men could push through. I did not attempt to pull it away with the grapnels as I considered the fire too heavy to justify me in exposing men so prominently at so short a distance from the work, our fire being insufficient to keep the Russian soldiers off the parapet from which they were firing on us. I am of opinion that under a less severe fire it would be easy to break it up by means of axes and the iron grapnels. I am not aware that any of our men passed the abattis. I regret to state that Capt. Jesse, R.E., was shot through the head while speaking to me. Lieut. Graves is missing. He is supposed to have been killed under the abattis.'' (Then comes a list of N.C.O.'s and privates of R.S. & M. killed and wounded). " I must not conclude without bringing under your notice the very gallant conduct of Sergt. Fandry, R.S. & M., whose steadiness in the advance and exertions in cheering on the men were most praiseworthy.''

The Engineer casualties in this unfortunate business were Capt. Jesse, Lieuts. Murray and Graves, killed; Lieut.-Colonel Tylden, died of wounds ; Major-General Jones and Capt. Bourchier, wounded. The only success gained on the occasion was at the left attack where the cemetery at the head of the Dockyard Creek was captured, and a communication made from it to the advanced trenches. This was effected by the promptitude and zeal of Lieut. Donnelly, R.E.

On June 28th the army had to deplore the death of the Commander-in-Chief, Lord Raglan. He had been for some time in feeble health ; but there is no doubt that the recent disaster was the cause of his sudden collapse. He was succeeded by Lieut.-General Simpson, who for some months had acted as Chief of the Staff.

It was now determined to add greatly to our weight of metal, and no efforts were spared to establish fresh batteries, and to bring up the ammunition that so large an armament would require.

On August 16th the position on the Tchernaya, which was held by the French and Sardinian troops was attacked in force by the Russians. After a heavy battle the enemy were driven back with great loss.

On the following day the batteries opened a certain amount of fire, intended to prevent the garrison from annoying the advanced trenches, which were being steadily pushed nearer and nearer to them, especially in front of the Malakoff ; and this fire was maintained with more or less intensity until the beginning of September.

By this time the following additions had been made to the British attacks :—On the Left six new batteries had been constructed. In the Right Attack also, six new batteries were formed. Two new parallels, the 4th and the 5th, with their communications, had been established, and a trench was pushed out in front of the 5th Parallel, towards the salient of the Redan, reaching to within 190 yards of it.

The losses in the Royal Engineers had been very heavy. Lieut.-Colonel Tylden, Capts. Jesse and Dawson, Lieuts. Murray, Graves, and Lowry had all been killed. Major Montagu and Lieut. James had been taken prisoners but the former returned to duty having been exchanged early in August. Many other officers of the Corps had been invalided, of whom Capt. Belson and Lieut. Somerville had died at Scutari.

On September 3rd the chief Artillery and Engineer officers of the two armies were once more summoned to assemble. They gave in their joint opinion " that the siege works have arrived at such a point that the assault ought to be given to the place after a short delay." They observed that the French left attack on the town had been stationary for a long time, no further advance being practicable. The British advance on the Redan could also not be carried further. At the Malakoff the French artillery had obtained a marked superiority, and in consequence the approaches were within 25 metres of the *enceinte*. Although it might be possible to push farther forward, and blow in the counterscarp, they thought the delay to enable this to be done would be prejudicial. The French extreme right attack in front of the Careening Bay (or little Redan) was also within 25 metres of the place, and could approach no nearer owing to the rocky soil. Under these circumstances " the moment to give the assault has arrived." It was decided that the principal attack should be on the Malakoff and little Redan.

" If we succeed in seizing and lodging ourselves securely in these works, the fall of the Karabelnaia suburb becomes inevitable."

It being decided that these were to be the main attacks, it was considered necessary to distract the garrison by subsidiary assaults.

" For this purpose, as soon as the success of the Malakoff front shall appear certain, the English at a concerted signal should give the assault to the Redan, and the French would at the same time advance on the enceinte of the town."

This project was approved, and on September 5th the bombard-ment became general, every gun that could be brought into play having opened on that morning. The British batteries consisted of 202 guns and mortars, and the French of 627. The calibre of the British guns was, however, in many cases superior to that of their allies. By these figures it will be seen that the weight of bombard-ment was of a most stupendous character, far exceeding what had ever before been brought into play on a similar occasion.

On September 6th the orders were issued for the British assault on the Redan. The assault was ordered for 12 noon on September 8th. Punctually at that hour the French columns rushed from their trenches, and the Malakoff was in their possession in a few moments. As soon as the tricolour was hoisted on the parapet as a token of capture, the signal was given for the British advance on the Redan. The story of this attempt and failure is best told in the words of the two principal Engineer actors, Capt. Montagu, attached to the General leading the column, and Lieut. Ranken, who had charge of the ladder party. The report of the former ran thus :—

" Upon the signal being shown that the French were in possession of the Malakoff Tower, the order was given for the troops to get ready. Such, however, was the excitement of the moment, that 100 men or more mistook the order, and went over the parapet before it was possible to stop them, and it was found necessary to let them all go, although by doing so the ladder party under Lieut. Ranken had not sufficient time to get all the ladders on the move and placed before the assaulting party arrived, they having less difficulty in passing the abattis, the passing of which, however, did not prove any serious obstacle. The first parties formed and moved off very well, but after that the showers of grape and rifle balls, etc., upon the succeeding parties sent from the flank of the Redan and Garden Batteries caused the men to run to the head of the single sap, from whence, after a short halt to take breath, they made another rush towards the salient angle, but by this means they were no longer in regular formation. All the men crowded on the salient angle so as to be out of the way of the flanking fire. To prevent this first check, I obtained permission from the General to allow the men pressing up from the left of the 5th Parallel to go up the single sap and start from the head of it. After about two hours' heavy firing the men all returned to the 5th Parallel, and no further attempt was made during the afternoon. General

Wyndham, who was in charge of the assaulting column, informed me that he had been inside the Redan with some 60 or 80 men who got behind a traverse and could not be induced to go further.   .   . I have great pleasure in informing you that Lieut. Ranken performed his very dangerous service to my great satisfaction, placing the ladders very judiciously, and he afterwards succeeded in making the descent and ascent such that the troops experienced no difficulty in getting up without ladders, and he has expressed himself perfectly satisfied with the conduct of the sappers under his charge.   I regret to say that Capt. Sedley, R.E., who was in charge of the working party to form the lodgments, was wounded, also Lieut. Elphinstone, R.E., who was on duty in the trenches ; and of the sappers two were killed, and eleven wounded."

General Jones, who was at the time too ill to move, insisted on being present.   He was carried down into the trenches in a litter, and remained with General Simpson throughout the attack.

In addition to the casualties among the Royal Engineers, Major Chapman, 20th Regiment, Assistant Engineer, was mortally wounded and died on September 20th.

This was the last operation of the siege.   The French had made good their grip on the Mamelon in spite of the most furious attempts of the Russians to secure that vital point.

There is no doubt that the British storm of the Redan, unsuccessful as it was, enabled their Allies to secure themselves within their prize.   For two most critical hours the enemy were compelled to divide their forces, and to devote a large portion of them to the retention of the Redan.   During those two hours the French were able to block up all the rear openings by which access was obtained to the Malakoff from the interior, and at the same time create a communication with the trenches.   A flying sap was established to the crest of the counterscarp, and a bridge of planks thrown over the ditch.   The troops were therefore poured into the work rapidly and without confusion or exposure.   Unquestionably this operation was much aided by the distraction caused by the other attacks, although they all failed.   Most fortunately, the one point that was secured was the key of the position.   The Russians were well aware of that fact, and shortly after darkness set in they began that masterly retreat to the north side which reflects so much credit on those who planned it, and also on those who so steadily and quietly carried it out.   Before midnight the first of the explosions took place, by which the magnificent forts erected at such cost to protect the harbour, were being destroyed by their own constructors, and a constant stream of men was observed to be passing across the bridge that led from the south to the north side of the town.

At the end of two days the British entered the place and occupied the Karabelnaia suburb, the French being posted in the town. A mixed commission was formed, composed of officers of both armies, to take an inventory of all ordnance and military stores that were found in the fortress, in order that an equitable division might be made between the two armies. Twelve British members sat on this commission.

The number of Engineer officers who from first to last took part in the Crimean War was sixty-nine. Of these thirteen were killed, six died of disease or accident, thirteen were wounded, and twelve invalided. Of the nineteen Assistant Engineers, two were killed, and five wounded. Of non-commissioned officers and privates of Engineers who landed in the Crimea, fifty were killed, ninety-two wounded, and sixty died of disease.

The following are approximately the numbers of the principal engineering materials used at the siege :—Common gabions, 17,015 ; iron gabions, 2,307 (these were made of the strap iron by which the compressed hay trusses were bound) ; fascines, 2,780 ; sandbags, 336,345 ; bread bags, 7,413 ; hide bags, 40.

The main object of the Siege of Sebastopol having been the destruction of the Russian fleet and the magnificent docks that had been constructed for its maintenance, the place had no sooner fallen into the possession of the Allies than orders were given to prepare a project for the demolition of the docks.

The docks were demolished by means of a series of three lines of mines, one under the centre of the floor, and the other two behind the revetments of the side walls, continued so as to meet round the semi-circular end. For the three docks there were 134 such mines, and 22 additional ones for the half of the basin that fell to the British share. As soon as this operation had been carried out the destruction of what was known as the White Buildings, an extensive range of barracks, was undertaken. The officers employed in this work, under Lieut.-Colonel Lloyd, were Major Ranken, and Lieuts. C. G. Gordon and G. Graham.* The demolition of the buildings was satisfactorily effected with one sad casualty. Major Ranken himself undertook to fire the form of four charges in the gable of one of the buildings at 5 p.m. This was to be done by means of a 3-ft. length of fuze. Unfortunately some loose powder became ignited, and exploded the four mines before Major Ranken could escape. His body was not found until the next morning when it was extricated from the ruins in a very mangled and crushed condition. This was the last British life lost in the war, and the sadness of the accident was accentuated by the fact that he had led the storming party on September 8th with the most dashing gallantry, and had escaped unhurt.

* Afterwards Lieut.-General Sir Gerald Graham, v.c., g.c.b.

CHAPTER THIRTEEN

THE SIEGE OF DELHI.

June—September, 1857.

In the early months of 1857, signs of unrest began to be prevalent among the native regiments of the Bengal Army, but it was not until May that the outbreak of the Indian Mutiny actually burst forth in all its violence.

At the large military cantonment of Meerut, the headquarters of the Meerut Division, 89 men of the Third Bengal Cavalry had been tried by court-martial for refusing to use the cartridges issued from the arsenals, which they declared to be made with lard or pig's fat, thus destroying their caste and religion. They were sentenced to long periods of imprisonment, and heavily manacled, were removed to the military jail. On Sunday, May 11th, the native troops at Meerut broke into open mutiny, setting fire to the bungalows, releasing the prisoners, and murdering their officers, and any unfortunate Europeans whom they happened to meet. After committing these outrages they made off to Delhi and were not pursued.

On arrival at Delhi, being joined by the inhabitants of the city, they proclaimed the old pensioned King of Delhi as Emperor of India and committed similar massacres to those at Meerut, shooting down the English officers of the native regiments and murdering the Europeans. A force under the command of Brig.-General Wilson—afterwards Sir Archdale Wilson, G.C.B., marched out of Meerut on the 27th May and completely defeated the rebels with great losses on the Hindun River, capturing all their guns. After the junction of this force with that under the Commander-in-Chief, General Sir W. Anson, which had marched from Umballa, the combined forces under Major-General Sir H. Barnard (General Anson having died of cholera at Kurnul) marched towards Delhi and defeated the rebels who had taken up a strong position at Badle-ka-Serai on the Grand Trunk Road about 4 miles from the city.

The result of the successful action on the 8th June, 1857, at Badle-ka-Serai was to give to the field force under the command of Major-General Sir Henry Barnard complete possession of the low ridge of hills to the westward of the city. The highest parts of the ridge rise to a height of about 50 to 60 ft. above the general level of the interior of the city, while the average command may be taken for practical purposes at about 40 ft. The greatest length of the ridge occupied at any time during the preliminary operations was a little more than 2 miles, and of this position the extreme left was so far retired from the place as to be in no serious danger at any time, while the right invited attack from the moment of occupation to the close of the operations.

Along the crest of the ridge, posts of considerable strength existed. They were formed either of ancient or modern buildings of good materials and substantial construction. Of these the group on the extreme right, distinguished during the progress of the siege as Hindoo Rao's house, was at once the most important and most exposed. The Mahratta Prince by whom it was built had occupied it for many years, regarding it as his home, and had surrounded the principal house with many inferior offices, all of which were capable of supplying shelter to men and cattle, though not by any means shotproof.

Hindoo Rao having died some time before the mutiny broke out, the place was unoccupied. About 180 yards to the left of Hindoo Rao's house stands the Observatory, an ancient structure suited to the purposes of Hindoo astronomy, built by the Rajpoot astronomer, Rajah Jai Singh. It is of irregular form, dark and ill-ventilated, but as a support to Hindoo Rao's house was found very useful, and was permanently occupied during the siege. About 650 yards further to the left there was an abandoned mosque of the oldest Pathan type in a somewhat ruinous condition, but still affording accommodation for an outpost of respectable strength. This also was suited for a permanent position.

At the distance of nearly a mile from Hindoo Rao's house stands the Flagstaff Tower, a double-storied circular building of Gothic design, which commands an excellent view of the ground lying between the city and the ridge. This building offered sufficient means of shelter to make it useful as a post. Other posts were decided upon from time to time during the siege. On driving the enemy from every point of the ridge on the 8th June, Sir Henry Barnard occupied at once, in strength, the four points just alluded to. He established the headquarters of the Sirmoor Battalion, 2nd Goorkhas, under Major Charles Reid, in Hindoo Rao's house, and there this distinguished corps remained unrelieved from the first day of the siege to the last. Each of the picquets mentioned was supported by two field guns.

The headquarter camp was established on the plains to the westward of the ridge, and occupied the old parade ground of the

Delhi Cantonment. Immediately in rear of the camp there runs a broad, rapid stream, being a drainage channel from the Nujufghur Jheel to the river Jumna, and along the right flank, at a distance of about a mile, flows the Western Jumna Canal, which, crossing the ridge by a bold cutting through the solid rock executed in the time of the Emperor Shah Jehan, passed through the suburbs of Kissengunge, and enters the city through a culvert in the wall near the Lahore Gate, and traversing the entire breadth of the city, falls into the river Jumna close to the Begumabad Gateway.

Three main lines of road only were immediately connected with the operations before Delhi. The first and most important was the Grand Trunk Road, by which communication was maintained with the Punjab, and along which all reinforcements and supplies were necessarily brought from the country lying to the rear of the force, on the resources of which it was mainly dependent. The second was merely a branch of the first, connecting the camp with the Grand Trunk line at about $1\frac{1}{2}$ miles to the rear.

It formed the old cantonment road to the city, crossing the Nujufghur Drain by a substantial bridge, damaged, but not destroyed, by the enemy during his retreat from the field at Badle-ka-Serai on the 8th June. The third was the line of road connecting Delhi with Rohtuk, Hissar, and other places to the south-westward, along which the enemy drew a considerable portion of his supplies. All the other roads centring at Delhi were completely commanded by the enemy, and it was only by long and precarious détours that any communication was maintained with the districts to the eastward or southward.

The ground around Delhi which was traversed by these canals and roads was, at the time of the siege, a tangled mass of old ruins, dense woodland, rice fields, and swamps of notorious insalubrity. It offered innumerable facilities for occupation by armed men of any degree of discipline, and, indeed, so incompatible were its features with the action of a mass of disciplined troops, that the many combats of which it was the scene were rather trials of skill between small bodies than operation by masses.

At the beginning of the siege the ordnance available for operation consisted of :—

24-pounders	..	..	..	2
18-pounders	..	..	..	9
8-in. howitzers	..	..	..	4
6-in. mortars	..	..	..	6
Total	..	..	..	21
$5\frac{1}{2}$-in. Coëhorns	..	..	..	12
Grand total ..	..	..		33

Many fluctuations in the strength of the force occurred and it is of little practical use attempting to give the precise numbers, but from 500 to 600 sabres, from 2,500 to 3,000 bayonets, and 22 field guns, may be taken as fairly representing the strength during the earlier operations. It is, of course, also extremely difficult to form any accurate estimate of the strength of the enemy, but as some of the most important accessions which he received did not occur until the siege had been for some time in progress, it may be inferred that on the 8th June the garrison of the place did not exceed 8,000 or 9,000 disciplined soldiers, supported by probably about the same number of half-disciplined and wholly undisciplined though armed men. For operations in the open field the sole strength of the garrison was in the trained soldiers, but for the operations in the rugged ground around Delhi, resolute men, familiar with their weapons and profiting by the universal cover everywhere supplied in some house or other, were antagonists whom it was necessary to respect.

In all the important materials and munitions of war the command of the arsenal in Delhi made the resources of the enemy, practically speaking, unlimited. Food was drawn with unrestricted freedom from the whole of the open districts to the east, south, and south-west, and there is no reason to suppose that money was deficient. With all the primary elements of a successful and vigorous defence the enemy was, therefore, abundantly provided.

The permanent posts for the ridge had scarcely been occupied on the 8th June when the enemy, rallied with such reinforcements as the garrison could supply, attacked the position on its whole length, but were immediately driven back on the picquets being reinforced. The most notable point in connection with this attack was the vigorous support it received from the fire of the heavy guns on the Moree and Cashmere Bastions, and the first engineer operations resolved on were directed against the former of these works.

It was determined by the Chief Engineer, in communication with the brigadier commanding the Artillery, to commence on the night of the 8th—9th June two batteries in the neighbourhood of Hindoo Rao's house for two guns each. These were designated Salkeld's and Wilson's Batteries. The armament of each was an 18-pounder and an 8-in. howitzer, and it was supposed that the fire of these four pieces would suffice to subdue, if not to silence, the guns on the Moree and Cashmere Bastions. The range to the Moree Bastion was about 1,500 yards ; to the Cashmere Bastion 2,100 yards, and to the Martello Tower, between these two main works, from which occasional support was given to them, about 1,830 yards. Several casualties occurred from round shot. The enemy again attacked on the right flank in great force, but were beaten back with heavy loss.

By the morning of the 9th June Salkeld's Battery was completed, armed, and opened fire on the Moree Bastion, and by noon of the same day Wilson's Battery was also completed, its howitzer being directed on the Cashmere Bastion, and its 18-pounder on the Martello Tower, where the enemy had placed a gun *en barbette*.

Heavy fire continued uninterruptedly on both sides, and it very soon became apparent that the enemy held a decided superiority. The fire of the four guns in Salkeld's and Wilson's Batteries produced no apparent effect on any of the enemy's works ; casualties became serious, and it was clear that if any result was to be produced it was essential that the strength of the batteries on the ridge must be increased. Accordingly, Maunsell's mortar battery* (two mortars) was commenced, and an additional gun portion was added to Salkeld's, Wilson's, and Maunsell's Batteries respectively. While these works were in progress the enemy attacked the right of the position with great vigour, but was repulsed, and on the 11th the whole of the guns, aided by the mortars, opened fire.

The effect of the increased fire from the ridge batteries was so far satisfactory that the enemy's fire was somewhat subdued, but the general result was not encouraging. The enemy still maintained a most effective fire action, and having a vast reserve store of heavy guns, he was more reckless in his method of firing, and took much more out of his guns than the British could venture to do with their scanty supply of pieces of large calibre, the disabling of even one of which was a great misfortune. Hence no real progress had been made.

On the morning of the 12th another resolute attack on the whole position was made by the enemy. It was carried out with unusual determination, and had partial success, a picquet at the Flagstaff post having been cut off, and the two guns there being nearly captured. Ultimately, however, the enemy was driven back at all points with loss. The weakness of the left centre of the position was, however, made so apparent by the partial success of the enemy's first attack that means of strengthening it were essential. Between the ridge and the river in front of the part of the position now under notice lies a low, flat piece of ground traversed by the main road from the cantonment to the city, and on the eastward of this road is Metcalfe's house, a large building which had been sacked and partially destroyed during the outbreak on the 11th and 12th May ; about 200 yards to the right of the house there was a substantial masonry building formerly used as a cow-house, while about 400 yards further in advance, or nearer to the place, there was at that time, a large roomy row of stables. The stables and cow-house were occupied on the evening of the 12th June by strong infantry

* Named after Capt. Maunsell, afterwards General Sir Frederick Maunsell, k.c.b., R.E.

picquets, supported by a troop of cavalry at first, and afterwards by some field guns stationed on a high artificial mound, probably an old brick kiln, near the dwelling house. Considerable variations in details for the tenure of this advanced position subsequently occurred, but throughout the whole of the preliminary operations the stable and cow-house picquets were regularly maintained and proved of great value in protecting the left and left centre of the main line of picquets on the ridge. The distance of the stable picquet from the Water Bastion was about 1,300 yards, and from the centre of the British camp about 2,830 yards, or rather more than 1½ miles.

On the night of the 11th—12th June a new mortar battery, called Perkins' Battery, named after Lieut. Perkins (afterwards General Sir Æneas Perkins, K.C.B., R.E.), was commenced, and during the action of the 12th a working party of 60 Sappers, under Lieut. Geneste,* employed at the time on the batteries, made a very gallant attack on a large body of the enemy, beat them back from the position, and killed a considerable number of them. The casualties among the sappers were three men wounded.

On the 13th the new mortar battery, having been armed during the previous night with two guns, opened fire. The enemy was found to have erected substantial earthen works on the Cashmere and Moree Bastions for the protection of the guns placed there *en barbette*, and the firing during the day was not vigorous. An attack was, however, again made on the right of our position, but was repulsed without difficulty, although supported by a very heavy fire from the whole of the batteries of the place. In the course of this attack the enemy made one very dangerous movement of advancing from Kissengunge with field guns up to the crest of the ridge on the extreme right, and from thence enfilading the entire line of the British batteries. The movement, however, was not persisted in, but it was plain that the enemy had observed a very weak point in the position, and was likely to renew his attempt upon it.

On the night of the 15th—16th June a trench of communication was made between Salkeld's and Wilson's Batteries, revetted inside with stones ; the soil being very rocky, the work was one of great difficulty, and proceeded slowly. The enemy was very quiet all night and day, and no attack was made on the position.

It was observed, on the 17th, that the enemy had commenced work on a battery in the suburbs of Pahareepore, and although the mortar practice from the batteries on the ridge was excellent, progress was not stopped. It being of the greatest importance that no permanent lodgment should be permitted on a site where guns

* Lieut. Geneste died very soon after the siege from the result of the exposure he had undergone.

would take all the ridge batteries in reverse with disastrous effect, Sir Henry Barnard determined on an attack in order to clear the suburb. This duty was effected with characteristic brilliancy by Major Charles Reid* and Major Henry Tombs† with the small columns under their respective commands, supported by four guns. The enemy's battery was captured and entirely destroyed, some loss was inflicted, and the only gun he had brought out from the place was taken.

The great danger of leaving the extreme right of the position unprovided with permanent means of defence now became apparent, and accordingly, on the night of the 17th, a new 3-gun battery, called Johnson's Battery, was traced out on the rocky plateau, about 300 yards to the right of Hindoo Rao's house. Not a spadeful of earth was locally available for the construction of the battery, the soil being bare rock. Material had, therefore, to be brought from the low ground in rear of the ridge, and the progress of the work was accordingly slow. In the morning the enemy kept up such a constant hot fire, that during the remainder of the day progress was virtually suspended. On the night of the 18th—19th it was resumed as vigorously as circumstances permitted, and by the morning of the 19th the parapet of the battery and epaulments was raised to a height of 5 ft. on the left and 6 ft. on the right. The rocky terreplein was raised by aid of the jumper ; and platform space for two guns secured. But more could not be done by daylight as the enemy's fire was incessant and heavy, causing some casualties among the working parties. By incessant labour on the part of the sappers and pioneers employed, the battery was at last completed, and mounted with three guns by the 22nd June. But while this work was in progress on the extreme right front of the position, movements of most critical importance were taking place on the right flank and rear. The garrison having been powerfully reinforced about this time by the junction of the Nusseerabad Brigade, a general attack on the British position seems to have been resolved on.

The various outlook posts reported on the afternoon of the 19th that masses of infantry, supported by artillery and cavalry, were steadily defiling through the Lahore and Ajmeer Gates, and gradually extending through all the strong ground in front and on the right flank of the position. About an hour before sunset the high ground immediately in rear of the camp was seen to be occupied by a powerful detachment of the enemy, strongly posted in the gardens and among the ruined walls thickly strewed over the neighbourhood. The crisis was very grave, for the enemy immediately attacked the camp from this position, directing a vigorous fire of artillery upon

* Afterwards General Sir Charles Reid, G.C.B.
† Afterwards Lieut.-General Sir Henry Tombs, K.C.B.

it, while so general was the threatening aspect of affairs on the front and flanks that only a very feeble fire could be spared to meet this most dangerous movement.

The cavalry and field artillery, however, under Brigadier Hope Grant, after a severe engagement, checked the advance of the enemy for that night, and on the morning of the 20th he was found to have retired from the ground. His retirement was, however, merely momentary, and the position being reoccupied almost before the troops reached camp, it was necessary to repeat the attack. A vigorous fight ensued, ending in the complete rout of the enemy, but with heavy loss in officers and men to the column engaged, which had about one-third of its number killed or wounded out of 600 strong of all arms. The result was, however, so far decisive that no attempt was again made by the enemy to operate on the camp itself from the rear, and the construction of a strong breast-work and battery for two 24-pounders added still further to the security of this part of the position. During the fighting, on the 19th Major Yule, of the 9th Lancers, was killed ; Daly (afterwards General Sir Henry Daly, G.C.B.), of the Guides, and Becher (afterwards General Sir Arthur Becher, G.C.B.), Quartermaster-General, were wounded.

On the night of the 23rd a working party, under Capt. Maunsell, accompanied by Lieut. Jones,* of the Engineers, destroyed the only other bridges across the drain in the immediate vicinity of Delhi. Both bridges were completely demolished, and, as it instantly appeared, with excellent results, as the engineer detachment had scarcely left the ground when a strong party of the enemy, with artillery, occupied it in preparation for a general attack on the British position. On the 24th it was found impossible for him, however, to transport his guns across the broad, deep, and rapid stream which had unexpectedly interposed, and it followed that during the vigorous assault of the 24th that the rear of the camp was not threatened as before. The whole of the right of the position was, however, enveloped by the enemy's attack on that day. The suburb of Subsee-Mundee was occupied by him in force, and held with much tenacity. Johnson's Battery was attacked, and from Pahareepore the works near Hindoo Rao's house were taken in flank by a battery of field guns, and some loss inflicted on the troops occupying them.

But the result of the fight was, as it had ever been, the defeat of the enemy at all points, heavy loss being inflicted on him while he retired sullenly into the city. Subsee-Mundee was subsequently held in strength by a regiment of Europeans ; a large serai, or travellers' resting place, and a Hindoo temple being prepared for occupation by the troops, and fortified as efficiently as means would

* Killed during the siege.

permit. Considerable clearances of old ruins and jungle were effected in the vicinity of this post, and its maintenance in support of the advanced battery on the ridge was found to be of much use.

In the many attacks of the enemy on the position, the detachments of artillery with the light guns at Hindoo Rao's house suffered seriously, and cover was accordingly provided for them in a new battery marked " Champain's." * This work was rather of the nature of a breastwork than a regular field battery, the object being to cover the men as much as possible without excessively restricting the sweep of the guns. A similar covering breastwork was provided for the guns at the Mosque, with great labour and difficulty, however, owing to the scarcity of materials. Reports having been received of the intentions of the commander of the garrison to convert the dry ditch of the fort into a wet one by turning into it the waters of the West Jumna Canal, it was determined to cut off the supply at the ancient aqueduct before mentioned. This was done in the first instance by a party of sappers, under Lieut. Champain, who cut through the bank of the canal above the aqueduct, and this turned the whole stream into the Nujufgurh Jheel Drain. Subsequently the partial demolition of the aqueduct was effected by powder, and the passage of the canal permanently interrupted. From the 28th June, accordingly, no water entered the city through the canal channel, but no practical inconvenience was thereby caused to the garrison, as they had complete command of the river Jumna. The fact is noteworthy, as very erroneous conceptions on this, as on many other points, prevailed in England at the time and since.

On the 28th June the Engineer Brigade was strengthened by the arrival of Capt. Alexander Taylor (afterwards General Sir Alexander Taylor, G.C.B., and W. W. Greathed (afterwards Major-General and C.B.), who had up to that time been acting as extra Aide-de-Camp to the Major-General commanding. Capt. Taylor relieved Major Laughton on the 29th.

During the first three weeks of the siege the Delhi Field Force was engaged in repelling the enemy's sorties. There were usually three or four sorties in each week, and some of these were on a very large scale. Large bodies of the rebels (cavalry, artillery, and infantry) could be seen issuing from the Lahore Gate. The general plan of the sorties was to turn our right flank by a large force, and to penetrate into our camp, while smaller numbers advanced under cover of the rocks and bushes for a direct attack on the ridge. In crossing the road leading from the Lahore Gate to the Subsee-Mundee the cavalry and artillery came under the view of our right battery, which poured a heavy fire into the enemy's troops. Those that

* Named after Lieut. Champain, Bengal Engineers (afterwards Colonel Sir John Champain, K.C.M.G., who died in 1887).

escaped this ordeal apparently swerved to their left, and returned in a disorganized state by the Kabul Gate or by some of the other gates. The repelling of these sorties sometimes occupied several hours. The enemy also made night attacks on our position, and a continual roll of musketry would be kept up for hours. There was a small post among the rocks on the right hand of this position called the Sammy House, and the corpses of the mutineers after one of these attacks were piled in heaps, there being no men available to bury them. How great was the disparity of numbers may be conjectured from the fact that on our arrival on the Delhi Ridge on the 8th June, the Delhi Field Force did not muster more than 3,800 men, and on the day of assault, on the 14th September, were only about 14,000. The number of revolted Sepoys and men in the city varied during the siege from 12,000 to 35,000, in addition to the armed inhabitants. Scarcely a house in the old cantonment was left untouched by the rebels. At this time about 20 native regiments of the Bengal Native Army had mutinied, and accounts were received daily of the mutiny of some regiment.

On the 18th June the rebels were reinforced by the brigade from Nusseerabad, which had joined the mutiny, bringing six guns with them. To celebrate the event, they came out in force, and made an attack on our rear. The contest was most desperate, and the loss on both sides was great. Major Yule, of the 9th Lancers, was killed; Daly of the Guides, and Becher the Quartermaster-General, were wounded.

The Commissioner of Delhi, Sir Theophilus Metcalfe, was in camp at this time. His house, as before mentioned, which had been completely gutted by the rebels, was occupied by our picquets. The mutineers used our bugle calls, and frequently came out to fight wearing their red coats. The buttons on the uniforms of the corpses bore the numbers of the regiments that had mutinied. The work of the artillery in the batteries at this time was most arduous. The most dangerous part was getting into the batteries, as the enemy had constructed a battery on the right of our position, at a place called the Eed Gurh, from which their shot enfiladed the ridge, the shot and shell crashing along the ridge, and striking down anyone who happened to be exposed. One shot fired from this battery entered the doorway of Hindoo Rao's house and killed an officer, Lieut. Wheatley, and eight men of the 2nd Goorkha Regiment, and wounded seven men. After this a large earthen traverse was thrown up in front of the doorway, which prevented the shot from entering the building. The Goorkha Regiment (Sirmoor Battalion) made use of the upper storey of Hindoo Rao's house as a hospital.

At this time news was received of the revolt of the whole of the Province of Oudh and of the Gwalior contingent. The enemy received reinforcements almost daily. The strains of the bands of the mutineer regiments could be heard as they marched into the city across the bridge of boats. They played "Cheer, boys, cheer," and other English tunes. However, we also received some welcome reinforcements. A battalion of the 8th King's, a detachment of the 61st Regiment, and two regiments of Sikhs marched into camp at this period.

Lieut.-Colonel Baird Smith took command of the Engineer Brigade on the 3rd July, having travelled about 75 miles the previous day by such aid as he was able to procure, in the hope of being present at an assault of the place planned for the morning of the 3rd. On reaching camp, however, at about 2 a.m., the Chief Engineer learnt that the project, like others of the same kind previously entertained, had been abandoned. He also learnt that the enemy was threatening in force the road from Badle-ka-Serai. On the same day, a strong column, under Major Coke (afterwards Major-General Sir John Coke, K.C.B.), was directed to proceed to Alipore, a point on the line of communication with the Punjab, where the enemy had established himself, having turned the position of the English force by a movement past its right flank on the 3rd of July. Happily, however, he withdrew, abandoning the advantages of his position, after inflicting some loss on the Commissariat post at Alipore.

After carefully inspecting the ground, and becoming acquainted with the details of the position occupied by the force, its capabilities, resources, and future prospects, the Chief Engineer arrived at the following conclusions :—As regarded the plan of defence adopted by the enemy, it was quite clear that two leading ideas pervaded it ; first, to drive Sir Henry Barnard from his advanced position on the heights by incessant attacks on the position itself ; and secondly, to force him to abandon that position by operations on his line of communications with the Punjab.

Of these two ideas, the enemy held the first with perfect clearness, and acted on it with an unswerving tenacity of purpose, which repeated defeats could scarcely shake. The second was neither apprehended distinctly, appreciated properly, or acted on vigorously by him. It is scarcely necessary to add that this want of discrimination influenced most gravely the fortune of the siege.

The garrison by the beginning of July must have consisted of not less than from 15,000 to 18,000 trained soldiers, and irregulars in even larger numbers. The besieging force numbered of all arms under 5,500 fighting men, Europeans and natives. An enterprising enemy might, therefore, with perfect ease, have maintained one or more strong movable columns, operating constantly on the communication, stopping convoys, harassing small detachments, disturbing the whole tract of country whence supplies were obtained, and finally, in all human probability, compelling the General to raise the siege from the impossibility of procuring subsistence for his army in a position so utterly insecure. Instead, however, of obstinate and continuous operations of this class, the enemy was satisfied to make feeble efforts, never sustained for any considerable time, and easily warded off by corresponding movements of columns detached from the force. It was necessary, however, at the time now under notice, to take precautions against both forms of attack. The vast numerical superiority of the enemy converted the position of Sir Henry Barnard's force from the very first into that of a besieged, instead of a besieging, army.

Commencing on the 8th June, the attacks by the garrison on all points of the ground held outside the walls were incessant. The casualties of the force day by day were most serious. Many of its bravest and best officers had been killed or severely wounded ; the daily average of casualties among the soldiers averaged from 30 to 40, and on occasions of vigorous combats the loss rose from 100 to 150. It was scarcely possible to resist the conviction that the army was steadily and surely being used up by the ordinary process of the siege, and it seemed as though a simple calculation would show that at such a rate of waste of life the status of a force numerically so feeble could not be sustained for long. To shorten the siege, or limit the waste of life, were the urgent necessities of the position. The former could be effected only in one of two ways, the first by regular operations against the place, or second by an assault *de vive force*. The insufficiency of artillery and engineer *matériel* for even the most limited formal operation made the first plan wholly impracticable. An official return supplied to the Chief Engineer on the 4th July showed that in the Artillery Park the entire ordnance supplies of the force were :—

Round shot, 24-pounders	150
,, ,, 18-pounders	628
Shells, common, 8-in.	2,016
,, spherical, 8-in.	192
,, common, 24-pounders	240
,, spherical, 24-pounders	43
,, 5$\frac{1}{2}$-in., 24-pounders	3,200

These details tell their own tale, and require no emphasis.

The whole supply of ordnance powder for 17 siege pieces in position was no more than 11,600 lbs., barely sufficient for one day's active firing, and even the musketry powder had sunk to 12,900 lbs. The Engineer Park was quite as insufficiently supplied for even the briefest formal operations. It is questionable whether batteries could have been maintained, even if their first construction had been practicable, as revetting materials were in extremely small numbers. Hence there was no hesitation whatever in abandoning all idea of operations of this class.

The second course, viz., an assault *de vive force*, was plainly a most desperate expedient in the actual condition of the force at the moment. It could only have been justified by assurances of the highest authority that the critical emergency of political circumstances had been such that all risks must be run to achieve a success.

The possibilities of success were sufficient to have warranted the General in making an attack even so desperate as that on Delhi would have been. The Chief Engineer came to this conclusion at the time, and adhered to it until circumstances to be explained hereafter had completely changed.

Assuming, however, that an assault involving such undeniable risks might be deferred, systematic provision for reducing the waste of life on the ridge was of the most urgent necessity, and though the means were small, both in men and material, it was absolutely necessary that they should be used and multiplied if the position were to be maintained for even a day.

On the morning of the 5th July, Sir Henry Barnard received the Chief Engineer at a confidential interview, which lasted about three hours.

The General in command explained to the Chief Engineer in most unreserved terms his views of the position of the force, and at first, especially, was evidently and most justly impressed with the deepest anxiety for its safety, and felt acutely the heavy weight of personal responsibility that must attach to his decisions. The general conclusions to which the Chief Engineer had come, as briefly detailed above, were duly submitted to the General, and were fully discussed. Reserving his final decision, however, at the moment, he appointed a second meeting at noon of the same day, when he expected to be prepared to give definite orders.

There were no external signs of fatal sickness at that time apparent about Sir H. Barnard. A worn and anxious expression of face, with a certain heaviness and dimness of eye, not at all natural to him, were the only signs of suffering that attracted the Chief Engineer's notice. And even these passed away as the discussion advanced, till the general cheerfulness of bearing under all difficulties, which did so much to win for him the warm affection of the whole force he commanded, resumed its usual glow, and the Chief Engineer left Sir Henry Barnard at the close of the interview as resolute for the present, and as hopeful for the future as ever. Scarcely an hour or two passed before the General was stricken with an attack of cholera, and on the Chief Engineer's return to headquarters at about 11 a.m. he was met by the medical attendants with the assurance that Sir Henry could now see no one, and that the worst was to be feared as to the issue of the disease. The anticipation was realized the same afternoon, and it was with the truest sorrow that the army learnt of the loss it had sustained in the premature death of a chief admired by all for his undaunted courage, his unwearying activity, his single-hearted devotion to duty, and beloved by all for his thoughtful care, courteous bearing, generous appreciation of the efforts of his officers and men, and the general spirit he diffused around him. No one can make the conduct of Sir Henry Barnard during that terrible month of June, 1857, a careful study without feeling that few soldiers have ever faced sterner perils with a stouter heart, and none have surpassed him in devotion to the Crown, or in the resolute discharge of duty under physical and moral conditions, so exhausting that life sunk beneath their pressure. On the death of Sir Henry Barnard, Major-General Reed, c.b., assumed the command of the Delhi Field Force.

CHAPTER FOURTEEN

The Siege of Delhi (*continued*).

The Major-General having communicated to the Chief Engineer his opinion that an assault *de vive force* was not expedient, attention was sedulously given to strengthening the position on the ridge, providing cover for the troops, clearing jungle and brushwood on the slopes, so as to diminish as much as possible the cover for the enemy, and finally to the security of the communications, by the demolition of all the bridges by which the enemy could cross the western Jumna Canal or Nujufghur Jheel Drainage Cut with his artillery.

On the 7th July a detachment of sappers and pioneers destroyed the Shalimar and Badlee Bridges, as well as a third bridge. These bridges had all superstructures of wood on masonry abutments and piers, and the demolitions were effected by the use of small charges sufficient to clear away the masonry retaining the girders, and by the subsequent removal of the latter and the roadway resting on them. The beams were required for use in the Engineer Park, and it was important to save them. On the 8th, the Busaye Bridge, the only remaining work of the kind on the drainage channel within moderate distance of the city, was also destroyed. On the 9th, the remaining bridges between the camp and Alipore were dismantled. On the same day, the Poolchuddun Aqueduct, of which the demolition had previously been only partial, was completely destroyed.

As part of a concerted scheme, apparently, a detachment of the enemy's cavalry charged into the camp on the 9th, and after causing considerable confusion and some loss was repulsed with heavy slaughter. A general attack was also made on the position under cover of a very hot fire from the place. A strong column under Brig.-General Chamberlain advanced through the suburbs, clearing them of the enemy, and driving him into the city. It suffered most severely however, the loss on this day being 228 in killed and wounded, considerably heavier than any other action in which the force had previously been engaged.

The Engineer Brigade was, however, happily strengthened the same day by the arrival of 300 Punjab sappers armed, under the command of Lieut. Gulliver, and 600 pioneers unarmed, under Lieut. H. A. Brownlow. The latter had been formed by the Chief Engineer, on receiving orders to take command of the brigade, by volunteers taken from the workmen employed on the Ganges Canal at Roorkee. Strange to say, these men, who were at once transferred from the peaceful tasks of day labourers to the most dangerous duties of working parties in siege operations, never exhibited a symptom of fear, but worked under the hottest fire like veterans, and were invaluable. The casualties among them were inevitably very numerous, but no instance occurred of their having hesitated to obey any order, whatever its consequences might have been. Lieut. Brownlow brought with him under their escort a large supply of stores of various kinds for the Engineer Park, drawn from the workshops of the Canal Department.

Between the 10th and 14th July active work was carried on in strengthening the right flank of the position. Early in the siege, a lofty mound, evidently a disused brick kiln, had been taken possession of, its crest roughly formed into a battery for three heavy guns, and an approach of easy slope cut along its face. It was called " The General's Mound," from having been a favourite position of Sir Henry Barnard during the many fights of which he was an eye-witness. It was between this mound and a mass of ancient Mahomedan buildings abutting on the Nujufghur Jheel Channel that the enemy's cavalry broke through on the 9th, and it was necessary to make the ground impracticable for horsemen. Strong parapets, deep ditches, and thick abattis of trees and brushwood were carried over all the open spaces ; provision was made for placing field guns in battery behind the bank on the right of the mound. The line to the drainage channel was thereby strengthened to be safe against attack.

Part of the ground in front of the Pagoda picquet being wholly unflanked and supplying cover frequently taken advantage of by the enemy, it was determined that a small battery for two field guns should be constructed on the right of Perkins's Mortar Battery, a position commanding the ground in question. There being reason to anticipate another general attack on the right of the position, the battery, for the sake of expedition, was built of sandbags, covered with a screen of gabions. The pioneers completed the work between 3 a.m. and 11 a.m. on the 15th, notwithstanding interruption from the enemy. This battery was called " Taylor's Battery," named after Capt. Taylor.

About sunrise the enemy attacked, as was expected, and the contest continued with variable vigour throughout the day. The position had been gradually so strengthened in all its parts that no impression could be made upon it. The troops remained quietly under cover of their parapets, and the artillery inflicted heavy loss on the enemy from all the batteries on the right. Scarcely any casualties had occurred until it was determined to move out and drive the enemy from the strong and rugged ground he usually held. This was done, of course, but with some loss, and in the impetuosity of pursuit the column followed the retreating enemy close up to the walls of the city.   There they were received with a murderous grape-shot fire, and officers and men fell thick and fast. The commander of this column, Brigadier Chamberlain, was struck down by a dangerous wound, and before the troops could be extricated from their position, 13 officers and 209 men were placed *hors de combat*. The casualties in the Engineer Brigade included three officers, Lieut. J. T. Walker, Bombay Engineers, severely, and Lieuts. Geneste and Perkins slightly, wounded.

The total casualties in the two actions of the 10th and 15th having risen to nearly 500 men, it was necessary to abandon all idea of any active operations against the place from the latter date. Up to that date it had been the personal conviction of the Chief Engineer, duly submitted to the consideration of the Major-General commanding, that the possibilities of success by assault were such as would justify the attempt being made, should the political necessity for it be so great as to warrant very grave risks being accepted. It was no matter of regret to the Chief Engineer that his judgment on this point was never put to the test, it having been held that the risks were greater than the circumstances of the moment would warrant the General in meeting, but from this time his views were entirely in accordance with that conclusion, and thenceforward but one idea regulated the operations of the Engineer Brigade, to prepare, namely, by economy of men and material on the spot, and, by collection of the same from every available point for the breaching of the city walls, and the attack of the place by siege operations, followed by open assault.

On the 16th and 17th, the breastwork at the Pagoda picquet was strengthened, and a traverse constructed, batteries were repaired, and a magazine made for Taylor's Battery. Metcalfe's picquet was strengthened by a ditch in front of the cow-house. On the 18th a party of Major Coke's Corps raised and strengthened the breast-work between Johnson's Battery and the Crow's Nest. At Metcalfe's picquet, an officer and 40 men were employed during the night in endeavouring to ascertain the truth of the supposed existence of an enemy's mine under the stable. The noise of what seemed to be miners at work was distinctly heard, but ceased on our party commencing to drive a shaft in the stall of the stable where the noise was most distinctly heard. On the 19th another desultory attack was made on our right, which continued for some hours. Our men suffered but little loss while behind their trenches and breastworks ; most of those hit being struck by shots from the Subzee-Mundee taking them in reverse. In the afternoon, a column under Brigadier Jones advanced and drove the enemy out of the Subzee-Mundee and Trevelyan Gunge. Lieut. Crozier, of the 75th Regiment, was killed on this occasion. On the 21st and 22nd the rear breastwork at the Metcalfe picquet was completed, very much improving the defences at that part, and placing them in a most satisfactory condition.

On the 25th—26th July, the lines of fire of the centre battery were altered and readjusted, so that one embrasure should bear on the Moree, a second on the Cashmere Bastion, and the third on Ludlow Castle. Lieut. Greathed, with 40 sappers, completed the demolition of the Rohtuk Road Bridge, leaving a gap exceeding 60 ft. in width.

Heavy rain fell on the 27th. The clearance round the Subzee-Mundee post was, however, continued, and the interior defences at the Pagoda picquet were strengthened and completed. On the left front the Flagstaff breastwork was improved. In addition to the above works, the preparation of gabions and fascines in the Engineer Park was continued daily without interruption.

By the 26th July no letters had been received for six weeks, all having been stopped or lost, and reinforcements were still expected. The enemy continued to make attacks on our position three or four times a week. Their average losses on each occasion amounted to some 300 or 400 men killed and wounded. Our position at this time was thoroughly entrenched on all sides, and perfectly secure from the enemy's attacks. About this time some attempts were made to destroy the bridge of boats across the Jumna River near the Selimgurh Fort, by floating down rafts, but without success. At this time we had been seven weeks in front of the city with a force of about 3,000 men, and had to repulse the enemy's sorties, which were sometimes made with a force of 10,000 or 12,000 men. One of the greatest discomforts at this period of the siege was the great plague of flies.

It was usual to watch the enemy's sorties from the batteries on the ridge. They sometimes occupied an hour in issuing from the city—cavalry, artillery, and infantry. The ground between the ridge and the city was very favourable for the enemy, being covered with rocks, trees, and bushes, from behind which they were able to pick off our men.

It may be remembered that the siege took place during the rainy season, so that the troops were continually drenched. The Engineer officers had to take parties of unarmed coolies out at dusk, and to work between the ridge and the city, their work usually consisting of felling trees and bushes, and clearing the ground in front of the picquets.   Attacked by the enemy in the darkness and rain, it was really wonderful how patiently these poor coolies bore their sufferings, and their conduct was a matter of universal admiration.   All the troops suffered alike.   The officers received a daily tot or ration of rum like the men.   Many now suffered from dysentery, and cholera had broken out.   The commander of the Delhi Field Force, Sir Henry Barnard, as has been stated, was seized with cholera on the 5th July, and died in a few hours.   Sales of effects of officers who had been killed, took place almost daily ; a bottle of beer sold for 4 or 5 rupees, and a bottle of brandy for 20 rupees.   Capt. A. Taylor was at this time second in command of the Engineers.   He had a charmed life.   It was his habit to go about alone, sometimes mounted, but more frequently on foot, between the ridge and the city, reconnoitring the enemy's position, and he seemed to have the faculty of dispensing with sleep.   On several occasions he succeeded in penetrating, alone and in daylight, through the enemy's outposts, to study the ground on which our operations would have to be conducted.

Although during the sorties that were of almost daily occurrence the fighting generally ranged along the whole of the front of our position, the picquets stationed at the Subzee-Mundee may, perhaps, be awarded the palm for the deadly nature of the combats which they sustained, and for the severity of the fighting.   Hand-to-hand combats were of frequent occurrence.   On one occasion, during one of these fights, a rebel Sepoy thrust his head through an opening of the wall of the serai.   A Goorkha Sepoy below the wall seized him by the hair and chopped off his head with one stroke of his kookree.

The route by which the troops marched from the camp to the ridge before arriving at the latter was much exposed to fire from the enemy's shot and shell throughout the siege.   The shot fired from the city which missed the batteries on the ridge just cleared the top of the ridge and fell in the valley beyond.   Dead camels, horses, and bullocks lay in every direction in this valley.

It now began to be understood in the camp that the mutineers had broken out into mutiny some days before the time decided upon by the confederation, at the head of whom was the Moolvie of Fyzabad.   This is also the view taken by Colonel Malleson in his history of the Indian Mutiny, and he states that the date fixed upon was the 31st May.   The punishment at Meerut of the 89 troopers of the 3rd Light Cavalry, who were sentenced by a court-martial to periods of imprisonment varying from six to ten years for refusing to take the greased cartridges, precipitated the Mutiny. It was commonly reported that out of 74 regiments of infantry in Bengal, only five remained staunch.   News was received at this time that the Europeans at Agra had been compelled to retire into the fort, and also of the capitulation of Sir Hugh Wheler, at Cawnpore, and the subsequent massacre of all the Europeans at that station with the exception of Lieuts. Mowbray Thompson and Delafosse, and two privates, who escaped after undergoing wonderful adventures and sufferings. It was frequently believed, and stated both by officers and men at this period of the siege, that death would be preferable to falling into the hands of the rebels.

There were present at the siege two officers who subsequently rose to high rank, Lieut. Roberts (afterwards Commander-in-Chief in India, and Field Marshal Lord Roberts of Kandahar) and Capt. Donald Stewart (afterwards Commander-in-Chief in India, a baronet, and G.C.B.). Lord Roberts was D.-A. Quartermaster-General of Artillery during the siege, was wounded on the 14th July, and his horse was shot under him on the 14th September. Sir Donald Stewart commanded the volunteers serving in the Allygurh District in May and June, 1857, and all communications with the upper provinces having been cut off, he volunteered to carry dispatches from the Governor of the North-West Provinces to the officer commanding at Delhi. On arriving at the camp he was appointed D.-A. Adjutant-General of the Field Force, and served throughout the siege, and afterwards as Assistant Adjutant-General at the Siege and Capture of Lucknow, and in Rohilcund. Among other distinguished officers who were present at the siege were General Sir Henry Norman, G.C.B., Governor of Queensland, who was Adjutant-General after the death of Colonel Chester, killed at the Battle of Badle-ka-Serai, General Sir Charles Reid, G.C.B., who commanded all the advanced posts on the right of the Delhi Ridge, including Hindoo Rao's, the key of the position, during which 26 separate attacks were made, and also a column on the 17th June for the attack of Kissengunge, and the 4th column of assault on the 14th September, being severely wounded on that occasion, General Sir D. Probyn, K.C.B., V.C., who commanded the 2nd Punjab Cavalry, General Sir John Watson, V.C., and many others.

At dawn on the 12th August a column consisting of 350 1st Bengal Fusiliers, 100 2nd Bengal Fusiliers, 100 8th King's Regiment, 100 75th Regiment, 300 Coke's Rifles, 100 Sirmoor Battalion, 100 4th Sikhs, total 1,150 infantry, with cavalry and six guns in support, moved down to Ludlow Castle, to capture the two field guns which had been annoying us from the front of the stable of Metcalfe's house. The operation was successful, four light guns being seized on the road by Ludlow Castle, many of the gunners being bayoneted, and considerable loss inflicted on the enemy. Our loss was 19 killed and 90 wounded. Lieut. Sheriff, 2nd Fusiliers, was wounded mortally; Brigadier Showers and Major Coke, severely; Lieut. Owen, 1st Fusiliers, and the orderly officer to Brigadier Showers, lightly.

On the night of the 19th August, reports having been received that Lieut. Hodson—who had gone in the direction of Rohtuk, to watch a body of mutineers, supposed to have moved in that direction—was in difficulties, a force consisting of about 1,000 infantry, 200 Mooltanee Horse, some Guide Cavalry, and six guns under Major Tombs, the whole under Brig.-General Nicholson, marched at 11 p.m. to relieve him. The rain fell in torrents, and the column returned, having found the road impracticable beyond Alipoor. On the 22nd the enemy brought out three light guns, and about midday made a feeble attack on the centre battery, occupying the gardens below it, and firing up into the embrasures, but they retired again in the afternoon. On the 24th, Capt. Taylor, with Lieuts. Medley, Home and Thomason, made a reconnaissance of the ground from the Pagoda picquet to Marshall's house. The enemy's skirmishers fired heavily at the party, and one Goorkha was mortally wounded.

On the 25th August, Brig.-General Nicholson, with a force consisting of about 2,200 men of all ranks, and 12 guns, started at 4 a.m. to meet a body of the enemy, which, it was understood, had left the city on the previous day for Nujufgurh, with a view of coming upon our rear. In the evening he came upon them posted in strength near the village of Nujufgurh, and drove them from it with small loss, taking 13 guns. Several men from Coke's Corps and the 61st were wounded in an attack on another village, in which the enemy had taken refuge, and which was walled and difficult of access. Here Lieut. Lumsden, Acting Commandant of the Corps, was, unfortunately, killed, and also Lieut. Gabbett, of the 61st, and Lieut. Elkington, of the same regiment. The rebels left all their camp equipment behind them.

On the afternoon of the 26th the rebels attacked our right, bringing out six guns. Apparently, they supposed that the main body of our troops had gone out with Nicholson's column. About 50 sowars rashly charged up to within 50 yards of Salkeld's Battery, where many paid the penalty of their rashness with their lives. Our casualties were 12 in this affair. General Nicholson's column returned at dusk.

On the 27th a battery for six light guns was marked out in the Pagoda left trench. The enemy fired a good deal at our working parties, but without doing any harm, and our batteries sustained their fire.

On the 1st September, a shell fired from the other side of the river bursting in the Metcalfe stable killed and wounded nine men, these being the first casualties that had occurred from this battery.

On the night of September 3rd—4th, Lieut. Tennant (afterwards Lieut.-General, C.I.E., F.R.S.) was sent down to construct a battery for two light guns on the right of the 6-gun battery, to fire across the front of the Sammy House. A road for light guns was made to the 6-gun battery. A magazine was commenced for the 6-gun battery, but little progress was made owing to the stony soil.

The siege guns arrived on the 5th September, the remainder of the 60th Rifles on the 6th, and the Jummoo Contingent, led by Richard Lawrence, on the 8th. All was now ready for the breaching of the city walls and the subsequent assault.

Assault of Delhi and Capture of the City.

Before describing the siege operations which commenced on the 7th September, it will be as well here to mention briefly the leading characteristics of the place, the description being taken from the Chief Engineer's Report.

The eastern face of the city rests on the Jumna, and during the season of the year when our operations were carried on the stream may be described as washing the base of the walls. All access to a besieger on the river front is therefore, impracticable. The defences here consist of an irregular wall, with occasional bastions and towers, and about one-half of the length of the river face is occupied by the King's Palace, and its outwork, the old Mogul Fort of Selimgurh.

The river may be described as the chord of a rough arc formed by the remaining defences of the place. These consist of a succession of bastioned fronts, the connecting curtains being very long, and the outworks limited to only a crown work at the Ajmeer Gate, and Martello Towers mounting a single gun at such points as require some additional flanking fire to that given by the bastions themselves.

The bastions were small, mounting generally three guns in each face, two in each flank, and one in embrasure at the salient. They were provided with masonry parapets about 12 ft. in thickness, and have a relief of about 16 ft. above the plane of site. The curtain consists of a simple masonry wall or rampart, 16 ft. in height, 11 ft. thick at top, and 14 or 15 ft. at bottom. This main wall carried a loophole for musketry 8 ft. in height and 3 ft. in thickness. The whole land front was covered by a berm varying from 16 to 30 ft. in width, and having a scarp wall 8 ft. high. Exterior to this is a dry ditch about 25 ft. in width and from 16 to 20 ft. in depth. The glacis was a very short one, extending only 50 or 60 yards from the counterscarp. The ground occupied by the besieging force presents some features deserving of notice as having exercised a most important influence on the plan and progress of the works of the attack. On the western side of Delhi there appear the last outlying spurs of the Aravelli Mountains, represented here by a low ridge, which disappears at its intersection with the Jumna about 2 miles above the place. The drainage from the eastern slope of the ridge finds its way to the river along the northern and north-western faces of the city, and has formed there a succession of parallel or connected ravines of considerable depth. By taking advantage of these hollow ways, admirable cover was constantly obtained by the troops, and the labour of the siege was materially reduced. The whole of the exterior of the place presents a mass of old buildings of all kinds, of thick brushwood, and occasional clumps of trees, giving great facilities for cover, which during the siege operations proved, on the whole, more favourable to us than to the enemy.

In anticipation of the siege, means had been taken to store the Engineer Park with all the materials and tools required during the operations. The arrival of the siege train having placed the artillery in an equally satisfactory condition, ground was broken as soon after its arrival as possible, being on the night of the 7th September, 1857.

The project of attack submitted by the Chief Engineer to the Major-General commanding, and honoured with his sanction, provided for a concentrated rapid and vigorous attack on the front of the place included between the Water or Moree and Cashmere Bastions, provision being made at the same time for silencing all important flanking fire, whether of artillery or musketry, that could be brought to bear on the lines of advance to be taken by the assaulting columns. Due care was also taken to protect the exposed right flank of the trenches from sorties. The left was secured by being rested on the river, and by the occupation of the Koodsea Bagh, a very strong post in front.

The best information procurable indicated that on the front of attack the fire of some 25 to 30 pieces would have to be subdued. To effect this, 54 siege guns were available.

Capt. Taylor, as has been before mentioned, succeeded on several occasions in penetrating alone through the enemy's outposts, for the purpose of studying the ground, and on the general information so obtained, and his own knowledge of the locality, Major Baird Smith prepared the project of the attack. On the evening of the 6th September the project was formally considered by General Wilson. General Nicholson volunteered to accompany Taylor to see the ground and the points selected for the batteries. It was now dark, and they did not know the strength or disposition of the rebels. They went to some of the places of most importance, and found them unoccupied. Nicholson was satisfied, and reported what he had seen to General Wilson, who then gave his sanction to the Chief Engineer's proposals.

The plan of attack consisted, in principle, in establishing on the front of the fortification selected an artillery fire so much more powerful than that of the enemy on the same front that the result must be to silence his guns and crush his works. The Chief Engineer had good information that on the front between the river and the Cashmere Bastion not more than 30 heavy guns could be brought to bear upon our approaches. So arrangements were made for placing 56 pieces of siege ordnance, of various calibres, against this front, and in about four days the whole opened with terrific effect. Two excellent breaches were made in the walls within 48 hours ; the cover for the enemy's infantry was at the same time utterly swept away ; an incessant storm of shot and shell poured into the place, and on the 14th September all was ready for the final assault, which was accordingly given with brilliant success.

On the 7th September General Wilson issued an address to the troops, complimenting them upon their past conduct, warning them that the hardest part of their task was now about to begin, but assuring them that if they maintained their discipline they could not fail to succeed, and bidding them spare women and children, but give no quarter to mutineers. About the same time the last reinforcements arrived from the Punjab.

The officers and men were regularly practiced in the loading and unloading of the siege materials on camels, and every vicissitude that would be likely to occur was duly provided for. It was necessary that the attack should be directed against the northern face, represented by the Moree, Cashmere, and Water Bastions, with the curtain wall between them. The evening of the 7th was fixed for the commencement of the tracing of the assailing batteries. Under the orders of Lieut. W. Greathed, No. 2 Battery was traced. This battery was situated in front of Ludlow Castle, 500 yards distant from the Cashmere Gate. It was designed with the object of silencing the fire from the Cashmere Bastion, to dismantle the parapets of the walls to the right and left which gave cover to the defenders, and to open a breach to the stormers. About 1,400 camels were employed to carry the fascines and other siege materials. The camels were quietly loaded, and the working parties marched off at dusk on the evening of the 7th.

For about a fortnight previous to the commencement of the siege batteries, large working parties were sent out to cut the trees and bushes near the sites proposed for the batteries. The men were at work from dusk to dawn, groping and stumbling about in the long, rank jungle, wet through with the rain and dew, and frequently attacked by the enemy.

On the 9th, 10th, 11th, and 12th, the batteries were completed. These were of great size, built up to the soles of the embrasures entirely of fascines. 1,500 camels were employed nightly in carrying down the fascines. The third battery was completed on the night of the 11th. This battery was traced by Capt. Medley on the evening of the 9th. With a boldness which was not rare, but the display of which in this instance testified to remarkable negligence on the part of the enemy, the engineers supported by volunteers traced this battery within 160 yards of the Water Bastion. Seeking for a fit site for the battery, Capt. Medley discovered a small ruined building, an out-office of the Custom House, totally unoccupied by the enemy. Capt. Medley took possession of the Custom House, and determined to trace the battery inside the small ruined building, the outer wall of which would conceal the work, and give cover to the workmen. This daring measure completely succeeded.

Everyone expected that the attention of the enemy would be attracted on the first night to the grunting and noise of the camels, but, strange to say, the animals were unusually quiet. Strange, also, though it may seem, the enemy fired very little on the batteries which were under construction, although a heavy fire was concentrated upon them after they were completed and had opened fire. Almost all the engineer officers present, and fit for duty, were on duty for three nights continuously at this period.

On the 12th the batteries opened fire, and the first salvo carried away a large portion of the wall of the Cashmere Bastion. No. 1 Battery consisted of five 18-pounders, one 8-in. howitzer, four 24-pounders. No. 2 Battery was placed in front of Ludlow Castle, and consisted of two 18-pounders, nine 24-pounders, and seven 8-in. howitzers. A battery of six 9-pounders and two 24-pounders, under Major Remington, had been placed below Hindoo Rao's house, so as to play on the Moree Bastion. No. 1 Battery, which was within 700 yards of the walls, was planted in advance of this. Four guns of this battery were directed against the Cashmere Bastion, and six against the Moree Bastion. The batteries in this position were under the command of Major Brind.

There was also a battery of 10 mortars under Major Tombs, and another battery at the Custom House under Major Scott. During the construction of the former battery, a rocket fired from the Moree Bastion ricochetted among the coolies employed in the battery, killing 13. Their comrades placed the bodies in a row, and went on with their work as before.

From the 9th to the 14th, the morning of the assault, the pounding went on day and night from about 50 guns and mortars. The Moree bastion was soon silenced, and the line of parapet which sheltered the sharpshooters was stripped. The Cashmere Bastion was silenced in 10 minutes after the Ludlow batteries opened upon it.

In a letter from the Chief Engineer to Major Brind, commanding the artillery, the former wrote :—" No. 1 Battery was unquestionably the key of the attack, on its success depended the opening of Delhi to our assaulting columns. The progress of the other batteries depended essentially on its efficiency, and but for your moral courage, clear perception, and unwavering resolution in arming and working it in spite of all obstacles, consequences would have followed causing the greatest embarrassment."

The fire from the left section of No. 1 Battery had been steadily directed against the Cashmere Bastion, when about noon on the 10th the half-battery caught fire from the constant discharge of the guns. The rebels at once directed on the burning battery every gun they could command, and it was only saved by the gallantry of Lieut. Lockhart, who was on duty at the battery with two companies of the 2nd Goorkhas. Calling for volunteers, this officer jumped on the parapet, followed by six or seven Goorkhas, and, taking the sandbags from the top, they smothered the fire with the sand. Two of the Goorkhas were shot dead, and Lockhart was shot through the jaw, but by great exertions the survivors succeeded in extinguishing the fire.

On the 11th, the mortar battery opened fire, and Scott's heavy battery was unmasked.

An hour before noon on the 12th, No. 3 Battery on the left was unmasked. It was situated in the Old Custom House, and was constructed to a great extent of sandbags. It was here that Major Fagan, of the Artillery, was killed on the afternoon of the 13th.

In the Water Bastion the fire from the heavy guns at the Custom House, at 160 yards, played with fearful effect ; the guns were dismounted and smashed, and the breach opened ; while under the play of Tombs's mortars the curtain was literally stripped. The losses of the British from the enfilading fire of the enemy were very heavy, but the assault was no longer to be delayed and on the night of the 13th the order was issued for it to take place at daybreak on the following morning.

The dangerous duty of examining the breaches was performed by three engineer officers, Lieuts. Medley,* Lang,† and Greathed.‡ Medley and Lang crept out and reached the edge of the ditch undiscovered, descended into it, and although they saw the enemy was on the alert they carefully examined the breach. A volley was fired at them, but they returned unhurt, and reported the breach practicable. A similar report was received of the breach in the Water Bastion.

There were to be four columns of attack, with a reserve ; the first was to storm the breach in the Cashmere Bastion, the second that in the Water Bastion, the third to enter by the Cashmere Gate, when, blown in by the engineers, and the fourth on the extreme right to clear the Kissengunge Suburb, and then enter by the Lahore Gate, while the reserve was to follow in the wake of the first three columns, and throw in supports when necessary.

The columns consisted of :—

No. 1.—Under General Nicholson, 1,000 men; engineer officers, Lieuts. Medley, Lang and Bingham.

* Lieut.-General Medley entered the Service in 1847, and died in 1886.
† Colonel Lang, c.b., r.e., subsequently head of the Thomason Civil Engineering College, Roorkee.
‡ Major-General W. W. Greathed, c.b., died December, 1878.

No. 2.—Under Brig.-General Jones, 61st Regiment, 800 men ; engineer officers, Lieuts. Greathed, Hovenden, and Pemberton.

No. 3.—Under Colonel Campbell, 52nd Light Infantry, 1,000 men ; engineer officers, Lieuts. Home, Salkeld, and Tandy.

No. 4.—Under Major Reid, Commanding Sirmoor Battalion, 780 men ; engineer officers, Lieuts. Maunsell and Tennant.

Reserve.—Under Brig.-General Longfield, 1,200 men ; engineer officers, Lieuts. Ward and Thackeray.

After being told off to the different columns, the officers joined the storming parties, and marched with the column to their respective posts. The guns from the batteries, which had kept up a heavy fire during the night, suddenly ceased, and for a few minutes there was a lull in the firing, and an unusual stillness seemed to prevail. This was suddenly broken by a loud explosion from the Cashmere Gate, and by a fierce battle of musketry from the different columns of assault.

It was just daylight when the third column halted at a turn in the road which concealed them from view of the walls, but close to the Cashmere Gate. Lieuts. Home and Salkeld, of the engineers, and Sergts. Carmichael, Burgess and Smith, and four sappers, with Havildar Madho and Bugler Hawthorn, H.M. 52nd Regt., advanced from the column up to the gate. It was an immensely heavy wooden gate, flanked on all sides by the walls. Home laid the powder bags at the foot of the gate. The party was instantly discovered, and a heavy fire opened upon them from all sides. Sergt. Carmichael took the fuze, and was on the point of firing it when he was shot dead by a Sepoy who placed his musket through a hole in the gate. Sergt. Burgess took the fuze from his hand, and was also shot dead, Lieut. Salkeld then took the fuze, and was shot through the arm, and fell into the ditch, breaking his leg by the fall. As he fell he threw up the fuze, which Sergt. Smith seized, and fired the charge, and jumped into the ditch. At the same time the bugler sounded the advance, and on rushed the column. The charge blew up the gate, and about 17 of the enemy who were close to it. The following native officers, N.C.O.'s, and sappers formed part of the explosion party :—Subahdar Tooloo, Havildar Tillok (wounded), Havildar Madho (wounded), Sepoy Rambeth (killed), Sepoy Jahub Singh. Our troops rushed in at the gate, up the bastion, and along the walls. At the same time the first and second columns attacked by the breaches, and the walls were cleared of the defenders. The Cashmere Gate presented a terrible sight ; several Sepoys had been blown up by the explosion, and others bayoneted or shot by the assailants, were lying all about. The same scene of carnage and destruction was visible along the walls and bastions. No quarter was asked or given. Almost every gun was dismounted and smashed by the fire from our guns, large pieces

226

of iron being in many cases knocked out of the guns. Dead Sepoys lay about in all imaginable positions. The troops took up positions in the College and Church, but the enemy fired constantly during the whole of the night of the 14th. Hundreds of wounded men were carried by in doolies ; General Nicholson was shot near the Burn Bastion while endeavouring to rally the men. At dusk a battery was constructed near the College, and commenced shelling the town and palace. The battery was under the command of Capt. Hamilton (afterwards Lieut.-General Sir W. Hamilton), and a heavy fire was kept up on the city from this battery during the whole of the night of the 14th. The losses in the assault and taking of the city were 64 officers and 1,380 men killed and wounded.

Surgeon H. T. Reade (now Surgeon-General and C.B.) was one of the first in the breach, and succeeded in spiking a gun. Capt. R. H. Shebbeare, 60th N.I., was severely wounded while endeavouring to capture a loopholed serai. The name of Ensign Phillips, 11th Bengal N.I., was proverbial on the Delhi Field Force for the number of gallant acts performed during the siege. He was thrice wounded, and captured the Water Bastion on the 14th September with a small party of men. This gallant and promising young officer was killed during the street fighting on the 18th. These officers were awarded the V.C. for their conduct on the 14th.

Among the non-commissioned officers who greatly distinguished themselves on the day of the assault were Colour-Sergt. Waller, 60th Rifles, by charging and capturing a gun ; Sergt. MacGunnis and Drummer Ryan, of the 75th Regiment, by throwing ammunition boxes into the water, thus saving many lives ; Lance-Corpl. H. Smith, 52nd Regiment, by removing a wounded comrade under a heavy fire at the Chandnee Chowk ; Sergt. J. Smith and Bugler Hawthorn, who were with Lieuts. Home and Salkeld at the Cashmere Gate. All these men obtained the V.C., and Sergt. J. Smith afterwards obtained a commission. Scott's Field Battery, which had entered the city by the Cashmere Gate, had during all this time rendered splendid service to the several columns, but at a large expenditure of life.

At the assault on the 14th, the storming party under Capt. Baynes, H.M. 8th Regiment, lost the greater part of their number. On the same day, from a detachment of 200 men of the 9th Lancers, the losses were 6 officers and 42 men. Of the 17 engineer officers engaged, Lieut. Tandy was killed, and Salkeld died from his wounds a few days afterwards. Lieuts. Greathed, Maunsell, Chesney,* Medley, Hovenden and Pemberton were wounded. The losses during the fighting on the 14th were 8 European officers and 162 rank and file killed, and 510 wounded. Of natives 103 were killed and 310 wounded.

* Afterwards General Sir George Chesney, k.c.b., c.s.i., c.i.e., R.E.

On the 16th the magazine was stormed by H.M. 61st Regiment, Wilde's Punjabees, and the Beloochees, the whole under Colonel Deacon, of the 61st. The enemy was surprised, and offered very little resistance, but in the afternoon made an attack in great force on the magazine. A heavy fire was opened on the turrets, where men of the 61st were posted to keep down the enemy's fire. The rebels set fire to the roof of the magazine, the fire being extinguished with much difficulty, and Renny, of the Artillery, got upon the roof with some 10-in. shells, which were handed up to him, and which he dropped on the enemy's heads. He dropped five or six shells in this manner, and many of the enemy must have been killed, as they ceased their attack soon afterwards. Capt. Renny and Lieut. Thackeray were awarded the V.C. on this occasion.

On the 18th a reconnaissance was made by Major Taylor who penetrated as far as the Chandnee Chowk ; he found the houses partly occupied by their usual inhabitants, and not by an armed enemy. On the 19th, with a small detachment, Taylor worked through the houses and captured the Burn Bastion. The enemy kept up a slack fire during the night and shortly afterwards the palace was captured, and the whole city was in our possession. The defeated rebels fled in every direction, and the British flag once more waved over the walls of the capital of Northern India.

A memorial monument commemorates the capture of Delhi. The besieging army subscribed one day's pay towards its erection but this sum, though amounting to nearly 20,000 rupees, falling short of the estimate, the building was taken in hand by the Government, and completed at a cost of 21,400 rupees. It is built on the ridge, on the site of the right battery and being 110 ft. high, is visible from every point. It bears on its faces the names of the officers and men of the several British regiments, and of the British officers of the native regiments, who fell during the siege.

CHAPTER FIFTEEN

The first practical intimation that the contagion of the cartridge question had reached Oudh was manifested early in April. Here it is necessary to state ·the troops by whom the newly annexed province was garrisoned. At Lucknow itself were quartered H.M.'s 32nd Regiment about 700 strong ; a weak company of European Artillery ; the 7th Regiment Light Cavalry (native) ; the 13th, 48th, and 71st Regiments of Native Infantry. Besides these there were at Lucknow, or in its immediate environs, two regiments of Irregular Native Infantry, raised for local service in Oudh, the 4th, and the 7th ; one regiment of Military Police, the 3rd ; a large proportion of Mounted Military Police ;* one regiment of Oudh Irregular Cavalry; and two batteries of Native Artillery. Thus the native armed troops were in the proportion of nearly ten to one Europeans, the actual numbers being 7,000 to 750. At Sitápúr, in addition to local troops, the 41st Native Infantry was stationed having a detachment at Maláun ; at Sultánpúr, the 15th Irregular Cavalry. The other stations, Daryábád, Faizábád, and Bahraich, were garrisoned by local corps.

On the 20th March, 1857, Sir Henry Lawrence had assumed the Chief Commissionership of Lucknow. Of all the men who have ever attained a prominent position in India, Sir Henry Lawrence was, perhaps, the most qualified to remove a discontent engendered by action—too fast, too hard, too reckless—on the part of the Government. He had great sympathies with the people, and thoroughly understood them. He did not, however, confine himself solely to the work of pacifying and of reasoning with the people. He realized at a glance the danger that threatened India ; he felt that at any moment the handful of Englishmen in the country might have two hundred millions on their hands. Whilst then he used every per-

* The Oudh Military Police consisted of 1,000 cavalry and 3 regiments of infantry, commanded by Capt. Gould Weston, an officer of great ability, who, prior to the annexation of the province, had been engaged for some years in the suppression of Thagí and Dakaití.

suasive argument, and put into action every precautionary measure to avert a crisis, he prepared to meet one.

He began his preparations in April. His own headquarters were at the Residency situated in the city close to the river Gúmti, and upwards of a quarter of a mile from the iron bridge leading to the Mariáun Cantonment. The native infantry regiments, a light horse battery of European artillery, and a battery of native artillery were at Mariáum. At Múdkipúr, 1½ miles further still from the Residency, was one cavalry regiment. In an opposite direction, in a line in fact forming a right angle with the road to Mariáun and at a distance of 1½ miles from the point of the angle, the Residency, was H.M.'s 32nd Regiment about 700 strong. Nearly 1½ miles directly north of the barracks of the British Regiment, and on the opposite bank of the river Gúmti, was the only remaining regiment of native cavalry. South of the river again, at or near Músa Bágh, 3 miles from the Residency, were two irregular native regiments, and between them and the Residency was a magazine containing a considerable stand of arms. About the Residency itself were clustered several substantial buildings of solid masonry occupied by the higher European officials. Here also were the Treasury, the Hospital, and a gaol. A detachment of native troops guarded the Residency and the Treasury. The whole of the Residency buildings were known to the natives throughout Oudh by the name Baillie Guard.*

Rather less than 1 mile from the Residency, on the same side of the river Gúmti, is a castellated stronghold called the Machchí Bhawan. The attention of Sir Henry was, in the first instance, directed to making the Residency defensible, and to a better location of the British troops. With this end in view he began to clear away the huts and other obstructions which occupied the ground close to the Residency ; to lay in supplies of grain of all sorts, and European stores ; to accumulate powder and small-arm ammunition and to dig pits for their reception ; to arrange for a constant water supply ; by degrees to send for the treasure from the city and outlying station ; and to form outworks on the ground encompassing the Residency. At the same time he moved to the vicinity of the barracks of the 32nd Foot four guns of the native battery stationed at Mariáun. His preparations had not been made too soon. On the 30th April the storm threatened. On the 3rd of May it broke.

The 7th Regiment of Oudh Irregular Infantry was stationed at Músa Bagh, about 3 miles from the Residency. The adjutant of the regiment was Lieut. Mecham, a cool, determined, and reso-

* The guard in question commanded by a Subadar was first stationed at this gate by Colonel Baillie, a former resident at the Court of Oudh. Hence the name.

lute officer. On the 30th April when he took his men to ball practice, these suddenly showed a disinclination to use the new cartridge. Mecham pointed out to them that the cartridge was similar to that they had been using the previous fortnight. This seemed to satisfy the men, and they proceeded with the practice. But the next morning the sergeant-major reported that the men positively refused to bite the cartridge, that many even declined to receive or even to touch it.

The day following was spent by the men in brooding over their grievances. They worked themselves to the state of fanaticism which will not bear reason, and at 10 o'clock, on the 3rd, they had arrived at the conclusion that they must kill their European officers. The latter warned in time by the quartermaster-sergeant of the disposition of their men, nobly did their duty, and succeeded after a time in inducing the Sepoys to return to their lines, though they refused to surrender their arms.

But Sir Henry Lawrence was not content with this doubtful triumph. The men of the 7th were paraded. The question was put to them whether they would continue to bite the cartridge, or whether they would refuse. The men, after some hesitation, promised to obey, but their manner was so sullen and so insolent that Sir Henry felt he could not trust them. He at once proceeded to the spot with the force he had organized, consisting of the 32nd Foot, a European battery, three regular native regiments of infantry, and one of cavalry. It was dark, but Sir Henry at once brought the 7th to the front, and ordered them to lay down their arms. In the presence of the imposing force in their front and on their flanks and of the lighted port-fires of the gunners the courage of the mutinous Sepoys gave way. Many of them panic-stricken fled wildly from the spot, but, on being followed and assured that no violence would be used if they obeyed orders, they returned, and before midnight all their arms were secured.

The next day the ringleaders were seized, and it transpired from their admissions that a treasonable correspondence with the view to a general rising had been going on for some time between them and the men of the 48th Regiment of Native Infantry.

On May 12th Sir Henry Lawrence held a great Durbar to which the native aristocracy, the European and native civil officials, the European and native officers were invited. Sir Henry concluded an eloquent speech delivered in the native language, by warning his listeners against becoming the dupes of designing men, and of the fate which would inevitably follow the neglect of his advice. He then caused the deserving native officers to be brought up to him, and in the name of the Government delivered to them the rewards they had merited.

The city of Lucknow 42 miles distant from Cawnpore extends

for about 3 miles on the right bank of the river Gúmtí. All the principal palatial buildings, the Residency, and the Machchí Bawun are between the city and the river bank. South of these buildings and covering an immense space is the city. This is intersected by a canal which falls into the Gúmtí close to the Martinieré College, about 3 miles south-east of the Residency. A little to the south of this is the Dilkushá, a hunting-box or palace within an enclosed park. The space between the Residency and the Martinieré was occupied by palaces among which the Motí Mahal, the Shah-Munzil, the Sikandrabágh are the most conspicuous. South of the city, about 4 miles from the Residency on the southern side of the road leading to Cawnpore, is the Alumbágh, a large walled garden, with a high and pretentious gateway.

Not counting the position of the native cavalry at Múdkipún, Sir Henry possessed now three military posts. Two of these, the Residency and the Machchí Bawun, he made as strong as he could. Having regard to possible eventualities he removed the spare ammunition from the magazine into the Machchí Bawun. He seized the earliest opportunity of garrisoning that place with Europeans, of storing supplies there, and of mounting on the ramparts guns of all sorts. Many of these were taken from the King's palaces, and were useful only to make a show. In the Residency compound, over the Treasury, he posted a mixed guard of 200 Sepoys, 130 Europeans and 6 guns—the guns being placed so that at the first alarm they could be brought to bear on any mutineers. The third post was the old cantonment of Mariáun. It was garrisoned by 340 men of the 32nd Foot, 50 European artillerymen, and 6 guns ; the three native regiments, and a battery of native artillery. Here, Sir Henry, for the time, took up his quarters.

Having made these preparations, Sir Henry Lawrence took an early opportunity to move the ladies and children into the houses within the Residency enclosure. Here also were brought the families and the sick men of the 32nd Regiment. At the same time, the clerks, copyists, section-writers, and others of that class were armed and drilled. On the 27th May he was able to write to Lord Canning, " Both the Residency and the Machchí Bawun are safe against all probable comers." On the same day, Capt. Hutchinson (afterwards Major-General Hutchinson, c.b., c.s.i.), of the Engineers, Military Secretary to the Chief Commissioner, an officer of great talent and daring, was ordered by Sir Henry Lawrence to accompany into the district, as political officer, a column composed of 200 men of the 7th Cavalry, and 200 men of the 48th Native Infantry. The object of sending this column was to rid Lucknow of the presence of men who might then be dangerous, but who posted on the northern frontier of Oudh, might be employed with advantage to restrain the turbulence of the inhabitants. Marching from Lucknow on the 27th,.

the column reached Sandila, 32 miles to the westward of Lucknow, on the 1st of June. There Hutchinson received accounts of the mutiny of the 30th May at Lucknow. The Sepoys heard of it at the same time, and it at once became apparent that they were biding their time. Hutchinson, after vainly endeavouring to pacify them, and noting the increased insolence of the men, urged the officers not to allow themselves to be taken in the net which was preparing for them on the other side of the river Ganges. But they were deaf and would not hear him. The regiment crossed the sacred stream. On the 7th or 8th the men rose, massacred all their own officers but one, Lieut. Boulton, who fled to perish elsewhere, and went off to Delhi. Hutchinson, accompanied by the paymaster of pensioners, Major Mariott, who with him had declined to cross the river, returned in safety to Lucknow.

The precautions before stated had not been taken at that city a moment too soon. On the night of the 30th May the insurrection broke out. At 9 o'clock the evening gun fired as usual. The men of the 71st Regiment, previously told off in parties, started off at the signal to fire the bungalows and murder their officers. A few men only of the other infantry regiments, and some men of the 7th Cavalry joined them.

Sir Henry Lawrence was dining that night at the Residency bungalow at Mariáun. An officer of his staff had informed him that he had been told by a Sepoy that at gun-fire (9 p.m.) the signal to mutiny would be given. The gun fired ; but all for the moment seemed quiet. Sir Henry leaned forward and said to the officer, " Your friends are not punctual." The words were scarcely out of his mouth when the discharge of muskets proved that his staff officer had been well informed. The horses were brought up, and Sir Henry followed by his staff started for the lines.

On his way he found 300 men of the 32nd, four guns Major Kaye's battery, and two of the Oudh force, posted in a position on the extreme right of the 71st lines, and contiguous to the road leading from cantonments to the city. Recognizing the necessity of preventing as far as possible communication between the mutineers and the evil-disposed in the city, Sir Henry took with him two guns and a company of the 32nd to occupy the road leading from the canton- ment to the bridge. He sent back shortly for the remainder of the Europeans, and for two more guns. Meanwhile, the officers of the native regiments had hastened to the lines to endeavour to reason with the men. Many of those, however, had already begun the work of plunder. A considerable body had marched straight to the 71st mess-house, and failing to find the officers, who had just left, they fired it. Very soon after a musketry fire from the 71st lines opened on the Europeans. These replied with grape, and with such effect that the Sepoys made a rush to the rear. In their hurried course they passed the infantry picket, composed of natives, and commanded by Lieut. Grant, 71st Native Infantry. Some of his own men tried to save this officer, but a Sepoy of his own regiment discovered his place of concealment to the mutineers and by these he was brutally murdered. Meanwhile, Lieut. Hardinge, taking with him a few of the Irregular Cavalry, had been patrolling the main street of cantonments to maintain order and to save life and property. He was not, however, in sufficient force to prevent the burning and. plundering of the officers' houses and the bazaars. The mutineers were prowling about in all directions. One of them fired at Lieut. Hardinge, and when his shot missed fire he came at him with his bayonet and wounded him in the arm.

During this time there had been great excitement in the lines. Gradually, however, some satisfactory symptoms evinced themselves. First, about 300 of the 13th Native Infantry, with their British officers, their colours, and the regimental treasure, marched up and enrolled themselves with the British. They were followed by a very few of the 71st but without their colours or their treasure. Of the 48th nothing was heard that night. The Europeans still remained formed up in the position assigned to them in case of alarm by Sir Henry Lawrence, their front flanking that of the several native regiments. About 10 p.m. some of the mutineers crept up to and occupied some empty lines bearing on that position, and opened a musketry fire. Brig. Handscomb, riding from his house straight into the 71st lines, was immediately shot. The fire, however, soon ceased, and arrangements having been made to protect the Residency bungalow, and the part of the cantonment next the city road, and strong guards having been posted, the force piled arms and waited for the morn.

At daylight next morning, Sir Henry placed himself at the head of the forces, and learning that the rebels had retired on Múdkipúr followed them thither. Crossing the parade ground the men came upon the body of Cornet Raleigh, a newly-joined officer who, left sick in his quarters, had been murdered by the rebels. Almost at the same time the mutinous regiments were discovered drawn up in line. At this critical time an officer on Lawrence's staff noticed, or thought he noticed, a mutinous disposition on the part of the 7th Cavalry, till then loyal. Their attitude appeared to him to betoken an intention to charge the British guns. To set the matter at rest the officer directed the guns to open fire on the distant line Then the men of the 7th Cavalry with the exception of about 30, raised a yell, and galloped over to join the enemy, who turned and fled with them. Our troops followed them up for about 10 miles and took 60 prisoners. In this pursuit Mr. Gubbins greatly distinguished himself, capturing several of the enemy with his own hand.   By 10 a.m. our force had returned to cantonments, the heat being excessive.

Sir Henry Lawrence had been on the point of returning to Europe for the benefit of his health before the storm arose, when he was summoned by Lord Canning to Oudh. Regarding that summons as a call of duty, with characteristic forgetfulness of self, he had obeyed it. But under the fatigues, the excitement, the anxiety of his new life, his physical condition had become worse than when his medical advisers had ordered him home from Rajputana.

Sir Henry Lawrence feeling his strength daily failing despatched to Lord Canning, on the 4th May, a telegram, in which he earnestly recommended that in event of anything happening to himself, the office of Chief Commissioner might be conferred upon Major Banks, and the command of the troops on Colonel Inglis. "This," he added, "is no time for punctilio as regards seniority. They are the right men—in fact, the only men—for the places."

Major Banks was the Commissioner of the Lucknow Division. He was the most promising political officer who had not actually attained the highest grade in that branch of the Indian Service. For languages he had a remarkable talent. He was familiar alike with Persian, with Hindí, and with Sanscrit. He had filled several offices with distinction and was esteemed by everyone.

Lieut.-Colonel Inglis (afterwards Major-General Sir J. Inglis, K.C.B.), the other officer referred to, commanded the 32nd Foot. He was in the prime of life, an excellent soldier, active, energetic, and quick-sighted. The native army having mutinied, and the only remaining reliable troops being European, it was practically necessary that the officer commanding the European regiment should have the chief military authority.

Sir Henry Lawrence was particularly desirous to retain the services of a large portion of the native troops. He believed that those who had stood the ordeal of the 30th May would thenceforth remain faithful. He believed that without the aid of native troops his position at Lucknow would not be tenable. He collected all the Sikhs from the three native regiments and formed them into one battalion. He also collected about 170 men who had served in the Company's army prior to the annexation, and placed them under separate command. The number of the native brigade was thus brought up to nearly 800.

On the night of the 9th June the whole of the cavalry of the military police remaining at their headquarters at Lucknow broke into revolt. Capt. Gould Weston at once rode down to their lines, followed only by his two native orderlies. He came upon them as they were starting and exhorted them to listen to the voice of duty and of honour, but his efforts proved unavailing. On the morning of the 12th of June the 2nd Regiment of Infantry of the Military Police mutinied at the Motí Mahal about 1½ miles from the Baillie Guard.

Since the mutiny of the 30th May, efforts to make the Residency defensible had been pushed on with extraordinary vigour. The outer tracing had been connected by breastworks ; ditches had been excavated in front of them, and parapets erected behind them ; at certain points ramparts had been thrown up and embrasures had been pierced ; slopes had been scarped ; stakes and palisades fixed ; some houses had been demolished, the roofs of others had been protected ; windows and doors had been barricaded ; walls had been loopholed. All the ordnance belonging to the ex-King of Oudh that could be found in the city had been brought within the defences. Some houses outside the walls of the Residency were left solely because time had not remained to level them as had been intended. The omission to destroy them was at a later period much regretted, for they were used by the rebels as shelter houses whence to watch the movements of the garrison and to keep up a heavy fire on the defences.

Nor was the Machchí Bawun neglected. Sir Henry Lawrence had originally resolved to hold this post in conjunction with the Residency, only to concentrate on the latter when threatened in overwhelming force. With this view he had strengthened it and made it habitable for Europeans. He then stored it with food and ammunition. On the 13th of June, Sir Henry was able to write to Lord Canning in the words quoted :—" We hold our ground in cantonment, and daily strengthen both our town positions, bearing in mind that the Residency is to be the final point of concentration." Sir Henry continued to strengthen the Machchí Bawun till the very last, believing that the preparations made would be greatly noised abroad, and would affect the moral of the enemy.

A terrible anxiety which preyed upon Sir Henry Lawrence about this time was caused by his inability to assist Sir Hugh Wheler, then beleaguered in Cawnpore. The cessation of communication with that station on the 6th of June had made it clear that the native troops there had mutinied. That they had gone further and under the leadership of Nana Sahib had besieged the British General in his barracks shortly became known. Writing to Sir Hugh Wheler on the 16th of June, the Chief Commissioner said : " I am very sorry indeed to hear of your condition, and grieve that I cannot help you. I have consulted with the chief officers about you, and except Gubbins, they are unanimous in thinking that with the enemy's command of the river we could not get a single man into your intrenchment. . . . We are strong in our intrenchments ; but by attempting the passage of the river, should be sacrificing a large detachment without a prospect of helping you . . . " etc.

A week later he wrote to Lord Canning : " It is deep grief to me to be unable to help Cawnpore; I would run much risk for Wheler's sake, but an attempt with our means, would only ruin ourselves without helping Cawnpore." No military critic will question the soundness of these views. To cross the Ganges, even with the entire force at the disposal of Sir Henry Lawrence, in the face of the army serving under Nana Sahib, would have been impossible.

A few days later a letter reached Sir Henry with the information that Wheler had agreed to treat with Nana Sahib. He then knew that all was over. His forebodings were confirmed by the receipt of details of the massacre on the 28th June. The following morning the advanced guard of the enemy's force marched on Chinhut, a village on the Fyzabad Road, within 8 miles of the Residency. This gave Sir Henry an opportunity for which he had been longing. With the foresight of a real general opposed to Asiatics, he felt that for him to await an attack would be to invite a general insurrection, whereas an effective blow dealt at the advanced troops of the rebels would paralyze their movements, and spread doubt and hesitation among them. To say that because he did not succeed his plan was bad and impolitic is not a logical argument. His plan was justified alike by military science and by political considerations. Whilst he fought a battle in which victory would have been decisive, he lost little by defeat.

Sir Henry's first step was to withdraw the troops from the cantonments and to bring them within the Residency. He then ordered that a force composed of 300 men of the 32nd Regiment ; 230 men of the regular native infantry ; the small troop of volunteer cavalry, 36 strong ; 120 troopers of the Oudh Irregulars ; ten guns and an 8-in. howitzer, should assemble at the iron bridge at daylight the following morning to march at once in the direction of Chinhut.

Of the ten guns, six were manned by natives and four only by Europeans. The howitzer was on a limber drawn by an elephant driven by a native. This work being mainly concerned with the siege operations it is not proposed to give a very long and detailed account of the Battle of Chinhut.

The following is the official report of that action by Brig. Inglis, commanding the Garrison of Lucknow, to the Secretary to the Government Military Department, Calcutta :—

Dated LUCKNOW, 26th September, 1857.

SIR,—In consequence of the very deeply-to-be-lamented death of Brig.-General Sir H. M. Lawrence, K.C.B., late in command of the Oudh Field Force, the duty of narrating the military events which have occurred at Lucknow since 29th June last, has· devolved upon myself.

On the evening of that day several reports reached Sir Henry Lawrence that the rebel army in no very considerable force, would march from Chinhut (a small village about 8 miles distant on the road to Fyzabad) on Lucknow on the following morning ; and the late Brigadier-General therefore determined to make a strong reconnaissance in that direction, with the view, if possible, of meeting the force at a disadvantage, either at its entrance into the suburbs of the city, or at the bridge across the Goterai, which.is a small stream intersecting the Fyzabad road, about half-way between Lucknow and Chinhut.

The force destined for this service—the details of which have been given above—moved out at 6 a.m., on the morning of the 30th June.

The troops misled by the reports of wayfarers—who stated that there were very few or no men between Lucknow and Chinhut—proceeded somewhat further than had been originally intended, and suddenly fell in with the enemy, who had up to that time eluded the vigilance of the advance guard by concealing themselves behind a long line of trees in overwhelming numbers. The European force, and the howitzers, with the native infantry held the foe in check for some time. and had the six guns of the Oudh Artillery been faithful, and the Sikh Cavalry shown a better front, the day would have been won in spite of an immense disparity of numbers. But the Oudh artillerymen and drivers were traitors. They overturned the guns into ditches, cut the traces of their horses, and abandoned them, regardless of the remonstrances and exertions of their own officers, and of those of Sir Henry Lawrence's staff, headed by the Brigadier-General in person, who himself drew his sword on these rebels. Every effort to induce them to stand having proved ineffectual, the force exposed to a vastly superior fire of artillery, and completely outflanked on both sides by an overpowering body of infantry and cavalry, which actually got into our rear, was compelled to retire with the loss of three pieces of artillery which fell into the hands of the enemy, in consequence of the rank treachery of the Oudh gunners, and with a very grievous list of killed and wounded. The heat was dreadful, the gun ammunition was expended, and the almost total want of cavalry to protect our rear made our retreat most disastrous.

All the gun ammunition was exhausted in this disastrous action. In this dilemma Sir Henry showed a nerve and decision not to be surpassed. He placed the guns on the bridge and ordered the port-fires to be lighted. The feint had all the hoped-for effect. The enemy shrank back from a bridge apparently defended by loaded guns. They at once relaxed their pursuit, and the little army succeeded in gaining the shelter of the city and in retiring in some sort of order on the Machchí Bawun and the Residency. Their losses had been most severe and they had left the howitzer and two field pieces behind them.*   On arriving at the Residency Sir Henry ordered out 50 men of the 32nd under an officer, Lieut. Edmonstone, to the iron bridge over the Gumtí, with a view to their being posted in the two houses on either side of the bridge, to defend it.   Towards this bridge the elated enemy surged in crowds, but they never forced it.   The 50 Englishmen covered by a fire from two 18-pounders in the Redan battery, held it successfully though not without loss, till noon.   The enemy then desisted, and crossed the river by another bridge.   Our men were then finálly withdrawn.   This defence was a very gallant affair.

The first consequence of the defeat was the occupation of the city by the rebels and the uprising of the discontented spirits within it. That very afternoon they began to loophole many of the houses in the vicinity of and commanding the Machchí Bawun and the Residency.   They even succeeded in bringing a 6-pounder to bear on the outer verandah of the post afterwards known as Anderson's post. Subsequently in the same afternoon, they brought another gun into position, and soon demolished the outer defences, including a loopholed mud parapet but recently erected.   The post, however, was so important, that orders were sent to the garrison to hold it to the last extremity.

The following morning the enemy opened a heavy fire on the Machchí Bawun and on the Residency.   Sir Henry had foreseen this action and had prepared for it.   Resolved to concentrate all his defensive efforts on the Residency, he signalled the following night to the garrison of the Machchí Bawun, to evacuate and blow up that fortress.   These orders were admirably carried out by Capt. Francis, 13th Native Infantry, then commanding at that post.   A quarter of an hour past midnight the garrison of the Machchí Bawun entered the Residency with their guns and treasure without the loss of a man.   Shortly afterwards the explosion of 240 barrels of gunpowder, and of 594,000 rounds of ball and gun ammunition announced the destruction of that post.

The garrison, consisting, including civilians, of 927 Europeans, and 765 natives were now concentrated in the Residency.   To all appearances the situation was desperate.   Not only were the fortifications incomplete, but the enemy had at once occupied and loopholed the houses which had been left standing, outside and close to those fortifications.   The west and south faces of the enclosure were practically undefended, the bastion which had been commenced at the angle of the two faces having been left unfinished.

Since the retirement of our force within its lines of defence, the

* These were however spiked by Capt. Wilson, the A.A.-General, before they were left.   The heroic efforts made by Lieut. Bonham, of the Artillery, to save the howitzer would most assuredly, had Sir Henry Lawrence lived, gained for that officer the Victoria Cross.

fire of the enemy upon it had been continuous. Night and day, from the tops of surrounding houses, from loopholed buildings, from every point where cover was available, they had poured in a perpetual fire of round shot, of musketry, and of matchlock balls. Many of the garrison who were in places considered before the siege perfectly safe were hit. But no place was so exposed as the Residency itself, and on it a well-directed fire was constantly maintained. Moreover, the enemy had recourse to digging deep approaches to their batteries and guns, and these effectually concealed them from our sharpshooters. But long before this cautious system of attack had attained its full development, the garrison sustained an irreparable loss.

Sir Henry Lawrence occupied in the Residency a room convenient for the purpose of observing the enemy, but much exposed to their fire. There the day after the defeat at Chinhut, he was seated, conversing with his secretary, Mr. Cooper. Suddenly, an 8-in. shell fired from the very howitzer that we had lost at Chinhut, fell into the room, close to them. It burst, however, without injury to either. The whole of the staff then implored Sir Henry to remove to a less exposed position. But this he declined to do, remarking with a smile that another shell would never be pitched into the same room. Later in the day, when it was evident that the enemy's round shot were being directed at the Residency and were striking the upper storey, Capt. Wilson and Mr. Cooper again pressed Sir Henry to go below, and to allow his things to be moved. He promised to comply on the morrow. The following morning he went out to post and arrange the force which had come in from the Machchí Bawun, and to place the field pieces in position. He returned tired and exhausted about 8 o'clock. He lay down on his bed, and transacted business with the Assistant Adjutant-General, Capt. Wilson. He was engaged in this work when a howitzer shell entered the room, and bursting, wounded him mortally. He lingered in extreme agony till the morning of the 4th when he died.

" Few men," wrote Brig. Inglis when commenting on his death, " have ever possessed to the same extent the power which he enjoyed of winning the hearts of all those with whom he came in contact, and thus ensuring the warmest and most zealous devotion for himself and for the Government which he served." The deep affection with which he was regarded when living survives to the present day. Of no man is the recollection more warmly cherished. He devoted all his energies to the country he served so well. In a word, he was a striking type of that class, not a rare one, of the public servants of England in India, who give themselves without reserve to their country. That Sir Henry Lawrence felt to the last the inner conviction that he had so given himself wholly and without stint, is evidenced by his dying wish that, if any epitaph were placed on his tomb, it should be simply this : " Here lies Henry Lawrence, who tried to do his duty."

The credit of the successful defence of the Residency of Lucknow is due in the first place to Sir Henry Lawrence. He alone made it possible to successfully defend it. Three weeks before anyone else dreamed of the chance even of a siege he began to lay in supplies. He caused to be brought into the Residency the treasure from the city and, wherever feasible, from out-stations. He collected there the guns, the mortars, the shot and shell, the small arms, the ammunition, and the grain. He strengthened the fortifications, formed outworks, cleared away the obstructions close up to the Residency. He did all this before the siege commenced.

Sir Henry died on the 4th July. In consequence of his death-bed instructions, Major Banks assumed the chief civil authority, whilst the command of the troops devolved upon Brig. Inglis.

The ground on which were built the detached houses now about to be attacked was an elevated plateau, the surface of which was rough and uneven. The defences traced around it had the form of an irregular pentagon. The accompanying plan will show that regarding the point indicated as " Innes's house " as the northern-most point, its eastern face ran irregularly parallel with the river Gúmti as far as the Baillie Guard. The line from that point to " Anderson's garrison " constituted the south-eastern, and from Anderson's garrison to " Gubbins's battery " the south-western face. The western face comprehended the line between Gubbins's battery and Innes's garrison.

Innes's garrison occupied a long, commodious lower-roomed house, containing several rooms, two good verandahs, and having a flat roof. It was commanded by Lieut. Loughnan, of the 13th Native Infantry, a most gallant officer.

Overlooking this post on the eastern face was the Redan battery, at the apex of the projecting point of high level ground. This battery was armed with two 18-pounders, and a 9-pounder. It was com-manded by Lieut. Samuel Lawrence of the 32nd Foot. The line of intrenchments between the Water Gate and the Banqueting Hall, transferred into a hospital, was commanded by Lieut. Langmore of the 71st Native Infantry. It was entirely without shelter.

Passing over the Residency and the Banqueting Hall, we come to the Treasury buildings situated below and to the eastward of the latter, known under the name of the Baillie Guard. This was armed with two 9-pounders and an 8-in. howitzer, commanded by Lieut. Aitken, 13th Native Infantry. Following the outer tracing we come to Fayrer's house* with one 9-pounder, commanded by Capt.

* Named after Surgeon-Major Fayrer, afterwards Surgeon-General Sir Joseph Fayrer, Bart., K.C.S.I.

Gould-Weston, to the Financial garrison post commanded by Capt. Sanders, 13th Native Infantry; and to Sago's house commanded by Capt. T. T. Boileau, 7th Cavalry. The two last-named buildings were commanded by the Post Office armed with two 18-pounders and a 9-pounder, and whose garrison was under the orders of Lieut. Graydon. Following the line of outer works we arrive at the Judicial post, an extensive upper house, commanded by Capt. Germon, 13th Native Infantry. Next to that, and forming the south-eastern angle of the position, was Anderson's post—a two-storied house surrounded by a wall, with two good verandahs, and intrenched and loopholed. No battery was attached to this post. It was commanded by Capt. R. P. Anderson, 25th Native Infantry.

The Cawnpore battery, constructed of earth and palisades, was the new post. This was armed with an 8-pounder, and two 9-pounders. This was the only post the commandant of which was constantly changed. The reason was that it was so entirely commanded by the enemy's works, that when they concentrated a heavy fire upon it no man could live in it. But neither could the enemy occupy it, for it was entirely commanded by the house behind it. It thus remained to the end a part of our defences. The Thag Gaol, occupied by the boys of the Martinieré College, and commanded by their principal, Mr. Schilling; the Brigade Mess, a high and convenient building, commanded by Colonel Master, 7th Light Cavalry; and the Sikh squares led to Gubbins's post, armed with two 9-pounders, and an 18-pounder, and commanded by Major Apthorp, 41st Native Infantry. Between this post and the Church Garrison were the Bhúsá intrenchments and sheep pens, slenderly manned by the officers and soldiers of the Commissariat Department. The Church Garrison consisted of about a dozen Europeans. The church was stored with grain. Of the garrison within the lines of defence may be mentioned Ommaney's post, connected by a lane with Gubbins's post and supported by the residents of the Begum Kothí, few in number and principally on the staff.

Far from taking that prompt advantage of their victory at Chinhut which a capable general would have seized, the rebel leaders for nearly three weeks did everything but assault these slight defences. They occupied in force the houses which commanded them, they erected batteries, they placed guns in position, they dug trenches to protect their men from our shells, and from the 1st to the 20th July, they kept up a terrific and incessant fire day and night, not less than 8,000 men, and probably a larger number, firing at one time into the defenders' position. Their fire was very effective. The mosques, the houses which from want of time to destroy them had been allowed to stand, the not very remote palaces, afforded them commanding positions.

Their shells penetrated into places before considered absolutely

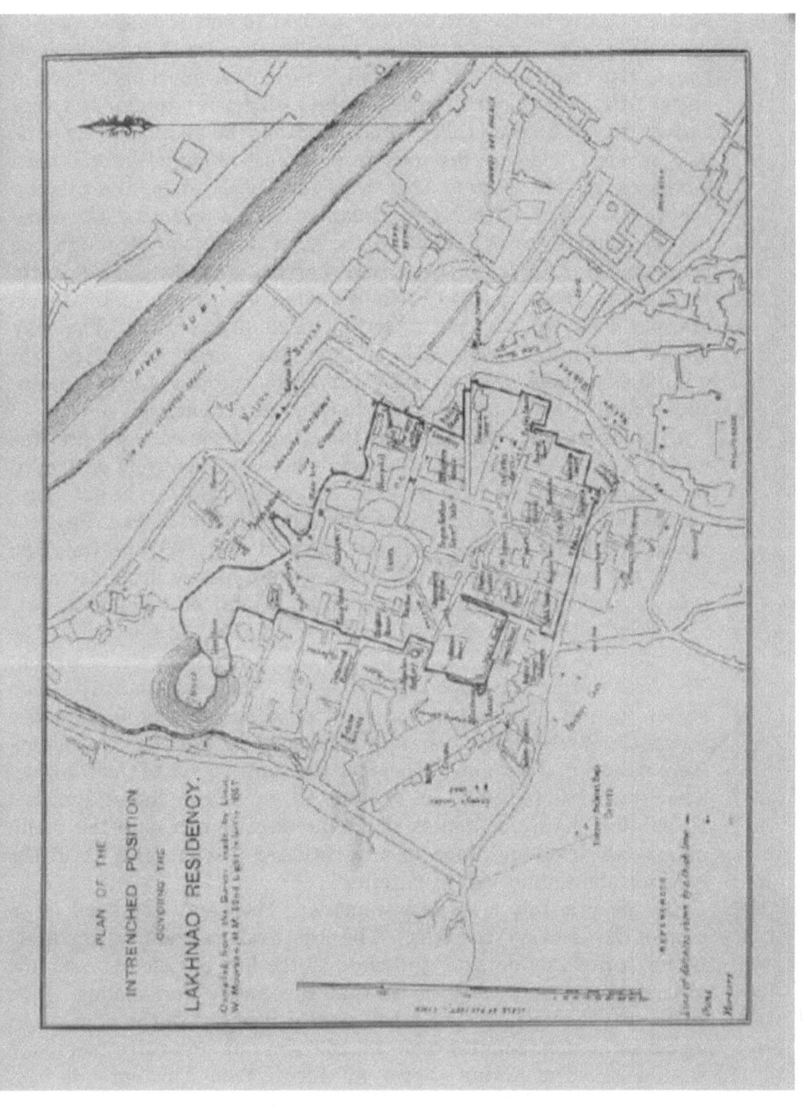
PLAN OF THE
INTRENCHED POSITION
COVERING THE
LAKHNAO RESIDENCY.

secure. Many of the garrison succumbed to this incessant rain of projectiles. Mr. Dorin was killed in an inner room of Mr. Gubbins's house, Mr. Dunmaney, of the Civil Service, was mortally wounded on the 4th July, Major Francis, of the 13th Native Infantry, a very gallant officer, on the 7th, Mr. Polehampton, the chaplain, the same day, severely. Before the 20th July, the list of casualties had been increased by Mr. Bryron shot through the head on the 9th, by Lieut. Dashwood, 48th Native Infantry, who succumbed the same day to cholera, by Lieut. Charlton, 32nd Foot, shot through the head on the 13th, by Lieut. Lester mortally wounded on the 14th, by Lieuts. Bryce and O'Brien wounded on the 16th, by Lieut. Harmer wounded, and Lieut. Arthur killed on the 19th. That day Mr. Polehampton, wounded on the 7th, died of cholera. In addition to these officers, many privates, Europeans and natives, succumbed. A few of the latter deserted to the enemy.

Upon the improvised defences the effect of the enemy's fire was even greater. On the 15th Anderson's house was entirely destroyed by round shot, though the post was still nobly held by the garrison ; on the 18th many round shots were fired into the Post Office, Fayrer's house, Gubbins's, and the Brigade Mess House. At one time the rebels succeeded in setting the Residency on fire by firing carcasses into it. At another they threatened an assault on Gubbins's post.

A large number of the bullocks perished, and the burying of the animals was no slight addition to the labours of the garrison. The heat during this time was excessive. Cholera was busy. The stench from putrid animals was most offensive. Few officers had a servant. Whilst the days were consumed in fighting, the nights were passed in developing means for the continuance of the struggle. Then stores had to be dug out and carried, guns to be shifted, trenches to be dug, shafts for miners sunk, the dead buried, and the many necessities devolving upon men so situated attended to. Still the garrison showed no sign of faltering.

On the 7th July a sortie was made. The party consisted of 50 men of the 32nd and 20 Sikhs. The object was to examine Johannes' house, a building outside, and close to the line of defence, near the Brigade Mess, as it was believed that the enemy were mining. The sortie was successful. The rebels were driven out of the house, and 15 or 20 of their number were killed. On our side three men were wounded. The daring shown by Lieut. Sam Lawrence on this occasion obtained for him the Victoria Cross.

At midnight on the 20th July, the enemy's fire almost ceased, nor was heavy firing resumed in the early morning. A little after 10 o'clock the rebels sprang a mine inside the Water Gate, about 25 yards from the inner defences, and close to the Redan. Immediately after the explosion they opened a very heavy fire on the defences near which the mine had been sprung. Under cover of this fire as soon as the smoke and dust had cleared away, they advanced in heavy masses against the Redan. The garrison, however, received them with so heavy a fire that they reeled back sorely smitten ; nor, although they made a second attempt, and penetrated to within a very few yards of the English battery, were they able to effect a lodgment. Again they fell back, baffled.

Simultaneously a heavy column advanced against Innes's house. The garrison here consisted of only 12 men of the 32nd Foot ; 12 of the 13th Native Infantry ; and a few non-military servants of Government. Against this handful of men the rebels pressed in large numbers, and made their way to within 10 yards of the palisades, and were received with a rolling fire which drove them back. They came, however, again, and again, and again, but always with the same result.

The enemy's attack was not confined to these two points. They made also a desperate and very determined attempt on the Cawnpore Battery. But their leader being stopped by a well-directed bullet, they became disheartened and fell back. Very soon afterwards another detachment advanced with scaling ladders against Anderson's and Germon's posts. But their reception at both was so warm that they retreated, not to renew the attack.

These attacks made in great force and with considerable resolution were defeated by the British with a loss of but 4 killed, and 12 wounded. By sharp experience the garrison had learnt the wisdom of keeping themselves as much as possible under cover.

But the day following this inspiring victory the garrison sustained a loss which it could ill afford. Major Banks, who had succeeded Sir Henry Lawrence as Chief Commissioner, was shot through the head. His fearlessness, his courage, and his sympathy with suffering had endeared him greatly to the garrison. His place was not filled up. The Brigadier then issued an order intimating that the office of Chief Commissioner would be held in abeyance until such time as the Government of India could be communicated with.*

From the 20th of July to the 10th of August the rebels contented themselves mainly with keeping up an unremitting fire upon the garrison, loopholing more houses, and bringing the attack closer and closer. They made no general assault. On their side the defenders were so fully occupied in repairing damages, in countermining, and in replying to the enemy's fire that they could not find sufficient time to remove the carcasses of horses and bullocks. The stench from these carcasses and from others partially buried became almost unbearable, and aided in fomenting the pest of flies, as well as the spread of cholera, of dysentery, of scurvy, and of small-pox. The badness and insufficiency of the food, the want of cooks, and the indifferent cooking, aided greatly the working of these diseases.

* Subsequently entirely approved by the Governor-General.

But in the midst of these trials a spark of hope of aid from outside glimmered in the horizon. Many letters had been despatched by messengers believed to be faithful, but up to the 25th July no reply had been received to any of them. Early on the morning of the 22nd the pensioner Angad came in from Cawnpore, but without a letter. On this occasion he did not carry one with him for fear of being detained by the enemy ; but he stated that the English had been victorious, and that he had seen two European regiments at or near Cawnpore.

At 11 o'clock on the night of the 25th, the same pensioner, who had been sent out again on the night of the 22nd to General Havelock's camp, returned with a reply to that letter from that officer's Quartermaster-General, Lieut.-Colonel Fraser-Tytler. The letter stated that " Havelock was advancing with a force sufficient to bear down all opposition and would arrive in five or six days."

And now the occasional sound of firing on the road between Cawnpore and Lucknow continued to confirm the hopes raised by the opening of this communication in the minds of the garrison.

Four days later, on the 10th August, the rebels made their second assault. About 10 o'clock that morning a body numbering perhaps 1,600 was observed by the garrison massed behind their trenches, opposite the southern face of the defences. Very soon after, a large force was noticed approaching the bridge of boats from the Marián cantonments. The word was passed that an assault was impending. Instantly all the occupants of the posts were on the alert. Half an hour later the enemy fired a shell into the Begum-Kóthí, a building in the centre of the intrenchment. This was apparently a signal, for immediately after they sprang a mine between Johannes' house and the Brigade Mess House. The effect of the explosion was terrible. The greater portion of the Martinieré house was blown in, the palisades and defences, for the space of 30 ft., were destroyed. On the smoke and dust clearing away a breach was discovered through which a regiment might have marched in unbroken order. The enemy advanced with great resolution, occupied Johannes' house and garden and the buildings close to the Cawnpore Battery, and made a desperate effort to take that post. But, whilst they were met by a withering fire from its defenders, the garrison of the Brigade Mess House, composed of a large number of officers, many of them excellent shots, and armed with their sporting guns and rifles, poured upon their flank from its roof a well-directed and continuous fusillade. This front and flank fire quite paralyzed the assailants. Some 30 of their number, however, more daring than their comrades, penetrated into the ditch of the battery within a few feet of our guns.

The following extract from Brig. Inglis' official report dated Lucknow, 26th September, 1857, to the Secretary to Government

Military Department, Calcutta, relates the events that occurred between the 10th August and the arrival of the relieving force on the 25th September :—

" On the 10th August, the enemy made another assault, having previously sprung a mine close to the Brigade Mess which entirely destroyed our defences for the space of 20 ft., and blew in a great portion of the outside wall of the house occupied by Mr. Schilling's garrison. A few of the enemy came on with the utmost determination but were received with such a withering flank fire of musketry from the officers and men holding the top of the Brigade Mess, that they beat a speedy retreat, leaving the more adventurous of their numbers lying on the crest of the breach. While this operation was going on, another large body advanced on the Cawnpore Battery, and succeeded in locating themselves for a few minutes in the ditch. They were however dislodged by hand grenades. At Capt. Anderson's post they also came boldly forward with scaling ladders, which they placed against the wall ; but here, as elsewhere, they were met with the most indomitable resolution, and, the leaders being slain, the rest fled, leaving the ladders, and retreated to their batteries and loopholed defences, from whence they kept up for the rest of the day an unusually heavy cannonade and musketry fire. On the 18th August the enemy sprung another mine in front of the Sikh lines with very fatal effect. Capt. Orr, Lieuts. Mecham and Soppit were blown into the air, but providentially returned to earth with no further injury than a severe shaking. The garrison, however, was not so fortunate. No less than 11 men were buried alive under the ruins, from whence it was impossible to extricate them, owing to the tremendous fire kept up by the enemy from the houses situated not 10 yards in front of the breach. The explosion was followed by a general assault of a less determined nature than the two former efforts, and the enemy were consequently repulsed without much difficulty. But they succeeded under cover of the breach, in establishing themselves in one of the houses in our position, from which they were driven in the evening by the bayonets of H.M.'s 32nd and 84th.

" On the 5th September the enemy made their last serious assault. Having exploded a large mine, a few feet short of the bastion of the 18-pounder gun, in Major Apthorpe's post, they advanced with large heavy scaling ladders, which they placed against the wall, and mounted, thereby gaining for an instant the embrasure of a gun. They were, however, speedily driven back with loss by handgrenades and musketry. A few minutes subsequently they sprung another mine close to the Brigade Mess, and advanced boldly, but soon the corpses strewn in the garden in front of the post bore testimony to the accuracy of the rifle and musketry fire of the gallant members of that garrison, and the enemy fled ignominiously, leaving their leader—a fine-looking old native officer—among the slain. At other posts they made similar attacks, but with less resolution, and everywhere with the same want of success. Their loss upon this day must have been very heavy, as they came on with much determination, and at night they were seen bearing large numbers of their killed and wounded over the bridges in the direction of the cantonments. His Lordship in Council will perceive that the enemy invariably commenced his attacks by the explosion of a mine, a species of offensive warfare, for the exercise of which our position was unfortunately peculiarly situated ; and had it not been for the most untiring vigilance on our part in watching and blowing up their mines before they were completed, the assaults would probably have been much more numerous, and might perhaps have ended in the capture of the place. But by countermining in all directions, we succeeded in detecting and destroying no less than four of the enemy's subterraneous advances towards important positions, two of which operations were eminently successful, as on one occasion not less than eight of them were blown into the air, and 20 suffered a similar fate on the second explosion. The labour, however, which devolved upon us in making these countermines in the absence of a body of skilled miners, was very heavy. The Right Honourable the Governor-General in Council will feel that it would be impossible to crowd within the limits of a despatch even the principal events, much more the individual acts of gallantry, which have marked this protracted struggle. But I can conscientiously declare my conviction that few troops have ever undergone greater hardships, exposed as they have been to a never-ceasing musketry fire and cannonade. They have also experienced the alternate vicissitudes of extreme wet and of intense heat, and that too with very insufficient shelter from either, and in many cases without any shelter at all.

" In addition to having had to repel real attacks, they have been exposed night and day to the hardly less harassing false alarms which the enemy have been constantly raising. The insurgents have frequently fired very heavily, sounded the advance and shouted for several hours together, though not a man could be seen, with the view of course of harassing our small and exhausted force, in which object they succeeded, for no post has been strong enough to allow of a portion only of the garrison being prepared in the event of a false attack being turned into a real one. All, therefore, had to stand to their arms and to remain at their posts until the demonstration had ceased ; and such attacks were of almost nightly occurrence. The whole of the officers and men have been on duty night and day during the 87 days which the siege has lasted, up to the arrival of Sir J. Outram, G.C.B. In addition to this incessant military duty, the force has been nightly employed in repairing defences, in moving guns, in burying dead animals, in conveying ammunition and commissariat stores from one place to another, and in other fatigue duties too numerous and too trivial to enumerate here.

" I feel, however, that any words of mine will fail to convey any adequate idea of what our fatigues and labours have been—labours in which all ranks and classes, civilians, officers, and soldiers, have all borne an equally noble part. All have together descended into the mines, all have together handled the shovel for the interment of the putrid bullock, and all accoutred with musket and bayonet, and relieved each other on sentry without regard to the distinctions of rank, civil or military. Notwithstanding these hardships, the garrison has made no less than five sorties in which they spiked two of the enemy's heaviest guns, and blew up several of the houses from which they had kept up their most incessant fire. Owing to the extreme paucity of our numbers, each man was taught to feel that on his own individual efforts alone depended in no small measure the safety of the entire position.

" This consciousness incited every officer, soldier, and man to defend the post assigned to him with such desperate tenacity, and to fight for the lives which Providence had entrusted to his care with such dauntless determination, that the enemy despite their constant attacks, their heavy mines, their overwhelming numbers, and their incessant fire could never succeed in gaining one single inch of ground within the bounds of the straggling position, which was so feebly fortified that had they once obtained a footing in any of the outposts, the whole place must have inevitably fallen.

" If further proof be wanting of the desperate nature of the struggle which we have, under God's blessing, so long and so successfully waged, I would point to the roofless and ruined houses, to the crumbled walls, to the exploded mines, to the open breaches, to the shattered and disabled guns and defences, and lastly to the long and melancholy list of the brave and devoted men who have fallen.

" These silent witnesses bear sad and solemn testimony to the way in which this feeble position has been defended. During the early part of these vicissitudes, we were left without any information whatever regarding the posture of affairs outside. An occasional spy did indeed come in with the object of inducing our Sepoys and servants to desert ; but the intelligence derived from such source was, of course, entirely untrustworthy. We sent our messengers daily, calling for aid and asking for information, none of whom ever returned until the 26th day of the siege, when a pensioner named Angad came back with a letter from General Havelock's camp, informing us that they were advancing with a force sufficient to bear down all opposition, and would be with us in five or six days. A messenger was immediately despatched, requesting that on the evening of their arrival on the outskirts of the city two rockets might be sent up, in order that we might take the necessary measures for assisting them while forcing their way in. The sixth day, however, expired and they came not ; but for many evenings after officers and men watched for the ascension of the expected rockets, with hopes such as make the heart sick. We knew not then, nor did we know until the 29th August—or 35 days later—that the relieving force after having fought most nobly to effect our deliverance, had been obliged to fall back for reinforcements ; and this was the last communication that we received until two days before the arrival of Sir James Outram, on the 25th September.

" Besides heavy visitations of cholera and small-pox, we have also had to contend against a sickness which had almost universally pervaded the garrison. Commencing with a very painful eruption, it has merged into a low fever, combined with diarrhœa ; and although few or no men have died from its effects, it leaves behind a weakness and lassitude which in the absence of all material sustenance save coarse beef and still coarser flour, none have been able entirely to get over. The mortality among the women and children, and especially among the latter, from these diseases, and from other causes, has been perhaps, the most painful characteristic of the siege. The want of native servants has also been a source of much privation. Owing to the suddenness with which we were besieged, many of these people who might, perhaps, have proved otherwise faithful to their employers, but who were outside the defences at the time, were altogether excluded. Very many more deserted, and several families were consequently left without the services of a single domestic. Several ladies have had to tend their children, and even to wash their own clothes, as well as to cook their scanty meals entirely unaided. Combined with the absence of servants, the want of proper accommodation has probably been the cause of much of the disease with which we have been afflicted. I cannot refrain from bringing to the prominent notice of His Lordship in Council the patient endurance and the Christian resignation which have been evinced by the women of this garrison. They have animated us by their example. Many, alas, have been made widows, and their children fatherless, in this cruel struggle. But all such seem resigned to the will of Providence, and many among whom may be mentioned the honoured names of Birch, of Polehampton, of Barbor, and of Gall, have, after the manner of Miss Nightingale, constituted themselves the tender and solicitous nurses of the wounded and dying soldiers in the hospital."

General Inglis concludes by bringing to favourable notice the names of those officers who had distinguished themselves, and had afforded him the most valuable assistance during the operations.

CHAPTER SIXTEEN

Brig.-General Neill was pressed by the Commander of the Forces, Sir Patrick Grant, to hasten to Cawnpore to join General Havelock as soon as possible, in order that he might be on the spot to take command of the force should Havelock from any cause become unfit for the duty, and left Allahabad on the 16th July, and proceeding with all possible expedition, reached Cawnpore on the 20th.

On his way General Havelock informed him that he was anxiously awaiting his arrival, as, immediately he did, he intended " to strike a blow that would rebound through India." Neill on his arrival at Cawnpore was informed by Havelock that he intended to begin the passage of the Ganges on the morrow, leaving Neill in command at Cawnpore with about 200 men, the majority of whom were sick and wounded. In this arrangement, Neill anxious that Havelock should take with him every available man, entirely concurred.

Before deciding on making a desperate effort to relieve Lucknow, General Havelock had traced out a position resting on the river, which it would be easy for a small force to hold against very superior numbers. The work was being entrenched and some guns mounted there at the time of Neill's arrival. He was to complete and hold it.

Although General Havelock's force consisted of only about 1,500 men, owing to the breadth of the swollen river, the rapidity of the current alone presented formidable obstacles. The crossing occupied four days.

On the afternoon of the 24th General Havelock crossed, and marched the force about 5 miles on the Lucknow Road, halting for the night at the little village of Mungulwár. The force consisted of 10 guns imperfectly equipped and imperfectly manned ; the remains of the 64th, the 84th, the 75th Regiments, the Madras Fusiliers, and of Brazer's Sikhs ; and some 60 volunteer horse. Small as were the numbers they were possessed of the best spirit, and had unbounded confidence in their general.

On the night of the 24th of July this force bivouacked at Mungul-wár. It remained halted at the village four days, to enable the General to complete his dispositions for carriage and supplies. On the 28th these had been completed so far as the disorganized state of the country permitted. At 5 o'clock on the morning of the 29th the force began its onward movement. After marching 3 miles the advanced pickets of the enemy were discovered. These fell back as our men pressed on, disclosing the enemy occupying a very strong position. Their main force rested on the town of Oonáo, a straggling place, extending about three-quarters of a mile, and which the heavy rains and the nature of the soil rendered it impossible to turn. In advance of this town, and between it and the British force, was a succession of walled enclosures, filled with skirmishers. These enclosures joined a village united with Oonáo by a narrow passage, and all the houses in which were loopholed and defended.

It was impossible to turn such a position ; it was murderous work to attack it in front. But if he was to get on at all Havelock had no option. After a steady reconnaissance, Havelock gave his orders. Covering his main body with skirmishers, armed with the Enfield rifle, he opened a heavy fire from them, and from his guns on the more advanced positions of the enemy. This fire drove them from those positions and forced them to take refuge in the loopholed houses. At these Havelock then sent the 78th Highlanders, and the Madras Fusiliers. Gallantly did they advance. But to dislodge an enemy from loopholed houses, singly, one after the other, is deadly work ; Havelock therefore ordered up the 64th. Their advance decided the day. The enemy were either bayoneted in the houses or sought refuge in flight.

But the town of Oonáo was still in the enemy's possession, and, what was of more consequence, fresh troops were observed hastening down the Lucknow Road in its direction. Havelock at once made preparations to meet them. Drawing off his force to a dry spot of ground between the village and the town, he placed his guns in a position to command the high road, by which alone he could be attacked, and waited for the movement of the enemy further to develop itself. In a short time it was evident he would be attacked. The rebels were marching in dense columns upon him. Havelock's joy was great for he felt that he had them. Restraining his impatience until when they were well within distance, he suddenly opened a withering fire upon them from both arms. It stopped them and they attempted to deploy, but on either side of them were swamps and marshes. Consequently, their horses and their guns stuck fast, their infantry floundered. All this time they were exposed to a continuous fire. Meanwhile some of our men, wading in the marshes, made their presence perceptible on either flank. This was the final blow. The rebels gave way, and fled precipitately leaving in our possession 15 guns.

Notwithstanding that he and his men were under the terrible sun of India, he determined to push on after the enemy, as soon as his men should have satisfied the cravings of exhausted nature. He ordered a halt ; and while the cooks prepared the food, and the doctors attended the wounded, he had the 15 captured guns disabled as he had no cattle to take them with him.

At the end of three hours the men again fell in, and pushed forwards, always towards Lucknow. They had marched 6 miles, when suddenly they came in sight of a walled town, situated in the open, and intersected by the road which they must traverse. This was the town of Bashíratgunj. It looked very formidable. In front of it was a large pond or tank, swollen by the surrounding inundation to the form of a river. On the Lucknow side of it was another pond or lake, traversed by a narrow causeway. It possessed besides a wet ditch, and its main gate was defended by an earthwork and four guns, and flanked on both sides by loopholed turrets. He poured a tremendous fire on the town, whilst the 64th made a flank movement to his right ; then, when he deemed the moment to have arrived, he sent on his infantry to the main gate. But the 64th had not reached the causeway—and the larger body of the enemy escaped across it.

Still the loss of the rebels that day had been severe. It was computed that not less than 400 of them had been killed or wounded. On the British side 88 had been placed *hors de combat*, but two battles had been gained.

But the thoughts of the General that night were not consoling. It was not alone, or even mainly, that his losses in the fight had been heavy, for sickness also had done its work. On the morrow of the two battles he could not, deducting the necessary guards, place in line more than 850 infantry. He knew that in front of him were places to be traversed, or stormed, the means of defence of which exceeded those of the places he had already conquered. Then too he had no means of carrying his sick, and he could not leave them, for he could not spare a sufficient force to guard them. But perhaps his greatest difficulty lay in the fact that every step forwards would take him further from his base, and he had information that that base was threatened. Náná Sahib, in fact, had no sooner heard of the onward move of the British, than he sent a considerable body of cavalry across the river to cut off their communications with Cawnpore. No one can doubt that the resolution at which Havelock arrived on the following morning, to fall back on Mangalwúr, and to ask for reinforcements was the right one. From Mangalwúr it would be possible to send the sick and wounded to Cawnpore without permanently weakening his force. He effected this movement the following day without haste, and in the most perfect order. From Mangalwúr he despatched his sick and wounded into Cawnpore, and a letter to General Neill, stating that he had been forced to fall back, and that to enable him to reach Lucknow it was necessary that he should receive a reinforcement of a thousand men and another battery of guns. Neill had assumed command at Cawnpore on the 24th July. He had not been satisfied with the state of affairs as he found them there. The location of the troops appeared to him faulty, the camp pitched without method or arrangement, no effectual steps taken to put a stop to the plundering in the city—a plundering carried on by our European and Sikh soldiers.* His first acts on the 25th were to appoint a superintendent of police, to re-establish order in the city and bazaars, to put a stop to plundering. He announced his assumption of command, and notified the measures above stated in a telegram the same day to the Commander of the Forces, Sir Patrick Grant. The spirit of the man showed itself in the last sentence of this telegram :—" All well here. I will hold my own against any odds."

Not only was Neill aware that Náná Sahib, distant from him but 24 miles, was threatening to cross the river and to attack him, but he had received information that the mutinous 42nd Native Infantry were within 8 miles of the station, and that other native regiments were gradually collecting on the right bank of the Jumna with the avowed intention of making a dash on Cawnpore. But Neill was not disturbed. " If the 42nd are within reach," he recorded in his journal on the 30th, " I will deal them a blow that will astound them." With the levies of Náná Sahib he did deal. On the 31st he despatched a party of 50 Fusiliers and 25 Sikhs, with two 6-pounders, and a $5\frac{1}{2}$-in. mortar, manned by six gunners, under the command of his aide-de-camp, Capt. John Gordon, of the 6th Regiment, Native Infantry, in the steamer to Jajamáo, to seize the boats in which it was reported Náná Sahib intended to cross the river. The party destroyed several boats, carried off six or eight, and returned to Cawnpore the next day.

On the 3rd August Havelock was reinforced by Olphert's half-battery and a company of the 84th. Hopes had been held out to him that the 5th Fusiliers and the 90th Light Infantry would reach Cawnpore early in August. But owing to the mutiny of the regiments at Dinapore these regiments were retained though grievously required to reinforce Cawnpore. The disappointment only roused Havelock to renewed exertion. On the 4th August having then about 1,400 effective men under his command, two heavy guns, (24-pounders), two 24-pounder howitzers, and a battery and a-half

* Private journal of Brig.-General Neill, unpublished.

of guns, he started a second time in the direction of the besieged Residency. Having heard that the town of Bashíratgunj had been re-occupied in force, he bivouacked that night at Oonáo. Leaving that place early next morning he found the enemy occupying a position very similar to that from which he had dislodged them on the 29th July.

Havelock ordered the advance by the road of the heavy guns supported by the Madras Fusiliers and the 84th Foot, whilst the 78th Highlanders, the Sikhs and Maude's Battery should turn the village on its left. The heavy guns speedily dislodged the enemy from the outer defences. Meanwhile the turning movement greatly disturbed them. Bewildered by the progress it was making, and much embarrassed by the firing in front of them, they were stricken with panic, and fled across the causeway. In their flight across the causeway the rebels came under the fire of the guns of Maude's Battery and were mown down in numbers. The heavy guns continued all this time their destructive fire, silencing the guns of the enemy and forcing them back. The rebels did indeed for some time longer hold villages to the right and left of the town, but in the end they were forced out of these.

Still though the enemy was beaten " the whole transaction " to use the language employed by Lieut.-Colonel Tytler to Sir Patrick Grant, was most unsatisfactory, only two small iron guns, formerly captured by us being taken.

The loss of our force had not been large. Two had been killed and 23 wounded. The loss of the rebels was stated to be 300. But there were weighty considerations to stay further advance, cholera had broken out in the camp and that disease and fever had placed 75 men on the sick list. In the action at Bashíratgunj one-fourth of the ammunition had been expended. Between that town and Lucknow was a deep river, the Saí, and three strong places, guarded it was believed by 30,000 men. The Zemindars, too, had risen in bodies of 500 or 600, independently of the regular troops. " All the men killed yesterday," wrote Colonel Tytler, " were Zemindars." But even were the force able to reach Lucknow what could it effect, enfeebled and worn out against the myriads who would oppose it in the streets ? On the morrow of the fighting at Bashíratgunj it was impossible to parade 900 infantry. To what extent would this number be reduced in fighting its way to the Residency ?

Intelligence reached Havelock on the 6th that the men of the Gwalior Contingent had successfully mutinied against their own Maharajah, and were threatening to move on Calpee, a position which would threaten Cawnpore, and menace the communication with Allahabad. The intelligence regarding the Gwalior force then brought home to Havelock for immediate decision the question of advance or retreat ; the advance could scarcely be successful, and yet failure in his opinion involved the destruction of his force, and with it possibly a disaster at Cawnpore. Retreat only risked Lucknow, while an unsuccessful advance subjected Lucknow to a greater risk.

No sensible man will deny that under the circumstances of the case, Havelock exercised a wise judgment in deciding to retire and wait for reinforcements and he fell back on Mangalwár, when he lay there for four days recruiting his men. On the 11th he purposed to recross into Cawnpore, but learning that the rebels had established themselves in considerable force at Bashíratgunj, with advanced parties at Oonáo, prepared to disturb him while crossing, he resolved to anticipate them. For the third time he advanced along the Lucknow Road, pushed the advanced parties out of Oonáo, and bivouacked near that town for the night. At dawn he again attacked the enemy. Under his orders the 78th Highlanders precipitated themselves, without firing a shot, on the earthworks in front, while the Madras Fusiliers, to whom the turning movement had been entrusted, took them in flank. The result was decisive. Two of the enemy's guns were captured and turned on them and they fled in disorder leaving about 200 killed and wounded. Our loss amounted to 35. Having thus scared away the enemy, on the 13th Havelock leisurely fell back, and by 2 o'clock on that day had recrossed into Cawnpore without a casualty. His troops were taken over in the steamers and in country boats towed by the steamers, the current being still too strong to permit the putting together of the bridge of boats for which materials had been prepared.

The private journal of General Neill showed that he still held to his previous opinion that Havelock, in retiring after his first victory on the 29th June, had committed an error which could not be redeemed until he had received large reinforcements. Sir John Kaye in his *History of the Indian Mutiny*, Vol. III., does not concur in this view, and considering the immense temptation to Havelock to advance, the pain which the order to retreat caused him, the historian of the Mutiny cannot but regard his resistance to that temptation as the most heroic act even of his great career.

After the action fought at Oonáo and Bashíratgunj by General Havelock, and after three strenuous efforts to reach Lucknow by the small force under that great General's command, the retirement of the force to Cawnpore in order to await reinforcements was imperative.

Sir James Outram had been sent to Cawnpore to command the force which was to relieve Lucknow. In accepting that command he superseded the man whose daring efforts with an inferior force to effect that relief had won for him the applause and admiration of his countrymen. To the generous nature of Outram, it seemed revolting that he should obtain the glory where another had endured the trials and the dangers. He could not do it, and he was determined that it should not be done. Availing himself of the circumstance that whilst from a military point of view, he was commander of the forces about to march into Oudh, he would also enter that country in a civil capacity as its Chief Commissioner, he published, the day of his arrival at Cawnpore on the 16th September the following order :—" The important duty of relieving the garrison of Lucknow had been first entrusted to Brig.-General Havelock, c.b., and Major-General Outram feels that it is due to that distinguished officer, and to the noble and strenuous exertion which he has already made to effect that object, that to him should accrue the honour of the achievement. Major-General Outram is confident that the great end for which Brig.-General Havelock and his brave troops have so long and gloriously fought will now, under the blessing of Providence, be accomplished. The Major-General, therefore, in gratitude for, and admiration of the brilliant deed of arms achieved by Brig.-General Havelock and his gallant troops, will cheerfully waive his rank in favour of that officer on this occasion, and will accompany the force to Lucknow in his civil capacity as Chief Commissioner of Oudh, tendering his military services to Brig.-General Havelock as a volunteer. On the relief of Lucknow, the Major-General will resume his position at the head of the force."

On the 17th General Havelock found waiting him on his return from a successful expedition to Bithoor, and after the capture of that place, a copy of the *Calcutta Gazette* dated the 5th August, containing the nomination of Major-General Sir James Outram to the military command of the country in which he was operating. He learned in fact that he was superseded. He received this information from the *Gazette* alone. It was accompanied by no communication to break the news. He received the bald announcement only. Superseded as he regarded himself to be, he was as active, as daring, as devoted, as when he ruled, the unfettered commander of an independent force. Never indeed was the exercise of the great qualities of resolution and energy more needed than after his return from the expedition against Bithoor. Out of 1,700 English troops whom he had altogether under his orders from the time of his quitting Allahabad, but 685 remained effective.

Not only was he now compelled to abandon for the moment all idea of re-crossing into Oudh, but the action of the Gwalior Contingent threatening Calpee, rendered it doubtful if he could even hold Cawnpore. Were Calpee to be occupied by this force, consisting of 5,000 disciplined men with 30 guns, his communications with Allahabad might at any moment be cut off.

To the north, the Nawáb of Furruckábád was ready with 30,000 men—some sepoys, some raw levies—to take advantage of any difficulty which might threaten Cawnpore. It was too, in the power of the rebels in Oudh to cross the Ganges at any point below Cawnpore, and acting singly or co-operating possibly with the Gwalior troops, to endanger his communications. Of all these dangers Havelock had the fullest cognizance. Yet his judgment was never clouded. To remain at Cawnpore was undoubtedly a risk, but to fall back on Allahabad would have been a calamity. He resolved then to hold Cawnpore as long as possible and to await the reinforcements which were on their way.

CHAPTER SEVENTEEN

Arrangements were in the meantime made and carried out for sending all the sick and wounded who could bear the journey to Allahabad. Reinforcements gradually arrived in small parties, the troops were allowed to rest after their fatigues, the regulations for the maintenance of public order were rigidly enforced, and the works at the intrenchment were pushed on.

The feeling entertained by Neill towards Havelock had never been very cordial. The two men were not formed to act together. Neill had chafed much under the inaction to which, since Havelock's arrival, he had been subjected, and he had greatly feared that in the advance which was to take place, he would again be left behind. His gratification then, may be imagined when, on the eve of Outram's arrival, Havelock informed him that the command of the right wing of the relieving force had been conferred upon him.

Sir James Outram arrived at Cawnpore on the 15th September. If there could be anything which would reconcile a successful soldier to supersession it would be to be superseded by such a man as Outram. He had been called the Bayard of the Indian Army. He was without fear and without reproach. Engaged in many contests, he never fought for himself—he fought always for the cause of those whom he believed to have been wronged. He was appalled neither by the power, the talent, the interest, of the side to which he was opposed.

Well might Sir Colin Campbell write these glowing words when announcing to the army this deed of real glory. Seldom, perhaps never, has it occurred to a Commander-in-Chief to publish and confirm such an order as the following one :—

" With such a reputation as Major-General Sir James Outram has won for himself, he can well afford to share glory and honour with others. But that does not lessen the value of the sacrifice he has made with such generosity in favour of Brig.-General Havelock, C.B., commanding the field force in Oudh.

" Concurring, as the Commander-in-Chief does, in everything stated in the just eulogy of the latter by Sir James Outram, His Excellency takes this opportunity of publicly testifying to the army his admiration for an act of self-sacrifice and generosity, on a point which, of all others, is dear to a real soldier."

The force now at Havelock's disposal consisted of 3,179 men of all arms.* He divided it into three brigades :—two of infantry, the third of artillery. The 1st Brigade consisted of the 5th Fusiliers ; the 84th Regiment, and, attached to it, two companies of the 64th ; and the Madras Fusiliers. It was commanded by the gallant Neill.

The 2nd Brigade, composed of the 78th Highlanders ; the 90th Light Infantry ; and the Sikh Regiment of Ferozepore, was commanded by Brigadier Hamilton.

The 3rd Brigade included Capt. Maude's Battery, Capt. Olpherts' Battery, Major Eyre's Battery of heavy 18-pounders, the whole commanded by Major Cooper.

Besides these, there were 109 volunteers, and some 59 of the 12th Irregulars, believed to be faithful, under the command of Capt. L. Barrow. Major-General Outram was one of these volunteers. To defend Cawnpore during the advance on Lucknow, there remained the headquarters of the 64th Regiment, under the command of Colonel Wilson.

The whole of the reinforcements had reached Cawnpore by the morning of the 16th September to attempt the passage of the river when the bridge of boats was completed. On the afternoon of the 17th a party of the rebel cavalry and infantry, with three guns, came down to the opposite bank to reconnoitre. Their appearance was the signal for the withdrawal to the right bank of a party of Sikhs who had been sent across to cover the formation of the bridge, and a detachment of the rebel infantry crossed to an island and under cover of long grass opened fire on the men working at the bridge. A few round and shrapnel shot soon drove them away.

The bridge-head on the opposite side was covered by a detachment from the British force during the night, and on the 18th the bridge had so nearly approached completion that it was resolved to make arrangements at once to effect a successful passage. On the 18th no enemy was to be seen on the opposite bank. That morning four guns of Maude's Battery were crossed over to the island, and the 78th Highlanders and the 90th Light Infantry were marched to a position on the river bank, to be ready to take advantage of the completion of the bridge. Subsequently part of the

* The numerical strength of the component portions of the force was as follows :—Europeans : Infantry, 2,388 ; Volunteer Cavalry, 109 ; Artillery, 282. Natives : Sikh Infantry, 341 ; Native Irregular Cavalry, 59. Total, 3,179.

90th and three guns of Maude's Battery crossed the river. At 11 o'clock the enemy brought down their heavy guns, and opened fire on the British, whose guns answered. The cannonade lasted three hours, ceasing almost as suddenly as it had begun.

On the 19th the bridge was ready. During the previous month frequent reconnaissances had been made by Capt. Crommelin* of the Engineers who had completed all the arrangements and collected the materials and superintended the construction of the bridge. As soon as the troops had crossed they were formed into contiguous quarter-columns, and the 84th being in the line of the enemy's fire were ordered to lie down. General Neill's Brigade was then ordered to take up a position on the right of the line, and to drive the enemy from some sandhills about 600 yards in advance which they occupied. Neill immediately moved forward his brigade and attacked the enemy. They made a firm resistance but were driven from their position. Whilst the infantry fight was going on William Olpherts† brought up a half-battery in splendid style, and silenced the enemy's guns. The enemy slowly retired, and the cavalry having followed them up to observe, the force piled arms, and awaited the arrival of the camp equipage. The next day was devoted to the crossing of Eyre's heavy guns, and they were brought into camp by noon. The arrangements for the advance were then complete. On the morning of the 21st the force started on its arduous task. On approaching the village of Mangalwúr, it became evident that the enemy was massed there in great strength. Havelock upon this took ground to the left, and deployed into line, having the volunteer cavalry on the extreme left. This had scarcely been accomplished before the enemy's guns, five in number, opened fire. They had one gun defended by a breastwork playing on the road. The three English batteries at once replied, whilst the infantry marched through the swamp to the high ground from which they could act on the rear of the rebels. Before they could reach the road behind the village the enemy had evacuated it. A rapid pursuit ensued and was most successful.. The volunteer cavalry captured two guns, a set of colours, and an elephant, and killed about 120 men. This close pursuit drove the enemy helter-skelter through the village of Oonáo, no effort being made to defend it. The force had thus reached with but a skirmish the furthest point of Havelock's three brilliant inroads into Oudh.

The rain fell heavily next morning as Havelock's force left its night quarters, the 1st Brigade leading. After a march of 16 miles

* Afterwards Lieut.-General Crommelin, c.b., R.E.
† Regarding this officer, Lord Napier of Magdala once said " I have often seen Olpherts in action. but never without his deserving the Victoria Cross."

they reached the village of Banni, which was a strong and defensible position. To reach it a force coming from Cawnpore had to cross the river Sái, here spanned by a long masonry bridge. The river was not fordable. Strong as was the position, the enemy neither used the advantages it offered them, nor opposed to our troops the smallest opposition. They even neglected to break down the bridge, and although they had constructed two batteries on the Lucknow side of it, had not the spirit to use them. Panic-stricken by Havelock's rapid advance, they abandoned the best chance they had of stopping him, and evacuated their strongest position before even it had been attacked. Banni was but 16 miles from Lucknow, and in the hope of giving information of his approach to the garrison of the Residency Havelock that evening fired a Royal salute. His men lay there for the night, their indignation aroused and their slumbers troubled by the constant sound of the booming of the cannon fire against their beleaguered countrymen.

By 8 o'clock on the 23rd they were on their way again, marching in column of subdivisions right in front. The rain had cleared off but it was very close and steamy, without a breath of wind. Since 6 o'clock that morning the booming of the cannon discharged against the Residency had ceased. This silence seemed to indicate that the enemy was massing his big guns to oppose the relieving force. For some time no enemy was visible, but as the British approached the Alambágh, infantry began to show themselves on their flanks, and it soon became apparent that the enemy was prepared to receive them at the walled garden. A party of cavalry was sent on to reconnoitre, and reported that the mutineers had six guns in position, that their left rested on the Alambágh, and their centre and right were drawn up behind a chain of hillocks.

Havelock then halted his force, changed the order of the column from right to left in front, and brought up the 78th Highlanders and Eyre's heavy guns. These changes having been effected, the British force moved on. No sooner, however, were they within range than the enemy's guns opened with round and grape shot ; they must have studied the distance very carefully, for their first shot knocked over three officers of the 90th, all of whom subsequently died. The casualties among the men and camp followers were likewise considerable. But these losses did not check the advance. Whilst the 78th, the 90th, and the remainder of the 2nd Brigade pushed quickly on to gain the open ground on which it could deploy, Neill with the 1st Brigade took ground to the left, passing through deep ditches, through swamps, and over heavy ground.

Meanwhile Eyre's Battery on the road, and Olpherts' on the right, had opened out on the enemy, Maude's followed quickly. This fire had the effect of dispersing the rebel cavalry and cleared the way for the advance of our men. Neill now led his men over very heavy ground, and drove the rebels from several villages in succession. The key of the position, however, was the Alumbágh, and the upper-storied buildings adjacent to it. These the rebels defended with great resolution ; but they could not withstand the assault made by the 5th Fusiliers. Advancing with the bayonet, the men of this splendid regiment cleared the houses and stormed the position. Of the guns the rebels had brought into action five were captured by the Volunteer Cavalry.

Having driven the enemy from the Alumbágh, the force advanced to within sight of the domes, the minarets, and the gardens of Lucknow. But the day's work had been hard, and the General prudently determined to halt for the night. Our men, however, had scarcely taken up the ground assigned to them and had halted, when the rebels who up to that time had been fleeing in desperate haste, suddenly stopped, brought up fresh guns, and opened a heavy fire on the regiments as they stood or lay in line.

Just at this time the rain came down in torrents. Havelock met this action of the enemy by drawing back his line of fire, throwing his right on the Alumbágh, and re-forming his left. The movement was a difficult one, as darkness had set in, and the road was obstructed with horses, elephants, bullocks, guns, and men. The 5th Fusiliers occupied the Alumbágh. The other regiments were more or less provided for, some occupying hamlets, some lying in the open. The Madras Fusiliers bivouacked in mud ankle deep ; but they and the rest of the force " were as merry and jolly as possible."* The men had been greatly cheered by the news that reached them that day that Delhi had been captured.

The force halted throughout the day of the 24th. And the position was further changed so as to remove the men entirely from the range of the enemy's guns, which nevertheless continued their cannonade. The enemy's cavalry, likewise, creeping round to the rear, made an attempt on the baggage, but though they surprised and killed some ten or twelve of its defenders, they were eventually driven off. That night all the baggage of our men was stored in the Alumbágh, and a guard of 250 men was placed there. At last the day of trial dawned. General Havelock in consultation with Sir James Outram, had resolved to advance, not by the direct route to the Residency, but by another and more circuitous road skirting the Chárbágh Canal. Early on the morning of the 25th, the 1st Brigade headed by Maude's Battery, with two companies of the 5th Fusiliers leading, moved off in column of sections, right in front. They had advanced but a short distance when a tremendous fire opened upon them. From the Alumbágh to a house called the Yellow House, the advancing troops had to encounter

* MSS. Journal, kept at the time.

a perfect storm of round and grape shot and a sharp musketry fire.

Vigorously pushing on, they approached the enclosure called the Chárbágh, and a village, both filled with the enemy. From there the musketry fire was very galling. Our men, however, dashed at the enemy and expelled them. The next point to be reached was the Chárbágh Bridge, the only opening left into Lucknow. The bridge was barred by an earthen parapet about 7 ft. high. On this parapet were mounted six guns, two of them 24-pounders. On approaching the position the force halted ; Maude brought two guns to the front and opened fire, whilst Outram taking with him the 5th Fusiliers and the Sikhs, proceeded to drive the enemy from the enclosures on the right, with the view of bringing a reverse fire on the guns defending the bridge. The enemy had the advantage of numbers and position, and for some time the artillery duel raged with great fury. Maude had but two light guns and they were in the open. When the duel had lasted half an hour, it became evident that Maude could make no impression on the enemy. He had lost 21 men at the Yellow House, and others had fallen in front of the bridge.

Something had to be done. Under these circumstances, young Henry Havelock, always bold, daring and adventurous, imperilled his commission to carry out an idea which had flashed through his brain. Turning his horse's head, he galloped off in the direction of the post occupied by his father. After making the turn of the road, he halted, waited for three or four minutes, then galloping back to Neill, saluted him, and said, as if bringing an order from the General, whom he had not seen, " You are to charge the bridge, sir." Neill at once issued the order.

Arnold, of the Madras Fusiliers, dashed on to the bridge, with the advance of 25 men, Tytler and Havelock accompanying them mounted. Tytler was pierced through the groin and his horse killed. Every other man of the 25, except Havelock and a private named Jakes, was shot down by the enemy's six guns loaded with grape. Havelock, unable to pass the overlapping barrier, sat in his saddle, calling on the men to come on. Jakes stood by his side, loading and firing as fast as he could. A few seconds later the Madras Fusiliers swarmed over the parapet, and through the gap, and carried all before them. The entry into Lucknow was won. The 78th Highlanders of the 2nd Brigade followed and the captured guns were spiked.*

* For his gallant conduct on this occasion, Havelock was recommended by Sir James Outram for the Victoria Cross. He had previously received it for his conduct at Cawnpore. Maude also received the Cross for the persistent gallantry he displayed this day. " But for his nerve and coolness," wrote Outram, " the army could not have advanced." Private Jakes was killed later in the day.

On the regiments of the 2nd Brigade closing up, the whole force advanced, but in pursuance of the resolution already referred to, instead of moving straight on through the city, it took a turn to the right at the bridge, and pushed on by a very bad and narrow road along the outskirts. The troops pressed along this road, subjected here to but little opposition. Two regiments were detached to cover the advance of the remaining brigades, as well as to protect the heavy guns, the dragging of which over a bad road was found both tedious and difficult.

This road gradually led into the outskirts of the city, and the men were forced to penetrate through narrow streets and lanes, every one of which seemed alive with the enemy's fire. Suddenly they found their progress barred by a narrow bridge over a nullah, with high banks on the opposite side. This bridge lay under the lee of the Kaiserbágh, partially commanded by the two guns posted there, and by the infantry occupying it. The infantry and the guns were forced to cross that bridge, and to cross it almost singly. The fire from the Kaiserbágh was tremendous. It happened, however, that a sheltered position was attainable on the other side, from which the enemy might be fired on with advantage. The troops as they crossed the bridge, took up this position and opening fire to some extent covered their comrades. But the ordeal was a terrible one, and many men fell at this point. Having passed this obstacle, the force re-united, and halted under cover of some deserted buildings near the Chuttar Munzil and Faratbaksh Palaces.

Darkness was now coming on. The rear guard, with the heavy guns, the wounded, and the baggage, was behind, exposed to the fury of the enemy. In a consultation with General Havelock, Sir James Outram proposed that the force should occupy the Chuttar Munzil for a few hours, to permit the junction with the rear guard. The proposition showed judgment and prudence, for the Chuttar Munzil was a strong position, easy to hold, and virtually communicated, by means of intervening palaces, with the Residency. Had the suggestion been adopted, the safety of the rear guard would have been assured, and the entrance into the Residency enclosure could have been effected with comparatively little loss. But General Havelock considered that the importance of letting the beleaguered garrison know that succour was at hand outweighed every other consideration. The troops, re-formed, accordingly pushed on. The houses in Khás Bazaar were thronged with the enemy. As the men approached the archway a tremendous fire opened upon them. Neill, who was leading them, passed through the archway, then, suddenly pulling up his horse, he directed his aide-de-camp, Gordon, to gallop back and recall a half-battery which had taken a wrong road. He remained there sitting on his horse, when a Sepoy, who had taken post on the arch, discharged his musket at him over the parapet on its top. The bullet entered his head behind the left ear and killed him. .Thus fell one of the bravest and most determined men in the British Army. He was a born warrior, very cool and very keen-sighted. In a word he was a noble type of the northern land that owned him. Though 57 years have elapsed since he fell, his memory still lives alike in India and in England.

Undeterred by the loss they had sustained, the British troops pressed on through the Khás Bazaar, fiercely assailed by a musketry fire. Emerging from this, the sounds of cheering from the Residency suddenly gladdened the ears of the Highlanders and their comrades. Others of the advancing force, who had forced their way through side streets, appeared on the scene almost immediately afterwards, and took up the cheers most vociferously. Well, indeed might their hearts swell within them. But they are not yet within the enclosure. The night was dark, and before our troops could enter, it was necessary to make a way for them and for the guns. The displacement of the impediments at the gate of the Baillie Guard which had so long resisted the enemy's assaults caused some delay. But at last they were removed, and many of the victorious troops entered. Then ensued a scene which cannot better be told than in the words of Capt. Wilson's diary :—

" At 4 p.m. report was made that some officers dressed in shooting coats and solah hats, a regiment of Europeans in blue pantaloons and shirts, and a bullock battery were seen near Mr. Martin's house, and the Moti Mahal. At 5 p.m. volleys of musketry, rapidly growing louder, were heard in the city. But soon the firing of a Minié ball over our heads gave notice of the still nearer approach of our friends, of whom as yet little or nothing had been seen, though the enemy had been seen firing heavily on them from the roofs of the houses. Five minutes later, and our troops were seen fighting their way through one of the principal streets ; and though men fell at almost every step, yet nothing could withstand the headlong gallantry of our reinforcements. Once fairly *seen* all our doubts and fears regarding them were ended : and then the garrison's long pent-up feelings of anxiety and suspense burst forth in a succession of deafening cheers. From every pit, trench, and battery, from behind the sandbags piled on shattered houses, from every post still held by a few gallant spirits, rose cheer on cheer. Even from the hospital many of the wounded crawled forth to join in that glad shout of welcome to those who had so bravely come to our assistance. It was a moment never to be forgotten.

" Soon all the rear-guard and heavy guns were inside our position ; and then ensued a scene which baffles description. For 87 days the Lucknow garrison had lived in utter ignorance of all that had taken place outside. Wives who had long mourned their husbands as dead were restored to them. Others, fondly looking forward to glad meetings with those near and dear to them, now for the first time learned that they were alone. On all sides eager inquiries for relations and friends were made. Alas ! in too many instances the answer was a painful one. Such an operation as the relief of Lucknow by so small a force could not indeed be effected save at a heavy sacrifice of life. The actual loss of the relieving force up to the 25th September inclusive, in killed and wounded, amounted to 564 officers and men. This does not include the casualties sustained by the rear guard up to the morning of the 27th amounting to 61 killed, and 77 missing. As the missing were sick or wounded men, who had been intercepted or slain the number of killed of the rear guard may be counted as 138. This would raise the entire losses of the relief operation to 702 officers and men. Amongst the former was Major Cooper, commanding the Artillery Brigade. By his death the command of that brigade devolved upon Major Eyre."

The force which had with such daring and persistent bravery reached the beleaguered Residency discovered in a few hours that they had reached that spot only to increase the number of the garrison. Means of transport for the combined force were wanting, and the force was not strong enough to escort the ladies and children to Cawnpore. The result of the successful advance on Lucknow was that more mouths required to be fed—more lodgment had become necessary for the garrison. But to meet and overcome such difficulties is one of the natural tasks of a real man. How Sir James Outram who had resumed command on the 26th met and conquered them will presently be described.

CHAPTER EIGHTEEN

THE SECOND RELIEF OF LUCKNOW.

The Commander-in-Chief, General Sir Colin Campbell, reached Cawnpore on the 3rd November, 1857, with the resolution to relieve Lucknow before doing anything else, and he had previously made all his arrangements for an advance on Lucknow. Sir Hope Grant's column which had left Delhi after the capture of that city, had reached Cawnpore on the 26th October, where it was increased to an effective strength of 5,500. Something arrived daily in the way of provisions and carriage, for the certainty of having to carry back with him the women and children had not been lost sight of by the Commander-in-Chief.

Sir Colin Campbell joined Hope Grant on the 9th. The interval, from the 3rd to the 9th, had been spent by the Commander-in-Chief in arranging for the protection of his base at Cawnpore. He left behind at Cawnpore about 500 Europeans under the command of Major-General Charles A. Windham, C.B. Windham was directed by the Commander-in-Chief to place his troops within the entrench-ment which, on the occupation of Cawnpore by Havelock in July, had been hastily constructed on the river, and to send into Oudh the detachments of European infantry which might arrive, and on no pretext to detain them.

Having by these instructions secured his base, Sir Colin Campbell started on the 9th, accompanied by his staff, to join Hope Grant's camp in the sandy plain 4 miles beyond Banní. He reached it that afternoon, had a cordial meeting with Hope Grant and his old friends of the Delhi force, and after a short conversation gave his orders for the following day.

In pursuance of these orders Colonel Adrian Hope was sent for-ward to the Alumbagh, the following day, in charge of a large con-voy of provisions. The provisions were to be left there and the carts laden with sick and wounded to be sent back to Cawnpore. That same day a portion of the siege train, escorted by the Naval

Brigade arrived in camp. Early in the morning of the 10th there suddenly presented himself to the astonished gaze of Sir Colin Campbell, a European gentleman disguised as a native, and who in that disguise, had managed to make his way through the beleaguering forces, carrying on his person important dispatches. His name was Kavanagh. To understand thoroughly the nature of the information he brought the reader is asked to remember the account given in the last chapter of this history of the arrival of the relieving force under Outram and Havelock.

On the night of the 25th September the advanced portion of Havelock's force had entered the Residency. They were followed next morning by all but the rear guard. It had already been discovered that the advent of Outram's force constituted not a relief but a reinforcement, that means of transport for the ladies and children, the sick, and the wounded were wanting, that an enormous addition had been made to the hospital list, and that even had transport been available the combined force was not strong enough to escort it to Cawnpore. But one course then remained open to Outram, and that was to hold the Residency, until he should be effectively relieved by Sir Colin Campbell.

Outram's first care was to provide accommodation for the largely increased force. With this view he at once caused the palaces extending along the line of the river the Táráwálá Koti, the Chuttur Munzil, and the Farhat Bukhsh to be occupied, the enemy's works and guns in the vicinity being at the same time destroyed. These posts were taken on the morning of the 26th September.

The six weeks which followed the arrival of Outram's force have not been inaptly described as a blockade. ' His arrival had terminated the siege. The danger of being overwhelmed by the masses of the enemy had in a great measure passed away. Before the arrival of the reinforcements there had generally been the excitement of defence ; it had now become the more stirring excitement of attack.

On the 27th September, for instance, a party of the 1st Fusiliers and some men of the 32nd Regiment, under the command of Major Stephenson, made a sortie for the purpose of taking some guns in the enemy's Cawnpore battery. The British troops were met by a very heavy fire from the enemy, and although they succeeded in spiking three of the enemy's guns, they were unable to bring them back within the defences. On their return, they were exposed to so destructive a fire from the tops of houses and loopholes, that they found it most difficult to carry in their killed and wounded.

On the 29th September, three sorties were made simultaneously. One of these proceeded from the left square of the Brigade Mess, the second from the Sikh Square, the third from the Redan. The third party, composed of 200 men, with a reserve of 150 from the 32nd and 5th Fusiliers, drove the enemy from their guns, and advanced till they came to a lane commanded by an 18-pounder. In this advance they lost Capt. McCabe, of the 32nd, a most distinguished officer, who was then leading his fourth sortie. Major Simmons, of the 5th Fusiliers, was also killed, and it being ascertained that no further advance could be made without considerable loss, the party was recalled. The second party from the Sikh Square was composed of men from the 32nd, 78th, and 1st Madras Fusiliers, 200 in all, and supported by some men of the 13th Native Infantry, under Lieut. Aitken. They succeeded in demolishing several houses and batteries. The first party from the Brigade Mess, commanded by Capt. Shute, and composed of men from the 32nd, 64th, and 84th, succeeded in destroying a 24-pounder gun, and in spiking two mortars and four native guns of small calibre. Their loss was very severe. Again on the 2nd November Lieut. Hardinge led a party composed of the 32nd, 84th, and 1st Madras Fusiliers, and seven artillerymen, to destroy some guns on the Cawnpore Road. This was done effectively and almost without opposition. To write a detailed account of these operations would require a volume devoted wholly to the Siege of Lucknow. Constantly recurring are the names of Wilson, Aitken, Ouseley, Apthorpe, Forbes, Graham and Cubitt, of the infantry; McLeod Innes, Anderson, and Hutchinson, of the Engineers. Every native officer of the 13th Bengal Native Infantry was killed, wounded, or died during the siege. The subahdar of the regiment, Aman Singh, a gallant old Rájpút, received two wounds at Chinhut, but struggled back into the Residency with the beaten troops from that fatal field, and served throughout the siege, and for many years afterwards as a subahdar-major of the Regiment of Lucknow. All ranks of that gallant regiment the 13th as well as the 48th, and 71st Native Infantry received the Order of Merit.

On the 2nd October, Outram, finding that the garrison was greatly annoyed by a fire from a very strong battery, known as Phillip's Garden Battery, on the Cawnpore Road, ordered a party formed of detachments from several regiments under Colonel Napier to storm it. Napier conducted the attack with his usual combination of science and daring, and took the battery, with the loss of two men killed and eleven wounded. He captured three guns—two 9-pounders and a 6-pounder. There was nothing strange in this, but it was remarkable that he should have rescued a private soldier of the Madras Fusiliers, who had fallen down a well, and had remained there three days, undiscovered by the rebels who were occupying the place.

Outram had been much impressed with the advantages of adopting the direct Cawnpore Road as the mode of communication with the Alumbagh. To carry out this idea, he directed Major Haliburton, of the 78th Highlanders, to extend the position in that direction, working from house to house. This operation which was full of danger was begun on the 3rd. The next day Haliburton was mortally wounded. Stephenson, of the Madras Fusiliers, who succeeded him shared the same fate on the 5th. Still the work was persevered with. Several houses were pierced through and at last, on the 6th, a large mosque was reached. This place was in great strength of itself and was occupied in considerable force. The intermediate houses were blown up, and the 78th were located in the garden in which rested the battery captured on the 2nd. This became an important post, and not only protected a considerable portion of the old entrenchment, but connected it with the palaces which had been occupied previously.

The work of mining and countermining, so remarkable during the siege, was still further developed under the superintendence of Colonel Napier. Ably seconded by the Engineer officers, Crommelin, Anderson, McLeod Innes, Hutchinson, Russell, Limond, and by others, all the efforts of the enemy in this direction were frustrated. Some of the 32nd, trained during the siege, made themselves remarkable for their dexterity in mining. For general purposes a company of miners was formed of volunteers from the several corps, and placed under the orders of Capt. Crommelin. These " soon gave him the ascendancy over the enemy who were foiled at all points, with the loss of their galleries and mines, and the destruction of their miners in repeated instances." *

The effect on the enemy of the occupation as outposts of three strong positions commanding the road to the iron bridge, was remarkable. During the siege they had occupied positions within a few yards of our entrenchments. From these they were now driven back to a distance so great, that their musketry fire had no chance of doing mischief inside the old position. They accordingly, with considerable skill, altered their tactics. They withdrew their guns to a point whence the fire would clear the outer defences and fall within the entrenchment. The plan was ingenious, and was so far well worked that the point of fire was constantly shifted. It might have been very damaging but for one defect, viz. want of confidence in the success of the plan, which produced, therefore, want of continuity in the working of it and proved fatal.

* Sir James Outram's official report. "I am aware," he also said, "of no parallel to our series of mines in modern war. Twenty-one shafts, aggregating 200 ft. in depth, and 3,291 ft. of gallery have been executed. The enemy advanced 20 mines against the palaces and outposts; of these they exploded three which caused us loss of life, and two which did no injury; seven had been blown in, and out of seven others the enemy have been driven, and their galleries taken possession of by our miners."

On the 9th October the garrison was cheered by the news that Delhi had fallen and was completely in our power, that the King was a prisoner, and that Greathed had set out to lead a brigade to Cawnpore. This news was confirmed the following day by the further intelligence of the victory gained by Greathed at Bulundshahr. From this date relief became a question of time, and if relief could arrive before the 20th November, Outram felt that all would be well. He believed from the information officially given him that even on the reduced scale of rations allowed, the supplies in the Residency would not feed the force longer than the 20th. But this was an entire misconception on the part of the supply department, for the supplies would have lasted for a far longer period.

It was mainly the belief that Outram's supplies were nearly exhausted that induced Sir Colin Campbell to march to Lucknow before disposing of Tantia Topee and the Gwalior troops. Still, though the greatest enemy was impatience, the efforts of the enemy outside the walls never slackened ; nor were they wholly without effect. Many officers were killed or wounded between the 25th September and the 10th November, among the former being Lieut. Graydon, of the 44th Native Infantry, Capt. McCabe, of the 32nd, and Capt. Hughes, of the 57th Native Infantry, and among the latter, Browne, Edmonstone, Capt. Lowe, of the 32nd, and Assistant Surgeon Darby, of the same regiment. On the south side of the entrenchment the fire continued to be especially galling, several bullets entering the loopholes. Complete exposure on this side was certain death. On the 4th November, Dashwood of the Bengal Army, a very gallant officer, lost both his legs by a round shot, whilst sketching in the Residency compound. He had been warned by a first shot passing near him, but he would not stir.

On the 6th November, news reached the garrison that Hope Grant had encamped on the Lucknow side of the Banni Bridge, and that he was to wait there for Sir Colin Campbell, whose arrival at Cawnpore was also announced. Sir James Outram had previously forwarded to the Alumbagh a dispatch for Sir Colin, in which were contained plans of the city and its approaches, and his own ideas as to the best mode of effecting the junction of the relieved and the relieving forces. He had advised the Commander-in-Chief to make a détour from the Alumbagh to the right of the Dilkushá, and to advance thence by the Martinière and Sikandrabagh. By means of a preconcerted signal, he ascertained that his dispatch had safely reached the Alumbagh. The success of this mode of communication suggested the improvising of a semaphore telegraph, and the idea was no sooner conceived than it was carried out.

But though written descriptions might be useful to the Commander-in-Chief their value could in no respect equal that which might be conveyed by an intelligent member of the garrison, by one

who had undergone the siege and withstood the blockade, and who
could cast the light of personal experience on the insufficient description of a dispatch. But where was the man who would undertake
to penetrate the serried lines of the enemy, knowing that death was
synonymous with discovery? Disguise was necessary. To ask a
man to dare this risk everyone felt was impossible. But it has
often been found, amongst Englishmen, that the occasion produces
the man. A clerk in one of the civil offices, by name Thomas Henry
Kavanagh, caused General Outram to be informed, on the 9th
November, that he was prepared to traverse in disguise the hostile
lines, and to convey a letter to the Commander-in-Chief in his camp
near Banní. Mr. Kavanagh's offer was the more heroic, as of all
the garrison he was perhaps the most difficult man to disguise.
Taller than the ordinary run of natives he was also very fair. But
perfectly cognizant of these drawbacks, Mr. Kavanagh offered himself. General Outram loved a gallant deed ; but brave as he was,
and loving bravery in others, he yet shrank from exposing a man
to the consequences of a deed such as that which Kavanagh proposed. He told him frankly the risks he ran, the almost certain
fate that would befall him. But Kavanagh had made up his mind,
dangers there were he knew, but having in view the all-importance
of his mission he would brave them. Kavanagh chose the garb of a
Badmársh, a native " swashbuckler," a soldier for plunder, of the sort
which abounded in the ranks of the rebels. He wore a pair of tight
silk trousers, fitting close to the skin, a tight-fitting muslin shirt, and
over this a short yellow silk jacket. Round his waist he wound a
white band, over his shoulders he threw a coloured chintz cloth, a
cream-coloured turban being on his head, and he wore native slippers.
His face and down to the shoulders, and his hands to the wrist, he
stained with lamp-black dipped in oil, his hair being cut short.
Thus disguised and wearing the shield and sword peculiar to the
swashbuckler, Kavanagh at 9 o'clock on the evening of the 9th
November, accompanied by a faithful native spy, by name Kananjí
Lál, set out. His journey, though not without its alarms,* proved
that Mr. Kavanagh had not counted vainly on his brave and resolute
heart. He could not, indeed, reach the Alumbagh, but passing by
it, he fell in on the morning of the 10th, with a party of Punjab
Cavalry, by whom, after receiving their warm greetings and con-
gratulations, he was escorted to Sir Colin Campbell.

The information thus received by that gallant commander supplied the one link which till then had been wanting to complete his
mastery of the position. The following morning his engineer park
arrived, and orders were issued for an advance the next day.

* Mr. Kavanagh wrote an account of this journey, *How I Won the
Victoria Cross* (Ward & Lock). He died in St. Thomas's Hospital
in 1883.

The force under the command of Sir Colin Campbell consisted mainly of regiments which had already fought against the mutineers. They were the 8th, a wing of the 53rd, the 75th, and the 93rd Regiments of the Line, the 2nd and 4th Punjab Infantry (Sikhs), the 9th Lancers, Hodson's Horse, and other detachments; the Artillery consisted of 16 guns all tried at Delhi, a few Bengal sappers, and some Punjabi pioneers, and 250 men of the Naval Brigade, with eight heavy guns, and two rocket tubes mounted on light carts. The total number of fighting men, European and Native, was estimated at 3,400.

It was curious to mark the difference between the old Indian troops and the Highlanders in their reception of Sir Colin. Anxious and fixed was the gaze of the former as he rode down their ranks —men evidently trying to measure the leader who had been sent to them from so far. Enthusiastic beyond expression was his reception by the latter. It was seen at once that to him was accorded their entire confidence, that under him they would go anywhere and do anything. At sunrise on the following morning the troops advanced. The plan upon which Sir Colin Campbell had determined, and he was well instructed by Sir James Outram while possessing the advantage of the presence by his side of Mr. Kavanagh, was to move on the Alumbágh; to store within that enclosure all the tents, and, having drawn to himself the detachments still in rear, to make with a wide sweep a flank march to the right, on the Dilkoosha Park and the Martinière; starting afresh from these points, to force the canal close to its junction with the Gúmti; then covered by that river to advance, up its right bank on the Sikancharbágh. This point once secured, a portion of the force could make a dash southwards. The main body, meanwhile forcing the Shah Nujif, and the Moti Mahál, would open out the way for a junction with Outram. To support this operation, Outram would co-operate by a heavy fire on the intermediate positions held by the enemy from all the guns in the Residency; having forced them he would move out, with all his sick and wounded, women and children, and treasure, between the Gúmti and the Kaiserbágh, and effect a junction with the Commander-in-Chief. It was based upon the plan drawn up by Outram, and transmitted to Sir Colin by the hands of the gallant Kavanagh, on the 9th.

To carry out this plan, the little army set out at sunrise on the morning of the 12th November. It had marched barely 3 miles when the advance guard headed by a squadron of Hodson's Horse, commanded by Lieut. Gough, striking the road leading to Jalálábád came under the fire of some light guns, covered by a line of fieldworks. Capt. Bourchier at once brought up his field battery, and opened a fire which soon silenced the hostile guns. The rebels attempted to remove these guns, but Gough was amongst them like lightning, and drove them from the field with the loss of two of their pieces. No further opposition was offered to the progress of the force to the Alumbágh.   The camp was pitched under cover of the Alumbágh. Here the force halted for the following day.

The 13th was devoted by Sir Colin Campbell to making arrangements for a decisive advance on the next day.   He first despatched a small brigade under the command of Colonel the Hon. Adrian Hope,* of the 93rd Highlanders, an officer of great attainments and brilliant promise, to take possession of the fort of Jelálábád in the right rear of the position at Alumbágh.   Hope found that the fort had been evacuated, and returned after rendering it useless by blowing in one of its faces.

Whilst one brigade was engaged in this operation, Sir Colin caused all the camp equipage not required for the hard work in prospect to be stacked within the enclosure.   He directed, also, that whilst supplies for 14 days for himself and the troops in Lucknow should accompany him, every soldier should carry in his haversack provisions for three days' consumption.   By successive reinforcements and the junction with the Alumbágh garrison, the force had now been augmented to about 5,000 men of all arms.

The Naval Brigade, commanded by Capt. William Peel, consisted of 250 men of the crew of the *Shannon*, seamen and marines, having with them eight heavy guns and howitzers, drawn by bullocks. The Cavalry Brigade commanded by Brigadier Little was composed of two squadrons of the 9th Lancers and one each of the 1st, 2nd, and 5th Punjab Cavalry, and of Hodson's Horse.   There were also a company of Royal Engineers, a company of Madras Sappers, a few Bengal Sappers who had served at Delhi, and two companies of newly-raised Punjab Pioneers.   The Infantry Brigades were the 3rd, the 4th, and the 5th, commanded by Brigadiers Greathed, Adrian Hope, and Russell respectively.

On the evening of the 13th Sir Colin rode out to reconnoitre, and the following morning at 9 o'clock he gave the order to march.   The advance was made from the right, through the fields, crossing the several roads leading from the city at right angles.   The turning movement was made at the point expected and the advance bringing forward their right shoulders moved directly on the wall of the Dilkusha Park.   As the advance neared the enclosure a heavy matchlock fire was opened upon it from the left.   Reinforcements were at once sent to the front, and the British guns opened upon the group whence this fire proceeded, and silenced it.   The British skirmishers advancing drove back the rebels and the Dilkusha was thus carried almost without a blow.

The infantry composed of a battalion, made up of companies from

* This distinguished officer was killed at the attack on Fort Rohia in Oudh in April, 1858.

the 5th Fusiliers, the 8th, 64th, and 78th Foot, commanded by Lieut.-Colonel Hamilton of the 78th, and supported by the guns dashed down the slope and carried the Martinière, the enemy not waiting to receive them, but retreating across the canal with all speed, pursued by our cavalry.

Both these important places having been carried the Commander-in-Chief brought up the 4th Brigade and arranged it in position in the gardens of the Martinière. He located there also a troop of horse artillery, and the 5th Brigade was posted on the left in front of the Martinière. These arrangements had not been made one moment too soon. They were hardly completed, when it became evident from the massing of troops on their centre, that the enemy were contemplating an aggressive movement. About 400 yards to the right of the wall of the Dilkusha Park as one faces the canal is the bridge connecting the Martinière plain with the Hazrat-gunj main street. It was on this bridge that the rebels, about 5 o'clock in the afternoon, came down in great numbers and with several guns.

Bourchier's Battery and Peel's 24-pounders occupied a position on some high ground on the left of the bridge, whence they were able to direct a concentric fire on the angle formed by the canal near the bridge, and where the enemy was massed in large numbers. Their fire speedily crushed the enemy out of this position. Then Adrian Hope, forming up his brigade, pushed across the bridge, drove back the enemy with heavy loss, and secured a lodgment on the other side. The attack of the rebels had failed.

That night the men slept with their arms by their side, ready for prompt action. The following day, the 15th, was spent in making preparations for the grand advance. Then Sir Colin made his final arrangements. The whole of his heavy baggage, his supplies for 14 days, he stored in the Dilkushá. Into the palace all the sick and wounded were conveyed. Defences were thrown up round that building, and a force was detailed to guard it.

Having made all the arrangements which skill and foresight could suggest, Sir Colin signalled to Sir James Outram by a code previously arranged, that he would advance on the morrow.

Early on the morning of the 16th the heavy guns were withdrawn from the advanced pickets on the canal, and the detachments of Adrian Hope's Brigade which had been sent to the front rejoined their regiments. The advance guard moved forward from the extreme right. Following the advance guard marched Adrian Hope's Brigade, then Russell's; then the Ammunition and Engineers' Park. Greathed's Brigade followed the remainder of the force as its rear guard. The advance guard then marched along the bank of the Gúmti through the lane and enclosures without meeting an enemy.

Suddenly for the first time the enemy took the alarm. First from men occupying huts and enclosures in advance of the building, then from the mass of men in the Sikandarbágh* itself, poured an overwhelming fire on the troops forming the advance. Their position was in a military point of view desperate, for they were exposing their flank to the enemy. For a distance of 120 yards to the walled enclosure of Sikandarbágh, they were broadside on to the enemy's fire. The situation was indeed critical. One company of the gallant 53rd in skirmishing order lined the enclosures bordering on the lane, but their numbers were few, and the fire of the enemy was concentrated; the cavalry were jammed together, unable to advance, and the high banks on either side seemed to offer an impassable barrier to artillery. But, up the steep bank the daring Blunt led his gallant troops, and "conquering the impossible," brought them, guns and all, into an open space between the Sikandarbágh and another large loopholed building, exposed to a terrific cross-fire as he advanced. Here unlimbering, he opened with his six guns on the Sikandarbágh. Never was anything done better. Travers followed with his heavy battery, and the sappers and miners having demolished a portion of the high bank, he too was able, by the aid of the infantry, to bring two of his 18-pounders into position and to open fire against the angle of the enclosure. In less than half an hour their fire made a breach in the wall which might be practicable for stormers.

Meanwhile the infantry of Adrian Hope's Brigade had been ordered to lie down, covered by a small bank and some trees. But the moment the breach was considered practicable the bugle sounded the signal for assault. It was made by the 93rd Highlanders and the 4th Punjab Rifles, supported by the 53rd and a battalion of detachments. The Highlanders, under Lieut.-Colonel Ewart, and the Sikhs, under Lieut. Paul, and a native officer of the Sikhs, Subadar Gokal Singh, dashed forward. All ran towards the hole—a small hole in a bricked-up doorway, about 3 ft. square, and about the same distance from the ground. A Sikh of the 4th Rifles reached it first, but he was shot dead as he jumped through. A similar fate befell a Highlander in his track. A young officer of the 93rd, Richard Cooper by name, outstripping the majority of his comrades was more fortunate. Flying, so to speak, through the hole he landed unscathed. Cooper was immediately followed by Colonel Ewart, of the 93rd, and Capt. Lumsden and three privates, then by eight or nine men, Sikhs and Highlanders. Another officer, Capt. Burroughs, of the 93rd, also penetrated within the enclosure but was almost immediately attacked and severely wounded. Lumsden was

---

* The Sikandarbágh, Anglice, "the garden of Alexander," was a high-walled enclosure, about 150 yards square, with towers at the angles.

killed by a musket shot. Ewart, forcing his way into the court-yard, pushed forward with his following against the men at the other end of it. The few Highlanders and Sikhs then rushed at them and a desperate hand-to-hand encounter ensued. At the critical moment the bulk of the brigade, Highlanders, the Sikhs, and the 53rd, poured in to the rescue.

Impatient of the delay which would be caused by jumping singly through a narrow hole, the bulk of the storming party had turned to the left to force a way by the gate of the enclosure. This gate was locked and barred; and although the men used all their efforts, firing their pieces at the lock, some time elapsed before it gave way. But at last it yielded, and the 93rd and Sikhs dashed through it. Almost simultaneously the 53rd forced a barred window to the right of it and joined in the rush to the rescue of Ewart, of Cooper (still fighting in spite of his wound), and their comrades.

Through the gate and window, and through Cooper's hole which the sappers had succeeded in enlarging, the stormers poured as fast as they could make their way. As they entered the rebels fell back into the towers at the angle of the enclosure, and opened a heavy and continuous musketry fire on our men, occasionally diversifying this mode of fighting by descending to a hand-to-hand encounter. In one of these, Colonel Ewart succeeded in cutting down two native officers who guarded a colour, and in capturing the colour, which he presented with his own hand to Sir Colin Campbell. The fight for the possession of the enclosure was bloody and desperate the rebels fighting with all the energy of despair. Every room, every staircase, every corner of the towers was contested. Quarter was neither given nor asked for, and when at last the assailants were masters of the place more than 2,000 rebel corpses lay heaped around them.

About 300 yards along the road leading from Sikandarbágh to the Residency there was a small village with garden enclosures round it, while about 250 yards further on and 100 yards to the right of the road stood the Sháh Najif, a large mosque, situated in a garden enclosed by a high loopholed wall. This wall was nearly square and very strong. Between it and the Sikandarbágh amidst jungles and enclosure, to the right of the little plain, was a building on a high mound called the Kadam Rasúl.

The afternoon was now waning and Sir Colin Campbell deemed it essential to carry the Sháh Najif. The operation was dangerous and most difficult. On the right the Kadam Rasúl was assaulted and carried by a party of Sikhs. There was great confusion in the narrow lane leading up from the rear. The animals carrying the ordnance and engineer supplies unable to get out on either side got completely jammed, and the confusion near the Sikandarbágh had got to such a pitch that all passage had become impassable; and had it not been that a staff officer discovered a by-path leading into a broad road which abutted on the Sikandarbágh, neither men nor ammunition could have been brought up.

In front of the Sháh Najif the battle made no way, and the men were falling fast. It was now apparent that a crisis had been reached. Our heavy artillery could not subdue the fire of the Sháh Najif ; we could not even hold permanently our present advanced position under it. But retreat to us there was none. What shot and shell could not do, the bayonets of the infantry must accomplish.

Collecting the 93rd about him, the Commander-in-Chief addressed a few words to them. He told them that the Sháh Najif *must be taken ;* that the artillery could not bring its fire under, so they must win it with the bayonet. Giving them a few plain directions, he told them he would go on with them himself. The grey-haired veteran of many fights rode at the head of the troops. As they approached the nearest angle of the enclosure, the soldiers began to drop fast ; but without a check they reached its foot. There, however, they were brought to a stand. The wall, perfectly entire was nearly 20 ft. high, and well loopholed ; there was no breach, and no scaling ladders.

Unable to advance, unwilling to retire, they halted and commenced a musketry battle with the garrison. But all the advantage was with the latter, who shot with security behind loopholes, and the Highlanders went down fast before them. At this time nearly all the mounted officers were either wounded or dismounted. Two of Peel's guns were now brought up to within a few yards of the wall. Covered by the fusillade of the infantry, the sailors shot fast and strong ; but though the masonry soon fell off in flakes, it came down so as to leave the mass behind perpendicular, and as inaccessible as ever.

Success now seemed impossible. The dead and wounded were ordered to be collected and carried to the rear. Some rocket frames were brought up, and threw in a volley of these fiery projectiles with such admirable precision, that just skimming over the top of the rampart they plunged hissing into the interior of the building, and searched it out with a destroying force. Under cover of this the guns were drawn off. The shades of evening were falling fast and the assault could not much longer be continued. Then, as a last resource, Adrian Hope, collecting some 50 men, stole silently and cautiously through the jungle and brushwood away to the right, to a portion of the wall on which he believed some injury to have been inflicted, having observed signs of this before the assault. Reaching it unperceived, a narrow fissure was found, and up this, a single man was with some difficulty pushed. He saw no one near the spot, and so helped up Hope, Ogilvy, Allgood, the Assistant Quartermaster-General, and some others. The numbers inside soon increased, and as they did so they advanced, gradually extending their front.   A body of sappers, sent for in haste, arrived at the double, the opening was enlarged, the supports rushed in.   Meanwhile Hope's small party, pushing on, to their great astonishment found themselves unopposed.   Gaining the gate they threw it open for their comrades.   Panic-stricken, apparently, by the destruction caused by the rockets and the sudden appearance of some of the assailants within the walls, they fled from the place, and gave up the struggle just when victory was secure.   Never had there been a harder-fought day,* but never was a result gained more satisfactorily.   A lodgment had been made for the night and the order was then given to bivouac.   The main body of the 93rd garrisoned the Shah Najif; another portion of that regiment occupied the barracks.   The troops not occupying these two posts lined the roads and maintained the communications.   The field hospital for the wounded was established in some huts opposite the Sikandarbágh which might be regarded as the central point of the position taken up for the night.   The men lay down in line with their arms by their sides.

During the hours employed by the troops under Sir Colin Campbell in attacking the Shah Najif, the Residency garrison under Sir James Outram were using all their efforts to effect a diversion.   They captured some of the positions to the east of the Residency, and from these maintained a continuous fire of guns and mortars on the rebels.

The British and Sikh troops, lying in unbroken order with their arms by their sides, were awakened early in the morning of the 17th, not by their own bugles, but by the bells of the city and the beating of the enemy's drums.   The British soldiers sprang up with alacrity, each man in his place, ready for action.   But the enemy did not come on.   Sir Colin Campbell was, therefore, able to carry out his own plan and to choose his own time.   His plan was first to carry the Mess House, a large masonry building defended by a ditch 12 ft. broad, surmounted by a loopholed wall behind, about midway between the Sháh Najif and the Kaiserbágh.   Much would still remain to be accomplished.   The strong positions of the Kaiserbágh, and of the Begum's palace covering the vast city behind them would still remain in the occupation of some 30,000 unsubdued foes, and it was in the face of these that Sir Colin would have to withdraw the women and children, the sick and the wounded.   Sir Colin commenced his operations with great caution.   First, he deemed it advisable to secure his left flank.   To prevent the enemy from acting on our left rear he

* "It was an action almost unexampled in war."—Sir Colin Campbell's Dispatch, 18th November, 1857.

detached the 5th Brigade under Brigadier Russell to carry the house called Banks's house and four bungalows close to the barracks, to convert them into military posts. Possessing now the barracks and the Dilkushá the occupation of Banks's house and the bungalows would sever the communication between the Kaiserbágh and the Dilkushá and would cover the left rear of the attacking force.

Having thus made arrangements to secure his communications Sir Colin directed William Peel to open fire with his heavy guns on the Mess House. The fire continued from early morning till 3 o'clock in the afternoon. At that hour the musketry fire of the enemy having been almost completely silenced, it appeared to Sir Colin that the Mess House might be stormed without much risk. It was a building of considerable size, and surrounded by a loop-holed mud wall, covering a ditch about 12 ft. broad, scarped with masonry. The ditch was traversed by drawbridges, but whether these were down or up was unknown to the storming party.

Never was a daring feat of arms better performed. Leading his men at the double across the intervening space, exposed to a hot fire from the neighbouring buildings, Hopkins, of the 53rd, reached the mud wall, dashed over it, crossed the drawbridge, fortunately left down, and entered the Mess House. He had but just gained the place when Roberts (afterwards Field Marshal Earl Roberts and Commander-in-Chief in India) galloped up, handed him a Union Jack, and requested him to hoist it on one of the turrets. Followed by one of his men, Hopkins climbed upon the roof, and giving three cheers, planted the flag on the summit. The flag had not been up ten minutes before a round shot cut the staff and sent it down into the garden. Again did Hopkins plant it, and again it was knocked down. He asked to hoist it again, but just at the moment, an order arrived from the Commander-in-Chief forbidding the further display of it. Simultaneously Wolseley, moving on a different point, had attacked the houses to the right of the Mess House, whilst Irby with a company of the supports, attempted to clear those on the left. Both attacks were successful, and the rebels being driven out fled in panic to the Motí Mahal.

The victorious stormers followed the flying enemy. Wolseley hurried on to the wall of the Motí Mahal, but the opposition was great, and the wall was solid, and the gateway had been blocked up, he had therefore to send back for the sappers. These promptly came up and succeeded in making narrow openings in the wall. Through these Wolseley and his men eagerly rushed, and attacked the network of buildings within. The resistance they encountered was, however stout and desperate, every room being contested. At length, however, he expelled the enemy, and the Motí Mahal, the last building held by the rebels on the line communicating with Outram and Havelock, came completely into British possession.

An open space, nearly half a mile in width, still intervened between the assailants and the advanced positions of Outram and Havelock. This space was exposed to heavy musketry fire from the Kaiserbágh and could not be crossed without imminent risk. But the risk did not prevent the two gallant generals and their staff from crossing the space to meet the Commander-in-Chief.

They started, eight officers and one civilian. They were Outram, Havelock, Napier (afterwards Lord Napier of Magdala), Vincent Eyre, Dodgson, the Deputy Adjutant-General, young Havelock, the aide-de-camp, Sitwell, Russell of the Engineers, and the gallant Kavanagh. They had not gone many paces before they were seen by the enemy, and the musketry fire from the Kaiserbágh redoubled. Napier, young Havelock, Sitwell and Russell were struck down. Outram, Havelock, Eyre, Dodgson and Kavanagh alone reached the Motí Mahal uninjured; then to borrow from the appropriate language of Sir Colin Campbell, "the relief of the garrison had been accomplished." But a most difficult and dangerous task still remained. The garrison, with women and children, sick and wounded, guns and stores had to be withdrawn ; and to effect this in the face of the vast force of the enemy was no easy task.

One narrow lane alone led to the rear, and through it the whole force had to be filed. To protect the march of the convoy, the whole of the immense line, extending from the ruined walls of the Residency to the wooded park of the Dilkushá required to be held, and this gave a most hazardous extension to our forces—far too weak for the maintenance of so extended a position. To keep any considerable reserve in hand was impossible. The enemy still occupied the Kaiserbágh in great force. From the Kaiserbágh they threatened the flank and the left rear of the British Army. Sir Colin's first object was then to silence the fire from the Kaiserbágh. He directed the colonels of the 93rd, the 82nd and the 23rd commanding the posts covering the left rear, simply to maintain their positions, whilst he would himself personally superintend the delicate operations of the withdrawal, by the road already traversed, of the sick and the wounded, the women and the children. The order was simple, and was carried out to the letter.

On the morning of the 20th, as a preliminary measure, William Peel opened on the Kaiserbágh a tremendous fire from his heavy guns. This fire continued during that day, the day following, and the 22nd, increasing every hour in intensity. It gradually assumed the character of a bombardment. The enemy suffered enormous losses, and on the evening of the 22nd three breaches in the walls of the Kaiserbágh invited assault. Such however was not the intention of Sir Colin ; the bombardment had, in fact, been used to cover the withdrawal of the women and children, sick and wounded. Long before it concluded, these had reached the Dilkushá in safety.   The three breaches effected on the evening of the 22nd were used to carry out the retreat of the glorious garrison of Lucknow.   Whilst the rebels passed that night in devising measures to meet the assault which they expected on the morrow, the garrison which had so long kept them at bay, the veterans of Inglis's force, the victors in many fights of Havelock's and Outram's, began to retire at midnight.   The guns which they could not carry away they rendered useless.   Then behind the screen of Campbell's outposts, Inglis's and Havelock's toilworn bands withdrew. Then these began to retire also ; the pickets fell back through the supports, the supports glided away between the intervals of the reserve, the reserve when all had passed silently defiled into the lane, thick darkness shrouded the movement from the gaze of the enemy, and hours after the position had been quitted, they were firing into the abandoned posts.

Hope's Brigade, which had so nobly headed the advance had also covered the retreat.   Before daylight on the 23rd the last straggler had quitted the camp at Dilkushá.   The reunited force remained at the Dilkushá during that day and the ensuing night.   But there was no rest for officer or private.   The detachment parties who had come up with the relieving force had to be distributed to their different regiments ; carriages had to be allotted ; arrangements for the convoy of the women and children under responsible officers had to be made.   On this day a reorganization of the whole force was made to remain in operation as far as the Alumbágh.

Havelock died on the 24th.   On the morning of the 26th his remains were consigned to a humble grave in the Alumbágh.   His gallant son, the leaders who had been associated with him, Campbell, Grant, Outram, Inglis, Napier, and others and a crowd of officers, followed him to his last resting place.   He had fought a good fight ; he had died, as he had lived, in the performance of duty.   The life of Havelock had been a life devoted to his profession.   Gifted with military abilities of a very high order, and conscious that he possessed these abilities, he had borne without repining the disadvantages of slow promotion.   But every trial of Fortune had found Havelock, cheerful, resolute, and devoted.   To the smallest office he gave his best abilities, and had striven also to prepare himself for the eventualities which were to follow.   He had lived long enough to hear that his Queen and his countrymen had appreciated his noble qualities, that his name had become a household word among the homes and the hearths of England.

Sir Colin decided on the 26th that Sir James Outram should remain at Alumbágh with a force of about 4,000 men of all arms, 25 guns and howitzers and 10 mortars.   Outram would thus occupy a position threatening Lucknow, and would retain it till the Commander-in-Chief having placed his convoy in safety, and disposed of the Gwalior mutineers, should return to act offensively against the city of Lucknow.

The chapter which will follow with an account of the final Capture of Lucknow will comprise references to the very distinguished services of several officers of the Royal and Indian Engineers both at the Relief and Capture of the City, among whom should be noted the names of Field Marshal Lord Napier of Magdala, General Sir Lothian Nicholson, General Sir Henry Harness, General Sir Wilbraham Lennox, General Sir Frederick Maunsell, General Sir Richard Harrison, Major-General Greathed, Colonels A. Lang, E. Malcolm, J. G. Forbes and others.

CHAPTER NINETEEN

THE CAPTURE OF LUCKNOW, APRIL, 1858.

In December, 1857, Sir Colin Campbell commenced to concentrate
his forces for the final operations of the capture of Lucknow ; and
it was at this time that the outlines of his plans were drawn up.
In a memorandum to Lord Canning, dated December 22nd, 1857,
Sir Colin wrote :—

" Colonel Napier has given his deliberate opinion in which I coincide
as regards numbers, that 20,000 men will be necessary for the first
operation of subduing the city. That having been performed, it will
be necessary to leave a garrison in occupation, consisting of at least
10,000 men, viz. 6,000 in the city, and 4,000 in a chain of posts on
the Cawnpore roads, until the whole province should have been conquered, and the rebels driven out of their last stronghold."—(*Life of
Lord Clyde*, Vol. II., p. 68).

Early in January, 1858, Colonel Napier returned to his post as
Chief of the Staff to Sir James Outram at the Alumbagh, where
that General had been left with a force to hold the ground pending
the return of Sir Colin. Whilst there he soon formed the opinion
that the attack should be made on the east side, accompanied by
a flank movement on the north across the river Gúmti, which would
take the enemy's fire in reverse. He therefore devoted the intervals
between his arrival at the Alumbagh, and that of Sir Colin with his
force, to a careful inspection of the ground on both sides of the river.
The following reasons for these views were published in the *Professional Papers of the Corps of Royal Engineers*, Vol. X., New Series,
1861, p. 68.

" The east side offered : first the smallest front, and was therefore
the more easily enveloped by our attack ; secondly, ground for planting
our artillery, which would be located on the west side ; thirdly, it gave
also the shortest approach to the Kaiser Bagh, a place to which the
rebels attached the greatest importance ; more than all, we knew the
east side, and were little acquainted with the west."

Everything was decided in accordance with Napier's view, and on the 10th he was appointed to the command of the Engineer Brigade.

The city of Lucknow being upwards of 20 miles in circumference, it was utterly impossible to attempt an investment or a siege under ordinary conditions. The town is bounded on the north by the Gúmti, and on the east by a canal which runs northward from that river. About halfway between the canal and the Residency stands the King's palace—the Kaiser Bagh. This was the citadel of defence, and was covered by three lines. The first was a flanked rampart on the main side of the canal, which formed a wet ditch to it. The second, with a circular trace, enclosed a large building called the Moti Mahal, whilst the third consisted of a line of rampart to the north of the citadel. The first and second lines rested on the river to their left, and terminated on the right in the town itself, where it was impossible for an enemy to advance or turn them. Indeed, the only possible point of attack was from the east, supported by a corresponding advance on the other side of the river to take the lines in reverse. In front of the canal, and about a mile from it, was an extensive block of buildings called La Martinière, about 5 miles from Alumbagh.

Lucknow at this time was in the hands of the rebels, and had been occupied by them since the removal of the garrison with the ladies and children by the relieving force under Sir Colin Campbell. The Alumbagh, distant about 3 miles from Lucknow, however, was still held by a garrison under Sir James Outram, consisting of 4,000 men. At Futtegurh there were about 5,000 men at this period, and about 3,000 on the Ramganga. Materials had been collected to form a bridge to cross this river, but the orders to cross were not issued.

A serious attack had been made on General Outram's position at the Alumbagh on the 16th January. In the morning a body of the enemy, of which the strength is not mentioned in the dispatch, led by a Hindu fanatic, attired to represent the Monkey-god, made a sudden attack on the Jellalabad half-way picquet, at the time commanded by a subaltern, and was received by musketry fire which drove them back with the loss of their leader, who fell mortally wounded into the hands of the picquet, and of more killed and wounded than the enemy could carry off. Two 9-pounder guns, brought up from camp under the escort of a subaltern and 25 men from the right brigade to support the picquet, compelled an abandonment of the cover in front which the enemy had used as a *point d'appui*. The left front and flank were threatened throughout the day, and after dark the enemy's infantry assembled in great strength in front of picquet No. 5, reinforced to 200 men, commanded by a major, who allowed the rebels to approach within 80 yards, and then opened fire with three guns, and his infantry. As they withdrew with loss, he followed them up with shells from a mortar. Attempts by cavalry against the left rear had been watched and checked throughout the day by four horse artillery guns. The division had a bombardier killed and eight men wounded.

The successful repulse of this attack and the prospect of the arrival of the Commander-in-Chief now moving towards Lucknow relieved the General of much anxiety; but still he felt it necessary to warn headquarters that, owing to the enormous numbers of the enemy and the extent of his position, he was obliged to keep his men in readiness, and as there was a perceptible change in the temperature, the hospitals would begin to fill under so much exposure. Moreover that unless reinforced ere compelled to detach another convoy, he would have hard work in repelling the incessant attacks of the increasing hosts of the enemy, headed by the many territorial chiefs reported to be in the city or immediate vicinity. It must not be supposed that the General allowed his anxiety to be shared by his troops. Seldom has duty of any sort been performed with greater confidence and cheerfulness by all ranks. In the intervals between the attacks, as much as possible was done to relieve the monotony of camp life. Officers off duty were allowed to go for short distances shooting, and to get up races. During Christmas week the usual sports were organized for the men.

About this time the Intelligence Department received news that a grand assault was being planned, and that a particular day, the opening one of a festival, had been fixed for the purpose. The assault, however, did not come off, much to the disappointment of the General, who having been rejoined by the convoy escort and reinforced by some cavalry, had hoped to inflict a severe defeat on the rebels, and to capture some of their guns. The spies reported a day or two afterwards that the enemy's troops and guns had taken up positions during the night ; that in the morning their generals had ensconced themselves at a respectable distance in the rear, that the men were accoutred, and all were apparently in readiness. They did not advance, however, and the rebel leaders sent for the chief officers of divisions, to inquire the reason. They replied that they would attack, since it was better to die fighting than to be hanged, but they must have their pay first.

From this period till the 15th February the rebels evinced a nervous restlessness, which betrayed itself in constant assemblies of cavalry and infantry, and by demonstrations of attack, which were instantly stopped by a few rounds from the guns at the supports. About this time the concentration of troops and material for the projected attack on the city had commenced, and on the Cawnpore Road stood a succession of detachments at intervals of an easy day's march, somewhat resembling the system of stages by which a

German field army maintains communication with its base. The continued movement of troops and stores was known to the enemy, and caused the activity on his part which, though occasioning few casualties to the British division, constantly necessitated the turning out and remaining under arms.

On the 13th February the news from the *Court Journal*, as the epitome of daily intelligence was styled in the British camp, was to the effect that an attack on all points of the position was planned for the 15th. It seemed probable that under the mingled taunts, promises. and threats of the so-called " Queen Mother " the rebels might be induced to make one desperate last attempt, and that if, as was expected, she should come out, it was possible that the whole force then collected in Lucknow, regular and irregular, might be inspirited to join the attack..

The General, with a view of being able to inflict a heavy blow, requested when passing on this intelligence to army headquarters, now returned to Cawnpore, that the order for a battalion to be withdrawn from his command in exchange for a raw one of native sappers might be countermanded. The request was complied with, but the next day it was reported from the city that the expected movement of the rebels had been abandoned, and a message was sent to the bridge post for the battalion to resume its march on Cawnpore.

Notwithstanding, however, the failure of the rebel Court to induce their troops to come out in mass, a demonstration took place on the day in question, concealed to some extent by a violent dust-storm, round the left of the British position against the high road, along which a convoy was at the time marching. The horse artillery escorted as usual by cavalry, and dashing well out, supported also by the nearest battalion of the left brigade, sufficed to disperse the enemy's cavalry and infantry, wounding their chief, a Mussulman dignitary, who rode in a litter. The division had only one man wounded.

Next day, the 16th February, the rebels, while they threatened, as on former occasions, the left flank with cavalry and infantry, filled their trenches and the groves in rear of these with the latter arm, but although they began their demonstration in the morning, they did not muster resolution enough for the attack till about 5.30 p.m. when they suddenly issued in clouds of skirmishers against the guns of the centre and left, and in large bodies advanced against the village where the picquet had been reinforced to a strength of 200 men under a lieutenant-colonel. This picquet had three men wounded before it repulsed the enemy. For a couple of hours after dark a heavy musketry fire was kept up against the north and east faces of the Alumbagh without occasioning any loss to the defenders, who aimed grape and shrapnel against the line indicated by the flashes of the muskets.

On the 17th, while a partial advance against the right and left picquets was repulsed by artillery fire, some 2,000 infantry, sent by the enemy towards the right rear, withdrew towards the city on the appearance from camp of a couple of squadrons and two guns. The information received at this time was to the effect that the rebels proposed continuing these attacks daily and from all quarters. Consequently the picquets had to be maintained at abnormal strength, and the troops were harassed by being constantly turned out.

In échelon behind the line of two picquets, both of which were armed with guns, was established a fresh battery guarded by an escort. The Jellalabad half-way picquet was furnished from camp, strength 2 subalterns and 50 infantry. The Alumbagh detachment was increased to 275 rank and file. The proportion of men at the outposts to those in camp was, however, now so great that the reliefs of many of the picquets could only be effected every three days, sometimes only weekly. The General again remonstrated against his troops having under these circumstances to furnish the convoy escorts half-way to the bridge posts in rear.

On the morning of the 21st February, while the strength of the division, particularly in cavalry, was reduced by such an escort, a simultaneous movement took place threatening both flanks, as well as the whole front of the position, the points actually attacked being the north-east angle of the Alumbagh and the fort of Jellalabad with the half-way picquet. The troops holding these posts were reinforced, while a body of about 250 cavalry with two guns was sent to the rear of the fort, and coming suddenly on about 2,000 of the rebel cavalry drove them back on their infantry some 5,000 strong, which latter after advancing to within range of grape, retired with loss. The left flank was threatened by 8,000 to 10,000 infantry with 500 cavalry, against which force were sent with the usual result, four horse artillery guns escorted by about 120 troopers, and supported by the available strength of the left brigade.

The division had 9 men wounded, while the reports from the city gave the loss of the enemy as 60 killed and 200 wounded in front of Alumbagh, with some 80 or 90 casualties near Jellalabad.

A few days before the 25th, the first instalment of troops composing the force which the Commander-in-Chief was concentrating for the capture of Lucknow arrived within the lines of this division, and were temporarily at the disposal of the General. These consisted of a battalion which had for some days past been distributed on the line of communication with Cawnpore, of several squadrons, and of a troop of horse artillery. By this time a large quantity of combustible stores had been collected in the fort of Jellalabad. An attack was expected on the 29th, but did not come off.

On the 2nd March, the advance of the Commander-in-Chief began with a second division of infantry, a brigade of cavalry and four batteries, from the Cawnpore Road, by a line leading east from Jellalabad, into a position of which the right rested on the river Gúmti behind Dilkoosha, followed on the next two days by the closing up of the siege train and of a third division of infantry causing the withdrawal of the bulk of the rebel forces to the extensive defences which they had constructed along and in advance of the eastern end of the canal, and thus removed the pressure on the front of the 1st Division, which had stood for three months unsupported. It had been for some time previously made movable by provision of carriage for baggage and tents, and it was now gradually reduced by the withdrawal from its organization of the greater portion of the cavalry, of which part was sent to preserve communication between Jellalabad and the Commander-in-Chief's camp, while the remainder made up from fresh arrivals to the strength of a brigade was extended westward to watch the exits from the city in that direction, and by the successive dispatch of battalions and guns to reinforce the main attack from the east. The General was summoned on the 5th to conduct a turning movement on the north bank of the Gúmti. On the 12th there remained in his former camp but one brigade of infantry, and on the 16th only two battalions with the horse artillery.

Meanwhile the advance, from the eastward, of the army by a movement in échelon from the right, as the entrenchments and palaces held by the rebels were successively turned or stormed, had the effect of causing the old pressure on the Alumbagh position to be renewed to a serious extent. On the 15th most of the army was established on a line fronting to the south-west, and, therefore, towards the Alumbagh, from which post the left was distant 3 miles as the crow flies. The space between the Commander-in-Chief's inner flank and the canal was filled by a body of Nepaulese troops, which had arrived on the 12th as allies against the Oudh Pretender, and had come into line with a force of about 9,000 infantry and 24 field guns drawn by men. On the 15th one of their detachments after a short fight took possession of the Yellow House, a building midway between Alumbagh and the canal, but withdrew from it after dark without giving notice to the British outposts, who were in the sequel somewhat embarrassed by uncertainty as to whether that point was held by friend or foe.

During the whole time Sir James Outram held the position at Alumbagh, from the 22nd November, 1857, to the 17th March, 1858, Capt. Olpherts (afterwards General Sir William Olpherts, V.C., G.C.B.) commanded a battery and was present at all the engagements at this time. The previous services of Sir William Olpherts at Benares, and at the Relief of Lucknow by Havelock are well known.

On the 16th, the Commander-in-Chief's right led by the former General of the 1st Division gained another mile to the westward.

" And in short," as was the language of His Excellency's dispatch, " the city was ours." With like brevity it is stated that on the 16th, for the last time, the enemy showed in some strength before Alumbagh; that the Goorkha leader was requested to move to his left up the canal and take the position ; that His Highness executed this very well, and that he seized the positions, one after another, with little loss to himself, the enemy's guns falling into his hands. Some details, however, of this, the last brush that took place on the front of the position, may not be uninteresting. They are produced in nearly the identical words of the field officer who commanded in the Alumbagh enclosure.

Between 8 and 9 a.m. he observed from the roof of the palace a large body of cavalry coming out of the city, while infantry manned the batteries and trenches along the front of the position. An orderly was immediately dispatched to the brigadier in camp, who in consequence of this, and information subsequently received, tele-graphed in the course of the day to the Chief of the Staff with Army Headquarters :—" The enemy are coming on in immense force, both cavalry and infantry, with field guns on my left front and towards the dense wood close to Alumbagh. Nothing seen of the Goorkhas. I have drawn up my infantry and field guns, and my batteries have opened upon them. I have only 140 cavalry here." The rebels' movement continued to be observed from the Alumbagh roof, their cavalry in most regular order proceeding along the rear of their batteries. A few shots were fired from the heavy guns of the outpost, but the range of the nearest point of their line of march was upwards of 2,000 yards. They were accompanied by three horse and two bullock guns, and their numbers were estimated at not less than 3,000 sabres. The cavalry continued its march until it had passed the left flank of the position some distance, and then, developing upon the plain in order of battle, was seen to charge down in the direction of the village held by picquet No. 5. During this time the batteries and trenches in front of Alumbagh had become crowded with infantry. About 1,000 men with colours came out and took position in spite of the fire of the British rifles, about 400 yards in front of the Mosque picquet, and kept up a warm matchlock fire upon it and the enclosure. Some discharges of grape from all the available guns caused them severe loss as appeared from the bodies found next morning. The enemy's trenches had on the previous occasion been seen by the field officer to be crowded, and he esti-mated the strength of their infantry in front of him to be not less than 5,000. This attack commenced simultaneously with the cavalry charge, and was not abandoned till about noon. As here-tofore the more open left flank was freed by the dash and fire of the horse battery, supported by the available infantry from camp.

Thus the important duty of covering the Cawnpore Road which still formed the line of communication for the British Army Corps until the course of operations in the city had brought the left forward to the westward of Alumbagh, was successfully performed up to the last by the remnants of the 1st Division.

After the evacuation of Lucknow, Lieut. McLeod Innes, who had greatly distinguished himself during the Defence, was posted to General Frank's column during his march through Oudh and gained the V.C. at the Battle of Sultanpore. He afterwards joined the army before Lucknow, and was severely wounded on the day of joining. The amount of labour expended on the works by the rebels was enormous. Streets a mile long had almost every house loopholed, and guns pointed from many of them. The bridge across the Gúmti had also been ruined.

On the night of March 4th two bridges of casks were completed across the Gúmti, a very troublesome and difficult operation. General Outram with his division, consisting of the Queen's Bays, 9th Lancers, and the Highland Brigade and other troops, crossed the river on the 6th and met with little opposition. The remainder of the army being posted at Dilkoosha about 1,000 yards in rear of La Martinière.

Brigadier Franks joined the army about this time with Jung Bahadur and 4,000 Goorkhas. This manœuvre of crossing the river was a splendid success, and completely baffled the enemy. The rebels' earthworks on the south side of the river were enfiladed by the guns of Outram's Division on the other side of the river.

On the 7th the Sepoys made a sharp attack on General Outram, but were repulsed without difficulty, and retired within their lines, leaving him free to push forward.

While referring to La Martinière, special mention should be made of the excellent service rendered by the boys of the Martinière College, whose gallantry in the defence of the post assigned them in the Residency has rarely been surpassed, and forms a bright page in the history of that long siege. In the grounds of the Bailey Guard there may still be seen a masonry pillar with a marble slab inserted, on which are inscribed the words Martinière Post. The three companies formed from the students of the College wore as a badge on their accoutrements a turreted castle with the words " Defence of Lucknow," the same honour as was awarded to the 16th, the Lucknow Regiment of Bengal Infantry, which was formed in 1858 from the loyal remnants of mutinous native regiments who fought throughout the siege by the side of the British, and held firmly to the post called the Bailey Guard.

On the 9th March the Martinière was assaulted and captured with very little loss. The Engineer officers who accompanied the assaulting column were Lieuts. A. M. Lang, J. G. Forbes, E. T. Thackeray,

Swetenham, and H. J. Nuthall. Each officer was in command of a detachment of sappers, and formed up in rear of the Dilkoosha. At the signal the troops raced across the space between the Martinière and the Dilkoosha. After capturing La Martinière the column pushed on to a village on the right close to the enemy's first line of entrenchments. Here, an officer of the 1st Bengal Fusiliers, Lieut. Butler, was seen standing alone on the bastion waving his hand. He had swam across the river, and had climbed the parapet remaining there until the work was occupied by our troops. For his conduct on this occasion, Butler was awarded the Victoria Cross.

On the evening of the 9th, Sir Colin Campbell, who had secured La Martinière in the morning, was able to advance on the canal line which had been enfiladed and taken in reverse by the batteries already established by General Outram. He secured the line without loss. The forward movement was now continued, the houses and palaces being used as approaches. In this way the second line was turned to the left. Batteries were then thrown up to break a large block of palaces called the Begum Koti on the right which were then stormed and carried.

From thenceforward the Chief Engineer, Brig.-General Napier, pushed his approaches with the greatest judgment through the enclosures by the aid of the sappers and heavy guns, the troops immediately occupying the grounds, and the mortars being moved from one position to another as ground was won on which they could be placed. (Sir Colin Campbell's dispatch). At length the third line was turned, and the Kaiser Bagh entered. Supports were quickly thrown in, and the Mess House, the Tara Koti, the Motee Mahal, the Engine House, and the Chattar Munzil, were rapidly occupied by the troops, while the Engineers devoted their attention to securing their positions towards the south and west. Owing to being taken in flank by the fire from the guns with General Outram's Division, and to our advance, the enemy had not only evacuated the Martinière, but their first line of entrenchments as well. So the first line up to Banks's house was captured without great loss. While advancing from the Martinière to the village rather a heavy fire was met with from the village, and here the Highlanders lost a few men. The Sepoys could be seen running along the ramparts in hundreds.

On the 11th, the Artillery and Naval Brigade, under Sir William Peel, had battered and breached the Begum Koti with three 68-pounders. This was then assaulted and carried by our troops, the enemy losing about 500 men. Lieut. McBean, Adjutant of the 93rd Highlanders, here gained the V.C., and greatly distinguished himself, killing 11 of the enemy with his own hand in the main breach.

It was after this assault that Hodson, of Hodson's Horse, lost his life. He was the finest leader of irregular cavalry in India, and his loss was greatly mourned by everyone in the force. He had arrived at Banks's house just as the party going to attack the Begum Palace had started, and accompanied them. Previous to this he had remarked in a laughing manner to his friend Brigadier Napier (afterwards Lord Napier of Magdala) " I am come to take care of you, you have no business to go to work without me to look after you." The place had been taken before he was wounded. When the soldiers were searching for concealed Sepoys in the court-yard and buildings adjoining, he said to his orderly " I wonder if any are in there." He turned the angle of the passage and looked into a dark room which was full of Sepoys ; a shot was fired from inside. He staggered back some paces and then fell. A party of Highlanders hearing who had been hit, rushed into the room and bayoneted every man there. Hodson was shot through the right side of the chest, the ball entering in front and going out behind. He was taken in a dooly to Banks's house, where his wound was dressed. At daylight the following morning he was much better, his hands being warm and his pulse good. The medical officer hoped that if the bleeding, which had ceased, did not return he might recover. At 10 a.m., however, bleeding came on again profusely, and he rapidly became worse. He sent for General Napier, to whom he gave directions about his property, and sent messages to his wife. After this he rapidly sank, though he remained sensible, and was able to speak until he became too weak, and at 25 minutes past 1 he died. He was buried that evening, the Commander-in-Chief and his staff being present. Thus, on the 12th March, 1858, in his 37th year, closed the earthly career of this brave and talented officer. One of those best qualified to judge declared that Hodson with his regiment would have been worth a division, had he been spared to take part in the subsequent operations in Oudh. His particular qualifications for Asiatic warfare would have found an appropriate field for their display. Sir Colin Campbell, in a letter of condolence to his widow, dated March 13th, thus expressed himself :—" I followed your noble husband to the grave myself, in order to mark in the most public manner my regret and esteem for the most brilliant soldier under my command, and one whom I am proud to call my friend."

In the evening a battery was constructed by the sappers at the side of the Begum Kotí. The place presented an extraordinary sight with its palace, gardens, and lamps with enormous mirrors and chandeliers, dead Highlanders and Sepoys lying in all directions. The Engine House was captured by the 20th Regiment. The Sepoys seemed paralyzed by the suddenness of the attack, and had not time to escape. They were piled in heaps among the machinery. A portion of the room had caught fire, and this added to the horrors of the scene. At night a great part of the city appeared to be in flames.   Fires were seen in all directions, while the shells from our batteries continued to pour into the city.   The enemy was badly supplied with shells.   This was the last day of regular fighting, but the rebels hung about the native city for a few days.   The losses on our side during the operations were about 25 officers killed and 50 wounded, and 800 men killed and wounded.

The force under General Outram which had been advanced on the other side of the Gumti, now recrossed on a bridge of casks, and pushed forwards to capture the Residency.   This was the last move and the enemy abandoned the defences.   Still there were detached forts held by desperate bands of natives, and it was not till the 21st that all fighting ceased.

During the operations a most unfortunate accident happened. At the Jumma Musjid nine cartloads of powder were found in a courtyard which the General directed to be destroyed.   As there was a well on the spot it was considered that the best method of destroying the powder, which was in tin cases, would be to throw them down into the water.   A line of men was formed and the cases passed from hand to hand as quickly as possible.   By some fatality one of the cases exploded in falling.   A flame of fire flashed up, and ignited case after case along the line until the carts were reached when they also exploded.   Capt. Clarke, R.E., and Lieut. Brownlow, R.E., who were superintending the operations, received such injuries that they both died during the night.   With one exception every man forming the party, to the number of 22, were killed. Strangely enough the only man to escape was the man who was throwing the cases down the well.   He was rendered senseless, but eventually recovered.

The duties of the Engineer officers during the Capture of Lucknow, although arduous, were not of such a dangerous nature as at Delhi, and the operations lasted only for fifteen days.   The Kaiser Bagh at the time of its capture was a splendid mass of buildings with large gardens and gilt domes and statues.

The amount of loot obtained by some of the regiments was considerable.   Diamond necklaces, shawls, and swords of great value were sometimes obtained by private soldiers, and sold for a few rupees.   For two or three days after the capture of the town the troops were employed in extinguishing fires and destroying loose gunpowder, an immense quantity of which was found in the positions occupied by the rebels.

CHAPTER TWENTY

THE WAR WITH CHINA, 1860. CAPTURE OF PEKIN.

The cause of this war appears to have been the unwillingness of the Chinese Government to ratify the Treaty of Tientsin, which, according to the provisions of that agreement, should have been completed on or before 26th June, 1859.

On 17th June, Admiral Hope, Commander-in-Chief of H.M.'s Naval Forces in the Eastern seas, appeared at the mouth of the Peiho to announce the approach of the English and French Ministers. The Admiral was told that the passage had been closed by the Militia without the orders of their Government. These untrue representations were supported by false appearances ; the batteries of the forts were masked, no banners were displayed, and no soldier was seen. No communication was allowed with the shore. After promising to remove the obstacles at the mouth of the river the Militia repudiated the promise.

Such was the state of affairs when the British Minister, the Hon. F. Bruce, arrived outside the bar on 20th June. Finding that the Chinese officials kept aloof, while the Militia continued to assert that the obstruction was their own unauthorized act, he called upon the Admiral to take such steps as were necessary to reach the capital by the time appointed. This, on the 25th June, the Admiral was proceeding to effect, when the forts, which for eight days previous had appeared deserted, suddenly opened fire on the squadron, the result being that it was repulsed, and obliged to abandon some ships, guns, and *matériel*.

The British and French Governments then entered into a treaty to enforce the Treaty of Tientsin, by force of arms if necessary ; and it was agreed that 10,000 English and 7,000 French should be sent to China. Lieut.-General Sir Hope Grant was placed at the head of the *corps d'armée* of two divisions, and Major-General Sir Robert Napier, R.E., commanded the 2nd Division. The French Army had to be despatched from France, the British came chiefly from India. The former assembled at Shanghai, the latter at

Hong Kong, and the British were ready for action by the middle of June. The French were not so forward with their arrangements, and fixed the 25th July as the earliest date on which they could assume offensive operations.

On the 1st August the 2nd Brigade, 1st Division, supported by the French, had landed at Pehtang, a large village situated on a river of the same name, 10 miles north of the Peiho. They experienced great difficulty in getting through the mud, and passed the night on the mud-flats. The 2nd Division remained on board the ships. The forts looked formidable, but no serious opposition was offered to the disembarkation ; the chief difficulty was the mud.

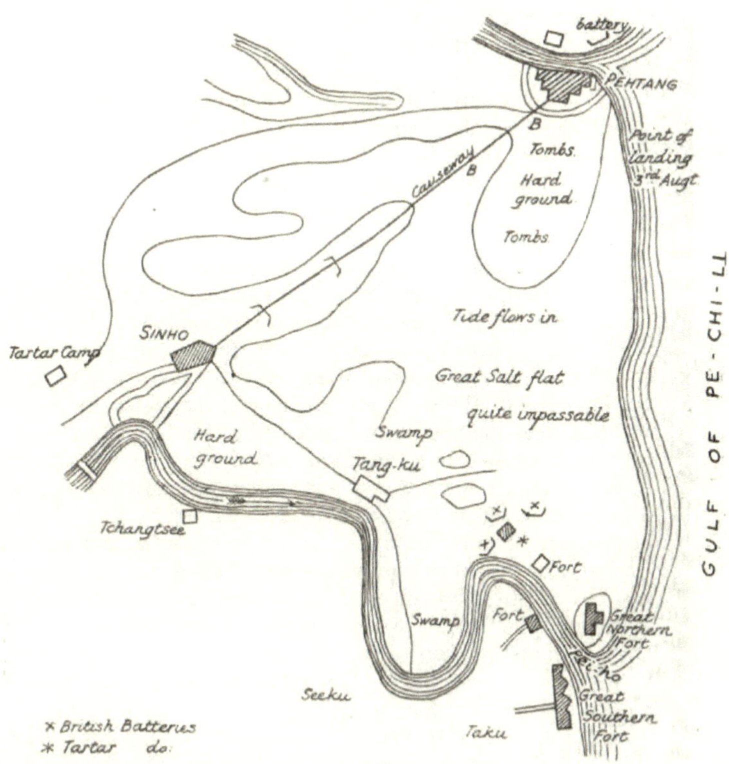

In the morning the forts and town were taken possession of. The Chinese, before withdrawing, had buried large shells with trains with spring-locks, so as to cause an explosion should the latter be accidentally pressed by the foot. Warning was, however, received in time to prevent damage. On the 3rd August the troops had a skirmish with the Tartars in which Major Greathed, R.E., was wounded.

By the 7th August all the troops had landed. The quarters allotted to the Sappers were found full of putrid matter, the Chinese having killed their animals prior to abandoning the town, and distributed parts of them over the different houses, doubtless with a view to cause a pestilence among the invaders. After making the houses habitable, the Sappers were employed in making a road through the marshes which surrounded Pehtang, and which had been rendered very difficult by heavy rain, so as to facilitate the transit of the heavy guns and baggage to the main embanked road, which led to the entrenchments in front and to the Taku Forts.

On the 9th Capt. Wolseley (afterwards Field Marshal Viscount Wolseley, O.M., G.C.B., G.C.M.G., etc., etc.) reconnoitred to the right by which the enemy's left might be turned. He ascertained that the country in that direction was practicable for all arms.

The allied force left Pehtang on 12th August, and marched in the direction of Sinho, a large village on the Peiho, about 8 miles from its mouth, the Tartars being known to occupy a strongly entrenched position on the lines of march. The 2nd Division went in advance, by the route to the right, to take the entrenched camp in flank. The 1st Division, and the French force moved along the causeway. On approaching the entrenchment, a large force of Tartar cavalry came out and hovered about our flank to charge but without effecting it. Upon one occasion the brigade to which the Sappers were attached was halted, and formed into squares to receive them ; but our fire kept them most effectually at a distance.

Notwithstanding the work of the Sappers, the marsh was so bad that the horses stuck, the guns sank up to their axles, and it was found absolutely necessary to leave behind many of the waggons. The start had been made at 2.30 a.m. and after many hours of hard work struggling against these difficulties, the guns were dragged through about 2 miles of marsh, and eventually landed on hard ground at 10 a.m., when the troops were halted, the enemy being known to be close in advance. After a short rest, the advance was ordered, and the Tartars were soon discovered. In spite of some gallant attempts at charges on their part, they had to retire and leave the Allies in possession of the entrenchment at Sinho ; and the army bivouacked there for the night.

Next day the force moved to the east of Sinho, within 2 miles of the fortified town of Tang-koo. An Engineer Brigade was then formed under the orders of Lieut.-Colonel Mann, commanding R.E. It consisted of the 10th and 23rd Companies, R.E., half of the 8th Company, with A and K Companies of the Madras Sappers.

On the night of the 13th a working party, consisting of details of R.E., and Madras Sappers, and a strong body from the Line, were sent in the direction of Tang-koo, for the purpose of throwing up cover for the riflemen. After reconnoitring the fort closely, the party was set to work, and by daybreak a good line of cover had been thrown up about 400 yards from the fort.

About 6 a.m., the 1st Division advanced to the attack, the English on the right close to the Peiho, while the French attacked the gateway. A strong body of Artillery and Engineers accompanied the force. Among the latter were parties of Madras Sappers, with scaling ladders and powder bags, Lieut. Filgate being in charge of the former, and Lieut. Swanston of the latter. The Artillery opened fire at a distance of 1,500 yards, and gradually approaching the fort, silenced the Tartar fire after a sharp cannonade of three hours. The pontoons and scaling ladders were then called for ; but before they reached the ditch, a few riflemen had crept round the work close to the river, and found that the Tartars had fled and were crossing to the south side as fast as they could. Twenty-four guns were taken in the fort. The capture of Tang-koo left us in a very strong position in rear of the Peiho Forts.

The following days were occupied in reconnoitring, and on the 17th the Commander-in-Chief, Sir Hope Grant, determined that the fort to the north of the Peiho should be first attacked. It was nearly square in shape, each side measuring 150 to 200 yards. In the centre was an immense tower of solid earth, on which were mounted three very large brass guns. The whole of the fort was strongly defended by smaller batteries.

The enemy had lost no time in strengthening the land defences ; all their heavy guns had been turned round, the parapet had been raised and strengthened with enormous piles, and fresh embrasures and loopholes had been cut. But it was in what may be called its " passive " defences that the fort especially excelled. Throughout a circuit of about a mile the country was intersected by numerous canals and deep ditches, running in every direction. The fort itself was surrounded by three wet ditches, the outer one broad and shallow, and the two inner ones varying in breadth from 20 to 25 ft., and 4 to 8 ft. in depth ; the intervening spaces, as well as the berm, were protected by very strong abattis, and by masses of sharp-pointed stones, and bamboo spikes, firmly rooted to the ground.

All were agreed that few places of the kind have ever been more perfectly supplied with obstacles of this nature. Nothing seems to have been neglected. *Trous de loup*, crows' feet, and strong iron spikes were scattered in abundance to impede our progress, while the garrison was defended against night surprises by alarm bells, which anyone attempting to cross the abattis must inevitably sound.

The 18th and 19th August were taken up in preparing small bridges to carry the artillery over the canals and ditches. At 5.30 p.m., on the 19th, a party started to place these bridges in position. The Sappers who were employed on this work were under the orders of Lieuts. Du Cane and Filgate. They returned at 8 a.m. on the 20th having effected their purpose, besides making two dams to shut off the supply of water from the canals.

On the afternoon of the same day, Lieuts. Hime, R.E., and Trail, R.(M.).E., were directed to trace five batteries in positions which had been fixed after the reconnaissance and personal inspection of Sir Robert Napier. ˙ This duty was carried out without much opposition from the forts. When night closed in, all the available men of the Madras Sappers were marched out to complete the necessary works before daylight, by which time it was intended that the guns should be in position and ready to open fire. This intention was successfully carried out, and the Tartars did not notice that the English were in position till 4.30 a.m., on the 21st, when they opened fire.

The elevation of the enemy's fire was fortunately too great, and, as by their arrangements they could not readily be altered, their fire did comparatively little harm. Our guns at once returned the enemy's fire, and a very heavy cannonade was kept up for about four hours, when the Taku Fort was somewhat silenced. The 44th and 67th Regiments were pushed forward as skirmishers, followed by the Sappers, etc., with pontoons and ladders. There was some delay in crossing the ditch, owing to the size and weight of the pontoons, and during this slight halt our troops suffered severely from the heavy cross-fire.

The Sappers accompanying the storming party were divided into four subdivisions ; the pontoon party under Lieut. Pritchard, R.E. (afterwards Lieut.-General Sir Gordon Pritchard, K.C.B., Colonel Commandant, R.E.) ; the ladder party under Lieut. Hime, R.E. ; the detachment for removing obstacles under Lieut. Trail ; and the powder bags under Lieut. Clements, R.E. Once over the ditch, the scaling party were not long in effecting a lodgment in the work, ˙despite the fierce attempts of the Tartars to dislodge them. Lieut. Trail was with the ladder party, and was among the first of those who entered the fort. Lieut. Filgate, with a party of Sappers, was highly praised for the rapidity with which, under a heavy fire, he made a causeway for heavy artillery across a canal close to the fort. The escalade was greatly facilitated by the Chinese coolies from the south ; who rushing into the ditch, and throwing ladders across their shoulders, formed a temporary bridge, over which the assailants passed. Many of the coolies were wounded, but instead of retiring to the rear, they took up their position behind the first mound which offered the slightest shelter, and thence viewed the attack going on in front. In the afternoon an advance was made against a second fort. We were allowed to take possession of it without opposition, and one after another the remaining forts capitulated.

This was a very fortunate circumstance, as almost immediately after heavy rain came on, which so saturated the mud, that moving the guns would have been a task of a very serious nature in the face of the enemy. During the 22nd and 23rd, all the forts on the south side of the river were evacuated and surrendered to the Allies.

It was now thought that the campaign was finished. The 1st Division moved up to Tientsin on the 30th, and the 2nd followed on 1st September. On the advance of the expedition towards Tientsin, orders were given for the demolition of the forts on the south side of the river, while the French undertook the destruction of those on the north.

In accordance with these instructions, the Wasp and Artillery Forts were completely destroyed, and the mining of the South Fort proceeded with until stopped by the conclusion of peace at Pekin. Owing to the unexpected interruption of the negotiations at Tientsin, a large part of the force then at that place was ordered to march in the direction of Pekin. The army marched by Poo-kow, Yang-tsin, and Hose-woo, which last place it reached on the 13th.

On the 14th, a mission, consisting of Messrs. Parkes, Lock and a small escort started for Tung-chow. The army moved forward on the 18th. Although carrying a flag of truce, Messrs. Parkes, Lock, and their whole party were taken prisoners, and most shamefully treated. Many of these were cruelly tortured to death. On the 18th, was fought the Battle of Chang-kia-wan, when the enemy were signally defeated, and driven back with great loss on Tung-chow.

Tung-chow was occupied, and the army remained there till the 21st. All this time negotiations were going on with the object, if possible, of rescuing the prisoners in the hands of the Chinese, who were then imprisoned at Pekin. These failed, and at last it was decided that force must be employed. The Engineer operations and the subsequent destruction of the Summer Palace were thus described by Capt. C. G. Gordon (afterwards General Gordon, the hero of Khartoum) in one of his letters :—

" On the 11th October we were sent down in a great hurry to throw up works and batteries against the town, as the Chinese refused to give up the gate we required them to surrender before we would treat with them. They were also required to give up all the prisoners. . . .

" To go back to the work, the Chinese were given until 12 on the 13th to give up the gate. We made a lot of batteries and every-thing was ready for the assault of the wall which is battlemented and 40 ft. high, but of inferior masonry. At 11.30 p.m., however, the gate was opened and we took possession so our work was of . no avail. . . .

" Owing to the ill-treatment the prisoners experienced at the Summer Palace the General ordered it to be destroyed, and stuck up proclamations to say why it was ordered. We accordingly went out, and after pillaging it burned the whole place, destroying in a vandal-like manner most valuable property which could not be replaced for four millions. . . . Quantities of gold ornaments were burned, considered as brass. It was wretchedly demoralizing work for an army. Everybody was wild for plunder. You could scarcely conceive the magnificence of this residence, or the tremendous devastation the French have committed. The throne and rooms were lined with ebony carved in a marvellous way ; there were huge mirrors of all shapes and sizes, clocks, watches, musical boxes with puppets on them, magnificent china of every description, heaps and heaps of silks of all colours, embroidery, and as much splendour and civilization as you would see at Windsor ; carved ivory screens, coral screens, large amounts of treasure, etc. The French have smashed everything in the most wanton manner. It was a scene of utter destruction which passes my description."

On the 12th and 13th Messrs Parkes and Lock, with a French officer and a Sikh duffadar were released ; a few more Sikhs and French were subsequently sent in, and the Mandarins then stated that no more of the prisoners remained alive. They afterwards sent in the bodies of all who had been murdered, with the exception of two, Capt. Brabazon and the Abbé de Luc, who had been beheaded at the bridge of Pa-li-chow, having met the Tartar Army on its retreat on 21st September. The bodies of the murdered prisoners were buried on the 17th with great solemnity.*

Lord Elgin's terms were that 300,000 taels should be handed over by the 22nd October to be distributed among those who had suffered and the families of those who had been murdered. He notified also that it was intended at once to utterly destroy all that remained of Yuen-ming-yuen, within the precincts of which several of the British captives had been subjected to the grossest indignities. Before the 20th Prince Kung was to inform Lord Elgin that he was willing to sign the convention.

On the 18th October the 1st Division, under Sir John Michel, marched on Yuen-ming-yuen, and set fire to all the palaces. On the 19th the fires were still burning, and the wind carried the smoke over our camp right into the city. By the evening the summer palaces had ceased to exist. On the 20th Lord Elgin received Prince Kung's absolute submission. On the 24th the convention was

* Prisoners returned safe—Messrs. Parkes and Lock, Monsieur L'Escoyrac de Lauture, 11 Sikh soldiers, 5 French soldiers; total, 19. Prisoners murdered—Lieut. Anderson, Mr. de Norman, Phipps, K.D.G., Mr. Bowlby (*Times* Correspondent), Capt. Brabazon, R.A., Abbé de Luc, 4 French officers and soldiers, 10 Sikhs; total, 20.

signed by Lord Elgin and Prince Kung (brother to the Emperor). Sir Hope Grant was present at the proceedings, while Sir Robert Napier had charge of the military arrangements connected with them. The French convention was signed next day. Both treaties were afterwards sent to Gehok, where they received the Emperor's signature.

The position selected for our breaching batteries is a point ot interest worthy of record. It was about 600 yards to the east of the Au-ting Gate. The guns were to be placed within the high wall which surrounded the Te-tsu or Temple of the Earth. Four 8-in. guns were to make a breach between the second and third square flanking towers east of the gate. Two Armstrong 12-pounders were to play upon the breach, whilst two others fired down the road leading to the gate, two more to be in reserve. A battery of 9-pounders to counter-batter. Our mortars to play on the breach. Our guns were placed on wooden platforms laid down behind the massive brick wall of the Temple. The French had no regular breaching guns, but they hoped to make their heaviest field battery serve instead. Their battery was to our left and only 60 yards from the walls. Ours was 200 yards. Shelter was dug in advance for our infantry, so that the Chinese gunners and the breach should be well plied with rifle fire.

Nothing now remained for the army to do in the north, and the march to the south shortly commenced. The weather in the latter part of the campaign was extremely cold and trying to the troops, especially the natives of India. On the march from Pekin the thermometer at night was often below 20 degrees Fahrenheit.

Sir Hope Grant in a letter to the Viceroy, dated 21st November, 1860, thus writes :—" The two companies of Madras Artillery under Capt. Hicks, and the two companies of Madras Sappers under Capt. Shaw-Stewart rendered good and useful service in the operation which preceded and led to the fall of the Taku Forts. The latter corps was most energetic in working without reliefs at the construction of the batteries. . . ."

CHAPTER TWENTY-ONE

Capture of Magdala, 1868.

His Royal Highness the Duke of Cambridge in describing in the House of Lords the operations in Abyssinia under General Sir Robert Napier (afterwards Field Marshal Lord Napier of Magdala, G.C.B., G.C.S.I.) declared that " his every step had been a success and a triumph." As Commander-in-Chief of the expedition, before he took the field Sir Robert Napier, as a philosopher in his study, planned a piece of mechanism, of which every piece of military arm, every military department, and every branch of military science were the polished *wheels*, the whole to be kept in motion by one highly tempered *main spring*.

In the Abyssinian War, Sir Robert Napier's " thin red line " was an arterial line of communication a few feet only in breadth, but in length extending from the Red Sea to the Amba or Citadel of Magdala; upon the vitality of this arterial line, the life of the invading army depended. If, throughout its enormous length, pulsation at any one point had ceased, mortification at the extremity must inevitably have ensued. From Zoulla, in spite of physical obstruction of every description, it stretched itself onwards for nearly 400 miles, through the scarped and counterscarped gigantic outworks of the Citadel of Magdala, until within its second gate, it reached the self-condemned, self-executed, ghastly corpse of King Theodore. And then as the victorious army returned it instinctively contracted, until on the embarkation of the last regiment at Zoulla, as if its commander signalled to it to depart, it vanished. On the march through a region of the world in which war had always been disgraced by robbery, murder, and mutilation, he induced the troops " to be true and just in all their dealings." To keep their hands from picking and stealing, and in the battlefield, to do unto their wounded enemy " as they would he should do unto them."

Bearing no malice or hatred in his heart, he offered not only to forgive, but also to give honourable treatment to King Theodore, who for many years had trespassed against Her Majesty the Queen and her subjects. King Theodore shortly before he gave the fatal pull to the trigger of his revolver, wrote to his conqueror, as his last dying speech and confession : " Since the day of my birth, whenever my soldiers began to waver in battle, it was mine to arise and rally them. Yesterday, though I killed and punished my soldiers they would not return to the battle. You have prevailed against me by people brought into a state of discipline."

At sunrise on the morning of Easter Monday, April 13th, 1868, Theodore arose and calling to his troops said : " Warriors who love me, gird yourselves ; leave all behind, take nothing but arms and follow me ; the time has come to seek another home." He had apparently determined to make an attempt to escape, and went out of the fortress near the Kiffir-bir Gate at a place where it was possible to descend towards Sangallat. He was followed by two chiefs of rank, and about 2,000 men, variously armed. As he passed down he asked where the advance guard was, and on being told that they were in rear, ordered them to the front. They refused, saying that they would never flee before an enemy again, and would rather seek death in Magdala. Theodore pondered for a brief space, and then saying " Let it be so " re-ascended the mountain. It would have been impossible for him to continue his journey alone, as the cries of the Gallas, who, under the guidance of Meer Akber Ali, were watching the issue from the fortress on that side, could be distinctly heard. On re-entering the fortress, he told all who were not prepared to share his fortunes to the last to provide for their own safety. Thousands thereupon left him, and ultimately surrendered to the British.

It was a fine sight, the long line of red, Royal Engineers, toiling under their scaling ladders, Sappers, 35th and 45th Regiments, the 4th King's Own, the Beloochees in their dark green, the Royal Artillery in blue, and the mountain batteries on mules, toiling up the steep ascent that led to the Fahla saddle ; while down by the side of the hill by every sheep track, streamed the soldiery of Theodore, who had surrendered to Capt. Speedy, and laid down their arms. Old men and boys, mothers, and families, with their household treasures, were seeking an asylum in the Arogi Valley till the storm of war should be over above. Sword and helmet sparkled in the morning sun, the banners were unfurled, the breeze was just enough to display their gay colours, and all nature seemed to contribute to the splendour of the pageant.

Inspirited as the soldiers were by the thought that their toils were now almost over, and that success was about to crown their enterprise, their ardour was also strengthened by the uncertainty which surrounded everything up to the very last moment. For all anybody knew to the contrary, Theodore might have 10,000 armed men in battle-array on the top.

About 4 p.m. the order to storm was given. The mountain batteries kept up as long as possible a fire over the heads of the troops advancing to the assault. The 33rd Regiment led by Major Cooper, and keeping up a continuous fire from its skirmishers, soon surmounted the steep precipitous cliff which lay between it and the outer gate, notwithstanding the fire of the garrison from behind its defensive line, which consisted of a wall surrounded by thick and strong barricades of thorny stakes, with a narrow stone gateway. The gate being closed, the progress of the assailants was arrested, and for the moment the powder bags with which to blow it in were not at hand. On arriving close to the gate the enemy opened fire through loopholes, by which Major Pritchard, R.E. (afterwards Lieut.-General Sir Gordon Douglas Pritchard, K.C.B., Colonel Commandant, R.E.), two non-commissioned and one sapper were wounded, and Lieut. Morgan at the same time received a severe contusion on the head and shoulders from stones.

Major Pritchard thus describes the affair : " About 2 p.m. when it was decided that Magdala should be taken by assault, I received orders to send back for the ladders, powder barrels, bags, etc. (these by order of Sir C. Staveley had been left at the foot of the cliff). I accordingly sent a detachment who brought up the ladders, the two barrels of powder, the fuze, etc., but not the powder bags, which on inquiry I found had been taken by the natives for their original purpose of carrying water. I reported the circumstance to Sir C. Staveley and informed him that I could if necessary, blow open the gate of Magdala with one of my barrels of powder and fuze. About 4 p.m. the Engineers took the post of honour, carrying our entrenching tools, ladders, two barrels of powder, fuze, etc., and led the way along a path on the side of a precipice to the gate, on the right of which over the wall we effected an entrance by climbing and using our ladders."

The entrance was made at two points, Corpl. M'Donough, R.E., being the first man in at one, whilst Major Pritchard, Lieut. Le Mesurier and Sapper Bayley (one of the flag signallers) entered at the same moment by escalade at another. Immediately following them the 33rd Regiment forced its way over the stockade at the right, and joined Pritchard and his small party within the gateway. They then made a dash at the upper gateway which was not defended, the enemy flying in all directions. Here they found the body of King Theodore, who had shot himself on realizing that his troops could make no stand against the British forces. The summit of the fortress was quickly occupied, the British standard was planted upon the African rock which had been so long the prison-house of British envoys, and Magdala was captured. The followers of Theodore immediately threw down their arms and prayed for quarter, which was of course granted, and no further loss of life occurred.

So ended the war and the prisoners were rescued. On April 17th Magdala was burnt to the ground, and the fortifications destroyed. The army wended its way back as rapidly as possible and re-embarked on reaching the base. This fortress, which was comparatively easily carried, might (owing to its outworks, Fahla and Selassie which added so much to its strength) have been made impregnable.

If Theodore had been properly supported by his soldiers, the British could not have escaped severe loss in its attack. As it was however his army had been so completely demoralized by the severity of the loss inflicted two days before, that the troops remaining faithful to Theodore were few ; and when they found that their unscientific defences gave them no opportunity to inflict loss on the assailants, without exposing themselves to the fatal fire of the breechloaders, they abandoned the contest as soon as their first line of defence was carried by the stormers.

This campaign has a peculiar interest for the Royal Engineers, in that it is the first in which the supreme command was entrusted to one of their Corps. The difficulties attending the operations were probably more considerable than would be encountered in most campaigns, but it was universally admitted that, great as those difficulties were, they were clearly foreseen and admirably provided for.

Officers of Artillery and Engineers have since been employed in high positions in command of troops other than those of their own services, and the results have proved as satisfactory as in the case of the Abyssinian Campaign. The peerage earned by Lord Napier of Magdala shows the value set by public opinion on his work, but he has received beyond this the warm gratitude of his brother officers, for having demonstrated how fallacious was the idea that men of the scientific corps were wanting in the military genius necessary for the command of an army.

CHAPTER TWENTY-TWO

CAPTURE OF KABUL, 1879.

After the massacre of the Resident, Sir Louis Cavagnari, with the greater part of his escort at Kabul on September 3rd, 1879, orders were immediately issued for a new advance on that city and for the retention of Kandahar.

It was decided that the movement on Kabul should be made by the Kurum Column under the command of General Sir Frederick Roberts (afterwards Field Marshal Earl Roberts, V.C., O.M., G.C.B., G.C.S.I., etc.). General Roberts who at the time was at Simla hurried down to reassume command of the force, and reached Alikhel on the 12th September. The column which numbered about 6,000 fighting men, began the advance the following day, and after defeating the enemy at Charasiab, entered Kabul on the 8th October. The Engineers at once set to work to repair the fortifications. The Sherpur Cantonment had to be repaired, its defences improved, and its accommodation remodelled. The Chief Engineer with the force was Colonel Æneas Perkins, C.B., R.E. (afterwards General Sir Æneas Perkins, K.C.B., Colonel Commandant, R. (Bengal) E.), an officer who had greatly distinguished himself in the Indian Mutiny, in the Bhootan War, and latterly in the Kurum Valley. The advance guard of the force had reached the Shutargurden as early as the 11th September. Lieut. Nugent, R.E.,* was with this force, and he immediately began entrenching the position with the 23rd Pioneers.

The Bala Hissar had also to be made fit for occupation by troops. Among the public buildings in Kabul, the Bala Hissar or Citadel claimed the first importance, but not from its strength. Kabul is enclosed to the south and west by high rocky hills, and at the eastern extremity of these the Bala Hissar which commands the city, is situated. There was another fort under it, also called the Bala

* Lieut. Nugent was unfortunately killed while engaged in blowing up some towers near Kabul on the 23rd December, 1879, owing to a defective fuse.

Hissar. It was a poor, irregular and dilapidated fortification. The upper fort is small, but that below will contain about 5,000 people. The Bala Hissar was built by different princes of the House of Timur, from Baber downwards. Aurungzeb prepared extensive vaults under it to defend his treasures.

A new line of communication had also to be opened out, the Shuturgurden Pass, by which the advance had been made, being blocked with snow in the winter. The new line of communication with Kabul from Peshawur by the Khyber Pass was adopted and the route by the Shuturgurden was abandoned.

The streets of Kabul City are narrow, and the houses built with flat roofs. To many of the better sort of private dwellings there were gardens. The town is situated in a gorge between two lofty hills, up and along whose steep and rocky ridges a long line of massive wall is discernible, with numerous half-ruined towers, once forming an imposing barrier of defence against the sudden and devastating inroads of the western tribes.

The largest portion of the city stands on the right bank of the river, the opposite side being principally lined with walled gardens and small forts. The covered bazaar consisted of five open squares connected by four arcades, down the centre of which a marble aqueduct conveyed a small running stream, the sides being lined with shops. The great Bazaar or Chunhut, an arcade nearly 600 ft. long, and about 30 ft. broad, was divided into four equal parts, the streets being intersected with small covered aqueducts of clear water, a great convenience to the people. Kabul was a compactly-built city, but the houses had no pretension to elegance. They were constructed of sun-dried bricks and wood, and few of them were more than two stories high. It was thickly peopled, the population being about 60,000. The Kabul River flows through the city. There could not be a dirtier place in rain.

At the period under notice signs of unrest were becoming apparent in the neighbourhood of Kabul, and by the end of the first week of December the Afghans assembled in such overwhelming numbers that General Roberts had to withdraw the outposts, and on December 14th assembled the whole of his small force within the walls of Sherpur. Entrenchments were hastily constructed to strengthen the position against the overwhelming force of the enemy. Under the direction of Colonel Perkins gun emplacements and abattis were rapidly constructed, blockhouses were built on the Bimaru Heights, walls and villages dangerously near the cantonment were blown down and levelled, and a second line of defence within the enclosure was improvised. The perimeter of the cantonment was over 4 miles, only 1½ of which were enclosed by a wall.

A scheme had been prepared by the Engineers in November for its improvement, and this was now put in hand ; the northern face was formed by the Bimaru Heights on which some towers had been constructed. It was now further fortified by a line of breastwork with emplacements for guns at intervals. The north-west face was defended by a ditch and breastworks made with ammunition waggons, abattis, and wire entanglements. The eastern face, the weakest, was defended by detached buildings, and Bimaru Village was loopholed. Garden walls and villages dangerously near the cantonment were blown down and levelled. It was considered necessary to clear carefully 800 yards all round the cantonment enclosure.

In November a force was dispatched from Kabul under Brig.-General Macpherson (afterwards Lieut.-General Sir Herbert Macpherson, K.C.B.), to join hands with the Khyber Field Force that had advanced through the Khyber to Jellalabad and Gundamuk, under the command of Lieut.-General Bright. The two commanders met near Kota Sungh on the 6th November. General Macpherson's column then returned to Kabul, and General Gough's Brigade returned to Gundamuk. Detachments were left at the various posts between Gundamuk and Kabul, viz., Soorkhab, Jugdulluk Kotul, Jugdulluk, and Latabund.

On Monday, 8th December, 1879, General Roberts ordered a great divisional parade at Kabul. On the afternoon after the review (the village of Arghandi, a great centre of discontent on the direct road to Gharni having been selected for attack), Macpherson's Brigade moved into the Chardeh Valley and encamped at Killa. On the 9th the forces halted to allow General Baker (afterwards Lieut.-General Sir Thomas Baker, K.C.B.) to develop his turning movement by the Logan Valley, and across the hills by Maidan. Warnings had not been wanting. The deportation of Yakoob Khan and the various tentative means for securing tranquillity, excited nothing but enmity and distrust among the tribes.

A large contingent from Kohistan was reported to be creeping round from the north to join the gathering at Arghandi. General Macpherson by a skilful manœuvre placed his brigade in the hollow of a commanding ridge, before the Kohistanis or the Arghandi columns were aware of its presence. On the guns opening fire the hostile masses dispersed, and the infantry, Sikhs on the right, English in the centre, and Goorkhas on the left, raced down the slopes towards the enemy. The affair lasted little more than an hour. The enemy's loss was between 50 and 100.

On the 11th December, Brig.-General Massey, with four horse artillery guns and four squadrons of cavalry, rode out from the camp at Killa. This was part of General Roberts' general plan for surrounding and crushing the enemy at Arghandi. General Macpherson was to push straight along by the Pughman Hills, while General Baker was to take the enemy in rear from Maidan. The

Killa Kasi, 2,000 yards off, made a good target for the first shells, but as villages and enclosures were rapidly left behind, the battery became hotly engaged. Round after round of shrapnel was hurled forward, but the enemy had taken the measure of the little force, and swept down with great determination.

Then it was that the want of a few hundred good rifles was severely felt. After 30 dismounted horsemen had in vain striven to make up for the deficiency, it became evident that a desperate effort must be made to save the honour of the day. Side by side the British and Indian Lancers dashed forward on their hopeless errand. The ground was unfitted for cavalry, and the enemy's loose formation offered no resistance to the shock. Of all the officers of the 9th Lancers who took part in that charge, but three escaped unscathed. Hearsey and Ricardo, of the 9th, and Forbes, of the 14th, were killed, and Lieut.-Colonel Cleland, 9th Lancers, was dangerously wounded, and he died of his wounds some months afterwards.

Retreat was still possible, but before a practicable roadway in the required direction was hit upon, the leading gun toppled over into a deep ditch, hopelessly blocking the passage for those that followed. Groups of troopers made charge after charge without checking the enemy's masses. At last, when the case was desperate, orders were given to the gunners to cut the traces and gallop off, thus avoiding the sacrifice of many valuable lives.

General Macpherson's infantry was pushing forward so rapidly, that with another hour's grace the guns would have been saved, and the brigade actually got within view of the field before the fighting was over. General Macpherson chased the enemy on the right up the hills for some miles, while his force was thus employed the guns were recovered. The carriages had been stripped and left lying by the enemy in their haste when captured; and Colonel Macgregor with a very small party of officers and men, collected as he went, was able to sally out and bring them back. At midnight the Guides' cavalry and infantry marched in from Seh Baba, having covered that day over 30 miles, the first of which over the Lataband Pass was by far the worst on the line.

None now knew better than General Roberts the arduous task that was before him, and that to re-establish our shaken prestige many valuable lives must be sacrificed, and many desperate deeds attempted.

On the morning of the 12th December, the enemy's flag waved from the lofty Takht-i-Shah, and from a lower and more advanced peak, but the Sher Durwaza and the command of the city were in the hands of the 72nd. Part of Macpherson's force moving up early from Siah Sung, the attack began along the ridge. The base of the Takht-i-Shah was reached in the afternoon, but a murderous fire from the sides checked all further advance. About eight in the morning of the 13th, General Baker marched out past the city with a strong brigade. He sent the 92nd Highlanders straight at the heights above Bala Hissar, telling them this was the post of honour. The gallant regiment sprang forward and carried crest after crest at the point of the bayonet. A severe fight ensued. The rabble, too, from the city commenced sharpshooting from the Bala Hissar and from the walled villages on the plain. But the fire from all these quarters was steadily quelled, and finally the Guides cavalry swept across the valley, while the 9th Lancers and the Punjab Cavalry rode along the ridge itself. The enemy stood up boldly to meet them with their rifles, but the Guides charging to the cry of " Bala Hissar," had not forgotten the massacre of September, and the enemy suffered severely. On the 14th there was again heavy fighting with severe losses on both sides, and General Roberts wisely decided upon instant concentration within the Sherpur defences. The enemy failed to press his advantage, and General Macpherson's brigade reached Sherpur without serious mishap.

General Roberts now took up a defensive position, and he chose Sherpur rather than Siah Sung, or the Bala Hissar, in virtue of a decision arrived at two months before, and not under pressure of immediate necessity. The wisdom of this change of tactics after the events of the 14th was apparent to all. Reinforcements might reasonably be expected to arrive in a week. There had been no direct defeat, but five days' marching and fighting and climbing, fasting, and watching, is a severe ordeal for any troops.

From Deh Afghan right round to Bimaru, villages and walled gardens had been left standing at a convenient distance from Sherpur. These were now occupied by the enemy. The position of the little garrison that held the Latabund Pass caused great anxiety. Communication could only be held by heliograph, and at this time the sun was much obscured by clouds.

At last the tiny intermittent flash from Latabund reached Kabul and gave the welcome message that the post was safe, and the advancing brigade under General Charles Gough (afterwards General Sir Charles Gough, V.C., G.C.B.) was expected on the 22nd.

To supply the deficiency of cavalry with General Gough's Brigade, and also to secure, if possible, the bridge over the Logar, the 12th Bengal Cavalry were ordered to make their way through the enemy's position, and to join hands with that brigade. This exploit was carried out in the most gallant and spirited manner. The bridge at the Logar was found unoccupied ; but at Butkhak a regiment of Afghan regulars turned out and received the brave Sowars with volleys of musketry, so they rode on 10 miles further to Lataband without drawing rein.

The hours of Mahomed Jan's greatness were now numbered. On the 23rd December, an hour before daybreak, a clear beacon fire shone out from the Asmai Hill. Every man in Sherpur was at once at his post, for this was the signal for the long-threatened attack. The enemy collected in thousands under Bimaru, and were rapidly increasing in numbers, running in groups of 10 and 12 from one village to another.

When the direction of the main attack became evident, General Roberts was at liberty to concentrate reserves in sufficient force to roll back the most determined assault. On the other side the attack hung fire all day, never getting past the stage of a demonstration. When the first wave of the attack on Bimaru seemed spent, and before another could gather force, General Roberts sent four guns, well escorted, through the gorge in the centre of the ridge, with orders to wheel to the right and take the enemy in flank. The moment was perfectly judged. No sooner did the Afghans perceive the cavalry and guns on their flank, than they began to retire from the nearest villages, and this retreat soon became a rout. The main body made for the Pai Manar Kotul, while on either side a multitude of stragglers dotted the snow-covered fields. The mass of the fugitives escaped unscathed, but a number of stragglers were cut up by the 5th Punjab Cavalry, and others streaming back were raked by a searching fire by the 67th from the cantonment walls.

In the afternoon the two infantry brigades moving out to the east of Sherpur, blew up the towers of some of the villages that lay in the path of General Gough's advance. In performing this service the lives of Capt. Dundas, v.c., and Lieut. Nugent, two most distinguished officers of the Royal Engineers, were sacrificed owing to a defective fuze, a mine which they had prepared exploding before they could get clear.

The enemy though they made a last demonstration on Siah Sung fell back that night upon the city, disheartened and ripe for flight. Next morning there was not an armed man to be seen, and the cavalry had a 20-mile ride, in vain pursuit, without firing a shot.

Thus ended the great Jehad of Mahomed Jan and the Moolah, Mushk-i-Alam. On the 24th General Gough with his brigade marched into Sherpur.

During the occupation of Kabul the Commanding Engineer, Colonel Æneas Perkins, had under his direction the following works to complete :—10 forts, 15 detached works, 3 large trestle bridges, numerous small ones, 4,000 yards of defence, 45 miles of road. 9 posts, also quarters for 8,000 men.

The operations carried out by the Khyber Field Force under General Bright, and by the 1st Brigade under General Charles Gough on his advance through the passes were of an extensive, varied, and arduous nature. General Gough marched from Gundamuk on the 14th December, 1879, with the following troops :—10th Bengal Lancers, 130 men ; No. 5 Company, Sappers, 73 men ; 2nd

Battalion 9th Foot, 487 men ; 4th Goorkhas, 375 men. The outpost at Perwan, near the Soakhal River, was held by 157 men of the 2nd Goorkhas ; 6th Company, Sappers ; 4 guns Hazara Mountain Battery ; 50 men of the 10th Bengal Lancers. At Jugdulluk Kotul there were the 2nd and 3rd Company, Sappers, and 40 men of the 2nd Goorkhas. Jugdulluk Fort was held by 180 men of the 2nd Goorkhas, 2 guns Hazara Mountain Battery, and 90 men of the 10th Bengal Lancers.

On General Gough's arrival at Jugdulluk the whole country seemed to have risen in arms to bar his further progress, and daily skirmishes took place between the troops escorting the convoys between Pezwan and Jugdulluk. The post at Jugdulluk Kotul commanded by Major Thackeray, v.c., R.E., was attacked on three occasions, the last being on the 23rd December when he was severely wounded, and the enemy were driven off in all these attacks. On the 21st December, after seven days' severe fighting in the passes, a large convoy bringing supplies and ammunition having arrived, General Charles Gough was in a position to advance towards Kabul. The road was covered with snow, but all difficulties were overcome. The force reached Lataband without opposition, relieving the garrison at that place, and on the 24th December General Gough's force reached Kabul.

CHAPTER TWENTY-THREE

The Siege of Ladysmith.

The environs of Ladysmith lend themselves to a policy of pure defence far more readily than is generally supposed. The perimeter eventually held gave the defenders a clear field of fire for 1,400 yards and upwards along almost its whole extent.* Before October 30th, 1899, a series of fieldworks calculated for the defence of the town itself had been constructed by Major S. R. Rice, R.E., and these formed the basis, at any rate on the north-eastern side, of the defence scheme which was now formulated and put into execution. The whole perimeter was divided into four sections, A, B, C, and D, under the command of Colonel Knox, Major-General Howard, Major-General Ian Hamilton and Colonel Royston.

Section A extended from Devonshire Post, the easternmost of the kopjes on the northern edge of the Ladysmith Plain, to Cove Redoubt some 3 miles to the west. Devonshire Post, Helpmakaar Hill, Cemetery Hill, Tunnel Hill and Gloucester Post, to the east of the railway, were at the opening of the siege held by the Devons, half the 1st K.R.R., half the Liverpools, and the remnant of the Gloucesters. Immediately west of the junction of the Harrismith and Newcastle railways was Junction Hill, with a naval 4·7 gun guarded by two companies of Liverpools. The other 4·7 and the remaining two companies of the Liverpools were on Cove Redoubt, while the naval 12-pounders and the chief station of the Naval Brigade were between the two on Gordon Hill. This section had the smallest clear field of rifle fire, and was exposed to converging artillery fire from every quarter. But it was strongly manned, and its commander, Colonel Knox, had not been at Plevna in 1877 for nothing. Under his direction and by the willing exertion of officers and men, the open stone breastworks already in existence were improved, connected with a curtain of stone wall, and made accessible by covered ways, till eventually the whole section became one continuous fortification. The scrub on the plain in front of the eastern portion was cut down, and converted into three parallel lines of abattis, 100 yards apart. West of Knox came Howard's section manned by the Leicesters,

---

* On the north-east there was at one point cover to within 800 yards from the British trenches, and on the south-west a gap of only 900 yards separated Wagon Point from Mounted Infantry Hill.

Rifle Brigade, and the bulk of the two battalions of the K.R.R. This section extended westwards from Leicester Post, past King's Post to Ration Post, along the north side of the valley in which the " tin camp " of the permanent garrison was situated, and then southward and south-eastward by Rifleman's Post to Range Post on the right bank of the Klip River. The northern face of this section was strongly fortified and practically continuous with A Section. On the western face the works were lighter and more isolated. This was even more the case with Hamilton's section, the longest and most weakly held of them all, which continued south-eastward from Range Post, past Highlanders Post, and Maiden's Castle up to Cæsar's Camp, the latter held by the Manchesters, and the other points by half the Gordons and the two surviving companies of the Irish Fusiliers.

From halfway down the slope of Cæsar's Camp to Devonshire Post the plain was picketed and patrolled by the Natal Volunteers, under Royston. A proportion of the artillery was assigned to each section. The most powerful weapons of the defence were the naval guns, posted along the northern portion of Knox's section. In addition Helpmakaar Hill and Devonshire Post were strengthened by the inclusion in their system of works of the field guns of the 13th Battery and of two 6·3 howitzers of obsolete pattern which had been sent round from Port Elizabeth at White's request. Although these guns had only a range of some 3,000 yards they proved of signal service throughout the siege and kept down the fire of any gun which the enemy pushed within their range. The 42nd Battery was sent as soon as a practicable road was made to Cæsar's Camp, and posted in sections in skilfully designed pits along the main plateau. The 69th Battery was held in support of Howard's section of the defences. The remaining three batteries—the 21st, 63rd, and 67th—together with Brocklehurst's cavalry brigade and half the Gordons were kept as a central reserve. These dispositions and the composition of the reserve were however considerably varied in the course of the siege. A very complete system of telephonic communication was established between the different posts and Sir G. White's headquarters in Ladysmith. The total length of the perimeter was about 14 miles, and the force available for its defence amounted, inclusive of the reserve, to over 13,000 men.

The details of the force in Ladysmith were as follows :—

Naval Brigade.—Two 4·7-in., four 12-pounders, four Maxims, 284 officers and men ; Natal Naval Volunteers.

Mounted Troops.—6th Dragoon Guards, 5th Lancers, 18th and 19th Hussars, Natal Carabineers, Natal Mounted Rifles, Border Mounted Rifles, Natal Mounted Police, Imperial Light Horse ; about 2,800 men.

Royal Artillery.—13th, 21st, 42nd, 53rd, 67th, 69th Batteries, R.F.A. ; four 15-pounders, two 6·3 howitzers, two 12½-pounders (captured at Elandslaagte), two 9-pounders (No. 10 Mountain

Battery), two 3-pounder Hotchkiss (Natal Hotchkiss Detachment), Ammunition Column.

Royal Engineers.—23rd (Field) Company, Balloon Section, Telegraph Section.

Infantry.—1st Liverpools, 1st Devons, 1st Gloucesters, four companies 1st Manchesters, 1st and 2nd King's Royal Rifles, Royal Irish Fusiliers (two companies), 1st Leicesters, 2nd Gordons, 2nd Rifle Brigade, 2nd Dublin Fusiliers (half-company) ; total over 6,000 men.

Army Service Corps and Army Ordnance Department.

Town Guard about 250 men.

The Battle of Ladysmith had created for the Boers an opportunity to inflict a crushing blow on their enemy, such as was never to present itself to them again. With nearly 22,000 men concentrated round White's shaken and dispirited force, they might with every prospect of success have attempted to rush Ladysmith during the first day or two after the battle, when it was still practically unfortified. But such an attempt, involving both promptitude of decision and a readiness to face heavy losses, was foreign alike to the cautious character of General Joubert and to the constitution of the force which he commanded. With the deliberation which had marked the whole of their invasion of Natal, the Transvaalers confined themselves on October 31st to occupying the eastern edge of the Ladysmith plain, not so much to secure positions for a further offensive, as to utilize the immunity from attack thus assured in order to settle down in their laagers and discuss the situation in comfort. The Free Staters similarly settled down with their main body to the north-west of the town. That evening, however, General A. P. Cronje led out some 2,000 men of the Harrismith, Heillbron, Winburg and Brede Commandos, with two guns, and by a night march across the open plain west of Ladysmith established them in the hilly ground to the south-west where they would be conveniently posted either to check an attempt on the part of the British to break out on that side, or to cross the hills and descend upon Colenso, into which place they in fact began to drop shells a few hours later.

On November 1st a joint council of war was held at Joubert's headquarters when it was decided that the commandos should invest the town on all sides to prevent the escape of White's force, while their artillery carried on a bombardment which it was confidently expected would bring about a surrender before the end of many days. The different sections of the investing line were duly apportioned, gun positions were selected, and during the next few days the burghers busied themselves in putting their policy into execution. In this they were not seriously disturbed by the British who were too preoccupied with the task of strengthening their own defences to attempt to take advantage of the confidently negligent movements of the commandos. The cavalry reconnaissance of November 2nd did indeed succeed in surprising the Winburgers; but that of the

Imperial Light Horse on the 3rd, developing as it did into an inconsequent general engagement, only seemed to encourage the burghers, who greatly enjoyed shelling the British back into camp, and believed that they had repelled a determined attempt to break through the investing line with very trifling loss to themselves.

The positions taken up by the Transvaalers for the investment were, with small modifications, those in which they had encamped on their first arrival and from which they had fought on October 30th. Joubert's headquarters were behind Long Hill, a little distance south of the railway siding at Modderspruit, which was now converted into an advanced base for the whole Transvaal force round Ladysmith and subsequently on the Tugela. Here, the commissary-general established his supply park, and separated from the British positions by the valley through which runs the Harrismith Railway was General Erasmus's section, 3,500 to 4,000 men in all. The centre of the Transvaal position was under Vice-President Schalk Burgen, Joubert's second in command, and was manned by some 6,000 to 6,500 burghers. Behind Lombard's Kop and Lombard's Nek were the strong Middelburg and Heidelberg commandos. The southern section was held by Lukas Meyer, temporarily replaced by Louis Botha, with some 4,500 burghers. Wakkerstrom, Krugersdorp and Standerton were securely camped behind Balwana and Interbagone. Utrecht, Vryheid, and the Pretoria Germans, in the order named, held the ridges across the Klip river facing the plain, and Cæsar Camp with their laagers in the valley of Herman's Spruit. The rest of the circle was completed by some 7,000 or more Free Staters. The head laager under Martinus Prinsloo with part of the Winburg commando, was at Smith's crossing on the Harrismith Railway. The large Kronstadt commando, laagered in several camps, held the line eastwards to Thornhill's Kopje adjoining the Pretorians on Surprise Hill, and south-westwards to the Sand Spruit, including the ridge crossed by the telegraph line from Ladysmith to the Free State and known to the besieged as Telegraph Hill. South, Harrismith held Lancers Hill, commanding the road from Potgeiters Drift, and the Long Valley across to Middle Hill, while beyond them the burghers from Ventenburg and Winburg, on the extreme right, kept touch with Vryheid and the Germans on the Transvaal left.

The whole of these positions were admirably adapted to the work intended to be accomplished, which was not so much to facilitate the capture of Ladysmith as to prevent the escape of the garrison. The broad valleys around Ladysmith were as defensible from one side as from the other, and furnished the Boers with an outer circle of defences corresponding exactly to the perimeter held by the British garrison. By their dispositions the Boers, no less than Sir Geo. White, made all transition from the defensive to the offensive difficult for themselves, and thus prepared for the long and weary stalemate of the siege.

The Boers placed the greatest confidence in the speedy and complete success of the artillery bombardment. The available guns some 17 in number increased afterwards to about 22 were dragged up under Colonel Trichardt's directions on to the various heights commanding the town on the British defences. These included two 6-in. Creuzot " Long Toms " firing a 96-lb. projectile with an effective range of nearly 10,000 yards, and four 4·7-in. Krupp howitzers, firing a 34-lb. projectile with a range of over 6,000 yards. For the rest, the Boer siege artillery consisted of their ordinary Krupp or Creuzot guns. A comparison of the gun power of besiegers and besieged is instructive, for it brings out the fact that, except in long range weapons, the Boers were less than half as strong as the enemy whom they were attempting to reduce. This inferiority prevented their bringing their field guns into effective range, and threw practically the whole task of bombardment on the long-range guns. Even with a very small target and a carefully concentrated fire it would be difficult to hope for much result from the fire of half-a-dozen guns. But so elated were the Boers by the success of " Long Tom " in driving Yule out of Dundee, and by the more recent prowess of the Pepworth guns on October 30th, that they attributed a well-nigh magical efficacy to the bombardment, convinced that it would force White into almost immediate surrender.

The bombardment may be said to have begun on November 2nd, when the Creuzot on Pepworth opened a desultory fire first on the town and then on the naval 4·7, which had just been mounted on Junction Hill, one of its shells mortally wounding Lieut. Egerton, R.N., in command of the gun. That same evening other guns joined in from Lombard's Nek, and on the 3rd and 4th the bombardment increased in intensity as new guns were brought into position. Trifling as the fire was from the military point of view, it induced the mayor to address Sir Geo. White on the removal of non-combatants, more especially of women and children, to some place of greater security. The principal medical officer also pointed out that the sick and wounded in the Town Hall, which had been converted into a hospital, were exposed to grave danger from the fire. The result was the opening up by White of negotiations with Joubert which resulted in an armistice till midnight on the 5th and the formation of a neutral camp for sick, wounded, and non-combatants at the southern end of the plain along the Intombi Spruit. Trains were run down to Intombi on the 5th, hospital tents pitched, and before the armistice expired most of the sick and wounded were transferred to the new camp. The camp was placed under the control of Mr Bennett, the Resident Magistrate of Ladysmith, while Major Mapleton, R.A.M.C., was made responsible for the hospital arrangements. Under agreement with the besiegers, a daily train was allowed to ration the camp, provided it made the journey in daylight.

The armistice was actively employed, alike by the British in strengthening their positions, and by the Boers in mounting and protecting their guns. With much labour the second " Long Tom " which now arrived from Lang's Nek, was dragged on to the summit of Bulwana, and on the morning of the 8th opened fire, at a range of 7,500 yards, from a projecting spur on the west side of the hill— to the great consternation of the Ladysmith staff, who had never anticipated such a feat of gun transportation, and now found many of their defences enfiladed or taken in rear by its far-ranging and alarming projectiles. Meanwhile a week had passed since the opening of the bombardment, and to the surprise and chagrin of the Boers there were no signs of surrendering from Ladysmith.

A Krygsraad was held on the 8th, and it was agreed that the policy of investment should make way for one of active offence which should place the Boers in possession of some point commanding the town and the British positions at closer range.

The obvious key of the whole position was the great ridge of Cæsar's Camp, and Wagon Hill, known to the Boers as the Platrand which with its northern underfeature, Maiden's Castle, completely domi- nated the whole of the town, and of the western defences at from 2,000 to 5,000 yards range. Another point known to be weakly defended and not trenched whose occupation would seriously cramp the defences of the garrison was Observation Hill, a ridge some 1,700 yards in front of Cove Redoubt and separated by a valley only 1,400 yards across from the bush-grown plateau of Bell's Kopje held by Van Dam's " Zarps." It was decided not to waste a single day but to capture the Platrand and Observation Hill by a sudden attack that very night.

The commandos along the sections opposite these points were warned to start soon after midnight; the rest were to support or assist by a demonstration in the morning under cover of a grand bombardment. Late at night the attack on Cæsar's Camp was sud- denly countermanded, for on reconsideration of the plan from his own standpoint Joubert thought this part of it too venturesome. The rest of the plan held good, and at 1.30 a.m. on the 9th Field-Cornet Zeeder- berg's section of the Pretorians left their laager and established themselves by daybreak in a donga within 800 yards from Observation Hill. Had they come a little earlier they could have pushed on at once and could have occupied the hill itself without opposition.

At 5 a.m. all the Boer guns began the artillery preparations for the attack, that is to say, they dropped their missiles into the town, the tin camp, and on to different points of the defences according to the gunners' fancy. An hour later the squadron of the 5th Lancers which as usual took up its position on Observation Hill at daybreak, was heavily fired at by the Pretorians, who were now advancing from the donga. Two companies of the Rifle Brigade were sent forward in support from Leicester Post, being shelled in rear from Bulwana as they reached the hill, and forced by this fire to send forward their exposed supports in order to prolong the more sheltered firing line. The advance of the Pretorians had already been checked by the fire of the Lancers who had held their ground manfully, and the Riflemen now effectually drove back the Boer supports, who were coming on from Bell's Kopje in considerable numbers, but with no great resolution. Firing was heavy all day but the attack was never pressed, though a small party of the Pretorians remained till dusk in the donga, and even behind rocks and out-hills some distance in front of it where the road ran close under Gun Hill. Before coming to this the force halted. Leaving 100 of the Border Mounted Rifles across the road to guard the left flank, and sending Royston with the main body of his Volunteers to the right to check any counter-attack from Lombard's Nek, Hunter with the storming party (the Imperial Light Horse and 100 Natal Volunteers of various corps) struck straight across the stony donga, intersected with thorn scrub, for the middle of Gun Hill. Arriving at the foot of the hill at 2 a.m., the assaulting column deployed into line ; the Light Horse under Colonel A. H. Edwards and Major Kani Davies on the left; the Natal troop under Major Addison on the right. Then the ascent of the 250 ft. of steep boulder-strewn slope began. Slowly and steadily the men scrambled up what seemed an endless black wall of perpendicular rock. Suddenly from 'the darkness to their left rear came a faint uncertain challenge—" Wie daar ? "—repeated again and again, and then with a sudden realization of what was happening, rising into an agonised cry of warning to the sentry on the summit : " Schiet, Stephanus, hier kom de verdomde rooineks, schiet, schiet ! " With that the whole picket fired wildly into the rear of the assaulting line, which was clambering on with silent, desperate energy, and was now within 20 paces of the summit. A fringe of fire broke out along the crest, for the defenders had waited for them. A few men began to reply, but the officers stopped them, and then Edwards' voice ran out clear—" Fix bayonets ! " There were no bayonets, but taking up the cry the men rushed the skyline. The thought of the cold steel was too much for the Boer gunners who fled into the darkness. At the head of his men Edwards groped his way across the plateau to the battery, annexing " Long Tom " in the name of the Imperial Light Horse. The 4·7 howitzer was found soon after, and then Capt. Fowke, and Lieut. Turner with a few sappers, inserted the guncotton charge into the breech and muzzle of the guns while the stormers withdrew from the crest. Then followed the explosion leaving the guns as the Sappers thought wrecked and irreparably destroyed ; but they had yet to reckon with the resources of the Pretoria repairing shops.* Hunter called for three cheers for the Queen and then the descent began, the men taking with them as

* " Long Tom " was repaired within three weeks, and, with shortened muzzle and a new breech,was sent off to help in the Siege of Kimberley. The howitzer was beyond repair but an exact reproduction was made of it.

trophies the breech-block of the 6-in. gun, and a Colt gun, and many other articles found in the battery. The return journey was unmolested. The total casualties were seven wounded, including Major Henderson to whose leading the success of this most gallant enterprise was so largely due.

Encouraged by the successful issue of the Gun Hill sortie Colonel Metcalfe asked and received permission to take out the Rifle Brigade on the 10th to destroy a 4·7 howitzer which had been pounding all the northern posts from Surprise Hill. At 10 p.m. five companies of the Rifle Brigade moved out of camp behind King's Post. Colonel Metcalfe was in command accompanied by Major King, R.A., the guides Thornhill and Ashby, and by Lieut. Digby Jones, R.E., in charge of the blasting detachment. The darkness was illuminated at intervals by the faint flicker of a flashlight on the broken clouds—they were signalling from the relief column 20 miles away. Then a harsher light would shine out from the enemy's position on Telegraph Hill, but the riflemen lay quietly in the nullah, the great beam left them undiscovered. At times there would be a rifle-shot in the distance, and perhaps a burst of firing, as some picket along the far line of defences imagined itself disturbed. But with the assaulting party all was still. Just before midnight the moon was lost in a bank of cloud, and the time for action had arrived. Silently the five companies of the riflemen filed out of the nullah and began slowly and steadily to pick their way across the uneven surface of the plain. Leaving half a company to protect their left as they crossed the Harrismith Railway, and another on their right in the shadow of Bell's Kopje, they moved on, every moment expecting to stumble on a picket, but finding none. Fortune was on their side, for till a few days before, a rise half a mile in front of Surprise Hill had been occupied nightly by a strong picket.

But Viljoen who had been responsible for that sub-section of the perimeter, had been withdrawn to the Upper Tugela, and his successor had not seen fit to continue his precautions. By 2 a.m. the foot of the hill was reached. Here two companies were halted and formed outwards to support the two other companies which furnished the assaulting line. The ascent now began, the boots and rifles of the men clattering audibly on the loose boulders of the slope. Yet it was not until the leading section was almost on the brow of the hill that the challenge came, and with it a burst of fire from the left shoulder of the hill. Heedless of the fire the Riflemen swarmed over the crest line. The battery was found in a few seconds, but for a moment the men thought their prize had been removed, until they unearthed it, covered with a tarpaulin, just outside the emplacement. The men were thrown out in a semicircle while the preparations for the destruction of the gun were made. When all was ready the party retired over the edge. But something went amiss with the fuze and Digby Jones returned to place another. This time all went well and after a ringing cheer the men started stumbling and slipping down the slope.

At the first outbreak of fire a Boer gunner on Bell's Kopje fired off a round to give the alarm, and in a few minutes the Transvaalers on that side, and the Free Staters at Thornhill's Kopje, streamed out of their laagers, and began firing furiously and blindly at the hill slope from both flanks. Through this fire, enveloping them at closer range every moment, the men stumbled down. Suddenly a ring of flame blazed forth at their very feet; a small party of Pretorians had boldly come round the side of the hill, and regardless of the heavy fire from their own side, had laid down in a line across the slope ready to intercept the storming party, of whose numbers they probably had no idea. But with implicit obedience to Metcalfe's orders, and disregarding the misleading orders shouted out by the Boers, the men charged forward in grim silence. The gallant band of Pretorians wildly emptied their magazines in the vain endeavour to stay the rush and then the Riflemen surged into and over them, killing or wounding several with their bayonets as they passed. From the foot of the hill the men, as arranged, made their way back as best they could under the lee of Observation Hill, getting home to camp by dawn. The casualties, 14 killed or mortally wounded, including Lieut. Fergusson, and 50 wounded were not excessive for a feat so gallantly and successfully performed.

The success of the sortie had a most inspiriting effect on the garrison, which was beginning to feel the depressing influence of inactive isolation. To the besiegers, who had gradually become more and more careless in carrying out the ordinary military pre-cautions, the sorties were a severe shock.

The indignation in Pretoria over the Gun Hill affair was intense. The government censured General Burger, who was in command, and he ordered a court-martial, the sentence of which suspended Commandant Weilbach and Major Erasmus of the Artillery from their commands. The second sortie led colour to the suggestion now made that the unfortunate sentries—men of English names as it happened—had been guilty of deliberate treachery. They were arrested and sent to Pretoria, but eventually released.

The time appointed by Buller for the beginning of the relieving movement was now drawing near, and with it White's hopes of achieving some really effective stroke in the way of co-operation steadily grew. On December 9th Buller announced that he would start for Potgieter's on the 12th and would reach Lancer's Hill on the western edge of Long Valley by the 17th. On the 11th on the ground of being uncertain as to dates, he suggested that White should not attempt co-operation before he himself got to Lancer's Hill, unless he felt absolutely sure as to Buller's whereabouts. On the 13th the Potgieter's route was abandoned for Colenso and Ouderbrook Spruit and the date for the move postponed to the

17th. Impressing upon his chief the all-importance of time as a factor of co-operation, and the necessity of keeping him informed of any change of plans, White set about his preparations. The mobile column was again brought into being. To free some of Royston's mounted troops for this work the town guard was on the 12th once more embodied. Some of the artillery was brought into camp from the defences, whilst a 4·7-in. gun and a 12-pounder were transferred from the northern defences to Cæsar's Camp and Wagon Hill. Arrangements were made for the feeding of Buller's force and the care of a large number of wounded. The special field force created by White's order of the 14th, which he intended to lead out in person, included almost all the best troops in Ladysmith, and left the merest skeleton of about four battalions, one battery, a cavalry regiment and a few volunteers to Colonel Knox for the defence of the town. For the first time since October 30th, White was determined to strike a blow with all the weight that he could put into it.

On the 15th Ladysmith woke to the noise of the fighting on the Tugela, but it was some time before White realized from the heliograms coming in, that Buller had anticipated the date fixed for the attack by two days without giving him warning. Even then White may have thought that Buller had good reasons for not calling in his aid until he had secured a footing across the river. Assuredly the summons to action would come in the morning.

The message, inexplicable and bewildering, came. As the actual text of the message has been made public it is here reproduced :—

BULLER TO WHITE.—No. 88 Cipher, 16th December :—" I tried Colenso yesterday but failed ; the enemy is too strong for my force, except with siege operations and those will take one full month to prepare. Can you last so long ? If not, how many days can you give me in which to take up defensive positions ? After which I suggest your firing away as much ammunition as you can, and making best terms you can. I can remain here if you have alternative suggestions, but unaided I cannot break in. I find my infantry cannot fight more than 10 miles from camp, and then only if water can be got, and it is scarce here.—Buller."

BULLER TO WHITE.—No. 92 Cipher, 16th December :—" My message No. 88 Cipher. Groups 31 to 43 were correctly sent, but in place of them, and first number of 44 group read as follows : How many days can you hold out ? Also add to the end of message : ' Whatever happens recollect to burn your cipher, and decipher and code books and any deciphered messages.'—Buller."

WHITE TO BULLER :—" Your No. 88 of to-day received and understood. My suggestion is that you take up strongest available position that will enable you to keep touch of the enemy, and harass him constantly with artillery fire, and in other ways as much as possible. I can make food last for much longer than a month, and will not think of making terms until forced to. You may have hit enemy harder than you think. All our native spies report that your artillery fire made considerable impression on enemy. Have your losses been very heavy ? If you lose touch of enemy it will immediately increase his opportunities of crushing me, and will have worst effect elsewhere. While you are in touch with him, and in communication with me, he has both of our forces to reckon with. Make every effort to get reinforcements as soon as possible, including India, and enlist men in both Colonies who will serve and can ride. Things may look brighter. The loss of 12,000 men here would be a heavy blow to England. We must not think of it. I fear I cannot cut my way to you. Enteric fever is increasing alarmingly here. There are now 180 cases all within last month. Answer fully ; I am keeping everything secret until I hear your plans."

The besieged garrison, ignorant of the inner story of Colenso, received the news with some depression, relieved by the cheerful tone of White's manly order, and by a calm consideration of the position. The defences had now been perfected and seemed practically secure against attack. Sickness was the worst enemy. There was food yet which with economy would last for two months. The most serious anxiety at the moment was the welfare of the horses. The supply of hard forage was almost exhausted. In fact in this respect the turning-point in the condition of the garrison had arrived. Up to December 15th it might have been used as a mobile force operating from its entrenched positions ; after this date it gradually ceased to be anything but a garrison to the perimeter it held. From December 15th to the end of the year little occurred. The inconveniences of the siege were however brought home to the garrison more severely than heretofore. Supplies had to be husbanded and the scale of rations was reduced all round. The Boer artillery practice improved somewhat, and there was an increase in the casualties from this cause. Sir George White was forced to change his headquarters owing to the damaging fire directed upon his house, which lent some colour to the suspicion that the Boer gunners on Bulwana had information supplied to them from within the perimeter. Christmastide was not marked by any special development. Few of the festivities which mark the season were possible ; but an impressive service was held by the Rev. J. G. W. Tuckey, Army Chaplain, and in the evening, Colonel Frank Rhodes, Colonel Dartnell, Major Doneton, and Major Kani Davies gave a Christmas party to the children of the garrison, an incident of pathetic interest amid the privations and anxieties of the siege.

On the morning of December 17th Lord Roberts received the news of his only son's death at Colenso. A few hours later at the call of duty he put his great sorrow behind him, and undismayed by the difficulty of the task, undeterred by the weight of his years, accepted the command of the forces in South Africa, conscious of his fitness to hold it, and to restore victory to the British arms. On December

23rd, a dreary winter day, the new Commander-in-Chief for South Africa left Southampton, and at his request Major-General Lord Kitchener of Khartoum was appointed Chief of Staff. At the moment of his appointment Kitchener was at Khartoum engaged in the task of building a new city, and creating a new administration on the ruins of the Dervish power, the last remnants of which had been crushed by his lieutenants. Leaving Khartoum on the 18th December, he reached Alexandria on the 21st after three days by steamer and train, was there taken on board by the steamer *Isis*, and joined Roberts at Gibraltar on the 26th.

As his Director of Intelligence, Lord Roberts took with him Major G. F. R. Henderson, at that moment Professor of Military History at the Staff College. A brilliant writer and a profound thinker on the great problems of strategy and tactics, Henderson was an officer who would have risen to the highest positions on the General Staff.*

Colonel W. G. Nicholson,† an officer of exceptional capability and of great experience of staff work, whose cautious critical judgment and skilled pen Lord Roberts had long learned to value in India, was another member of the Staff. It was from India where he was occupying the post of Adjutant-General that Roberts now summoned Nicholson to meet him at Cape Town. Originally appointed as Military Secretary, he was subsequently entrusted with the direction of the transport service, and on a variety of responsible and confidential duties.

On the south side Joubert had intended that there should be nothing more than a demonstration. But the Vryheid burghers, acting on their own initiative, endeavoured to convert this into an actual attack, and securing a lodgment in the bush-grown under-features of Cæsar's Camp, and in the valley between it and Wagon Hill, pushed forward with some vigour about 10 a.m., being supported by a hot fire from Mounted Infantry Hill, and from other points. But the Manchesters, who had been strengthened by the arrival of the 42nd Battery and by some 130 of the Imperial Light Horse, who occupied Wagon Hill, replied strenuously, and the attack soon died away into an exchange of long-distance rifle fire.

By mid-day Sir G. White was so satisfied that he had nothing to fear from the attack that he was able to order a salute of 21 guns to be fired in honour of the Prince of Wales' birthday. Artillery and rifle fire went on until evening put an end to a rather tame sequel to the resolutions formed by the Boers on the previous day. The total casualties of the day were 4 killed, and 27 wounded on the British side, and probably about the same on that of the Boers.

---

* Colonel Henderson died in March, 1903, leaving a gap in the ranks of British military thinkers which will not easily be filled.

† Now Field Marshal Lord Nicholson, G.C.B. Nicholson reached Cape Town on January 18th.

The direct result of this affair was that White's attention was drawn to two particularly vulnerable portions of his defences, and from this date Observation Hill, and eventually Wagon Hill, were included in the perimeter and scheme of the defence.

The moral effect upon the staff and the garrison generally of the weakness of the Boer attack was excellent, and did much to remove the depression which had weighed upon the whole force since the battle of the 30th. As for the Boers, their expectations of speedy results from the bombardment were no longer high as at first ; but, on the other hand the reports of Kaffirs, caught in trying to make their way out,' now led them to hope that famine and disease were already working fearful havoc with the garrison, and that the end could not be very far off. Meanwhile, as a concession to the clamour of the party of action, an expedition was organized for the invasion of Natal, south of the Tugela, and the first step taken was the reduction of the investing force which was gradually to bring it down to a mere skeleton of 5,000 to 6,000 men. Joubert himself accompanied the expedition to ensure its being conducted with due caution, leaving the command at Ladysmith in the hands of Schalk Burgher.

The departure of the Estcourt expedition on November 13th did not pass unobserved by the British outposts, and encouraged by this, and by the inactivity of the Boers since the 9th, White determined to essay a more active policy. On the 14th Brocklehurst went out with the 5th Lancers, 19th Hussars, two squadrons each of the Imperial Light Horse, and Border Mounted Rifles, and two batteries, with instructions to turn the enemy off Rifleman's Ridge. The Imperial Light Horse established themselves on Star Hill, north-east of Rifleman's Ridge, and the rest of the force endeavoured to work round by Field's Farm. The Boers on the Ridge, some 400 Trede and Bethlehem burghers, defended themselves vigorously, while three Boer guns joined in from different points. The British guns expended a great deal more shell than could be afforded for anything but a decisive operation, but no attempt was made to push home an attack which in the opinion of spectators from Wagon Hill might easily have succeeded, and early in the afternoon Brocklehurst withdrew. His withdrawal was a signal for a hot shell fire, in which Bulwana joined as the retreating force came within range.

From this date to the end of the month no incidents of great importance occurred to break the monotony of the investment. The bombardment continued as aimlessly as before. On the 14th and for a night or two after, the Boers fired a few rounds from their big guns in the middle of the night, a most harassing manœuvre, but one which they were too indolent to keep up. On the 23rd a single shell from Bulwana killed and wounded 11 men of the Liverpools on Junction Hill. On the 24th the Boer guns on Rifleman's Ridge and Telegraph Hill stampeded a herd of 228 oxen, and by a series of shells planted just beyond them, successfully shepherded them into their own lines.   The direct result of this incident was the reduction of the Ladysmith meat ration on the 25th.

On November 27th the Boers unmasked a third 6-in. Creuzot on Middle Hill, bringing Wagon Hill and Cæsar's Camp under fire at a damaging range.   To meet this new development the two old howitzers on Devonshire Post were removed by night, and mounted on the nek between Wagon Hill and its extreme spur, Wagon Point. They set to work to such good effect on the 30th that in a few rounds they completely mastered the fire of the " Long Tom," a lucky shot killing and wounding nine of the gunners and damaging the gun. It was withdrawn during the night, to reappear on December 11th on Telegraph Hill, whereupon the howitzers were sent round to Ration Post.   At the increased range (4,000 yards) they were less successful, and never managed completely to silence it, and to the end of the siege it continued to shell the tin camp and northern defences.   On the British side almost the only minor active measure undertaken at this time was the sending out one night of a locomotive containing some explosives up the Harrismith line in the hope that it might run into something.   It successfully ran into the veld, where it overturned, its fate providing the garrison with many humorous sallies at the expense of the staff.

All this time Ladysmith had been in intermittent touch with the outside world by native runners.   Maps of Ladysmith and the surrounding country, photographically reduced, were sent down to Maritzberg by carrier pigeons, and in this way Major Altham, White's A.A.G. for Intelligence, was able to give substantial help to the forces collecting south of the Tugela.   On the 27th White announced his intention of harassing the commandos that were now being withdrawn to oppose Methuen, and of breaking a gap in the Boer line; a scheme which had to be abandoned owing to the coincidence of the Boer reinforcement of Rifleman's Ridge.

On the 30th in answer to Buller's inquiries, White announced that he still had 70 days' provisions and could hold Ladysmith while they lasted.   On the 7th Colonel Knox was instructed to take out a small force that night and harass the enemy at Limit Hill and further along the Newcastle Road.   Knox reported to Hunter that there were no Boers within reach in that direction, and suggested as an alternative an attack on Gun Hill, which since the removal to it of the Pepworth Creuzot had made itself very obnoxious to Knox's section. Hunter took up the idea warmly, and Sir G. White's sanction was secured on the condition that Hunter personally conducted the expedition and that at least 500 men accompanied him.   Hunter selected for this bold enterprise 100 of the Imperial Light Horse, and 400 of Royston's Volunteers, entrusting the guidance of the force to Major David Henderson and his corps of Guides.   Knox, whose previous orders still held good, was to cover the left flank of the sortie.

Preparations were made with the utmost secrecy, and at 10.15

p.m. the little force started from Devonshire Post, marching along the road that leads round the northern slope of Gun Hill and Lombard's Kop. There was a Boer picquet, of whose existence Henderson was well aware, on a small spur.

This completes the narrative of the Siege of Ladysmith and of the situation at the close of the year 1899, and as this short compilation of the History of Sieges only extends to those that took place during the 19th century it is not proposed to narrate in detail the final operations of the siege which terminated in the relief of Ladysmith by General Sir Redvers Buller on March 3rd, 1900.

The memorable attack by the Boers on Wagon Hill ; the charge of the Devons ; the operations on the Upper Tugela ; the ineffective attack on Spion Kop and its abandonment ; the feint attack and capture of Vaal Krantz ; the operations on the Tugela Heights including the capture of Cingolo and Monte Chinto and the attack upon Inniskilling Hill, all these are fully and accurately described in the 3rd Volume of the *Times History of the War in South Africa*.

To quote from the latter history, " On March 3rd Buller's army made its formal entry into Ladysmith, and the bronzed and service-begrimed battalions of the relieving force marched proudly through the streets lined by the haggard and emaciated garrison. It was a stirring moment and one full of pathos, as men recognized old friends and comrades-in-arms, or looked vainly down the ranks for those whom they expected, but whom they were destined not to see again. After the parade was over, addresses read by the Mayor, and speeches delivered, Buller issued a special order to the troops of both forces, thanking them for their efforts."

Thus ended the campaign for the relief of Ladysmith. In the memory of the British people it will long live as a deeply dramatic event, with its alternations of hope and disappointment, with its tale of struggle oft renewed to be crowned with success at the last.

That Buller did at last break his way through to Ladysmith, was due to two causes ; to the weakness of his adversaries, and above all to the fundamental soundness of the material of which his army was composed. It was the virtues of the British regimental officers and the men whom he led, that in the end broke the Boer resistance and relieved Ladysmith.

Their fearless courage, their patient endurance, their imperturbable cheerfulness in defeat, their unquestioning loyalty to their leader, lend dignity and pathos to a story which would otherwise be depressing, and give a sure hope of better things. If there is one clear lesson to be drawn from the Tugela Campaign, it is that British soldiers, trained as they might be trained, and led with courage and science, need fear to match themselves with no army in the world.

THE END.